THE GRIEF PROCESS

THE GRIEF PROCESS
Analysis and Counseling

Yorick Spiegel
Translated by Elsbeth Duke

ABINGDON
Nashville

Library of Congress Cataloging in Publication Data

Spiegel, Yorick, 1935-
    The grief process.

    Translation of Der Prozess des Trauerns.
    A revision of the author's Habilitationsschrift, Bochum.
    Bibliography: p.
    1. Grief. 2. Death—Psychological aspects. I. Title.
BF575.G7S6413 1977   155.9'37   77-1547

                    ISBN 0-687-15880

The tables on pp. 47, 51 are reprinted with permission from D. Maddison and A. Viola, "The Health of Widows in the Year Following Bereavement," *Journal of Psychosomatic Research,* © 1968, Pergamum Press, Ltd.

Lines from B. Brecht's "On a Drowned Girl" (p. 307) are taken from *On a Drowned Girl,* trans. Eric W. White (Knotting, Bedfordshire, England: Sceptre Press, 1973). © 1973 by E. W. White.

MANUFACTURED BY THE PARTHENON PRESS AT
NASHVILLE, TENNESSEE, UNITED STATES OF AMERICA

Foreword

A few years ago I entitled a section in a book "The Neglect of Grief" and went on to state, "In the light of the universality of grief and its impact in human life, it is particularly surprising that the field of psychology, 'the science of human behavior,' has largely ignored this powerful human emotion."[1] Not only psychology but also other psychotherapeutic fields, including pastoral care and counseling, with a few notable exceptions, have not given the thorough and systematic investigation of this topic that its universality and potency in human life would seem to have demanded.

Such a statement read at this time, however, is clearly out of date and no longer appropriate. Quite to the contrary, during the last six years there has been what almost amounts to a flood of books, articles, and even whole journals that are dealing seriously with death, dying, and grief in a scientific, scholarly, and sensitive manner.

Those which focus on grief seem to be primarily of three types. First, there are those writings which are by and for people who have undergone or are currently undergoing grief, the sharing of the authors' own experiences as a form both of working through their own present reactions and of assisting the reader in dealing with his or her response to loss. The second category includes technical books which explore

---

[1]David K. Switzer, *The Dynamics of Grief* (Nashville: Abingdon, 1970), p. 13.

the various aspects of bereavement and its complexities and which are written by medical, psychological, and psychotherapeutic investigators. Finally, there are those that might be called professional in the sense that they focus directly on one's professional functioning in the situation.

One could almost say that death is an event whose time has come. It still remains for some competent research sociologist to make the analysis of our contemporary culture that will inform us concerning this surge of investigation and writing which had been taboo for so long. What factors have converged to make this the time? Of course, there have been earlier times in the history of the Western world when death, dying, and grief were openly acknowledged. Expression of the feelings and discussion of the events were supported by social custom and religious ritual, and they were the focus of some amount of writing. But as time went by, death became a major subject of massive denial both individually and societally as far as our own culture is concerned. Whether the current "popularity" of the event as a subject for articles, books, college courses, lay seminars, and numerous other methods of presentation means a genuine openness to the acceptance of death as a part of our life experiences, or whether we somehow believe that talking about it sufficiently while covering up our feelings of dread will make it go away for us, remains to be seen. I believe that I am observing both of these phenomena from time to time, both in others and in myself.

Perhaps one characteristic of our age that has contributed, if not to the desire, then to the necessity of the study of grief, is the rise of the psychotherapeutic professions and their increasing discoveries of the dynamic power of the response to loss by individuals, families, and society. Particularly has there been firm documentation of the power of those ego defense mechanisms that any individual must inevitably utilize in order to seek to maintain oneself as a person in the face of the threat to his or her own existence as a human being posed by the loss by death of a person with whom there has been a close emotional relationship. Especially when the relationship with the now dead person has been a very complex one, involving a strong ambivalence of love-dependence on the one hand and hate-anger-fear on the other, plus intense guilt, the mechanisms of denial and self-protection become so extreme that the grief itself is severely complicated, the process is blocked, and maladaptive behavior patterns become established. The attributing of these forms of emotional distress and dysfunctional behavior to sources other than the loss itself and the nature of the prior relationship with the person who died, has led to faulty diagnosis and therefore to inappropriate and ineffective treatment of these persons and even of whole families. Psychotherapeutic professionals are now being pushed by their new awareness of the power of grief to investigate the reaction in greater depth and thoroughness in order to be more accurate in diagnosis and more effective in the therapeutic treatment of pathological grief. In order to understand the pathological fully, however, important studies of the normal grief process are necessary. A number of these have already been published, and the work goes on.

Ministers, priests, and rabbis stand in a unique position among professionals in their opportunities to serve persons in many different ways. They are not primarily psycho-therapists, and they do not deal primarily with pathology, although they work with *all* persons in need, including severely disturbed ones, and such relationships should issue in therapeutic results. Their main opportunity, however, lies in the fact that a majority of persons are in touch with them in some way immediately following loss. Most people still have funerals for family members, and most funerals are still conducted by the clergy. If the minister is aware of the need for grief work's beginning immediately, knows the stages in the normal process, and is familiar with methods of facilitating grief work, he or she can make a major contribution to the lives of individuals and families. This is both an expression of their faithfulness to God in service to persons in times of distress and of preventive mental health at its best. Any book that contributes to our understanding of grief and leads to our more effective professional functioning commands our attention.

This is the first part of the answer to the very legitimate question, "Why, in the light of the substantial body of literature already available, another book on this subject?" The primary purpose of this introduction is to answer this question more completely and, in so doing, make some comment about the author, the book, and its place in the larger context of study and professional practice in this field.

In the fall of 1971 I was interested in meeting a number of persons working in pastoral care and counseling in Europe. It was strongly recommended to me that, given my strong interest in the subject of grief, I make a trip to Bochum in West Germany for a visit with Dr. Yorick Spiegel, who was in the process of writing his *Habilitationsarbeit*, a book-length project which qualifies a person in Germany to be considered for a university professorship. Dr. Spiegel was most gracious with his time, and our discussions were extremely useful to me. I was especially impressed with his bibliographical card file on grief and bereavement, what I would imagine to have been the most complete bibliography on the subject in the world at that time. In addition, he had actually gotten his hands on most of the material and read it! It seemed to me at the time that a book that would come out of such resources would stand a good chance of making a major contribution.

Two years later I had the opportunity to look over the two-volume* work that Dr. Spiegel had produced as it appeared in its publication by Kaiser-Grünewald in German. As I browsed through it, my judgment was confirmed to myself at least that the material and its organization would fulfill a useful role in the literature available in English. Now that Abingdon has arranged for its translation and publication, I am happy to discover in reading the English manuscript both of my earlier judgments reconfirmed.

Obviously, the writing of an introduction implies some stamp of approval on the book that follows. While I am not

---

*The second volume consisted of detailed footnotes, some additional material, and an extensive bibliography. The primary references have been incorporated in this translation. Scholars who want to consult the more extensive technical material will find it in the annotations volume (*Anmerkungsband*) of the German edition.

uncritical of Spiegel's presentation, I do recommend it for those interested in the serious study of grief. It is not light reading in many places, but its theoretical discussions always issue in practical procedures for the minister.

Spiegel's three professional orientations and competencies are reflected in the basic plan of the book, and the combination of these within one volume defines the volume's unique place in the literature on grief as I know it. He is an ordained minister and theologian, a professor of practical theology. A major thrust of much of his other scholarly work has been in sociology, with an emphasis on the utilization of social research methods for the investigation of church life, both congregations and ministers. At the same time, he has a keen interest in psychotherapy and has studied and had personal experience in this area. This makes for a book that is truly practical theology, an approach that is still somewhat rare in this country where most of what goes on under this designation is more "practical" and less "theology."

Each of the major mechanisms by which the grief sufferer seeks to adapt is discussed from the psychological or, more precisely, a psychoanalytic, point of view. This is followed by a presentation of the sociological or group-membership influences that are relevant for the particular mechanism. Finally, relevant theological material is offered. Here in this work is seen the dynamic interplay, the mutual input process of the raw data of human experience, the psychological and sociological analyses and implications of such data, and the application of theological thought to the process. In addition, there is the stimulation of the process of theologizing by the data, thereby testing and modifying the theological statements.

The organization and methodology of this book, then, is doubly useful, as it sets the study of grief in a multidisciplinary context, including theology, and offers us a model for the doing of practical theology. For these reasons, it deserves serious and careful reading.

DAVID K. SWITZER

Preface
to the German Edition

The investigation undertaken in this book was accepted by the department of Protestant Theology at Ruhr University at Bochum as a dissertation in the field of practical theology. The text was edited and shortened for publication.

The author is greatly indebted to the Deutsche Forschungsgemeinschaft for awarding him a habilitation scholarship and financing a trip to the U.S.A. for the purpose of study. His gratitude is extended to the Protestant Church of Berlin-Brandenburg, especially Bishop D. Kurt Scharf, for a contribution to the printing of the first volume and to the German Research Society for the second volume.

Manfred Josuttis and Rolf Zerfass, as well as the experts Hans-Eckehard Bahr, Joachim Scharfenberg, and Johannes Schreiber, have made important contributions. Elisabeth Pracht and Helmut Strack have been of great help in scrutinizing citations and in the process of reading the galley proof. Rosemarie Kurte and Liza Walter undertook the difficult task of typing the final manuscript. I want to thank them all.

This study appears in two volumes. The first volume contains the text together with an index of more detailed literature, including the most important and more frequently cited essays and monographs. Those who are interested in the exact bibliographical data of the citations and in special literature on that subject are referred to the second volume containing the annotations. There, the comments to the notes in the main text, as well as additional references to the subject under discussion, and an extensive bibliography of grief and related subjects, such as death, funerals, and depression can be found. *

Personal experiences were the reason for this study. They evoked the question of death and how to cope with it. I want to dedicate this book to Ina-Susanne who did not succumb to helplessness, but in her own way—in an intellectual struggle—sought to solve this crisis. She had collected the bibliography and literary material on dying and death for that purpose and stimulated the writing on the subject of grief. She followed the writing of this book with active interest.

YORICK SPIEGEL

---

*The primary references have been incorporated in this translation. Scholars who want to consult the more extensive technical material will find it in the annotations volume (Anmerkungsband) of the German edition.

Contents

1. Introduction. 17
    1.1   Objective 17
    1.2   Theological argument 20
    1.3   Arrangement of the material 24

PART I: GRIEF—The Individual Aspect
2. Theory and symptomatology of grief 29
    2.1   Sigmund Freud: the murder of the father 29
    2.2   Karl Abraham: incorporation 36
    2.3   Melanie Klein: the "depressive position" 40
    2.4   Grief as disease 45
    2.41   *The psychic symptomatology of grief* 45
    2.42   *The psychosomatic of grief* 48
    2.43   *Grief as disease entity* 53

3. The process of bereavement 59
    3.1   The four stages of bereavement 59
    3.2   The stage of shock 62
    3.3   The controlled stage 66
    3.4   The stage of regression 70
    3.41   *The concept of regression* 70
    3.42   *The bereaved in the regressive stage* 72
    3.43   *The function of regression* 77
    3.5   The stage of adaptation 80
    3.6   Anticipatory grief 83
    3.7   Inhibition of grief 86
    3.8   Symptoms of pathological coping
           with grief 91
    3.9   The work of the bereaved .94

PART II: GRIEF—The Social Aspect

4. Grief as status transition 101

    4.1   *Rites de passage (rites of passage)* 101
    4.2   New structuring 106
    4.3   The significance of the ritual 110
    4.4   The status transition of the deceased 113
    4.41   *The goal* 114
    4.42   *The release of the deceased* 118
    4.43   *Intercessory prayers for the deceased* 119
    4.44   *The new status* 122
    4.45   *Public recognition* 123
    4.46   *The community of the dead with
        the living* 125
    4.5   The status transition of the bereaved 125
 — 4.51 *The detachment from the deceased* 126
    4.52   *The controlled mourning* 126
    4.53   *Reducing anxiety* 129
    4.54   *The new status* 130
    4.55   *The publication of the new status* 131
    4.56   *The community between the bereaved
        and the living* 133

5. Care giving agents 134

    5.1   The physician in the hospital 134
    5.2   The general practitioner 136
    5.3   The funeral director 137
    5.4   The minister 138
    5.41   *The social position* 138
    5.42   *Pastor and funeral* 142
    5.43   *The minister's emotional problems
        in counseling* 144
    5.5   Counseling 149
    5.51   *Training in grief* 151
    5.52   *Counseling in the situation of
        anticipatory grief* 152
    5.53   *The visit prior to the funeral
        (stage of shock)* 153
    5.54   *The group for whom the funeral is
        intended (controlled stage)* 160
    5.55   *Postfuneral calls (regressive stage)* 165

PART III: The Mechanisms of Coping

6. The narcissistic coping mechanisms 173

    6.1   Survey 173
    6.11   *The defense mechanisms in grief* 173

CONTENTS

6.12   *Social promotion and inhibition*
       of grief work 177

6.13   *The threefold direction of*
       eschatological statements 178

6.2   The mechanism: breakdown of
       reality testing 181

6.21   *Psychological aspects* 181

6.22   *Sociological implications* 189

6.23   *Image, or "night of the loss of images"* 190

6.3   The mechanism: denial/repression 194

6.31   *Psychological aspects* 194

6.32   *Sociological implications* 200

6.33   *The reality of death* 201

6.4   The mechanism: searching 207

6.41   *Psychological aspects* 207

6.42   *The "new society" as home* 211

6.5   The mechanism: mania 215

6.51   *Psychological aspects* 215

6.52   *Sociological implications* 223

6.53   *Joy* 224

7. The aggressive coping mechanisms 230

7.1   The mechanisms: protest and lamentation 232

7.11   *Psychological aspects* 232

7.12   *Sociological implications* 235

7.13   *The question of natural death* 237

7.2   The mechanism: the search for the guilty 243

7.21   *Psychological aspects* 243

7.22   *Sociological implications* 248

7.23   *Death as penalty* 251

7.3   The mechanism: identification with
       the aggressor 256

7.31   *Psychological aspects* 256

7.32   *Sociological implications* 277

7.33   *The universal redemption* 280

8. The object-libidinal coping mechanisms 286

8.1   The mechanism: helplessness.................286

8.11   *Psychological aspects* 286

8.12   *Sociological implications* 293

8.13   *Hope and courage* 298

8.2   The mechanism: recollection 301

8.21   *Psychological aspects* 301

8.22   *Sociological implications* 309

8.23   *Commemoration and recollection* 311

8.3   The mechanism: incorporation...............316

8.31 *Psychological aspects* 316
8.32 *Sociological implications* 320
8.33 *Corporeality* 321
8.4 The mechanism: substitution 324
8.41 *Psychological aspects* 324
8.42 *Sociological implications* 331
8.43 *Representation and substitution* 339

9. Epilogue: the death of Jesus and the grief of the
   disciples (John 16) 343

10. Additional literature 349

Notes 356

1. Introduction

1.1 Objective

Mourning is, to use the words of S. Freud, "regularly the reaction to the loss of a loved person or to the loss of some abstraction which has taken the place of one, such as fatherland, liberty, an ideal, and so on."[1] Wherever an experience of loss occurs, grief can appear. Therefore, some authors speak of the grief of the one who is dying, of one who has lost a limb, or of one who has left a familiar living area. Even growing up may be considered to be a grief process, because the person growing up loses the protection provided by childhood. This book, however, refers to grief exclusively as reaction to the death of a close loved one.

Although grief is a very radical human experience with which individuals are unavoidably confronted, up to this point only a few monographs that deal with it in a scholarly way exist.[2] In addition to these few comprehensive surveys, there are, to be sure, a large number of individual articles and collected volumes on this theme. Especially since 1960, one can speak almost of a flood of articles that concern themselves with the various themes on the issue of death.

This present study is the attempt to deal with the results of research from several of the scholarly fields which concentrate in a special way on grief and relate them to one another, especially psychoanalysis, psychiatry, psychology, sociology, and theology.

Based on the contribution by S. Freud, in "Trauer und Melancholie" (Mourning and Melancholia, 1916), psychoanalysis has established fundamental concepts concerning grief which have influenced in one way or another all other grief theories. Together with dynamically oriented psychiatry, psychoanalysis has described not only detailed individual cases of pathological coping with grief but has developed forms of therapy as well. Together these two disciplines have examined psychic and psychosomatic reactions to the loss of a loved one. They have concerned themselves especially with the issue of the circumstances under which grief will lead to continuing depressive and paranoid behavior disorders.

Psychology as such has made few direct contributions to grief research. Somewhat more productive has been the indirect contribution by the field of stress research and crisis prevention theory, where coping mechanisms (as well as the psychoanalytical concepts of defense mechanisms) are emphasized.

During the first decades of this century, sociological contributions to grief research were based primarily on mourning rituals of less differentiated societies, for it was believed that there the primitive forms of human behavior could be better observed. This close connection between ethnology and sociology has generally been retained until today, in particular as it relates to the subject of grief. In recent years, interaction research has dealt more and more with the specific situation in which interaction partners find themselves when facing death. At the same time several important studies about the sociology of death were published. Here the attempt was made to determine the influence of value judgments and forms of behavior in the entire society upon the valuation of death and the individual's attitude toward it. However, with few exceptions, there was no significant communication between psychoanalytical studies that focused more on family constellation and the society-oriented ethnological and sociological studies.

On the whole, theology has made very little specific contribution to the study of grief, even though it must be recognized that almost all monographs on this subject have been written by American pastoral theologians. In recent years, however, representatives of a "theology of hope" have begun to discuss with theoretical sociologists the meaning of death in its social-utopian dimension, the theme of repression of death in modern society, and also the medically important subject of "natural death." However, these exchanges on an abstract theoretical level have not dealt with the question of the individual's coping with grief. Nor has their theoretical discussion grappled seriously with a central question, namely, to what extent individual therapy has helped to alleviate the psychic damages created by the social power structure, but without attacking the evil at its root by abolishing the system which created the circumstances leading to these psychic damages.

If a theology of grief is to avoid becoming narrowly dogmatic, then it cannot ignore the experiences of the individual and the social group with which he is in interaction when the death of a loved one occurs. It must deal with the ways in which the mourner himself views his own personal loss and take seriously his ways of attempting to cope with it. A theology that continues to develop its statements systematically and subsequently seeks to apply them to the existential situation is of no help. It has to be theology "from the ground up."

This theology "from the ground up" is precisely what this book seeks to accomplish. It will proceed empirically, based upon psychoanalytic case studies; the investigations of situations of unusual pressure, such as battle, natural catastrophies, and other social traumatic occurrences; by stress theory; the insights that crisis theory has gained from counseling; descriptions of physical symptoms resulting from reactions to grief as these are observed by psychiatry; ethnological field studies among less differentiated societies; and sociological material growing out of interaction studies concerning change of status. In comparison with this, theological statements about death and mourning up to this point can hardly be called empirical.

In comparison with the continuously growing body of empirical data concerning bereavement on the one hand and abstract theological statements on the other hand, theology has tended to set a methodological limit for itself in dealing with death and grief. This self-limitation is quite unsatisfactory. If theology by its own self-definition relinquishes any utilization of the data of the empirical disciplines and is content only with its own generalizations, it thereby forfeits its authority to speak of and to the human condition.

Of the various disciplines of theology with their differing methods, only practical theology has inherent in its methodology sufficient attention to empirical data, to theology changed into action, to ecclesiology expressed in church structures, and to actual experiences with death. Practical theology certainly will not stop merely with the observation and analysis of such materials, but its point of departure is determined by the real experiences themselves.

1.2 Theological argument

There are a number of reasons that theology has a special responsibility to deal with the subject of grief. It is already apparent, of course, that up to this point, psychiatry and psychotherapy have made the significant contributions and provide the best material for developing a comprehensive understanding and therapy of grief. But the task of theology is given from a number of sources.

(1) A clear biblical commission is given to "weep with those who weep" (Rom. 12:15). The Old Testament provides impressive examples of lamentations for the deceased, such as David's mourning for Abner (II Sam. 3:31ff.). The mourners are especially recognized by Jesus in the Beatitudes, because their grief experiences have made them amenable to an understanding of and hope for the kingdom of God (Matt. 5:4).

Again and again the Old as well as the New Testament states the urgent demand to take care of widows and orphans, to provide for them and claim their rights. According to Luke, the first disagreement in the community in Jerusalem arose over the neglect of widows of Hellenistic origin (Acts 6:1ff.). Even today, the death of a husband in his middle years can create difficult situations for the widow. Very often the widow has to work. What is even more important, the general depreciation of the aging person affects the widowed in a special way; at the same time, the mourner is still under the "taboo of contact." Especially because the bereaved's burdens have changed through the loss of the close neighborhood style of community, it is essential for the fulfillment of the biblical call to minister to the mourners.

(2) The church, more than other organizations, is faced with the problem of dealing with grief. For reasons to be discussed in another context, the funeral has become more and more a function of the church. The frequency with which ministers are called upon to respond to the situation of grief makes such work an eminently practical theological task.

(3) It is not uncommon that the pastor shows signs of confusion, anxiety, and cynicism during the process of the funeral. For instance, if the minister cannot comprehend the meaning of the ritual he has to perform, or if he does not know how to bring together the biblical message and the situation at the grave, he may feel unable and unprepared to talk to the bereaved in a helpful way. Anxieties arise in him because he himself is a mortal being, and each funeral reminds him of his own mortality. These anxieties are intensified through social as well as theological uncertainty. Because of this confusion and these anxieties, ministers as well as doctors will occasionally cynically devalue everything related to the funeral and the bereaved. They scorn the ritual that they carry out unwillingly. They accuse the mourners of insincere motives and they oppose the so-called death cult. It is the central, personal concern of this book to contribute to the provision of greater insight and better ways for the minister to cope with this very difficult part of his ministry.

(4) Since the age of the Enlightenment, the nontheological disciplines have increasingly withdrawn from the question of life after death. With the end of classical German philosophy, that field has to a large extent ceased to include the question in the scope of its reflection. Explorations of the subject in the field of parapsychology have not gained recognition by the scientific community. Almost the same holds true in regard to the meaning and value of death. For the most part these questions have been dealt with only by existential philosophy

(and there perhaps in an exaggerated manner). But the questions of death and immortality did not expire with the decrease of scientific interest. They were only repressed into the popular philosophical underground and stored in the subconscious, from which they have been resurrected by psychoanalytical research, which tried to explain them by introducing the concept of the death wish.

Theology deserves credit for keeping the question of death and immortality open, even though it was scorned by the academic world. These questions have on the whole been left to theology by university and society. Yet, although theology has been required by its own self-definition to deal with these issues, it is doubtful whether it has provided much insight concerning them. Nevertheless, it has guaranteed that the questions of death and resurrection would not be silenced, and therefore theology has been able to offer some real help to the bereaved. The death of a person always raises the question of the meaning of death and its conquest to the survivors. Theology has insisted that these are to be considered legitimate questions, questions that are not completely answered by considering death a natural event which has to be accepted without question and complaint. Seen in this light, theology makes an essential contribution to coping with grief. Certainly theology throws light on human thoughts and behavior as it deals with biblical material. Nevertheless, the theological approach also requires a study and utilization of secular knowledge, making its theological statements in the context of precise and sensitive observations of specific human phenomena.

This approach is the particular problem of *practical* theology in which it presumably differs essentially from other theological disciplines. The danger implicit in this approach is that theology might lose its own identity and be over-whelmed by the secular knowledge with which it is working. Nevertheless, practical theology must choose this road if it takes seriously its goal to help the bereaved in a concrete way.

(5) Another fact which has contributed to the character of theology is that it insists upon considering the "entire" person, having retained the awareness that one cannot split

up the science of man into ever smaller areas of specialty without considering that man is a unity and experiences himself as a unity, even if parts of him may be distinguished from another. Theology therefore with good reason has adhered to the idea that man is a whole "person." This study takes this theological premise seriously. But by working in an integrated manner it also strives to avoid the accusation of separation from other legitimate sources of knowledge. This means that the subject of grief and the mourner as a person will not be permitted to become split up into various scientific views but will be considered in their totality. As far as possible, this study intends to analyze the interrelated internal and external situation of the bereaved. The justifiable theological claim of keeping in mind the wholeness and unity of man is one aspect that legitimates this study as theological.

(6) There is one concept of theology whose basic principle can be stated as follows: A theological task is given when, in a society, groups or individuals suffer under an oppressive social system without being able to help themselves effectively in their sufferings, or to experience sufficient help from others. Who the persons are who are suffering under the power structure may change from situation to situation. What tax collectors and Gentiles are in the New Testament may be the homeless and juvenile delinquents in another social context. Certainly mourners belong to one of those groups which are exposed to societal as well as internal pressures. They are avoided by others, and none of the "care giving agents," whose profession it is to provide help and healing, feels himself responsible for them as long as the mourners keep within the limits of what is considered normal and do not fall into pathological forms of coping with grief. This makes it an urgent necessity for theology to take an interest in this issue. In many ways theology is less equipped for this task than other sciences. Therefore, it is a combination of disinterest on the part of the more relevant sciences in connection with the ignored need of the bereaved which makes focusing on their problem a theological task.

(7) Finally, this study legitimates itself as theological in that it shows a particular partiality. That does not mean it

purposely neglects the criteria that distinguish a work as objective and scientific. Nevertheless, it shows partiality insofar as it decisively takes the side of the bereaved (and the deceased). Therefore it intends to make their problems and their situation more comprehensible than the situation of those who are professionally dealing with them, whether the latter are theologians or other scientists.

1.3 Arrangement of the material

After this brief outline of the purpose of the book, the theological legitimation, the sources, and the methodology, the second chapter will describe the most important psychoanalytical theories about bereavement and investigations of the symptoms of grief.

A general survey of the grief process forms the content of the third chapter. At this point, we will deal more specifically with the four phases of the grief process (phase of shock; controlled, regressive, and adaptive phases), as well as with the special problems resulting from anticipatory grief, inhibited grief, and pathological coping with grief.

The second and third chapters concern themselves primarily with those aspects that make grief understandable as an intropsychic process. In the second section, grief will also be investigated as a sociological process.

The fourth chapter deals with theories of grief as status transition. The fifth chapter concerns itself with the care giving agents: the physician at the hospital, the general practitioner, the undertaker, and the minister. The functions of these care giving agents for the bereaved will be clarified, with particular attention being given to the possibilities of pastoral counseling in the individual phases of the grief process.

The three chapters of the third part form a unity. The defense mechanisms (which appear both during the regressive phase and in the adaptive stage of bereavement) are described. However, these defense mechanisms have frequently a different function and phenomenology in the two phases.

The sixth chapter deals with the narcissistic defense

mechanisms, whose common characteristic is a general refusal to recognize the fact of death. These are the mechanisms of "breakdown of reality testing," in which mourners believe they are seeing the deceased in reality or dream; the mechanism of "denial," in which the fact of death is denied almost completely or is only partially recognized; the mechanism of "searching," in which the bereaved still hopes the separation will not be final; and the mechanism of "mania" in which grief temporarily is pushed aside by the pleasant feeling of being united again with the deceased.

Coping mechanisms, which have an extreme aggressive component, are the concern of the seventh chapter. There is the mechanism of "protest and lamentation," which is mainly directed toward the deceased but can also turn against other persons. The mechanism "search for the guilty" looks for the cause and the originator of death. The mechanism "identification with the aggressor" turns the aggression released by death against the bereaved himself.

The eighth chapter discusses the object-libidinal defense mechanisms in which the attempt is made to adhere to the deceased in a positive way. With the mechanism of "helplessness," the bereaved tries to secure the help of others. The mechanism of "recollection" allows for a step-by-step detachment from the deceased, who is integrated as an image through the mechanism of "incorporation." In the mechanism of "substitution" the bereaved attempts to find a substitute for the lost love object.

In the three chapters describing the mechanisms by which the bereaved tries to cope psychically with the loss, the sociological factors affecting the facilitation or hindrance of certain mechanisms are analyzed. Value judgments and standards of more distant relatives, the social environment, and society may interfere with the various forms of coping. It is also necessary to consider what can be said theologically about the mechanisms in question and what significance can be attached to them in the practice of the church. An epilogue contains an analysis of the death of Jesus and the grief of his disciples as portrayed in John 16, offering a model for coping with grief.

PART I

GRIEF—
The Individual Aspect

2. Theory and symptomatology of grief

2.1 Sigmund Freud: the murder of the father

The classical text, in which for the first time mourning became an object of scientific investigation, is the brief essay "Mourning and Melancholia" written by S. Freud in 1915 and published a year later.[1] In order better to understand the various themes (and one-sided tendencies) incorporated in this study, we have to discuss a few of Freud's earlier writings, particularly *Totem and Taboo* (1912/13).[2]

In *Totem and Taboo* Freud is interested in the numerous areas of correspondence, which in his opinion can be verified, between the psychology of "savage races" and the psychology of neurotics. However, his interpretation is ambiguous. On the one hand, he interprets the insufficiently explained behavior of the "primitives" through the reaction of the neurotic, which has been made comprehensible through psychoanalytical theory. But on the other hand, he proceeds in the opposite way when he rediscovers the behavior of "savages" in neurotics. Like the "primitives," they are either inhibited in their development or regressed, because both are fixed on the infantile incest wishes, the "nucleus complex of neurosis."[3]

Among the many comparisons and analogies drawn by Freud between "savages" and neurotics there are three important points for the subject of mourning: (1) the strong ambivalence that obsesses "savages" and neurotics, (2) the death wish, common to both of them, and (3) the admiration and respect both feel for their deceased father.

(1) In explaining the ambivalence, Freud starts from the marked fear of the deceased, which often is to be found in "primitive" cultures and which seems to Freud so far not to be sufficiently explained. Why do beloved relatives suddenly become revengeful demons after death? Freud seeks an explanation for the compulsive self-accusations of the survivors who feel they have caused the death of the loved one through some carelessness or neglect. No recalling of the facts that there was no fault can put an end to the torture of such reproaches. The reason for it is explained in the case of a patient:

Not that the mourner has really been guilty of the death or that she has really been careless, as the obsessive reproach asserts; but still there was something in her, a wish of which she herself was aware, which was not displeased with the fact that death came, and which would have brought it about sooner had it been strong enough. The reproach now reacts against this unconscious wish after the death of the beloved person. Such hostility, hidden in the unconscious behind tender love, exists in almost all cases of intensive emotional allegiance to a particular person, indeed it represents the classical case, the prototype of the ambivalence of human emotions.[4]

Freud assumes that a similar high degree of ambivalence can be found among the "savage races"; they too feel a strong hostility toward the deceased and a certain satisfaction at his death. However, for them this hostility is transferred to the deceased in the defense process of projection; not the mourner but the soul of the deceased now entertains these hostile emotions against which the bereaved has to protect himself through complicated taboo regulations.[5] Now, the dead person "curiously enough has become an evil demon . . . who seeks to bring death upon us. The survivors . . . are freed from inner oppression, but they have only succeeded in exchanging it for an affliction from without."[6]

In all human relations there is a mixture of tender and hostile emotions, but they are for the most part not conscious. The hostility toward a person may actually have a real background in his domineering and vicious behavior. The feelings of hatred awakened mostly remain latent with respect to the next of kin so long as they live. Only with their death does the ambivalence become unbearable. "The mourning originating from the enhanced tenderness became on the one hand more intolerant of the latent hostility, while on the other hand it could not tolerate that the latter should not give origin to a feeling of pure gratification."[7] This problem could only be mastered by way of an outward projection on the dead person.

The neurotic has brought with him "an atavistic remnant in the form of an archaic constitution" and is now compelled to the most prodigious psychic efforts and compulsive reproaches in the interest of cultural demand.[8] What had been a collective effort among primitive societies is now left to the neurotic alone and has to be carried out with his private means.[9] To argue here simply in a global way with the "course of the ages" and "culture," as Freud does, nevertheless appears rather unsatisfying, since he neglects the fact that to a high degree this change has been brought about by Christian culture.

(2) The hostility in the ambivalence conflict finds its strongest expression in the desire that the other person may die. If we take into account the analysis of dreams of normal individuals and neurotics then, according to Freud, this desire to kill others is much stronger and more frequent then we had suspected.[10] The commandment "Thou shalt not kill" would not exist if it were self-evident. Another thing "savages" and compulsive neurotics have in common is the belief that death wishes are fulfilled. "A compulsion neurotic may be oppressed by a sense of guilt, which is appropriate to a wholesale murderer, ... it is based upon intensive and frequent death wishes which unconsciously manifest themselves toward his fellow beings."[11] They are unmotivated in terms of the reality of the act; but they are motivated to the extent that "primitive man" and the neurotic believe that through the omnipotence of their thoughts these death wishes become reality.

It is well known that Freud repeatedly dealt with the problem of the death wish after he became aware of it through Breuer's analysis of Anna O.[12] In a letter to W. Fliess (1897) he reports his death wishes against his brother Julius who died at the age of eight months.[13] In the "dream interpretation" that refers back to a self-analysis he describes how a death wish is hidden in a dream about the death of loved ones, felt by the dreamer at the present or an earlier time, concerning the person dreamt about.[14]

Above all, Freud was affected by and dealt with the death wish against the father. Already in *Interpretation of Dreams* he pointed out that in boys' dreams these death wishes are primarily directed toward the father, because the child sees in the father the most essential rival for the mother's love.[15] The desire to kill the father as an obnoxious rival and at the same time a certain respect for him lead to the ambivalence conflict toward him. Freud described this ambivalence in a few case studies, especially in a "case of compulsive neurosis," in which a solution was even more difficult, because here a death wish was "successful."[16] In his analysis of Dostoevski's writings, Freud points out his death wishes toward the father as a dominating theme.[17]

(3) In a later paragraph about "the infantile recurrence of totemism"[18] Freud developed a story about the slaying of the primal father by his sons. This story, a mixture of myth, symbol, and real history, relates that the sons could get access to the female sexual objects, tyrannized by the father, only by removing him. The group of brothers "were dominated by the same contradictory feelings towards the father which we can demonstrate as the content of ambivalence of the father complex in all our children and in neurotics. They hated the father who stood so powerfully in the way of their sexual demands and their desire for power, but they also loved and admired him."[19] After they had satisfied their hate by his removal and had carried out their wish for identification with him, "the suppressed tender impulses had to assert themselves."[20] They renounced their deed, established a lasting sense of guilt, and denied themselves mothers and sisters by erecting the incest prohibition. The same happened with the murder of the father, which is carried out only symbolically in the sacrifice of the totem animal and is limited to unrealized death wishes. In other words, the sons created a "natural"

solution to the Oedipus complex. In this context the important statement is made: "The dead now became stronger than the living had been, even as we observe it today in the destinies of men."[21] In becoming an ancestor spirit, the murdered father gained a much deeper influence on the lives of the survivors than he could have had while alive. "Society is now based on complicity in the common crime, religion in the sense of guilt and the consequent remorse, while morality is based partly on the necessities of society and partly on the expiation which this sense of guilt demands."[22] This pattern of murder, guilt, and return of the murdered father henceforth determined the character of every religion;[23] it justifies the statement that "God at bottom is nothing but an exalted father"[24] (which of course is taken back on the following page since there it is only referred to as "the share of the father in the idea of God"). Above all, the father, who had been wished dead and with whom one no longer identifies by renouncing the rivalry with him, establishes himself anew as conscience and superego.[25]

The beginning of World War I revealed how thin was the cultural varnish that keeps the death wishes from their actualization. In "Thoughts for the Times on War and Death," Freud formulates the disillusionment many people experienced, a disillusionment about how highly civilized nations were capable of such outbreaks of hate. He cannot share this disillusionment because "in reality they [our world compatriots] have not sunk so low as we feared because they had never risen so high as we believed."[26]

The selfish and aggressive instincts, repressed only under the constraint of cultural demands and internalized by all too few, liberate themselves and are set free when nations permit killing and even make it an obligation. For Freud, war merely becomes the occasion to show what he assumes in every close relationship, namely, that every altruistic and social erotic element can be found together with intense hatred. The ambivalence of feeling is a natural state of affairs.[27] The death of the enemy with whom we have nothing in common does not create great problems; it is different when a loved one dies. Here the unacceptable hostility and the unconscious death wishes definitely come into conflict with the tender and loving feelings toward parents, spouses, or children. At this point the idea of the immortal soul was born in "primitive" culture. "Man could no longer keep death at a distance for he had tasted of it in his grief for the dead, but still he did not consent entirely to acknowledge it, for he could not conceive of himself as dead."[28] Freud asserts that at bottom "no one believes in his own death, or to put the same thing in another way, in the unconscious, every one of us is convinced of his own immortality."[29] Out of the conflict of being unable to imagine the death of a beloved person, but, at the same time, not being able to deny the reality of death, "primitive man" invented ghosts, demons, souls, and the conception of life continued after apparent death. Death wish and the desire not to lose the love object, according to Freud, still constitute our attitude toward the deceased, no matter whether that person is one whom we love or an enemy who should be included in our love according to the cultural demand.

The conclusion drawn by Freud is the expectation that our attitude toward death must change. "In our civilized attitude toward death we are once more living psychologically beyond our means,"[30] and that means for Freud that we have not sufficiently enough given account of our hostile and aggressive feelings over and against our neighbor. For us to confess this has the merit of taking somewhat more into account the true state of affairs, of dissolving the disillusionment about the regression into barbarism, and of making life again more endurable for us.[31]

In the brief contribution titled "Vergänglichkeit" (Mortality) Freud also considers the subject of mourning. In the infantile development a part of the libido turns away from the ego toward other objects. If these objects are destroyed or become lost, then the capacity to love is set free again. Nevertheless, it still adheres to its objects and refuses to give them up, even if there is a substitute available.[32]

Against the background of Freud's three papers *Totem and Taboo*, "Thoughts for the Times on War and Death," and "Vergänglichkeit," we now can turn to "Mourning and Melancholia." In this contribution Freud is not interested in

34

the phenomenon of mourning itself but rather in melancholia. Mourning is "regularly the reaction to the loss of a loved person, or to the loss of some abstraction which has taken the place of one, such as fatherland, liberty, an ideal, and so on."[33] This will be overcome after a certain period of time and any interference can have only harmful effects. Mourning is characterized by painful discord, suspension of interest in the outer world through the loss of the capacity to love, and inhibition of all activity, all of this to the extent that an activity is not in some way related to the deceased. This inhibition and limitation of the ego is the expression of a total concentration on the work of mourning.[34] The work of mourning is described as follows:

The testing of reality, having shown that the loved object no longer exists, requires forthwith that all the libido shall be withdrawn from its attachments to this object. Against this demand a struggle of course arises—it may be universally observed that man never willingly abandons a libido-position, not even when a substitute is already beckoning him. . . . The normal outcome is that deference for reality gains the day. Nevertheless, its behest cannot be at once obeyed. The task is now carried through bit by bit, under great expense of time and cathectic energy, while all the time the existence of the lost object is continued in the mind. Each single one of the memories and hopes which bound the libido to the object is brought up and hypercathected, and the detachment of the libido from it accomplished.[35]

At this point Freud speaks quite hopefully about the possibility of a final detachment from the object. According to his observation the fact is, however, that when the work of mourning is completed the ego "becomes free and uninhibited again."[36]

Nevertheless, the essential significance of "Mourning and Melancholia" lies in the fact that Freud made it very clear that melancholia is a conflict of ambivalence toward an endangered or lost love object.[37] As soon as it could be demonstrated even more clearly through further research that even in so-called "normal" mourning the correlation of loving and hostile feelings toward the dead not only existed but were effective as well, Freud's insights into the manic-depressive could then also be applied to the mourner.

In summarizing, one would have to say that Freud's most significant contribution lies in the fact that he for the first time structured the subject of grief. The essential part of it is the clarification of ambivalence which has widened our understanding of the funeral ceremony. Just as important is his point that ambivalence can lead to pathological coping with grief. With his economical and topological theory of melancholia he created the presupposition for the clarification of analogical processes in mourning. Nevertheless, Freud himself never went that far, for he underestimated the full effects of ambivalence in "normal" grief. The analogy to mourning refers in particular to the reproaches and self-reproaches, to mania, to the identification processes, and to the psychosomatic symptoms.[38] The more it became obvious in further research how undefined the borderlines between "normal" mourning, pathological mourning, and manic-depressive conditions are, the more Freud's theory on melancholia could be evaluated fruitfully for the understanding of the grief process.

No doubt, Freud's studies led to a better understanding of the coping mechanism "identification with the aggressor," dealt with later on.[39] However, even though this is an important form of working through grief, it is not the only way.

2.2 Karl Abraham: incorporation

Karl Abraham, the first German psychoanalyst and founder of the first branch of the International Psychoanalytical Association (1910), dealt even before the publication of "Mourning and Melancholia" with the correlation of fear and neurotic anxiety and related it to that of mourning and depression in an address published in 1912,[1] without going further into the subject of grief. Only in 1924 in "A Short Study of the Development of the Libido Viewed in the Light of Mental Disorders" did he return to the correlation of grief and manic-depressive conditions. While Freud saw melancholia in the fixation on the conflicts in the genital phase, Abraham attempted, following his own earlier approaches, to understand depression and compulsion neurosis as fixations on the sadistic-anal phase and especially the oral phase, and as a regression to these phases.[2]

In the sadistic-anal phase, according to Abraham, it is the withholding or expulsion of the excrement in which the ambiguous attitude toward the loss of the object finds its expression. Thus, with the neurotic, either constipation occurs in order to avoid a loss or diarrhea in order to expell the object which has acted so maliciously and unreliably.[3] So, the attempt is made either to preserve and dominate the endangered object or to give it up and destroy it; it depends upon how strong the respective sadistic and destructive forces are. In any case, "to lose something" and "to destroy something" are closely related; in this context Abraham refers to the phrase "to cleanse an area from all enemies." Some things that could support his argument without being mentioned by him in this context are the numerous rites of cleansing and purification carried out after the death of a person in less differentiated societies.

The very common custom in the U.S.A. (found also in other areas) of cleansing and disinfecting the house or apartment to excess after the funeral could be seen in this connection as getting rid of the dead person.

However, Abraham himself draws the analogy between mourning and manic-depressive disorder only by dealing with the oral level. He refers back to Freud's observation that the melancholiac introjects the lost object. Yet he criticizes Freud for not having efficiently enough taken into account the ambivalence toward the introjected object. Indeed, we observed that Freud states that in introjection the lost object always is incorporated as an evil, punishing object ("shadow") which forces the melancholiac into self-reproaches and self-accusations. Abraham, on the contrary, wants to make the point that for the mourner also in the oral stage, the ambivalence conflict continues to hold firmly to as well as to destroy the incorporated object.[4]

On the other hand, Freud differentiated mourning and

melancholia by the following fact: The melancholiac introjects the lost object, but the mourner frees himself from it during the process of bereavement because the ambivalence conflict in him is not developed to such a great extent. Now Abraham demonstrates, in the dream of an analyzed patient, how the introjection takes place even in "normal" grief and thus with the intention of adhering as well as destroying. The man in question had lost his wife during pregnancy when premature, Cesarean delivery became necessary because of a serious illness.

At that time one of the most striking symptoms shown by the analyzed patient was lack of interest in nourishment for many weeks. This stood in obvious contradiction to his usual daily habits and instead was reminiscent of the denial of nourishment by a melancholiac. One day the lack of interest in eating vanished and that evening the patient ate a full meal. During the following night he dreamt that he observed the dissection of the recently deceased. The dream had two contrasting scenes. In the first one, the cut up pieces of the corpse grew together again, the dead began to show signs of life, and the dreamer caressed her with feelings of utmost happiness. In the other scene of the dream, the appearance of the dissection changed its character and the dreamer was reminded of slaughtered animals in a butcher shop.[5]

According to the interpretation by Abraham, the dream combined two contrasting intentions. On the one hand, there is the desire to bring the deceased back to life. On the other hand, the deceased is in a cannibalistic way incorporated; the dreamer in this case study associates explicitly the parts of the corpse, the butchery, and the meat eaten the night before. This dream, according to Abraham, signals that the normal process of bereavement, the work of mourning, has started; the mourner no longer plays with the thought of following the dead by denial of food,[6] but can support himself as before. "The grief contains this comfort: *The love object is not lost, for now I carry it within me and can never lose it.*"[7] Nevertheless, unlike the melancholiac, incorporation for the mourner serves "mainly the tendency to conserve the relationship to the deceased or—which is the same thing—to compensate for the loss suffered. Never will the consciousness be overwhelmed by it in such a way as it occurs for the melancholiac."[8] While the mourner copes in a positive way with his ambivalence toward the lost object by incorporating it, the depressed is under the compulsion to destroy it, either willingly or forcibly by chewing it up or biting it to pieces.

In "Mourning and Melancholia" Freud had found analogies between mourning and depression but did not observe in normal psychic life a process that corresponds to the change from melancholia to mania,[9] appearing as denial, liberation, and triumph in the depressive-manic cycle. In the manic phase, the melancholiac succeeds in disregarding and denying the demands and reproaches of the superego (conscience). The "shadows of the object" vanish. The individual feels liberated and indulges in a regular "freedom-ecstasy"; all the restrictions once enforced upon him become futile.

Abraham believes, however, that such manic behavior can be found in a lesser form in normal grief when the mourner has detached himself from the deceased. Abraham observes an increased sexual desire, partly in the sublimated form of a very high adventurousness and expansion of the original circle of interests. An increased oral desire appears.[10]

Abraham, more so than Freud, considers melancholia an archaic form of mourning. This refers in particular to necrophagia as a form of incorporation of the deceased, to the expulsion of the dead symbolized in the excretion, and to the manic triumph over the dead.[11] Dream analysis and psychosomatic symptoms lead him to the conclusion *"that the work of mourning of the healthy person also is performed in the archaic form at deeper psychic levels."* [12] However, the reference to the archaic forms of mourning may not always be convincing, especially since they are not at all universal, and contemporary ethnology no longer proceeds from a continuous development from "primitive" natives to more cultivated tribes. Nevertheless, Abraham has taken a step beyond Freud with the disclosure that incorporation and mania are found in "normal" grief. Moreover, his distinction between tendencies either to keep and control the threatened object or to dispose of and destroy it is of great importance for the more exact determination of the coping mechanisms employed in grief.

2.3 Melanie Klein: the "depressive position"

The contribution from Melanie Klein, who studied with Abraham in Berlin, consists primarily of three points: (1) She differentiated the significance of internalization and introjection in the grief process beyond Freud and Abraham; (2) she made the attempt to explain mourning and depression as a modification of a particular period of infantile experiences, which she called the "depressive position";[1] and (3) she succeeded in clarifying better theoretically the appearance of manic phases in depression and tracing and making understandable analogous symptoms in grief.

(1) Klein starts with the presupposition that from the beginning of life the developing ego of the infant introjects good and bad objects. The objects are good if they are available to him; they are bad if they are denied to him. A first object of this sort is his mother's breast, but soon this includes the entire person of the mother and extends to the wider environment. The infant builds up an internal world of fantasy filled with good and bad objects, just as fantastic as the external world from which he takes his images of his inner world.[2] Negative experiences with the environment as well as his own sadistic instincts, which the infant projects toward the "bad" objects in his internal world, make them appear as persecuting, destroying objects, in particular, chewing-up objects. The ego experiences the anxiety of an impending loss of "good" objects. This is the case particularly if "the ego identifies more strongly with his good inner objects and at the same time—because of the increasing understanding of psychic reality—realizes his own inability to protect and preserve his good objects against the internalized bad objects and the id."[3] The infant fears the "good" objects may die and drag his ego into death with them.

(2) Weaning and a temporary absence of the mother, confusingly experienced, are magnified in the world of fantasy to the death of the mother and other loving persons.

Only in a mutual enrichment of experiences in the outer and inner world and in a gradual adjustment of these two worlds to reality is it normally possible to overcome these anxieties. If this is accomplished, the "depressive position" is left behind, which Klein considers "the result of a mixture of paranoid anxiety and those subjects of fear, feelings of sadness, and defense mechanisms that are linked to the danger of the loss of the (entire) beloved object."[4] The "depressive position" belongs to normal development;[5] the inadequate overcoming of it creates the disposition for depressive and paranoid behavior disorders, in particular if no efficient reality testing is undertaken. Now mourning is essentially revitalizing that first realization of introjection, loss, and reality testing.[6]

The external loss appearing through the death of a loved one not only represents the loss of the loving care experienced before, but it endangers the totality of the internal "good" objects. The mourner feels that the destroying and disintegrating objects have won the upper hand. According to Klein the task at hand is not only to restore the deceased person in his internal world, as described by Abraham; he must also save his entire inner world from destruction. "With this the early depressive position and together with it anxieties, guilt, feelings of loss and grief deriving from the breast situation and from all other sources, including the Oedipus situation, are revitalized."[7] Just as the infant lives through the "depressive position," so the mourner painfully must experience the deterioration of his internal world and restore it again. Klein assumes that he "lives through a modified and temporarily manic-depressive condition."[8] The work of mourning is in danger of failure where the mourner as well as the manic-depressive has failed to establish and stabilize the "good" objects in his internal world in infancy.

(3) Freud recognized the triumph over the dead both by the "savages" as well as by the manic-depressives, but denied that it also appears in the normal grief process.[9] Based on her theory, Klein represents the viewpoint that in every death, some infantile death wishes against parents, brothers, or sisters are recognized as fulfilled, because the emotions the infant had felt toward members of his family are directed

toward every beloved person. Therefore, death becomes a victory and brings triumph—and at the same time guilt feelings with it. But the guilt feelings turn the lost "good" object into an enemy and persecutor of the mourner and shake the faith in the efficient help of all other internalized "good" persons. In this claim Klein follows Freud's analysis in *Totem and Taboo*.[10] No longer can the mourner accept the deceased as an idealized "good" object whose affection and good qualities can comfort him in his grief.[11] Because of the preponderance of destructive and persecuting objects, in particular the "bad" parents, the mourner must revitalize the defense mechanisms that proved helpful to him during the "depressive position." Their essential objective is to deny the reality of loss, both the inner and, in part also, the outer reality. Therefore the ego must attempt to get all objects, "good" and "bad," under his control, for only in this way is the destructive power of the "bad" ones averted and the loss of the "good" ones undone. This represents a renewal of the infantile experience of omnipotence, according to which the ego can send away and call back the parents at his pleasure and thus kill and revive them. The experience of omnipotence not only confirms the ability of absolute control, but also gives the impression that all these objects are of no real significance for the ego.[12] Thus the defensive mechanism of omnipotence has its effects in two directions. On the one hand, it provides power to destroy the "bad" objects and thus to prevent their persecution, be it the "bad" parents who demand revenge[13] or persons who threaten the "good" object. Whatever has caused the death could not prevent it, or whatever symbolizes death must be disparaged (made bedeviled). On the other hand, the defense mechanism of omnipotence results in the revaluation of the "good" objects; they are looked upon as extremely perfect and unusually helpful in order to be able to support the ego in its struggle against loss.

The defense mechanism of omnipotence, which awakens the belief of being able to control and dominate all objects, finds its contrast in the defense mechanism of escape. The escape may be made to internalized "good" objects; if it is not the deceased, it can be other "persons" who proved to be helpful. The escape may also turn outwardly to real persons who give promise of becoming substitutes for the loss. That this escape represents a defense mechanism is shown in the idealization of these inner and outer objects.[14]

The defense mechanisms of omnipotence and escape, and the disparagement and idealization connected with them, serve the purpose of restoring the inner world. They are given up step by step and always taken up again when the attacks of the "bad" lost object begin anew. But gradually the inner world achieves a greater security. The persecution diminishes and the yearning for the lost beloved object is experienced with greater intensity. "Hate recedes and love is set free."[15] The yearning for the lost love object also includes a dependence, but this dependence becomes encouragement for the restoration and preservation of the object. The longing is creative and dominated by love, while the dependence based on persecution remains fruitless and destructive.[16]

A painful experience such as grief can stimulate sublimations in a person, make it possible for him to become creative and more tolerant in understanding others and in his relationship to other people and subjects. "It seems that every step forward in the grief process results in certain symptoms: a deepening of the relationship between the individual and his inner objects, happiness if they are regained after they had seemed lost (*Paradise Lost and Regained*), and, finally, an increased confidence in and love for them, because in spite of everything they proved to be good and helpful."[17] At the same time it is a process that can lead to greater inner and outer independence.

The restoration of the destroyed inner world is characteristic of a successful work of mourning according to Klein, not only the detachment from the loved one and the transference of the libido to substitutes. In the normal grief process the superego is introjected as well. Freud recognized this only for the melancholiac, but it is a "superego organization"[18] that includes not only the parents but the total of the internalized "good" and "bad" objects.

Klein's attempt to understand the progressive form of mourning in adults as a reactivation of infantile "depressive positions" is quite significant. This insight has remained basic, no matter what the deciding separation experience in childhood was thought to be. She drew attention to the fact that coping with grief is to a great extent determined by the way former crises, particularly in infancy, were overcome. More than anyone before, she has described in detail the process character of mourning, with its progressions, retreats, and renewed thrusts. Another important point to recognize is that a positive coping with crisis can lead an individual to a deeper confidence in his internal and external world.

This characterization of grief as process became possible when Klein recognized depression, and in particular mania, as being, in part, defense mechanisms, certainly not without the influence of a study by Anna Freud published shortly before.[19] To understand the manic state as reactivation of infantile triumph and omnipotence feelings that are used as a defense against an imminent or real loss in the form of denial, disparagement, and idealization went far beyond the contribution made by Abraham on this subject.

Finally, with her dual system of the internal and external reality, in which "good" and "bad" objects are in a complex correlation, Klein laid the foundation for an understanding of the grief process that is not limited to the internal psychic processes. For instance, with her statement that "good" objects from the external world contribute very much to the restoration of the disturbed inner world, she made the first attempts to understand mourning also in its social dimensions in relation to the internal processes. While for her the superego is more than an internalized father, she at the same time has created a much wider basis for the understanding of what is commonly called conscience. It is regrettable that her essay "Mourning and its Relation to Manic-Depressive States" found so little recognition. In our opinion, this paper is the most remarkable study written so far on the subject of the work of mourning, even if it became possible only through the preparatory works by Freud and Abraham.

The psychoanalytical theory of mourning was continued in the sixties by the English analyst John Bowlby. In a series of publications he dealt with the grief process in infancy and early childhood and its connection with the grief of adults, with special emphasis on separation-anxiety in childhood. The American Gregory Rochlin should be mentioned here as well. He has demonstrated under the term "loss complex" how early defense mechanisms against loss are developed and how the first attempts to overcome death also shape the religious experience in childhood.

2.4 Grief as disease

2.41 The psychic symptomatology of grief

If in dealing with grief reactions we differentiate as follows between psychic and psychosomatic symptoms, then we cannot avoid pursuing the matter somewhat forcibly in a few places. In many cases the somatic reaction is so closely bound together with the psychic that they are difficult to distinguish. While, for example, loss of weight is definitely a somatic symptom, the question arises whether the loss of appetite that contributes considerably to this loss of weight is not a psychic symptom. Similar statements could be made about insomnia. Symptoms of general indispositions, such as exhaustion, lack of concentration, and apathy, are also recognized as psychic symptoms.

Freud saw as the distinguishing features in grief a painful resentment, an abolition of interest in the outside world, loss of the capacity to love, and inhibition of all activity.[1] E. Lindemann, who was the first one to concern himself with establishing a comprehensive symptomatology of psychic symptoms in grief, found that all his patients were dealing exclusively with the lost person as well as "silent" attacks of grief (sorrow). Ninety-six percent of the mourners showed signs of excessive tiredness, 84 percent an inability to carry out usual tasks, and 29 percent insomnia.[2] At another point he adds the following symptoms: guilt feelings, hostile reaction to the environment, a feeling of "derealization," and an aimless hyperactivity in speech as well as in gestures.[3]

If one excludes Lindemann because he does not give a basis for his sample, there are, as far as it can be established, only three investigations that make the attempt to collect in a statistically sustained way information about psychic symptoms. The investigations by C. M. Parkes[4] and by P. Clayton et al.[5] exhibit considerable deficiencies since they do not use control groups, and their samples are so small that significant differences can hardly be established.

So far, the most reliable study concerning the distribution of grief reactions has been worked out by D. Maddison and A. Viola.[6] Their sample included 375 widows and a control group of 199 nonaffected women. The study was based on interviews. For methodological reasons the sample was limited to women between the ages of forty-five and sixty. A third of the interviewed persons came from the Boston area, the rest from Sidney, Australia.

The average figures reflecting psychic symptoms, based on the statements by those interviewed, are considerably lower than those of Lindemann and Parkes. This is explained by the fact that Maddison and Viola's sample does not represent people who had asked for medical help. Forty-seven percent mention a reduced ability to work and 41 percent a general nervousness. Occurring noticeably often are general exhaustion, insomnia, and depressive mood. Between 20 percent and 10 percent speak of the anxiety of a nervous breakdown, feeling of panic, a continuous anxiety, and trembling (Table 1). Also obvious is increased use of nutritional, soothing, and sleeping pills, but also an increase of alcohol consumption and smoking. More than a third of those interviewed claim that they are free of symptoms; at a second interview the same number reported a considerable diminution of the symptoms.

A comparison between the observations by Freud and the investigations by Lindemann; Parkes, Clayton et al.; and Maddison and Viola is hardly possible. Freud and Lindemann never mention anxieties and the use of intoxicating drugs. Hostile feelings toward others are mentioned only by Lindemann, guilt feelings only by Clayton et al.; both are missing in the statistics from Maddison and Viola. A general agreement is seen in dealing with symptoms with a high degree of distribution, such as depressive mood, insomnia, exhaustion, inability to work, and general nervousness.

Table 1[7]

Psychic grief reactions of widows in Boston and Sidney

Symptom or complaint	Total widows N = 375 %	Total control N = 199 %	P*	Boston widows N = 132 %	Sidney widows N = 221† %	P
Psychological symptoms:						
General nervousness	41.3	16.1	0.001	40.9	41.2	n.s‡
Depression	22.7	5.5	0.001	17.4	25.3	n.s.
—requiring medical treatment	12.8	1.0	0.001	9.1	14.0	n.s.
—requiring hospitalisation	1.3	0	0.05	0.7	1.8	n.s.
"Fear of nervous breakdown"	13.1	2.0	0.001	12.1	14.5	n.s.
Feelings of panic	12.0	2.5	0.001	8.3	14.0	n.s.
Persistent fears	12.0	3.0	0.001	9.8	12.2	n.s.
Repeated peculiar thoughts	8.5	2.0	0.001	8.3	9.5	n.s.
Nightmares	8.8	1.0	0.001	6.8	9.0	n.s.
Insomnia	40.8	12.6	0.001	35.6	44.8	n.s.
Trembling	10.4	2.0	0.001	4.5	14.0	0.01
Habits:						
Drug intake—increase	37.3	11.1	0.001	20.5	48.0	0.001
—marked increase	5.9	0.5	0.001	2.3	8.1	0.01
Alcohol intake—increase	6.7	2.0	0.001	9.1	3.2	0.05
Smoking—marked increase	11.7	1.5	0.001	14.4	9.0	n.s.
General:						
Reduced work capacity	46.7	26.1	0.001	43.2	50.2	n.s.
Gross fatigue	29.6	11.6	0.001	26.5	31.2	n.s.

*Probabilities calculated by chi-square analysis with 1 degree of freedom.
†Not including widows of husbands under 45 yr at time of death.
‡Chi-square value does not reach 0.05 level of significance.

2.42 The psychosomatic of grief

S. Freud gave little consideration to the psychosomatic symptoms of grief, quite in contrast to his recognition of anxiety neurosis. Only occasionally can some observations be found. In the analysis of Mrs. Emmy v. N. (1895) he reports on a session after the death of her husband: "Once more she had slept very little because of a stomach ache, she had taken no supper yesterday, and also complains about a pain in her right arm."[8] In *Psychische Behandlung (Seelenbehandlung)* (Psychic Treatment, 1905) he points to the physical correlation of stages of affects: "Constant stages of affects of a painful or so-called 'depressive' nature such as grief, sorrow, and mourning reduce the overall nourishment of the body, cause the bleaching of the hair, the disappearance of fat tissues and the morbid alteration of the blood-vascular tissues."[9]

In a little-recognized article, "Equivalencies of Mourning,"[10] Karl Landauer in 1926 compiled his observations of psychosomatic symptoms, which capsulize the theme of almost all the results of later investigations on the subject. He divides these symptoms under the terms weeping, salivation, achylia, constipation, pseudo-Parkinson's disease, pain, and association-inhibition.

In the paragraph on weeping, Landauer refers to the occasional occurrence of a cramp-like contraction of the diaphragm, besides the flow of tears. The frequent symptoms of shortness of breath and the anxiety connected with it are seen most completely in asthma, which Landauer had diagnosed in neurotic patients as the result of a death occurrence.[11]

Furthermore, during bereavement "often a strong secretion of a thin, liquidy, sometimes stale, sometimes bitter-tasting saliva occurs, which is swallowed."[12] Through this increased secretion of saliva, oxygen is swallowed, according to Landauer, which can cause a feeling of a full stomach, belching, vomiting, and colic.

Referring to experiments, Landauer considers it a matter of fact that grief upsets the secretion of gastric juices or even stops it completely. The result is also "the feeling of stuffiness, lack of appetite which facilitates the seclusion from the outside world, belching, diarrhea shortly after taking in food ('nothing stays with me anymore'), all of which build the bridge to anal erotic."[13] The spastic constipation seems to be in contrast to this but alternates often with diarrhea, very often in rapid sequence.

Under pseudo-Parkinson's disease Landauer includes the observations of both general poorness and retardation of expression: "Imitation movements hardly exist any more than accompanying movements, for example, of the arms while walking. If movements of expression are visible, then their start is delayed, their course slowed down. Since they can be kept for a long time, long after the cause for it has abated, the face appears to be rigid like a mask and the gestures frozen."[14] Hypotonia may occur, in particular before going to bed or shortly after being asleep; as its consequence, there are disturbances in going to sleep and waking up frightened from sleep. As in the contrast between constipation and diarrhea, here too hypo- and hypermotility are combined.

In terms of pain Landauer refers to the popular phrase about grief as "heartbreak" or "heartsickness." The "heart aches," "it is wounded," "it burns." Accordingly, pain is usually described as pressure, soreness, burning, sometimes also as cramps and contraction near the heart,[15] comparable to the grief that lies like "a great weight on the chest."

Finally, Landauer draws attention to the association-inhibition which is, in his opinion, often the only palpable expression of an unconscious sad ill-feeling. "If one overlooks this possibility, one easily makes the mistake of ignoring the dragging, apparently affectless speaking and the absence of imagination from the patient. In doing so one deprives oneself of the opportunity of attacking the cause of repression, namely grief, by fixing exclusively on the things repressed."[16]

Surely one ought to remain critical toward the connection Landauer establishes between individual symptoms. He also does not proceed homogenously in etiology by partly making the physiological processes accountable for the reaction and partly their symbolical interpretation (particularly with gastro-intestinal disorders). Finally, he connects several symptoms to the fully intended self-withdrawal of the mourner. It is, however, a remarkable achievement to attain such a comprehensive account of the psychosomatic grief reactions based entirely on individual observations. Only in recent years has this been established again through systematic investigations.

Lindemann briefly mentioned psychosomatic reactions in his research published in 1944.[17] According to information given by widowed women and their physicians whom Marris interviewed, the following symptoms occurred: weight loss, rheumatism and fibrositis, asthma, bronchitis and chest pains, peptic ulcer and indigestion, swollen feet and leg ulcers, falling hair, skin irritations and rashes, abscesses of the gums, headaches, dizziness, and "nerves."[18]

The careful survey by Maddison and Viola, the only one that compares widows with a control group, discovered from statements made by the interviewed a noticeable deterioration in their health (28 percent against 4.5 percent in the control group; a greater percentage among widows in Sidney), particularly with the increase in age of widows. Class structure, number and age of the children left, on the other hand, resulted in no difference (Table 2). Anorexia and weight loss appeared in this survey also relatively frequently, while the opposite symptom of excessive appetite and weight increase were less frequent. Furthermore, increased pulse rate, chest pains, and shortness of breath developed as well as other psychosomatic symptoms, as already mentioned by Landauer and Marris.[19]

G. Engel tried to determine more precisely the conditions under which unacceptable experiences and emotions are turned into psychosomatic symptoms:[20]

(1) The conversion symptom expresses itself in "body language," either as a psychic experience in somatic suffering or a denial of the experience in the same way. Therefore, psychosomatic symptomatology expresses either: "I feel pain"; "I was hurt by the death"; or: "I cannot see" (and therefore do not have to convince myself that the beloved person is dead); "I see the deceased"; "I cannot swallow this"; "I cannot digest it."

(2) Through a somatic reaction a relationship should be

Table 2 [21]

Psychosomatic grief reactions of widows in Boston and Sidney

Symptom or complaint	Total widows N = 375 %	Total control N = 199 %	P*	Boston widows N = 132 %	Sidney widows N = 221† %	P
Neurological:						
"Migraine"	4.8	3.0	n.s.	1.5	6.3	0.02
Headache	17.6	9.0	0.01	14.4	19.5	n.s.
Dizziness	9.1	4.5	0.05	5.3	11.3	0.05
Fainting spells	1.3	0	0.05	0.8	1.8	n.s.
Blurred vision	13.7	7.5	0.02	12.1	15.8	n.s.
Facial pain	1.9	0.5	n.s.	1.5	2.3	n.s.
Dermatological:						
Skin rashes	6.1	2.5	0.05	0.8	8.6	0.05
Excessive sweating	9.3	5.0	0.05	10.6	8.6	n.s.
Gastro-Intestinal:						
Indigestion	9.9	4.5	0.01	10.6	9.5	n.s.
Difficulty in swallowing	4.8	1.5	0.02	6.1	4.5	n.s.
Peptic ulceration	2.1	2.0	n.s.	0.8	3.2	n.s.
Colitis	0.5	0	n.s.	0	0.9	n.s.
Vomiting	2.7	0	0.01	0	4.5	0.01
Excessive appetite	5.4	0.5	0.001	3.0	5.9	n.s.
Anorexia	13.1	1.0	0.001	9.8	16.3	n.s.
Weight gain	8.5	9.0	n.s.	10.6	6.3	n.s.
Weight loss	13.6	2.0	0.001	9.1	16.7	0.05
Genito—Urinary:						
Menorrhagia	3.4	0.5	0.05	3.0	2.7	n.s.
Cardio—Vascular:						
Palpitations	12.5	4.0	0.001	9.1	14.9	n.s.
Chest pain	10.1	4.5	0.01	4.5	14.0	0.01
Respiratory:						
Dyspnoea	12.0	4.5	0.001	8.3	14.0	n.s.
Asthma	2.4	1.5	n.s.	2.3	2.3	n.s.
General:						
Frequent infections	2.1	0	0.01	3.0	1.8	n.s.
General aching	8.4	4.0	0.001	6.8	9.5	n.s.
Neoplastic growth	0.8	0	n.s.	1.5	0.5	n.s.
Diabetes mellitus	0.8	0.5	n.s.	0.8	0.9	n.s.

*Probabilities calculated by chi-square analysis with 1 degree of freedom.
†Not including widows of husbands under 45 yr at time of death.
‡Chi-square value does not reach 0.05 level of significance.

restored by recalling a former physical experience or illness by the affected person in which the object-loss had not yet occurred. As in the former situation pain, breathlessness, nausea, or feebleness intensified the relationship with the person now lost and secured his help, so now the same effect should be induced through the same somatic reaction.

(3) Significant for the choice of suffering is the identification with the illness the lost object had suffered from, either in reality or in the imagination of the patient.[22] Through taking on the symptoms of the illness the relation is restored not only in fantasy but through the pain in the same part of the body or, for example, through the same digestive problems. This stimulates in mourners particularly difficulties in breathing, which can occasionally lead to chronic asthma, since constriction of the throat, gasping for breath and groaning, the impression of receiving no air, and the feeling of having a heavy burden on the chest can be observed especially frequently in dying persons.[23]

If it happens that the affected person had certain negative desires against the lost love object and wished him "to be infected with the plague," then the situation may occur in which the patient suffers from the very thing he wanted to bring upon the other person. In general, one must be careful not to relate a somatic illness following a death symbolically to the deceased, a danger to which Abraham in particular succumbed all too easily. There are, as pointed out, a series of investigations that emphasize that the death of a loved one is for the most part connected with unspecific physical discomfort, which can lead to a permanent illness under unfavorable conditions. This is confirmed in the connection between grief and asthma, for the hyperventilation syndrome, for psychogenic vomiting and dysphagia, for ulcerous colitis, for cancer, diabetes, rheumatic arthritis, hyperphagia, and anorexia.[24] Yet all the psychosomatic symptoms named above are not specific grief reactions (perhaps with the exception of asthma) but discomforts which generally can result from a real or a symbolic loss or by unusual external or internal stress (stress and life crisis).[25] It is the general stress through inner psychic or social factors that intensifies the "susceptibility to illness" of certain organs or already latent illnesses.

The "choice" of the illness probably depends in addition on what kind of reactions an illness will cause in a certain society. If a somatic illness elicits a common effort by the family members and the persons responsible for the value of "health" as seen in our society, then this can suggest to a person becoming ill and allowing himself to be nursed in order to overcome the feeling of hopelessness and helplessness.[26] This may be desirable particularly when psychic symptoms, such as apathy, hypermotility, nerve strain, and insomnia, do not evoke the same careful attention, and the mourner, instead of receiving constant care, is put off with tranquilizers and sleeping pills. In this way physical illness becomes a defense mechanism. To cope with separation through a psychosomatic illness suggests itself above all if a particular dependence on the deceased had existed, which represented protection and help and for which no substitute is available in society.[27]

2.43 Grief as disease entity

The psychic and psychosomatic symptoms described in the two paragraphs above leave us with the questions, from a medical standpoint, (1) how "normal" grief can be distinguished from pathological mourning and (2) whether grief in general should not be considered as disease entity.

(1) Freud differentiated "normal" grief negatively from the "pathological" and from depression by stating that he could not detect a distinct ambivalence or any mania in "normal" mourning. Both criteria of distinction proved to be invalid in view of the studies by K. Abraham and M. Klein. E. Lindemann, in relying upon Freud, has stated a number of distinctive features, but nevertheless they do not agree within themselves. According to his presentation, pathological mourning consists in part in intensifying normal grief reactions ("severe physical reactions without organic changes," "excessive hostility," "exaggerated reactions") and in part in a persistance of normal grief reactions ("severe physical symptoms with organic changes," "constant loss of

habitual kinds of activity," "changes in character," "severe continuous depression"); finally, Lindemann notes a third criterion, namely, whether the grief reaction develops immediately after the death or is inhibited by some factors and is therefore delayed.[28] Besides that, he does not indicate how intensively enduring and how strong delayed grief reactions must be in order to be considered pathological.

Other authors also fail to provide a clear distinction. The *Diagnostic and Statistical Manual for Mental Disorders*, published by the American Psychiatric Association, categorizes grief under personality disorders, subdivision of situational personality disorders, department of heavy stress reaction,[29] and thus makes as little a distinction as Redlich and Freedman, who deal with grief under "manic and depressive behavior disorders."[30] W. Bräutigam describes grief under "conflict reaction,"[31] which develops if the fulfillment of a need is delayed or stopped completely by external influences, and he calls the morbid grief reaction, which he does not define more clearly under the same main heading, a "depressive reaction."[32]

In clarifying the terminology one must keep constantly in mind that the distinctions between "normal" behavior, neurotic behavior disorders, and psychosis in general, as well as in the context of grief, are in a state of flux. Besides, the mourner can overreact in certain psychic and somatic symptoms, while he otherwise goes through an entirely normal grief process. For instance, he can occupy himself most intensively with the question of guilt in the case of death, blame doctors, relatives, and friends, and consider himself the victim of a conspiracy, and yet at the same time behave completely normally otherwise. Another person may indeed develop ulcerous colitis, but otherwise give the impression that he has coped with the loss. Thus the fluctuating transitions on the one hand and certain exaggerated individual features on the other very often make a precise classification of grief difficult. Moreover, vehement emotional reactions can reactivate past illnesses and bring out latent ones, which in addition make classification rather hard.

(2) G. Engel has in a certain way avoided the difficulty by

not making a distinction between "normal" and pathological grief and characterizes grief generally as a disease:

Certainly it involves suffering and an impairment of the capacity to function, which may last for days, weeks, and even months. We can identify a consistent etiologic factor, namely, real, threatened, or even fantasized object loss. It fulfills all the criteria of a discrete syndrome, with relatively predictable symptomatology and course. The grieving person is often manifestly distressed and disabled to a degree quite evident to an observer.[33]

Engel then quickly responds to several objections made against the characterization of grief as a disease. To the objection that grief is simply a normal reaction, he replies by pointing to the fact that a wound or burn also is something normal. Like an injury, grief too constitutes suffering which is a part of life. To the argument that grief is a self-limited process requiring no medical attention, Engel responds that cultural expectations determine when symptoms are regarded as morbid and require medical attention by the physician. Actually, the mourner quite frequently consults the physician, who just does not diagnose grief as an independent disease entity and treats the person suffering primarily from grief simply for insomnia or exhaustion. It is relatively easy to refute the objection that grief does not involve any somatic reactions and is not perilous: The experience of the disease and mortality rate[34] by mourners shows distinct increases over against corresponding control groups. In response to the argument that it is only a matter of a temporary and partial derangement in the functioning of the individual suffering a loss, Engel justifiably says one cannot speak of a disease only if every system on all levels of the person is disabled.

With respect to the question particularly interesting to us, that is, how it is possible to differentiate "normal" from pathological grief, Engel proposes that it would be better to speak of an uncomplicated grief and a grief complicated by other factors. He compares this with an infection caused by measles, which the body normally overcomes without special medical intervention, but from which complications can develop, depending upon the capability of resistance of the organism and other factors.

Therefore, and here we agree with Engel, grief is a disease entity with a clear etiology and a specific disease process which limits itself and ends with the restoration of the former total condition. Together with him, we distinguish the uncomplicated, "normal" grief from pathological, which is characterized by unusual intensity, persistency of some individual symptoms, or chronic disease. What constitutes "unusual" depends upon the general norms of society.

However, the question still remains to be discussed whether grief should be characterized as a psychic or as a somatic disease. Engel tends to relate grief more strongly to somatic diseases.

Even Melanie Klein considers grief a disease, but she attributes it to psychic behavior disorders:

In normal grief early psychotic anxieties are aroused. The mourner is in fact sick, but this state of mind is so common and seems so natural to us that we do not call it a disease. (For similar reasons the infantile neurosis of the normal child was not recognized as disease until a few years ago.) To state it more clearly: In mourning the bereaved goes through a modified and temporary manic-depressive state and overcomes it by repeating the process the child normally goes through during infancy, even though the circumstances and symptoms are different.[35]

Since the psychic symptoms determine the pattern of disease much more strongly than the psychosomatic ones, and the symptoms in the physical as well as psychosomatic area are largely in accordance with the manic-depressive behavior disorder, one might agree with Klein that grief is to be attached to the manic-depressive circle of appearances with which it has in common self-limitation, even though it is permanent in the manic-depressive state. In this case, just as in manic-depressive illness, the depressive phase prevails; mania is more uncommon (this depends upon what one characterizes as mania in grief); and, a circular course with rapid changes is quite possible.

The question remains as to what is gained if we consider grief as a self-limiting behavior disorder with preponderantly psychic symptoms. One can in justice ask, considering the attitudes of our society which adjudge a social status to the physically ill but not to the emotionally disturbed, if one does not add an additional burden upon the bereaved by making such a distinction. The disturbed person may be spared from this if he is considered "normal" or only in a physical sense ill. The bereaved often express the fear of "going crazy" and are proud if they can control themselves, at least in public, and are able to act as "normal people."

This may be true. However, it should be asked whether it is not an urgent social-political priority to give equal social status to the emotionally disturbed just as the physically ill enjoy in public. Consensus exists on the professional side that in this case, a change in public awareness and consciousness must be induced in order to prevent the "lunatic" from being continuously discriminated against and isolated, unlike the "patient." Such a change of consciousness could help, because a bereaved person who could no longer cope with himself would consult a minister, a counseling office, or a psychiatrist, where he could expect professional help, instead of seeing the physician.

If such a change of consciousness is presupposed, this would mean that the bereaved could also participate in the advantages attached to the status of a patient. Though it is generally conceded that the most grief stricken can take a vacation from their jobs until the funeral, it is very seldom that it is considered a legal right to do so. It would be a justified social demand to consider the most grief stricken equal to a patient and allow for an appropriate continuation of salary. Work may be a help in coping with grief, but it must be the decision of the bereaved as to the way he or she chooses to cope with loss and how much time is needed to do so. The threat to health imminent in an insufficient work of mourning is strong enough (especially if in the treatment of the disease the preventive viewpoint gains the recognition it deserves) to make the exemption of the bereaved from professional and other obligations not only a social claim but a matter of concern for his health as well.

For counseling the bereaved, the recognition of the patient status would bring a number of advantages, which Engel named as follows: (1) Research would be directed to this disease entity no less than to other disorders. (2) The therapist would no longer dismiss the inquiry with respect to the significance of the loss and personal circumstances, often reported by patients or their families, as etiologic and therapeutic factors, and he would not be content with prescribing tranquilizers and offering comforting words. (3) Therapy could concentrate more strongly on the possibilities for an adequate restitution for the loss.[36]

3. The process of bereavement

3.1 The four stages of bereavement

The American psychologist A. F. S. Shand stated in his book *The Foundations of Character* (1914): "The nature of sorrow is so complex, its effects in different characters so various, that it is rare, if not impossible, for any writer to show an insight into all of them."[1] One possible way of systematizing this complex phenomenon is to attempt to distinguish stages in the process of bereavement. As far as such an attempt succeeds, for example, in describing the "typical" course the healing process takes after the loss of a loved one, it helps at the same time in pinpointing much better at what points the process is inhibited and can change into pathological grieving.

Already, in dealing with several theories of grief, we have come across some attempts to divide grief into stages. Thus J. Bowlby speaks of the three stages—protest, disorganization, and reorganization.[2] B. Kreis and A. Pattie speak of the following stages: shock, suffering, and recovery.[3] Engel observes that following a stage of shock is the realization of the loss, which grows more and more strong, followed then by restitution.[4] G. Pollock distinguishes shock, grief reaction, and a final separation reaction.[5] While the division into three stages is the most frequent, and the shock experience is recognized by most of the authors as the first stage, the classification of the subsequent phases or stages depends very much on an author's particular theory.

Bowlby is oriented toward the behavior successions he observed in children who were separated temporarily from their mothers. Therefore, he can give a detailed analysis of the protest, and also, in part, of the depression following separation, but in terms of reorganization his data is rather meager. Pollock follows closely Freud's theory about the gradual detachment of the libido from the lost love object. Engel, who is influenced by stress theory, understands the grief process as an analogy to coping with other stress situations, in which, following perception and evaluation of the dangerous situation, an adaptation results. For Engel the cognitive factor plays a greater role, while Kreis and Pattie understand grief more as suffering.

The pastoral theologian W. Oates, in his own analysis of grief, departs from the three stages and adopts six phases: shock, numbness, struggle between fantasy and reality, breakthrough of mourning, selective recollection connected with stabbing pain, and, finally, acceptance of loss and the reaffirmation of life itself,[6] a succession of phases which again is following Freud's theory.

D. Fulcomer divides the course of the grief process into four stages. The first stage, beginning immediately after receiving news of the death, is characterized by shock ("immediate stage"). It is followed by a second stage ("postimmediate stage"), characterized by culturally patterned behavior controls. In the third stage ("transitional stage"), "trial and error behavior" is particularly evident. The fourth stage ("repatterning stage") completes the grief process. During this period a continuous adaptive behavior gradually becomes possible again.[7] In checking the available materials, this division seemed to me to be the most reasonable, even if a few emphases are to be placed differently.

The first stage is one of shock that initiates regression. But it does not yet fully manifest itself because in the second stage of control, family, environment, and work-related "crisis" situations intervene for a short time. In contrast, in the two final stages the bereaved is for the most part left to himself. In the third stage regressive behavior prevails, while in the fourth stage, a new adjustment to what society demands is accomplished step by step. *Thus we speak of a succession of the four stages of shock, control, regression, and adaptation.*

The stage of shock usually lasts only for a few hours, and even if it is of longer duration, normally after one or two days it is over. The controlled stage comes to an end with the funeral and the departure of relatives, usually between three and seven days. The regressive stage, according to Lindemann, is already completed after four to six weeks,[8] although, according to Clayton et al. after six to ten weeks.[9] In the study by Maddison and Viola, more than a third of the interviewed persons mentioned that within three months the grief symptoms had considerably diminished.[10] Marris, relying on a sample similar to Maddison and Viola's, found, on the other hand, only a slight improvement in the interviewed widows' psychic condition.[11] The individual interviews were not carried out within the same interval after the death in all cases. Finally, the adaptive stage, according to Parkes, ends about six months after the death,[12] while Hinton[13] and D. Peretz[14] speak of six months to a year. In all cases it is a matter of unexamined empirical data. Since the specifics of individual stages are defined very differently and no consensus about the division of the stages exists, it is not possible to make comparisons.

This division into stages is naturally relevant only for modern Western societies in which church rituals and local customs have largely disappeared, and those religious and social norms that demanded a much stricter observance of a certain mourning period have abated. Many non-Western societies tend to structure the grief period in a completely different way. One thinks here of tribes that observe "dual funeral ceremonies."[15] Therefore, we can hardly do more than make the very general statement that almost everywhere the mourning period is considered completed a year after the death occurred, and even the taboos which affect the widow in particular are lifted.[16]

Knowing the "normal" grief process of our society can provide certain criteria for discerning when a mourning can be characterized as pathological. Generally, we can speak of pathological grief if the grief process gets stuck in one of the first three just mentioned stages. Under certain circumstances the shock can be so severe that the regression of grief is not set in motion ("inhibited grief").[17] Grief can also become pathological if the mourner proves to be so helpless at the end of the second stage that he cannot live without the active and continuous support of people of his environment, or if he persists in the regressive stage.[18]

3.2 The stage of shock

In Western societies more than half of all the deaths occur in the hospital. In the United States the proportion of deaths taking place in hospitals rose steadily within the last few years, from 66 percent in 1955 to 73 percent in 1967; this indicates that the proportion of deaths occurring at home dropped commensurately, from 31 percent in 1955 to 24 percent in 1967. The number of deaths occurring elsewhere, outside of hospitals and the home, account for somewhat more than 3 percent and remains relatively constant over the same period.[1] The survivors receive the notice of accidents mostly through the police or, of accidents at work, for example, through the immediate superior. Because the majority of deaths occur in the hospital, generally the physician or head nurse in charge has the responsibility of informing the relatives about the occurrence of death.

D. Sudnow has reported that information about a death is clearly structured in the hospital.[2] Since the physician has the duty to give the death notice, it can happen that hospital personnel who long since knew about the death are employed in the waiting room or hallways without informing the waiting family members. When the doctor appears, his behavior already betrays what is to be expected. For example, after the successful birth of a child, the doctor approaches the family with quick strides and shouts the news from a distance. In contrast, in the case of bad news, the doctor proceeds gravely with measured steps right up to the waiting party and makes the announcement often in a soft voice. In anticipation of the coming reaction, when possible this does not take place in public but in a private room or a secluded part of the corridor. As Sudnow observes, the doctor's authority is so great that the death notice given by the physician is in no way doubted or denied. If a doorkeeper or a nurse's aide were to bring the news, it would, on the other hand, be subject to doubt.

When the doctor undertakes the task of giving information, exchange of polite phrases usually does not take place. The decisive message is communicated in the first or second sentence and at the same time contains a medical explanation of why death was unavoidable. Then silence is kept on his part, while the bereaved show different reactions, ranging from loud lamentation to silent, controlled acceptance. Although a doctor generally can, based on his experiences, estimate the reactions of relatives, he nevertheless cannot sufficiently structure the resulting interaction with them, since in such a case the bereaved are socially permitted to act uncontrolled and there is no duty to pull oneself together. The pause is nevertheless limited. In case it is difficult for the most grief-stricken to begin a "conversation," a few of the less affected relatives try to help the doctor in his efforts.

The first reaction to the news of death is mostly disbelief, which may be especially strong if the death notice comes entirely unexpectedly or when the bereaved has no opportunity to make sure in person that death actually has occurred, as in the case of police call reporting that a husband has died in an accident. Thomas D. Eliot cites several such responses:

Her reaction to the news was disbelief—for about a month after, since she felt that many come out alive due to misinformation or some mistake on the part of observers. . . . "I felt as if I had turned to ice, I was so chilly. I don't remember crying at first, but did not think it had actually happened. . . . I said, 'It can't be true.'"[3]

Most often the doctor waits for a sign from the bereaved that he is ready to begin a conversation. In general three subjects dominate, the question of the cause, the question concerning the suffering of the deceased, and the question of unavoidability. The bereaved frequently starts with the question: "What was the cause of his death?" With sudden deaths, such as those from heart attacks, the physician may respond by asking whether such attacks have happened before. This is followed by a discussion of the history of the illness, which, however, does not have the character of a diagnostic inquiry about the disease but only provides material for talking about the actual circumstances of the death and explaining to the bereaved that the doctors have done everything possible.

An important subject for discussion is whether the deceased suffered in a particular way while dying. Generally the answer is no, perhaps with some reference that the patient was under sedation. Sudnow supposes that doctors give such an answer even against their better judgment, just as the bereaved ask the question even though they were informed about the suffering. Finally, the question concerning the unavoidability of death is brought up. Even here the doctor most often takes the comforting position, that on the part of the family everything possible had been done in order to avoid the death. This has a therapeutic function, for the bereaved with great frequency reproach themselves about certain neglects and mostly overestimate them by far in their actual significance.

Together with the relatively brief stage of shock and the stage of control by family, neighborhood, and "transition technicians" described in the following section, regressive behavior may have already set in. Still, a rapid breakdown of psychic organization in the second stage can be brought under control with the help of family members, if only for a short time. But it may also be the case that the bereaved either is so benumbed through the shock or summons so much self-control that regressive features during the stage of shock hardly become visible. The controlled stage then may permit the bereaved to dispense with self-control and let himself go, because he can be confident that his environment will take care of him. Shock or self-control can also persist during the stage controlled by others, just as, on the other hand, a breakdown during the phase of shock cannot be brought under control in the following stage, in spite of all efforts made by the family.

How the death notice can trigger an overpowering shock is described by Fulcomer in a case study:

THE PROCESS OF BEREAVEMENT

The bereaved wife was a young woman, thirty-three years of age, the wife of a newspaper reporter. Death came to her husband the eighth day after he had been struck by an automobile. All eight of those days he hovered between life and death. Present in the room at the time of his death were the bereaved wife, the hospital staff doctor, a nurse, and a brother of the deceased. As soon as the doctor announced the death, the wife uttered a loud gasp and slumped in her chair. The brother and nurse grabbed her and prevented her from falling to the floor. Her eyes remained open but stared blankly at nothing in particular. Hospital attendants had to place her on a bed in an adjoining room and administer stimulants.

She was kept in the bed almost a half hour before hospital attendants informed her brother-in-law that he might take her home. By that time a second brother-in-law had arrived and together they managed to get her home. But they had to support her (almost carry her) on the way to the car and also half carried her into her apartment when they had arrived. On the trip back to the apartment the bereaved women sobbed quietly at times but said nothing. Two days later the brother-in-law wrote: "She acted so strange on the way home, too. She seemed to know what was going on but she didn't pay any attention to us. She certainly was struck dumb and I got worried about her. I felt a bit peculiar myself. Perhaps we were all in a trance."

The bereaved wife ate no lunch. She remained in a state of collapse until her only son returned from school in the afternoon. As soon as he entered the apartment, she burst into tears and wept for at least ten minutes. Later she wrote the following in her journal: "No one ever knows what it is to lose a husband until it happens. Even though I knew it might happen, it came as a terrific shock to me. I was told what happened, but I do not remember anything until they put me into the car."[4]

The collapse does not always take place in such a visible way. The psychic breakdown may also show up in an outbreak of tears, which is often accompanied by complaints and self-reproaches. During such a collapse the bereaved are difficult to talk to; they seem scarcely aware of their environment, questions, and answers. Frequently they are benumbed and incapable of having clear ideas or thoughts. On the other hand, the following case study by Fulcomer shows a bereaved who acts completely controlled.

65

The bereaved spouse in this case was a man fifty-four years of age. The death of his wife had been considered inevitable for only a few hours; but the possibility of death had been admitted for three years. Present in the house at the time of death were: the bereaved husband, the family doctor, a neighbor and his wife, and a young lady who had been a long-time friend of the family. The bereaved husband and his wife had no children.

Only the doctor and the husband were in the room when death came. When it did occur, the doctor quietly announced the fact to the husband, who immediately left the room and announced to the other people in the house that his wife had just died. This he did with complete self-control and without the slightest trace of a tear, although his facial expression was considerably strained and fixed.

The two women present burst into tears, but the bereaved husband simply sat down in one of the living-room chairs and did nothing. After some time he got up and asked his neighbor to help him call an undertaker and send out night letters to the relatives. After those things were taken care of the bereaved husband lay down on the davenport in the living room. He soon fell asleep although it seemed to be a light sleep for he tossed a great deal and awakened at various times.

On the day following the death the family doctor said to the investigator: "He is one of those calm fellows who can take a shock like that and never show it. He acted as if nothing out of the ordinary had happened."

Eleven days after the death the bereaved husband wrote these comments about his part in the death situation: "It didn't surprise me when the doctor told me she was dead. I could tell she was going. The first few hours or so—before I rested—I didn't feel so bad. Funny how it hit me all of a sudden." [5]

Fulcomer calls this a stoic response. As the remarks of the family doctor suggest, such a reaction finds the approval of society, in which the acceptance of realities and the repression of emotions are considered positive.

3.3 The controlled stage

The controlled stage is characterized by a dual form of control, by the control the bereaved exercises upon himself and the corresponding control demanded by family, friends, and the "transition technicians" in order to secure a socially appropriate carrying out of the funeral. In this stage, the part played by social activity is particularly high. Every possible relief is granted to the bereaved in order to make self-control easy for him. He finds himself in this stage to a great extent passive and hardly in a position to carry out his own decisions. The very activity of his environment makes the bereaved feel how great the distance has become between him and the world around him. These phenomena, described by the research in depression as derealization and depersonalization, apply to the bereaved, even if in an abated forms. The world becomes "unreal"—everything that happens in it takes place at a great distance from the bereaved; he is not involved but finds himself merely in the role of a distant observer.

A nineteen-year-old girl described this derealization to the author in a very pregnant way. The arrangements to take her deceased mother out of the house and the transportation of the casket seemed totally unreal to her and like a dream experience. The noises attached to it seemed very subdued and the people far away. She followed the church service and the funeral with great indifference, since she was absolutely certain that upon her return home she would find her mother at exactly those activities she used to perform at this time of the day.

Von Gebsattel very impressively illustrated this act of derealization in the case of a depressive patient and cites her own remarks:

Terribly dead is the relationship to my husband and my children—that is why I have such a dreadful fear of being with them, an anxiety that they could notice it. This horrible feeling of not being able to react. . . . The visit of my family is a nightmare, shadowy, the children so pale—so undesired on my part. The emptiness fills the space between me and my husband, so that I cannot go across. . . . The unrelatedness is so great, the nonpresence, the noninvolvement; my loved ones are lost to me, I am lost to myself—a terrible agony. One is dead, everything is dead, nothing moves, nothing stirs . . . one does not know where one is.[1]

Von Gebsattel summarizes the experiences of this patient under the idea of "emptiness." For her the world does not exist, there is only emptiness, nothing else, even though she recognizes intellectually the existence of the world. Bereaved persons tell of similar experiences. Particular places where they have had especially happy experiences with the deceased now appear to be distinctively unreal. The places and streets look strange and foreign; the people one meets move like shadows and phantoms.

Von Gebsattel, as a psychiatrist who is particularly influenced by existential philosophy, proceeds from the idea that derealization symptoms are not a matter of partial disorder of a cognitive kind, but that the basic relationship to mankind and the world is disturbed, a relationship that precedes all knowledge and aspirations, that builds the ground on which alone all the cognitive and volitional acts unfold, that even precedes individual perceptions and emotions.[2] Derealization, which von Gebsattel attributes to an interruption of the "total relationship" to the world, can, according to Bowlby, be due to the breaking off of interactions between the self and the world. In his opinion, with the loss of a person the interactions end in emptiness.[3]

The experience of derealization can be accompanied by the feeling of depersonalization. Here the feeling of distance from one's own self is dominant. The self appears somehow strange and unknown to the bereaved. The patient described by von Gebsattel talks about this split experience: "I am not myself, I am separated from my being, I am without connection to myself."[4] The self remains detached from all relations to the world, he looks upon himself without being able to identify himself with his speech and actions.

"Perhaps the patient acts—then the self does not enter his actions and the act is in terms of its existential meaning as if not done at all. Maybe he talks to people but then he does not participate in his conversation as a feeling and changing being, and the spoken word is as if not spoken at all; it remains dead, senseless, empty. And correspondingly, the self feels itself 'empty, dead, not there,' deprived of the fulfillment of his existence and of self-realization."[5] Such experiences show that, precisely observed, depersonalization and derealization are two sides of the same communication

68

disorder. However, based on our preceding considerations, we will have to say that not only is the bereaved's communication with his environment disturbed, but that he also feels empty and inferior because the love and attention bestowed upon him and the strengthening of his self-esteem have been disrupted with the loss of the love object.

An essential distinction between depressive conditions and mourning is that, because of the suddenness of the death notice, the bereaved experiences more totally the disintegration of his world and his own self than the depressed, who already has lived with this experience for some time. The bereaved experiences the process of "breaking down," "falling apart," and "going to pieces," much more forcibly than the depressed. The depressed suffers more intensely but has experience with his suffering, while the bereaved is overtaken by the loss as an overpowering experience, since in most cases he cannot refer back to earlier comparable events. "In every separation a core of madness lies; one has to be careful not to hatch and nurse it pensively," said Goethe at the death of his son Karl August.

The experience of being on the threshold of a psychic breakdown and to be utterly helpless can create a feeling of panic and extreme anxiety. The bereaved refer to themselves as "automatons" and "robots." They feel "cold" and "unmoved" and report that they "have no feelings at all."[6] The energy that self-control requires shows itself further in the fact that speaking is troublesome and ceases when it is not called for through questions by others or by external circumstances.

To such derived symptoms belongs a certain overactivity without an obvious goal and sustained intention.[7] All the time the bereaved attempts to act as if the loss had not occurred, but betrays himself in front of others and convicts himself through his inability to carry on with his daily routine.[8] C. M. Parkes speaks here appropriately of "vacuum activities,"[9] activities that no longer have a goal and find no recipient. A symptom of the effort at self-control is the often unexplainable irritability and vulnerability of the bereaved, sometimes even a deep unaccountable suspicion toward relatives and friends.[10] The bereaved notice very clearly that the relationship of their family to them changes but often do not see that the cause for it lies with themselves. In certain circumstances they reject offered help, since this would be an acknowledgment that an important change took place by the death, and they see in every support an unjustified interference in the seemingly intact relationship with the deceased.

3.4 The stage of regression

With the loss of the abundance of relations the bereaved once had with the deceased, and with the gradual realization of this loss, the former psychic organization which had been in tune with the interaction with this person can no longer be sustained and collapses. The mourner refers back to forms of coping less differentiated and more independent from the environment, that is, more narcissistic. In psychoanalytical terms this process is called regression.

3.41 The concept of regression

In *A General Introduction to Psychoanalysis* (1916/1917) Freud says, "If reality remains inexorable, even when the libido is prepared to take another object in place of that denied, the libido will then finally be compelled to resort to regression, and to seek satisfaction in one of the organizations it had already surmounted or in one of the objects it had relinquished earlier."[1] Through the denial enforced by the undisputable reality of death, the ego no longer can help the libido to obtain satisfaction in forms available before. Therefore it regresses to developmental stages in which a satisfactory solution was still possible. The regression resorts in particular to such developmental stages in which the reality of the environment had not yet acquired the same profile with respect to the ego as in the stage of maturity; it is therefore easier to deny the loss.

In *Interpretation of Dreams*, Freud distinguishes three forms of general regression that are not found in the theory of dreams alone but also in the neurotic symptom formation:[2] (1) *topical regression*: processes that normally take place in a higher system are now placed in a lower one; (2) *temporal* regression: "insofar as it is a regression to older psychic formations";[3] and (3) *formal regression:* this applies "when primitive modes of expression and representation take the place of the customary modes."[4] Words are experienced as pictures or as something alive; "thinking becomes archaic."[5] One form of regression is for the most part linked with another; usually all three forms occur together. Basically it is the same process, seen at various times from different viewpoints.[6]

(1) Topical regression signifies that in grief we deal with processes no longer under the unendangered control of the ego. The ego admits to helplessness and is ready for a breakdown. Weeping frequently is the acknowledgment that the ego can adhere neither to the habitual environment nor to the familiar self; it is surrender to a process of suffering in which the ego does not know how much support it still can find. It confesses itself no longer to be in command of the situation. Yet, at the same time, the ego activates defense mechanisms in the system of the preconscious, which replace the omitted control possibilities on a simpler level, even if insufficiently.

(2) Temporal regression means a partial withdrawal to an infantile phase, but the question is, To which former stage is the regression made in grief? O. Fenichel offers generally three different possibilities for discussion.[7] The first possibility is to withdraw to the developmental stage in which the ego received a high satisfaction and which the ego left only with regret. This is the stage of primary narcissism, meaning the stage in which in general no harm is done to the infant ego and in which the object relationship is so little developed that ego and id are not yet clearly distinguished.[8] This regression to primary narcissism during mourning is most clearly represented by Abraham (and with reference to him by Freud as well, even though limited to depressions) as well as by Klein. In the clinical picture this form of regression is recognizable by the marked withdrawal and ego-centeredness of the bereaved.

For the classical psychoanalytical school the phase of primary narcissism largely coincides with the oral stage of development.[9] The assumption that the bereaved would regress to the oral stage is suggested by such symptoms as anorexia, weight loss, indigestion, as well as through vomiting and difficulties in swallowing (Maddison and Viola).[10] It appears that the avoidance of food is more common in Western societies than excessive eating, which is found in hunting, nomadic, and farm societies, as a means of coping with grief. Nevertheless, the survey mentioned above shows increased appetite among a small percentage of the bereaved. Even the increased use of drugs, alcohol, and tobacco signifies (besides the unquestionable effect of sedation and narcotization) an oral fixation, according to psychoanalytical theory.[11]

A further possibility which, according to Fenichel, acts as an impulse for choosing a particular developmental stage, is the regression to the phase of a strong frustration or a traumatic experience. The bereaved can resort to former loss experiences and mechanisms that helped to cope with the loss at that time. Thus Bowlby sees in grief a regression to the separation-anxiety experienced by the infant in the absence of the mother.

Finally, a third possibility considered by Fenichel for selecting the point of fixation is the retreat to a time which, in contrast to the present negative experience, was the most positive and happy. There are widowed persons who live entirely in the memory of the happiest and most intensive time of their mutual togetherness, excluding all negative experiences.

(3) The last of the three forms of regression is the formal. This is the regression to archaic modes of imagination and thought. Though this kind of regression appears most obviously in schizophrenics and compulsive neurotics, it is also found in a more simple form in the bereaved. Magical modes of thinking are set free and form a mixture of superstition, unconscious belief in one's own omnipotence, and a primitive fear of punishment.[12]

3.42 The bereaved in the regressive stage

Without doubt, the regressive stage is the most critical period in the grief process. Here the bereaved faces experiences that are not only extremely painful but often also of a frightening nature. His reactions to these experiences appear strange not only to himself, but also to his family and society. The bereaved knows that to some extent he has lost control over himself and is given over to a process whose end is not predictable.

When trying to give a summarizing description of the modes of imagination and behavior of the bereaved, it is necessary to keep in mind that they not only have lost a person, but that this person at the same time represented a mutual world of existence, which has now fallen apart. This collapse releases a high degree of libidinal and aggressive energies which up to now were tied up in familiar interactions with the deceased and the common environment. This produces a greatly heightened emotionality that can evoke unpredictable and unaccountable outbursts of weeping, complaints, and aggressions, which often, for outsiders, are minor causes and events and which appear to stand in no direct relation to the death.

The breakdown of his own psychic organization together with the "world of being" makes it vital for the bereaved to activate all his energy to sustain a "normal" behavior to some extent, in order not to be totally engulfed in the collapse, which could as an extreme result mean following the deceased into death. Only a minimum of energy can be expended for interaction with the environment. The bereaved very often is apathetic and withdraws from all demands, decisions, and conversations. He is under great tension, consequently resulting in an increased irritability and vulnerability; he appears to be helpless, because he does not want to deal with outside responsibilities; he neglects his appearance, because to take care of himself would demand an increase in energy.

In order to maintain a certain degree of "normal" behavior, the bereaved exhibits modes of conduct that would make him seem psychically ill, if they were not to be expected after a death and if they were not tolerated, considering the experience and the knowledge that such a condition is restricted to a certain period. Modes of imagination and conduct that seem irrational and inappropriate in daily life are quite "rational" for the bereaved in the regressive stage, that is, they help to prevent the total collapse. They are for the mourner more "reasonable" than exerting himself to think and behave "reasonably" as in daily life by means of an overly strong self-control.

A general phenomenon of regression in grief is the *simplification of complex coherences*. One aspect of this simplification is personalization. Instead of thinking in terms of the interconnection of all things, the world is imagined only as the interaction of individual persons (see 6, "The narcissistic coping mechanisms"). Due to this personification, the bereaved frequently concentrates entirely on his relationship with the deceased, even though the death still has many more far-reaching consequences for the bereaved. Released aggressions also are highly personalized. Instead of realizing that generally a number of factors have lead to the death, a specific person is made responsible for it, for example, the doctor, the minister, relatives, or the ego of the bereaved himself. Even God is made personally responsible (see 7.2). Often, help and compensation are expected from a particular person, instead of recognizing and perceiving all the various possibilities available.

Part of the simplification of complex facts is that matters of fact that have nothing to do with one another, or that are logically on different levels, or are related only through a number of intermediate links, are directly linked together. Thus the death can be interpreted as an immediate interference by God for sins committed by the bereaved or as a consequence of the death wish. The death also can be attributed to certain neglect or disregard of symptoms which are in no way related to the fatal end (see 7.23).

Often, complex ethical behavior is simplified to a world order in which rigid moral principles are valid. In such a world order, it is considered that older people have to die before the younger, and the bad before the good. That the industrious and ambitious perish instead of the one who is less interested in work, the gifted child instead of the mentally and physically retarded, is a contradiction in the order of things which gives cause for complaints and doubts about the reliability of the world and God. All these value judgments serve the purpose of proving death unnecessary and, together with the denial of its necessitiy, even averting its reality.

A balanced judgment about the deceased does not seem possible. In rarer cases his death is welcomed and considered a relief. The dead can be pushed aside, avoided, and forcefully forgotten, for he has not proven worthy of the love given to him by the person now left alone. He can be accused of his "disloyalty" to the bereaved. Yet, in the majority of the cases the deceased is glorified; all his negative sides seem to be forgotten. The reasons for this unrestricted high praise of the deceased can be manifold. The death may make clear how insignificant are daily quarrels compared with a deep tie; or, one can banish arising guilt feelings through praise. Often, this praise is only presented in public, because the relatives want to prevent it being known that differences existed. They want to make it possible for the dead to go to heaven, since this is one of the few opportunities to do something for him (see 8.2).

Simplification of complex coherences applies also to religious behavior. The question may arise for the bereaved as to what he can do for the dead, because a person for whom one can still care cannot be entirely dead. Biblical ideas about the Last Judgment and the fire of hell become urgent questions about how to make sure of the future of the dead person. These may appear obscure to the theologian, but they gain immediate actuality for the bereaved. Anxiety about the dead may be the hidden motive, but also there is the hope to be reunited again in order to undo the loss. It may be a shocking experience for the bereaved who is guided by the Christian faith that in the very situation of highest distress he is tormented by doubts about the justice of God and that prayer is not possible, because together with the communication with the world, communication with God is also broken off. The sudden interest in religious questions as well as the strong doubts with respect to the Christian faith are typical for the regressive stage. This, of course, should not be interpreted to mean these responses will necessarily persist.

The awakening of such a primitive religiosity frequently gives the minister the misleading impression that in bereavement the listener shows a special interest in faith, since he is made insecure by the death. In the analysis of a conversation with the bereaved, H. J. Thilo mentions that the ideas of the bereaved represent, theologically speaking, something like a popular theology, "which hardly exceeded infantile childhood views about God and his rule of the world." [13] However, we may have to ask whether it is not a matter of regression, caused by the death and therefore short-term. In many cases these more primitive ideas of faith, as well as the religious question, sink back into the subconscious as soon as the psychic organization returns to its normal function.

The question of guilt gains considerable weight in the regressive stage. Even in cases where no connection between the death of the other and offenses of the self is established, guilt feelings are effective. They may, for example, originate from the relief felt after a long time of nursing which had become a burden and made death a wished for event; they may be due to reproaches unjustifiably made against the dead, relatives, or the "death agents." The guilt of surviving may be felt strongly, if the bereaved considers himself inferior and of lesser value in comparison with the deceased, and if he thinks that actually he, the bereaved, should have died, according to the moral principles described above (compare 7.3).

Even the problem of anxiety plays a remarkable role. It can be the anxiety for the dead and his future fate, but also the pangs of conscience through which the dead rules over the bereaved. At the same time, the anxieties about his own existence come alive—the threat to himself, the daily realization that he too must die. In addition to this there is the anxiety of not being free from the dead and being engulfed in his death, because life appears meaningless without him—the dead person demands this anxiety as a sign of submission—and the anxiety that the general regression will not come to a halt. Finally, the bereaved can have an abundance of anxieties about how he will cope with the future filled with many problems of loneliness, adaptation of new family situations, and financial security.

The self-esteem and self-respect of the bereaved is diminished to a considerable degree. He feels humiliated and deprived by the loss. Not only children feel inferior and defeated in relation to their peers if they no longer have a father or mother. The loss of the spouse can evoke the same feeling, the more so since the bereaved is cut off almost totally from the environment and senses society's shunning of him. He may feel worthless because an essential part of his activity was directed toward the deceased and now has become objectless. He no longer sees any sensible activity for his life, since this to some extent is linked to the overestimation of the relation to the deceased already mentioned above.

Whoever comes in close contact with a bereaved person will have to deal, at least in the regressive stage, with phenomena described best in summary as follows: personalization, preoccupation with the deceased, simplification of complex facts and value systems, misjudging the value of the deceased, guilt and anxiety feelings as well as self-devaluation. All of this is connected with the experience of heightened emotionality which can lead to either excessively affectionate behavior or aggressive behavior marked by vulnerability, irritability, and mistrust.

3.43 The function of regression

With Redlich and Freedman it can be said that regression has to be understood as an application of modes of behavior that once had been adequate for problem solving in an earlier period. "Regression can be partial and selective or total and massive, it might be temporary or persistent. It can at times refer to the perception, to single cognitive functions, to the affectivity, adaptation and defense mechanisms, or all these functions at the same time."[14] It can be set in motion organically or psychically and it may take place in an organized or completely chaotic form. Regression in an organized form is found in playful and artistic behavior.[15] It happens in a bereaved person mostly in a chaotic form, where it is not structured by rituals, in particular if no experiences are available to cope with a loss of this dimension.

Regression can be both the reaction to a traumatic event as well as *a mechanism to cope with this experience.* While the psychic organization regresses to a simpler form in which the loss still may be mastered, it creates at the same time a starting point from which to build up new relationships. In this sense regression can be considered a defense mechanism. However, an essential distinction from other defense mechanisms remains. In regression the ego is much more passive— regression is inflicted upon the ego. Therefore it is quite meaningful to understand regression not only as a disintegration of the psychic organization, but also (with Kris) to speak of a "regression in the service of the ego."[16]

This dual function can be explained by using the helplessness observed in regression as an example. On the one hand, helplessness is a sign that the bereaved has lost control of himself. On the other hand, it may also be an appeal to the environment to provide comfort and support for the bereaved. Weeping and crying, therefore, can at the same time be an expression that everything is lost and also of the wish to free oneself from the embrace of the dead and to reorganize one's own ego with the help of other people. Illnesses, which occur quite often after the death of a loved one, can have the same dual function: by becoming sick the bereaved expresses the wish to die like the deceased; at the same time he gains in the role of the patient relief from daily tasks. He receives affection perhaps not attainable otherwise, and, thanks to this relief, he can concentrate wholly on the psychic coping with the loss.

Another example of the dual function of regression is the apathy often shown by the bereaved, mostly bound up with the wish to withdraw and not to be disturbed by anybody. According to psychoanalytical interpretation, apathy is both an image of the deceased and of being dead. The bereaved has given up and no longer sees meaning and hope in his life.[17] The withdrawal from other people signifies that they have become insignificant for the bereaved and that he does not need them anymore, because the only person from whom he had expected something now no longer exists. At the same time, the positive side of this withdrawal and self-isolation indicates that the bereaved seeks to conserve energy in order to maintain, at least at this regressed level, his psychic organization. Like a patient who is physically ill, he preserves his energy in order to reach a psychic adaptation. Besides, this apathy and withdrawal enable him to concentrate entirely on the loss, and to clarify for himself what he has lost and how to substitute for the loss.

With the observing of these avoidance and defense maneuvers, carried out by the ego in order to regain the ability to live, it is possible to speak with I. A. Caruso of "regressive" and "progressive" maneuvers.[18] In every grief process it is undecided for the present whether in the long run the regressive forces will prevail, a reorganization will be reached, or a compromise will take place in the unsolved discrepancy of the death and life instincts that will result in a pathological fixation of mourning. There are dispositions and social situations that cause behavior analogous to death to become real dying. "Following-in-death" takes on the most varied forms. Death can be caused willingly and actively by the bereaved by committing suicide, but it also can be decided only precognitively and brought about passively. Society's ideas, based on the real possibility of reunion and demanding devotion toward the deceased or submission to him, can make "following-in-death" seem meaningful; for example, the custom of burning the widow can reinforce these ideas through social pressure and direct compulsion. L. Giudice described this intermediate stage with clarity:

Since I have daily contact with a dead person I no longer am fully in this life. I am in an intermediate stage and look for a new orientation. In this intermediate realm, the life on earth takes on another meaning, and the contact with the dead person makes me strong in a strange way: the everyday life does not touch me so much, it is only important with respect to the end. It is as if with the departure of the beloved, the realities of this life had lost some of their importance, and to the same extent, life after death has gained reality. Existence on earth is like a dream in which one suddenly knows that one will awake with death in order only then to live. In this intermediate stage one walks toward death in serenity, although still active in life, and the joy is greater than the pain.[19]

In this transition it remains open, so to say, in which sphere the bereaved belongs, whether to the deceased or to the living. He has not yet dissociated himself from the dead, and it is not decided whether he will succeed. The bereaved shares this in-between condition with the dead, who no longer lives in this world and yet also does not belong to the reality of memories. This in particular gives the world and the ego the character of unreality. The system of need and interaction of the bereaved with the deceased is not yet actually dead; neither can the bereaved realistically grasp how the world will be after an adequate coping with grief.

3.5 The stage of adaptation

A grief process is not predictable because the forms of ties that bound the bereaved with the dead person are too various; the environment reacts very differently and the resources and coping mechanisms available to the bereaved change from person to person. There is neither the normal grief process nor the appropriate readaptation. The following example by Fulcomer illustrates what a "normal" grief process and an "appropriate" adaptation can look like.

The bereaved woman considered here was the forty-two-year-old wife of a college professor. She had wept a great deal following the notification of death and assumed an attitude of protest during the time of the funeral. The sixteenth day following the death, the bereaved wife, with the help of close friends, definitely decided that she would keep the home, rent out rooms to students, and attempt to find some type of employment for which she was fitted. She promptly found a position on the staff of the university library.

That evening she wrote: "Today was my first at the library. I am sure that I shall enjoy the work, but it does seem strange to be there. It was difficult to keep my mind on the job. Several times I found myself sitting there, thinking of how often my husband had gone in and out of those doors, how he had worked with the students, how he would be missed by students and faculty alike. I realized that I should be working, but I must confess that I enjoyed those thoughts. Sometimes, however, things weren't so pleasant as, for example, twice when I saw his name on library cards and once when I saw a book which he had brought home not so long ago. Those things made me hurt deep down inside."

In the evenings she would work at preparing the two rooms she wanted to rent or she would pack away her deceased husband's personal belongings. On the twenty-fifth day following the death she wrote, "My days are rather pleasant now. They are filled with work and dreams and memories. When I see or think of things that I associate with him I hurt all over inside. Then it seems almost as if daydreaming relieves me of my suffering. . . . I cannot understand myself, for I seem to enjoy thinking and talking about him and what he has done, and at the same time I suffer when I do so."

During the first weeks after she had begun her work in the library, the bereaved woman took no part in the social life of the campus. She seldom called anyone on the telephone and she visited no one except her neighbor. She did, however, seem pleased when visitors came.

The bereaved wife, beginning with the twelfth night following the death, often dreamed of her husband. Often in the dream he appeared to be alive but would also possess some supernatural qualities. Sometimes he would disappear completely, then come back again. Sometimes she would awaken; other times she would merely have a vivid memory of the circumstances and events in the dream when she did awaken.[1]

Step by step the regressive forms can be given up and substituted by adaptive ones. The loss is recognized in its full extent; the bereaved begins to liberate himself from the image of the mourner. At the same time he begins to restore again the person whom he lost within himself. The dead person is pushed aside; he no more needs to be remembered in this direct way since he has become the "property" of the bereaved. Giudice writes about that as follows:

At some time or another the dead is thrust aside. As time goes on he takes up less and less space; at first one only needs a drawer and pushes his papers a little to the side; then half a closet is needed and his clothes are taken away. I pushed you aside, because I wanted to be closer to you, and it all started when I decided to work in your room. . . . Without giving any thought to it, I lived with my memories as if this were natural. I had not seen it as a gift, the privilege of remembering, and now I am shocked by the thought that remembrance is a function of the brain and that with its abatement I could lose you once more, but this time decisively.[2]

In a "normal" grief process, the bereaved not only restores the deceased person within himself, but also renews his internal world so suddenly broken.[3] He regains the feeling for reality and receives himself as a person again. Anne Philipe describes this experience:

I cannot remember the day when I felt for the first time that not everything was irretrievably lost. ... One day I noticed that I had ceased to be only a façade. I exist, I breathe. I wanted again to have influence over events. Slowly I regained consciousness and saw what was left of me. Then I began not simply to submit to loneliness but to let myself be tamed by it.[4]

Even though in the "normal" grief process the adaptive coping mechanisms become effective, coping with grief does not take a continuous course; rather there are days when the bereaved is sure of a positive coping, followed by new attacks of apathy and despair. Periods in which the bereaved has the feeling of being given back to the world again are followed by those in which the world seems as unreal as at the beginning of the grief process. Particularly days and times connected with the deceased, such as his birthday, the day when it became certain that he would die, the day of his death, but also times in which the remembrance of the dead is intensified, as, for example, November [the German memorial season], can bring back the entire weight of grief, even though those periods are shorter and fade away faster. Giudice reports:

In the beginning the pain broke out anew every day in the hour of Oki's death, and it took a long time until I went through this hour without disquietude. ... Since then I have experienced this again and again, even now when I am calm: the pain comes and goes whenever it will. It is sunk into a depth which we cannot fully explore in ourselves. One is exposed to that pain defenseless and has to be grateful when it abates, humble when it comes.[5]

It is possible to experience the regressive stage of grief as separating one more from the deceased than the adaptive stage. The effort to deny the loss and to find again the dead person in memories and active roaming around brings often a greater estrangement than the liberating feeling of not having him bound to oneself any longer, and no longer to be bound to him. Paradoxically, it is exactly this release and liberation which keeps the lost present. Clerk formulates this experience very vividly:

Looking back, I see that only a very little time ago I was greatly concerned about my memory of H. and how false it might become. For some reason—the merciful sense of God is the only one I can think of—I have stopped bothering about that. And the remarkable thing is that since I stopped bothering about it, she seems to meet me everywhere. *Meet* is far too strong a word. I don't mean anything remotely like an apparition or a voice. I don't mean even any strikingly emotional experience at any particular moment. Rather a sort of unobtrusive but massive sense that she is, just as much as ever, a fact to be taken into account.[6]

After a brief sketch of the four stages of shock, control, regression, and adaptation, we now have to consider three themes which are in close connection to the grief process. First we must point out that under certain circumstances the grief process not only starts with the immediate occurrence of death but is anticipated (3.6). Secondly, it can be the case that the full expression of grief is inhibited and the grief process does not get under way (3.7). Finally, it can happen that the process gets stuck in one stage and a pathological coping with grief becomes imminent. At this point, certain criteria shall be named which signal such a pathological coping. They reveal under what circumstances death is especially felt as a burden (3.8).

3.6 Anticipatory grief
Bereavement following a long-anticipated death presents special problems. The initial shock is often not so intense, because the bereaved are not suddenly, but instead with

increasing certainty, confronted with the death of the loved one. The necessary preparations have already been made; relatives and friends are informed about the impending event. Generally, the climax of the grief reaction has taken place already some time before the actual occurrence of death and has given way to a resigned acceptance. The actual event of the death then occurs as something long expected.

How much the anticipation of grief has its effect upon the shock and the intensity of the grief reactions is contested. From experience we can set a general principle: "I can say that the more unexpected the death, the more acute and disturbing the grief; the more prolonged the illness, the more one can accomplish the most painful part of mourning in anticipation of the loss."[1] Also, according to Clayton et al., certain differences are apparent in the symptoms. Yet, differences of almost 20 percent in intensity appear for the bereaved if the length of illness was less than six months, and these in terms of heightened unrest, depressive mood, a feeling of tiredness, and, because of these symptoms, a resulting increased use of tranquilizers and sleeping pills and a weight loss.[2]

After a longer illness through which the grief process comes to a definite end, the feeling of grief is reactivated for a short time but has no longer the full impact. Frequently, death is even related to a feeling of relief, particularly after a long period of nursing. It also can be quite a relief if one no longer must wait day after day for the event. However, if the environment shows no understanding for the bereaved who does not exhibit the extent of grief expression normally expected at the death of a loved one, the bereaved, who has already been through the grief process, is then forced to pretend more perplexity and pain than he really can feel.

Particular complications are related to anticipated mourning if the illness is chronic but constant hospitalization is unnecessary, and if the lethal termination is certain but no prognosis can be made about the exact time of death.

I am acquainted with a physiologist, on a university faculty, who for the past ten years has had Hodgkin's Disease. When his illness was first diagnosed, it was thought he would live for only a few months, but he recovered sufficiently to return to his teaching and research. Periodically, though, he has had a severe exacerbation of his illness which has required hospitalization for weeks or months. During each of these periods of hospitalization, he has not been expected to recover. Yet, he has recovered and returned to his family and to work. During his remissions, each of which usually lasts for several months, he performs most of his duties at a high level of effectiveness and continues to do creative work in research.

Each time he is discharged from the hospital and returns home, a genuine crisis in interpersonal relationships develops. Hostility seems to flow in every direction. His wife and four children seem to have great difficulty integrating him again into the life of the family. Thus diverse complications arise which almost break the structure of the group.

In discussion of this problem with the brilliant and perceptive wife who, like her husband, is a university professor, it became obvious what was happening. Each time the husband and father went to the hospital, the wife and children expected him to die because of the gravity of his condition. They began to mourn his loss. In order to prepare themselves for the seemingly inevitable death of their loved one, they began to mourn for him in advance. When he did not die, but returned home after weeks or months, the family members had already to a great extent broken their ties to him. Then they were faced with the problem of reintegrating into their lives the person they had already given up.[3]

Anticipatory grief is also found in cases in which no actual death occurred, but the person mourned for is exposed to special danger, such as in the case of a soldier who is drafted during wartime. The family can be so preoccupied with the possible loss of the spouse or father that it suffers all degrees of the grief process. This anticipated mourning certainly is a protection in case the family receives in fact a death notice, but it can create considerable conflicts upon his return. The conflicts will be even more aggravated if the soldier had been proclaimed dead or missing in action and then returned.

In case of a prolonged terminal illness, the important responsibility for the minister is not only to care for the family after the death has occurred. He has to recognize that grief under such circumstances begins much earlier. It should be considered here that with the detachment of the family, the dying person is even more isolated than is ordinarily the case. Here lies a particular danger of anticipated mourning. The dying person, who himself struggles with separation anxiety and the fear of death, must also bear the grief of his family and their gradual turning away from him. Nevertheless, if the family, in spite of the forseeable loss, has an open attitude toward death and dying, the mutual isolation of the dying patient and the mourning family can be avoided, since frequently it is precisely this isolation that makes the anticipation so painful and guilt laden.

3.7 Inhibition of grief

It is of significant importance that grief come to full expression and the regression connected with the loss of the love object be given intellectual and emotional room. A number of reasons can be named which inhibit "normal" grief, delay its full expression, or make it totally impossible: (1) opposition to giving oneself up; (2) undeveloped ability in mourning; (3) a succession of losses; (4) external circumstances, forcing the bereaved primarily to take care of his own survival; (5) doubt about the reality of death; (6) ambivalent attitude toward the deceased; and (7) social and religious norms that demand the self-control of the bereaved.

(1) The opposition to regression is based upon the anxiety of not being able to cope with the coming situation. "To let oneself go" means to enter a process whose consequences are unknown. This inhibition of mourning corresponds to the resistance during analysis, which Freud said is produced by the ego's clinging tenaciously to its anticathexes established for the purpose of avoidance of anxiety.[1] In grief, increased activity and a quick substitute for the love object can be understood as such a form of anticathexis.

(2) Grief presupposes that the bereaved has developed the ability for a full expression of grief. This is largely not the case with children, who frequently irritate adults through a

seemingly indifferent response to the news of death. That children nevertheless are affected is seen in changes in their behavior. In the words of Helene Deutsch, "the ego of the child is not sufficiently developed to bear the strain of the work of mourning and ... it therefore utilizes some mechanism of narcissistic self-protection to circumvent the process."[2] This is particularly true in the case of a death that is especially cruel, as for example the suicide of the father.[3]

(3) An earlier death or another loss, which because of certain circumstances could not be worked through sufficiently, may in the case of a new death also inhibit the ability of mourning. Thus G. Gorer tells of a forty-one-year-old wife of a schoolteacher, both of whose parents had died within a few weeks of each other. She was unable to mourn for them. Her first husband had been killed on the anniversary of her wedding day. This had been so traumatic an experience that even twenty years later, happily remarried and with three young children, she could not speak of it without tears welling up in her eyes.[4]

(4) There are situations where external circumstances do not permit mourning for the dead. These can be wartime events which do not allow for a full expression of grief. Odysseus refers to this in his words to the grieving Achilles:

> It is not well that we of Greece should mourn
> the dead with fasting, since from day to day
> our warriors fall in numbers. Where was then
> respite from daily fasts? Lay we our slain
> in earth and mourn a day. We who outlive
> the cruel combat should refresh ourselves
> with food and wine, that we may steadily
> maintain in arms the conflict with the foe.[5]

Natural catastrophies or the situation in a concentration camp can force the bereaved to be first of all concerned with survival. For this reason it becomes rather difficult later on to make up for the mourning inhibited by external circumstances.

(5) Even doubt about the reality of death can cause the absence of grief, for example, when it is not possible to see the

deceased, or if there is no certain information about his death. This frequently is true for war victims who perished in another country, as well as for persons missing in action in case of war or natural catastrophies. Even with families whose members are presumed dead, either in a concentration camp or during flight, the grief expression can also be very much inhibited. Such a case is depicted by J. Fleming and S. Altschul. The patient, a twenty-nine-year-old woman, was an only child who was separated from her parents at fifteen. As she related her history, she described her inability to establish warm relationships with other people. She had few girl friends her own age. With men she carried on a buddy-buddy relationship. She tended to avoid any close contact. The analysis revealed that she was an adolescent in her character structure. She was still defiant and rebellious toward her parents, which was the emotional tone at the time of separation from them, and which had continued through letters full of arguments. She heard first of their fate when her letters brought no reply. In fact, she occasionally had the fantasy that if they did come to visit her she might have to support them.[6]

(6) One of the best analyzed motives for inhibition of grief is a very strong ambivalence toward the dead (this also played a role in the case mentioned above).

Helene Deutsch describes the story of a thirty-year-old man who at the funeral of his beloved mother was terrified about the fact that he had no feelings whatsoever. He was struck by an agonizing indifference in spite of his efforts to develop some form of sadness. During the time following the death he suffered under heavy self-reproaches and attempted repeatedly to remember his mother, hoping finally to be able to cry. The death of the mother occurred at a time when the patient was in great difficulties. He was temporarily impotent, had failed in his studies, and was inefficient in all his activities. The analysis revealed strong conflicts with his mother. His strong dependency on her had contributed significantly to his passive attitude toward life. At the death of his mother, feelings of hatred and annoyance were reactivated. His aggressive impulses caused the sensation of coldness and indifference and inhibited the expression of grief.[7]

(7) Grief can be delayed if particular social or religious norms exist which consider self-control and composure exemplary. In the case study about the "stoic" mentioned above, the approval of the environment is clearly expressed. Frequently, such self-control also means an inner consolation and represents a source of pride for the bereaved. Finally, religious opinions, for example, that a Christian does not mourn because he has a profound hope, play a role. There are certain facts that can help to reduce the inhibition of grief. If the bereaved is incapable of a full expression of grief, an experience of less significant and more distant losses can trigger the mourning, a process that has been called "mourning at a distance."[8] The classical instance of it occurs in Freud's case of the "wolf man" in "From the History of an Infantile Neurosis." There he mentioned that the patient who, when the news of his sister's death arrived, felt hardly a trace of grief. Freud explains the inhibition of grief in this case as related to incestuous love. A few days after his sister's death, the brother visited the area where she had died and sought out Pushkin's burial place, and there he shed bitter tears upon the grave of a man who had died already more than two generations ago. This in itself strange reaction finds its explanation in the moment when he remembers that his father once had compared his sister's poems with those of the poet.[9]

There are other occasions, such as the anniversary of the death or a new event of death, that can help to remove the inhibition of grief. Thus, patients in group psychotherapy reacted to the assassination of President Kennedy by working through the death of their own father or mother, with which they had not coped.[10] M. Wolfenstein tells about a little boy who showed no grief reaction at the death of his mother. The only obvious change was that he began to read intensively and continuously in his spare time. Through close identification with the figures of the books, the breakthrough of the inhibited grief finally occurred after three years. When he came to the end of the novel series of The Three Musketeers he began to cry profusely and said, "My three favorite characters died today," and began at the same time to grieve over his deceased mother.[11]

There is a similar case about a girl who immediately reacted to the death of her mother with disbelief and denial and showed no open grief reaction. At the same time she was struck by the suffering of others and might shed tears about an orphaned child of beggars'. She felt sad if someone else suffered a loss and married at the age of seventeen a man who like herself had lost his mother at the age of ten. Only after she realized during analysis that she would not let the mother die was she able to mourn.[12]

It is crucial for the stage of shock that the work of mourning begin. This is not a modern insight, as St. Augustine's reaction at the death of his mother and his desperate efforts to mourn for her show.

But when they heard what we were doing, many brethren and religious women came together; and whilst they whose office it was were, according to custom, making ready for the funeral, I, in a part of the house where I conveniently could, together with those who sought that I ought not to be left alone, discoursed on what was suited to the occasion; and by this alleviation of truth mitigated the anguish known unto Thee—they being unconscious of it, listened intently, and thought me to be devoid of any sense of sorrow. But in Thine ears, where none of them heard, did I blame the softness of my feelings, and restrained the flow of my grief, which yielded a little unto me; but the paroxysm returned again, though not so as to burst forth into tears, nor to a change of countenance, though I knew what I repressed in my heart. And as I was exceedingly annoyed that these human things had such power over me, which in due order and destiny of our natural condition must of necessity come to pass, with a new sorrow I sorrowed for my sorrow, and was wasted by a twofold sadness.

So, when the body was carried forth, we both went and returned without tears. For neither in those prayers which we poured forth unto Thee when the sacrifice of our redemption was offered up unto Thee for her—the dead body being now placed by the side of the grave, as the custom there is, prior to its being laid therein—neither in their prayers did I shed tears. . . .

It appeared to me also a good thing to go and bathe, I having heard that the bath (balneum) took its name from the Greek . . . , because it

90

drives trouble from the mind. Lo, this also I confess unto Thy mercy, "Father of the fatherless," that I bathed, and felt the same as before I had done so. For the bitterness of my grief exuded not from my heart. Then I slept, and on awaking found my grief not a little mitigated; and as I lay alone upon my bed, there came into my mind those true verses of Thy Ambrose. . . .

And then little by little did I bring back my former thoughts of Thine handmaid, her devout conversation toward Thee, her holy tenderness and attentiveness toward us, which was suddenly taken away from me; and it was pleasant to me to weep in Thy sight, for her and for me, concerning her and concerning myself. And I set free the tears which before I repressed, that they might flow at their will, spreading them beneath my heart; and it rested in them, for Thy ears were nigh me—not those of man, who would have put a scornful interpretation on my weeping. (*Confessions*, Book IX, chap. XII)

"The process of mourning as reaction to the real loss of a loved person *must*," as Helene Deutsch emphasizes, "*be carried through to completion.*" [13] Whatever the reasons for an inhibition of grief may be, if a full expression is not possible, this results in a delayed, transformed, or compulsive grief reaction. [14] Goethe wrote to Schiller about this after the death of his child:

In such cases one does not know whether it is better to succumb to pain naturally or to pull oneself together with the assistance provided for us by culture. If one decides for the latter, as I always do, one is only better for a moment and I have noticed that nature demands its right through other crises. [15]

3.8 Symptoms of pathological coping with grief

A pathological coping with grief is indicated if everything fails to get the bereaved out of his fixation on one of the first three stages of grief. If the bereaved shows his inability to begin with the process of grief in spite of a great emotional attachment to the deceased, but rather persists under the impact of shock; if he is completely helpless and irritated at the end of the controlled stage and cannot exist without the help of others; or, if he cannot relinquish the employment of regressive mechanisms after a period of four to six weeks, then one must consider that the mourning behavior is pathological. It becomes obvious in the rejection of all outside help; continual apathy; isolation and the breaking off of all communications; constant disorders in perception of reality, such as visual and aural hallucinations and sensations of presence, not necessarily related to the dead person; sustained derealization and depersonalization; denial of death and the affective avoidance of everything that reminds one of it, overactivity and compulsive cheerfulness; severe accusations against the environment and toward oneself, as well as paranoid anxieties and mentioning of suicide and intensive perseverance in memories; continual insomnia, aggressive and destructive dreams; general or specific deterioration of health and general well-being; increased smoking and alcohol consumption as well as a greater use of tranquilizers.

Among children and adolescents pathological behavior shows itself, according to Kliman, if (1) they exhibit regressive phenomena longer than several weeks, for example, an unusual (manic) cheerfulness; (2) a disease occurs, lasting longer than six months; (3) new symptoms appear after a certain period of time, such as diminution of school efforts (which is not uncommon for a child in the regressive stage and does not represent a serious disorder); (4) children or adolescents refuse to go to school (this is a sign that they cannot leave the surviving parent for fear of being separated from him or her also, or that they wish to withdraw completely); (5) in adolescents, falling into sexual promiscuity.[1] Finally, threats of suicide have to be mentioned. They are relatively more frequent among children who have suffered the loss of a loved one than among the general population.[2] In literature generally the death of a loved one is stated as one of the motives, yet there is a lack of studies about statistical frequency. In a study of four cases of attempted suicide by children between the ages of eight and thirteen, three suicide attempts were related to the death of a loved one.[3] In evaluating how seriously such threats must be taken, motivation plays a decisive role. For instance, the desires to be reunited with the deceased or to seek a way out of despair and find peace of mind have much more weight than the aim of drawing attention from the adults by means of this threat.[4] Also to be taken seriously is the desire for self-punishment for certain wishes and failures allegedly related to the dead when frustration becomes inwardly directed aggression, or when the child is identifying himself with the dead person.[5]

According to experience, certain specific circumstances surrounding the death prove to have a particular impact and can have a pathogenic effect, especially if several of these circumstances coincide. These factors can be considered as particularly burdensome:

(1) In the case of suicidal death, the survivor presumably had been exposed to tension a long time before the suicide, and in addition to that, he is now overcome by guilt feelings.[6]

(2) The same is true if a strong ambivalence existed between the deceased and the survivor; the intense conflict of hate and love can make it difficult to mourn for the dead and to gain an undisguised relationship to him.

(3) The survivor was dependent on the deceased to a great extent, and/or has isolated himself from his social environment, so that the deceased actually was his only communication partner and almost no contact to family and neighborhood existed.

(4) Death was only the last of several crises that could not be sufficiently worked through because of their rapid succession (for example, if several deaths within the inner family circle follow shortly one after another); or, death coincides with the climax of a development or an "accidental" crisis (for instance, with a critical stage in adolescence, retirement, or a serious operation).

(5) The loss is that of a child or young adult, who cannot at all or rather seldom be replaced by a new child; the older the young person was, the more hopes had been placed on him, the more libido had been invested in him, and the heavier will be the impact through his death.

(6) There is susceptibility to disease or already existing illnesses, such as heart disease, diabetes, and stomach ulcers.

(7) General psychic condition is unstable, deriving from insufficient coping with earlier, above all, infantile losses.

(8) Death is sudden and unexpected, or, in particular,

violent, considered "untimely," and cannot in any way be justified by the religious and normative system.

(9) Finally, the situation is particularly hard if terminal illness caused long suffering, great pain, and physical deformation. The prototype of such a situation is death from cancer, which, in addition, causes anxieties in the survivor of suffering from the same disease, or feeling that he ought to suffer from it; it is similarly hard if the cause of death is due to an illness the survivor suffers from as well.

Under certain circumstances, infantile grief can be pathogenic, according to clinical records. If the child is in a kindergarten with therapeutically trained personnel, certain help can be given there in addition to that given by the parents. The following factors in grief must be considered as extremely hard on children: (1) suicide of one parent, (2) a difficult relationship either to the deceased or to the surviving parent, (3) either parent's exhibiting psychic behavior disorders, or (4) a girl's loss of her mother before the age of eight.[7]

In the opinion of Kliman, two of the following contingencies occurring together can provoke a serious imperiling of health and necessitate preventive treatment: The child suffering the loss is under the age of four; the child already has a psychic behavior disorder; a change of environment is necessary; the surviving parent develops pathological grief; an increasing physical intimacy between the surviving parent and the child can be observed; the terminal illness had resulted in a considerable physical deformation or psychic transformation; the death was caused through the birth of a child; the family concealed the disease from the child and told him the news of death considerably later than it was told to others.[8]

3.9 The work of the bereaved

In order to achieve a "normal" grief process, the bereaved has to perform a series of tasks which can be summed up in the following description: release of grief, structuring, acceptance of reality, the decision for life, expressing socially unacceptable emotions and experiences, evaluating the loss, incorporation of the dead, new life orientation.

(1) *Release of grief:* It is significant that the grief process is set in motion, that is, that the bereaved is not acting as if nothing had happened, that he does not deny the death and behave in a compulsory controlled way, but rather is able "to let himself go" and give way to pain and grief. It takes courage to submit to the process of regression, since the bereaved cannot be sure where the collapse of his psychic organization and his external world will end. In a society where activity is highly valued, it may be easier to distract oneself by being constantly overly busy. But without this "letting-oneself-go" there is the danger that grief will be inhibited and repressed; it then might show up in other symptoms. To let go presumes confidence in oneself, in the social environment, and in God that these will assist the bereaved and allow him to express his feelings freely, whether they be lamentations or accusations.

(2) *Structuring:* The bereaved finds himself exposed to emotional chaos. He in no way is able to estimate what he has lost; he is overpowered by love and hate; he has strange experiences he cannot handle. Since the loss affects various levels of his relationship with the deceased and his social environment, the task to find new orientation everywhere is rather extensive. The bereaved finds himself in the dark as to when and how he should start the task of reorientation. He assumes many activities without being able to finish them, since he either lacks the strength, realizes that this activity cannot be carried out without the deceased, or sees that it is all meaningless. It is an essential responsibility to structure this chaos of emotions and to set certain priorities. The most important part may be, first, to clarify the relationship to the deceased before further practical decisions have to be made. The preoccupation with the dead, already mentioned, as well as the "egocentricity" of the bereaved, is a quite correct attempt to structure the overpowering experiences and emotions and to set priorities in the work of mourning.

(3) *Acceptance of reality:* An indispensable task in bereavement is the acceptance of the fact of death. Only if death

is accepted can it actually be overcome. The recognition of the reality principle can take place only step by step and is always interrupted by stages of denial. Every form of remembrance, every visit to the grave, every return to a place where the bereaved has spent happy and meaningful hours together with the deceased, represent the happiness of reunion as well as the painful recognition that this is irretrievably lost. This experience is not bearable in its completeness, but rather is denied again and again. Yet, at the same time, the bereaved repeatedly tries to test himself as to how well he can bear the loss. The contradictory behavior of withdrawing and avoiding any communication on the one hand, and the strong desire to talk about the loss on the other, is explained by the following: The bereaved does not want to be reminded of the loss but repeatedly is driven to convince himself in conversation with others as to whether the loss may yet have occurred, for in the last analysis it is only the social environment that can provide this affirmation.

(4) *The decision for life:* The stronger the insight into the reality of the loss grows, the more aggravating the question becomes for the bereaved as to whether it makes any sense at all to continue to live; whether it would not be better to give up the efforts of coping and to let oneself die. In the regressive stage it is undecided for some time whether the life instinct or the death instinct will prevail. Sometimes both form compromises which fixate the bereaved permanently in the regressive stage and lead into pathological coping. Nevertheless, in most cases of bereavement, the will to live succeeds, but how decisive and how fast this develops can vary a great deal. The decision to live certainly is a task in which the bereaved needs the help not only of the internalized good objects, but depends on outside support as well.

(5) *Expression of unacceptable emotions and desires:* Often the bereaved is frightened by the amount of negative feelings and desires toward the deceased of which he now becomes conscious after the death has set free a whole measure of emotions. He must cope with these negative feelings in one way or another if he wants to meet the goal of bereavement, to enter into a relationship of solidarity with the deceased. He

can repress these feelings through unjustified glorification of the deceased; he can turn against himself and employ private attempts of penance through various forms of self-punishment. A more positive coping, however, is the expression of these ambivalent feelings and imaginings in front of a neutral third party.

(6) *Evaluation of the loss:* A further step in the work of mourning, possible only toward the end of the regressive stage, is the evaluation of the loss. Only if the bereaved has overcome the increased emotionality and the regressive form of reaction connected with it, does it become possible to estimate more clearly what actually has been lost with the deceased. The bereaved can judge more precisely whether a substitute is thinkable and what it could look like; it becomes possible to set priorities with respect to which substitutes will have to be considered first. It may be frightening to the bereaved to find out how difficult it is, even seen from a distance, to replace the loss or, on the other hand, to find out to what a small extent he was actually dependent upon the deceased.

(7) *Incorporation of the deceased:* The "normal" grief process moves toward its end if the bereaved succeeds in restoring his internal and external world in which the deceased is integrated and is neither totally expelled nor has to live a "shadow existence" in a split part of the ego. This can be accomplished only if the unbalanced feelings of hate and love toward the dead person collapse through forgiveness, and a realistic insight in terms of the merits and weaknesses of this dead person is acquired. Only when the deceased is accepted in his entire humanness and is neither glorified nor condemned can he be incorporated in the world of the survivor so that there is no compulsion to distort reality for his sake. Only so can he gain the reality that secures his survival in the bereaved.

(8) *The chance of a new orientation:* Through the commitment to a person, either a conjugal partner or a child, the survivor decides on a possible way of life and commits himself. Through death the chance for new orientation is given. The survivor can emancipate himself in a positive way

97

from the deceased, who so far always had interfered in his life decisively and suppressed any independent behavior. For example, children, even as adults, often were not given their freedom by their parents, or one spouse suffered under the other because the one left no chance for the partner's development. In such cases the death of the domineering subject can enable the bereaved to establish a new orientation. It is not at all natural that repressive relations are given up after death; the bereaved may still feel bound and limited because of obligations toward the dead and his children without being able to change this. Nevertheless, it is part of the task of the work of mourning to examine seriously the chances for a new orientation, even if this seems at first to the bereaved a disloyalty to the deceased.

This survey of the grief process and its stages must remain rather sketchy in this brief form. The responsibility and mechanisms of coping will be dealt with in more detail especially in chapters 6 through 8. It therefore will also become more clear in the following parts of the book what heuristic function the division into stages has, particularly for the time of counseling and for the examination of a "normal" or a pathological grief process.

PART II

GRIEF—
The Social Aspect

4. Grief as
status transition

In the first part, grief has been dealt with as an aspect of individual experience. However, grief is not only a personal event; it takes place within a network of relations. The bereaved must newly create his relations to the deceased and to his environment; however, his environment as well as himself is affected by such a change of status.

According to the concept of crisis theory, the grief process can be understood as interaction process between a psychosocial burden and an individual. Although it takes place in this social "arena," the crisis situation still appears to be very much the problem of the individual. The need for a more comprehensive concept is obvious.

4.1 *Rites de passage* (rites of passage)

In order to understand the grief process as interaction, it is necessary to turn to a concept that was developed in the sociological school of Durkheim at the beginning of our century. Only in recent years (after a long marginal existence in ethnology) has this concept increasingly been admitted into the social sciences. The concept of the *rites de passage* has more recently been termed "status transition." Even though the concept of *rites de passage* was first formulated and composed into a theory by Arnold van Gennep, the basic insights had already been developed by Robert Hertz in 1905 in his article "Contribution à une étude sur la représentation collective de la mort." [1] He proceeds from the assumption that death is not considered a natural event in simple societies but evokes fear and anxiety: "It seems that the entire community feels lost or at least immediately threatened through the presence of hostile powers." [2] Because of this sense of threat, most "primitive" tribes when death occurs expel the deceased and his family from their midst, as victims and captives of malevolent powers.

Nevertheless, this exclusion is only temporary, unless the dead are children, assassins, or criminals. The "primitive" society, according to Hertz, can neither believe in the necessity of death nor consider it final. Exclusion is followed by reintegration. The dead person unites with those who have left the visible world before him; he does not enter this world unchanged: "Because he joins his ancestors, the deceased is reborn in a transformed appearance, elevated to superior power and dignity." [3]

Hertz compares this transition from the visible into the invisible society with the transition from adolescence to the status of an adult. The young man who undergoes the intitiation rite is introduced to the secrets of the adult world through which, in the opinion of natives, a significant personality change takes place, just as with birth and marriage: "This transition from one group to another, be it real or imagined, always assumes a radical renewal of the individual which is characterized by the bestowal of a new name, the change of clothes or life-style." [4] With each change from one social group to another, "an exclusion, a death so to speak, and a reintegration, a rebirth as it were," takes place. [5]

Such a process requires a certain length of time: "The mere fact of physical death is not enough to overcome death in consciousness." [6] Hertz illustrates this (and upon this lies the main emphasis of his ethnological material) with the "double funeral," as it is found in Melanesia and Oceania. There, a temporary removal of the corpse until it has largely disintegrated is observed; only then follows the final burial of the remaining bones. Only with this closing act has the deceased found his way into the realm of the dead. The visible disintegration is a sign of the detachment from this world.

The surviving members of the family are involved in this transition: "Originally grief is the necessary participation of the survivors in the death condition of their father or mother." [7] Their grief lasts just as long as the passage of the dead into the other world. Seen on principle, death exists as a social phenomenon in the twofold and protracted work of spiritual separation and synthesis. Only if this work has been brought to an end can society, according to Hertz, return to peace.

The major contribution by van Gennep is his generalizing of this concept and his more precise analysis of it. He replaces the idea of society, established by Hertz, with the notion of family. In addition, he distinguishes between those passages that bring about a change in human life (les passages humaines) and those related to the cosmic cycle (le passage cosmique)[8] and instances when such rites can coincide[9]— for example, in Germany, the conclusion of the official mourning period is marked by the annual commemoration of the dead. Something similar happens if the memory of a certain death changes, through an annual mass for the dead, from a unique event in a life cycle into a periodic event.

It was especially the representatives coming from the school of G. H. Mead, "the symbolic interactionists," who conceptualized the question of status transition in our society more theoretically. In particular, A. L. Strauss, in his study "Mirrors and Masks" (1959), dealt with the "regulated status transitions," which are linked to the membership in a lasting group or social structure.[10] Both in the course of the life cycle and within an organization, such status transitions develop. For example, in the case of retirement, a complicated ritual is set in motion which ensures an appropriate form of status transition. Becoming a pensioner brings an essential change of one's identity and self-understanding and a change in the social environment. The less the participants observe certain rules, the greater is the uncertainty in the social field, for instance, when someone does not want to give up his position and his successor puts on too much pressure. At the same time, the former colleagues do not know how the successor will treat them, just as he himself cannot know or foresee entirely what problems and demands he will have to face. The status transition therefore requires some time for the new man in the position to find out what is expected of him, whose loyalty he can count on, and for superiors, subordinates, and colleagues to accept him fully in this position.

One such status transition, according to Strauss, takes place in bereavement. The deceased becomes the dead in a regulated process in which he is honored. The bereaved is allowed to defer certain daily obligations, such as pursuing his vocational duties. "Thus the dead are honored and the survivor actually withdrawn from the normal social circulation. Certain actions of the bereaved are not subject to judgment, since he is not 'himself,' in particular during the early stages of his painful loss." [11] He is allowed to withdraw in order to find a new orientation. He can count on finding mediators during the period of suffering. When the survivor starts again to participate in normal interactions, he wears an armband, or the interaction partners are warned in some other way to be very considerate in his presence.

In this interaction, temporal as well as geographical factors play a role. The grief process has certain phases, known within a society, which convey to the interaction partner how to treat the bereaved. The gradual discarding of mourning clothes and other mourning symbols might indicate this. Today in particular, the participation in social activities and the degree of involvement in them mark the beginning of readaptation. Location too is symbolic for grief, such as the symbolic removal of the dead from the house to the funeral home (or mortuary), from there to the chapel, and finally to the grave.

As A. Hahn has made clear, the length of the mourning rite and its intensity depend upon the significance of the deceased for the survivor. The more activities, attitudes and emotions, plans, intentions and wishes, sympathies and aversions, determined the relationship, the more the identity of the survivor, which of course was shaped in a significant way through the relations to the deceased, has to change. "Through his death they lose their 'meaning.' They must be 'reduced,' i.e., either abandoned completely or transferred to other persons. But this demands, above all, time, because the orientations of his actions and his inner attitudes related to the deceased survive his death." [12]

W. L. Warner, who is skillful in the use of ethonological material, described the behavior of the bereaved toward the dead person in a small town in New England and their ideas about his fate.[13] Like Hahn, he represents the viewpoint that for those survivors death does not signify the end of the "social personality," that is, its identity, which was determined by interactions with other people. "When a member of a community dies, his social personality is not immediately extinguished. His physical lifetime is ended, but social existence continues. It exists so long as memory of it is felt by the living members of the group." [14] The deceased enters the sacred world of the dead. He continues to exist with his grave at the cemetery, which represents the continuing connection between the living and the dead with their social status, sexual differences, and mutually shared values. The "city of the dead" is a sacred place, set apart. But in the structure and decoration of the graves it symbolizes the lasting unity between the two worlds and affirms the values that determine the social world of the living.[15]

More strongly than in the psychoanalytical theory, the notion of status transition touches the social aspect of grief, without separating it from the psychological. A status transition sets free libidinal and aggressive feelings, whereby the necessary reorientation and the indispensable change of identity become possible. The concept of status transition allows to a greater extent the inclusion of the interactions between the bereaved and the dead, the social environment, above all the family, and society in the analysis of the grief process. It thus can also make it clear what role the professional "transition technicians," [16] such as doctors, ministers, and undertakers, play in these rites de passage. In addition, the concept of status transition permits the recall of other changes of status within the life cycle, such as birth, adolescence, marriage, marriage of children, retirement, etc., in order to achieve further understanding by the process of analogizing. Since the concept originally was derived from the mourning rites of less differentiated societies, it also makes it possible to understand the significance of informal and formal rituals attached to the status transition.

4.2 New structuring

For the bereaved a world has fallen apart, or, to say it more specifically with von Gebsattel, for him "not the world but the world of being is disturbed, i.e., the world, as far as it is 'my' world, the world which becomes a center, meaning, peculiarity, abundance, reality only by the fact that I exist with regard to it."[1] If the interaction with a loved one is suddenly interrupted, if a person who had been closely attached to the life of the survivor dies, then not only this person has died but the world related to him; and, last but not least, the bereaved has died to the world and himself. He is dead to the world as the world is dead for him.

There are numerous relations that have linked him to the deceased. We can divide these relations into three groups: (1) the personal relationship with its three levels of intimate, familiar, and mutual interchanges of activities, (2) the relationship to the environment the bereaved had with and through the deceased, and (3) the relationship with the entire society. The bereaved may not have been in interaction with the deceased in all three groups of relationships. But wherever they had existed, such relations are broken and have to be reorganized.

(1) In the personal relationship, the loss of the intimate interchange, not understood in a narrow sense here, but rather covering the various forms of libidinal and aggressive ties, can be experienced not only at the loss of a spouse. Often libidinal ties also exist between one parent and a child, or between brothers and sisters. A person outside the closer family circle, one who had been a close friend of the deceased, can suffer such a loss as well.

The loss of familiar interchange is not simply a loss of something valuable yet not necessarily essential for life. It threatens much more, the ego at its roots and in its self-understanding. "Actually," as Caruso says, "an identity has perished: a self-identity through identification with the other.''[2] Simone de Beauvoir expressed this experience as follows:

No more sleeping in the warmth of a body! No more. The sound of a death march! When I was overcome by this insight, I fell into death. I had always been afraid of Nothing; but so far I died daily, without paying too much attention to this dying. Now suddenly a great part of my self collapsed; that was brutal, as a mutilation, and in addition inexplicable, because nothing else happened to me.[3]

Death raises the question of meaning for one's own life. The person is missing "for whom I lived," who gave significance to my own activity, because a great deal of it was directed toward this person. It made sense to take troubles, to bear insults, because this care for the neighbor also meant the affirmation of myself, that I had a right to live.[4] I can work ever so hard and find external recognition, but only the appreciation by this person, who is now forever lost, means something to me and this I could accept. The loss of appreciation and respect makes the self now appear worthless and demonstrates in an intensified way the senselessness of wanting to go on living.[5] At the same time the support the bereaved had found in the other is lost. Now nobody gives instruction or makes decisions. The familiar person to whom one could turn for advice and help is missing. The only person who knew one for a long time is missing, the person by whom one felt thoroughly understood and to whom one could talk very openly about one's own feelings, desires, and longings without the fear of reprisals. The loss makes the self unprotected and homeless; the world becomes strange and unfamiliar.

In many cases, the loss of interchanges of shared activity is suffered as well. The contribution the deceased has made through his work to the common way of life is missing. It may have been the income, the care for the children; it may have been activities which only the deceased "could perform."

(2) The loss of a loved one also means a change of status within the immediate social environment of the bereaved. Within every family a certain distribution of roles takes place,

which now no longer exists but needs to be reorganized. The bereaved therefore cannot rely upon a stable environment but is also facing a change in the family situation. Frequently, the survivor is, through and together with the deceased, a member of a circle of friends, a social group, or a club and loses the status in such a group with the death of the companion. Added to the inner loss is the external change of the social environment. It makes the bereaved uncertain; he does not know how the environment will react to the death.

(3) In most cases the death of a person is also combined with a change in social status for the survivors. A wife becomes a widow, a child an orphan. However the immediate neighborhood and family respond, this change in social status nevertheless means primarily a social deprivation. This deprivation not only is seen in the avoidance of the bereaved and a general shunning of contact with him by the environment (see below) but also has a long-term effect. A child can feel extremely inferior for not fulfilling the social demands that insist that he ought to have a father. The young widow finds herself confronted with expectations growing out of social images about the "merry widow," which make her sexually "free game."

A rupture in all three named groups of relationships and the necessity of a new orientation is the case especially in the loss of a spouse at a relatively early age, when an intensive intimacy, familiarity, and responsibility (particularly in terms of small children) existed. The extent of the loss most often will be recognized only step by step. The significance of mutual satisfaction of needs and the weight of social recognition is most often recognized only after the loss has already occurred; what another means to us becomes obvious only after he is irretrievably lost. Alteration of the environment and the social status change cannot be previously experienced emotionally, even though they can be intellectually anticipated and estimated. Therefore, the realization of the full dimension of the loss requires a longer period of time. This is the justification for Freud's strong emphasis on the task of reality testing in grief.

These reflections may make plain why grief is considered more than an inner psychic process. Not just a relationship between two persons is broken. The death affects a broad psychosocial network that up to now had been in general organized and had conveyed security and stability for the bereaved. The inability to estimate and to distinguish the various aspects of what has been lost exposes the bereaved to intellectual and emotional chaos. Considering such a situation it is understandable that the diffused feeling of having lost everything, literally everything, prevails. It is like declaring total bankruptcy in which only gradually the clarification of the confused situation can be obtained and the amount of capital still on hand ascertained. This is related to the helplessness which signals that the bereaved should begin with the reorganization; and increasingly is this so as he discovers more and more things which have been lost with the death of the companion.

There are, however, definite situations that do not leave a choice for the bereaved and force him first of all to reorganize specific relations and to structure in this way the experience of loss. Adults may be irritated if a little child, as the reaction to the news of the death of his mother, asks the question, Who will take care of me now? Yet the child does not react without feeling, but rather finds himself considering his situation without the help of others, confronted with an immediate threat to existence, and is forced first of all to receive a clarification about this side of the loss.

Nevertheless, in general the experience of loss is so unstructured that the bereaved is able neither to comprehend sufficiently what has been lost nor to know which area of loss needs special preference in the process of working through. Very often he also receives no advice whatsoever as to how the work of mourning should be approached and carried through. Since he cannot estimate to what degree the world was meaningful only through the deceased, the loss is overestimated and overcharged, so that the bereaved receives the impression of having lost all relations to other people and the world, with the loss of his relationship to the loved one.

4.3 The significance of the ritual

The application of the ritual of the *rites de passage* occurs when the status transition of an individual is performed within a social group. The status transition, which signifies physically usually a lengthy process of separation from the former status and adaptation to the new status, is anticipated in the ritual and is presented symbolically, whereby most importantly the one who performs the change of status becomes the bearer of the symbol.

To be sure, the mourning ritual does not replace the grief process but rather presents it as something that the dead person, the survivor, and his social environment have to cope with together. The ritual is an expressive act which in the ideal case aids the implementation of the process.[1] N. Luhmann said of social systems that an increase of their complexity can "only be gained in that the fulfillment of some needs are postponed, especially those of intermediate preservation of the system, continuing motivation, feelings of security, and the building of trust. Instead of immediate satisfaction of needs, those distant goals must be striven for and at the same time be anchored in the present as meaningful."[2] This can be transferred to the complexity of human interactions that must be structured anew in a status transition. In order to guarantee the long, drawn-out process of individual and social reorientation, there have to be "actions with symbolized involvement,"[3] which can only take place through an expressive action, namely, the ritual.

The concept of ritual, as W. Neidhardt emphasizes, does not necessarily have a religious meaning. "Even an atheist can participate in this, without being dishonest."[4] He does not deny that the customs can contain religious (i.e., theologically unacceptable) elements, yet does not see this as the essential element of the ritual. It is false to impute from the beginning a pseudoreligious attitude among participants in the funeral ritual and perhaps speak of a death cult.[5] To what extent superstitious motivations play a role is hard to say. In any case, it is not justified to assume them automatically. The only research known to the author about the attitude toward the funeral is that by G. Kehrer on the religious consciousness of industrial workers. According to that, only 4 percent of those interviewed indicated mystical or magical fear in view of the phenomenon of death;[6] in general, the function of the funeral is "completely world immanent. The lack of appropriate substitute institutions for the entire society conditions its maintainance."[7]

It is therefore necessary to emphasize the open character of the ritual, since in the literature of religious ceremonies the tendency exists of confronting the proclamation of the gospel in the sermon with the pseudoreligious elements of the ritual. A theologically faithful text interpretation is sabotaged because the ceremonial practice today and a genuinely Christian sermon so often appear to be in conflict with each other. However, such an opinion can only be formed if the functions of the ritual are not sufficiently recognized and are declared in an unquestioned manner to be a pseudoreligious activity. The funeral sermon then appears to be the rock in the storming sea of heathen magic and death cult.

We do not subscribe to this distinction between proclamation and ritual for the following reasons. First, the results of an analysis of collections of funeral sermons and statements by ministers in Germany with whom we worked together in seminars indicate that the funeral oration, too, has a strong ritual character. Since little time for preparation is available, and in most cases the minister is not familiar with the life of the deceased, his statements in the church and funeral home are limited in general to not more than about a dozen groups of phrases out of which individual series of statements are combined, depending upon the death concerned. We therefore proceed from the fact that, besides all the liturgical ceremonies from the temporary viewing place to the funeral, the sermon and the conduct of the participants in the funeral are included in the funeral ritual.

Second, compared with rituals that accompany the funeral in less differentiated societies, our customs appear to be comparatively simple and uncomplicated, even if they presumably still represent the ceremonial in our modern society that is most intensively worked out. Considering the reserved feelings with which not only the minister but also most congregation members face the ritual, we once again recall its social-psychological significance. Therefore we will only deal with the *rites de passage*, not those rites celebrated within the annual cycle (e.g., Christmas) or because of particular crisis conditions.

In the following paragraph we introduce first of all the fundamental potential functions of the *rites de passage*. In doing so, nothing is said about how much rituals of status transition practiced in a society in fact fulfill all these possible functions. Even in less differentiated societies the social norms are in themselves rich in conflict and the level of requirements of individuals too various to make a ritual of transition an expression of mutual faith and at the same time capable of fulfilling all individual expectations. Certain functions may be emphasized more while others are neglected. Nevertheless, the analysis of the functions provides the possibility of examining the rituals of transition in terms of whether they fulfill definite tasks or do not.

(1) *Goal:* In every status transition the individual leaves a specific, socially defined position and must reach a new one, which cannot yet be known to him out of his own experience. The ritual helps him to keep this goal in mind by marking symbolically the path the individual must take. The ritual connects this with the invitation to the other members of the status group the individual leaves, as well as the status group he enters, to assist him in reaching this goal. It also verifies whether the individual fulfills the requirements that the new status demands of him.

(2) *Control of emotions:* Status transitions are tied to the release of strong emotions which are distributed throughout and firmly bound in daily life. This release is necessary, for status transitions always represent a new distribution of emotional relations as well; libido and aggression, affection and distance, must be redistributed. On the one hand, rituals serve the purpose of allowing for a full expression of these emotions, yet at the same time limit them by bringing the emotional outbreaks into definite, approved forms of expressions and limiting the outbursts of feelings in terms of time.

(3) *Anxiety reduction:* Every status transition is connected with anxiety, especially for the one who makes the change of status, for he does not know whether he will acquire the new status. But anxiety is also felt by the ones left behind who fear for him, as well as by those who accept him, since they do not know beforehand how the person concerned will behave toward them and to what extent he will observe the norms and informal rules of the group. He could display a behavior that, in the long run, might turn out to be burdensome or destructive. At this point the function of the ritual is to reduce anxiety and convey to all persons concerned the quieting certainty that the status transition will succeed.

(4) *Granting the new status:* Even though, as already mentioned, the status transition requires a longer period of time, the ritual grants the individual performing the transition the new status already, even though he had not yet in fact reached it. However, this acceptance is primarily based on the obligation that the person concerned prove himself before he can be finally assured of the new status.

(5) *Publication:* It is the individual who has to perform the status transition, but the transition requires public recognition by the social group in which it is carried out and a proclamation that the individual concerned has performed it and now can be approached in his new status in terms of its rights and obligations. In general, this public recognition and proclamation takes place by honoring the individual in a special way.

(6) *Group integration:* While this ritual of transition is performed for a certain member of a social group, it follows the pattern of the many transition rituals individuals have undergone and will undergo on a specific occasion. This potentially infinite repetition of the ritual stabilizes the social organization in which such transitions take place and affirms the common values which were threatened by this transition.

4.4 The status transition of the deceased

The ritual of the funeral symbolizes a double status transition. The bereaved performs a change in social status from, for instance, a married to a widowed woman. The deceased proceeds to the status of those who wait for the future "new society." This theological statement maintains its validity even if the status transition is performed only in the recollection and imagination of the survivor.

In the following section it will be shown how the above developed functions of the *rites de passage* can become effective within the funeral ritual. Yet it cannot be individually verified in what way liturgy, funeral oration, and the conduct of the bereaved, the relatives, and funeral participants actually fulfill these functions. We shall analyze in this section how the funeral ritual contributes to the reorganization of the relations between the dead and the bereaved. It accomplishes this by (1) defining the goal the dead should reach, (2) defining the feelings of the bereaved toward the dead, (3) reducing the anxiety for the dead, (4) awarding the dead the new status, (5) publicizing the reality of his death, and (6) remembering the communion between the dead and the living.

4.41 The goal

In popular piety, such as in obituaries, the status transition of the deceased preferably is characterized as a "way." He "went home"; or, "he has climbed the mountain which still causes you trouble." Liturgies, too, use the formula of blessing from Psalm 121:8: "The Lord will keep your going out and your coming in from this time forth and for evermore." These are the present remains of the worldwide idea that the dead will have to walk a difficult and threatening path before reaching their destination.

Today a conception such as the "soul's journey to heaven" cannot be advocated. The deceased enter the status of the "dead in Christ" and are therefore like the living in expectation of the approaching "new society." They do not enter a "kingdom" described as "paradise" but a status of expectation which will become reality only with the realization of the "kingdom of God." Because in Christian faith the body is not a meaningless frame for an immortal soul but just as much the expression of the total person as acting and

114

speaking, the deceased is regarded with the same human respect as any other living human being, no matter how much he may be deprived of his mental activities or be physically disfigured. The carefulness with which the early Christians treated their dead found public recognition during their own time, as well as the care for the burial of the poor.[1] Joseph of Arimathea's care for the dead body of Christ became the shaping pattern for Christian behavior toward the deceased.

During the early part of the Reformation the respectful treatment of the dead was temporarily threatened, because the abolition of the mass for the dead frequently resulted in the lack of liturgical patterns as to how the dead were to be treated. The Church Orders tried to fight abuses and to set new standards for the treatment of the dead. For example, in the Church Order of Halle from the year 1543 we read:

Christ through his resurrection from the dead has made the funeral of all of those who believe in him so honest and glorious so that the grave is not a fatal pit but a divine chamber in which one rests until eternal life, and a fertile field of God in which one grows before God and blooms for eternity. Therefore Christians shall not carelessly discard their deceased members as dead beasts, but bury them honestly and respectfully. Not as if the service of the living were useful and contributing to the salvation of the deceased, but rather that the ones who are still alive and attend the funeral demonstrate their Christian compassion and thus are reminded of the resurrection of our Lord and are strengthened in their faith.[2]

The question about how the corpse should be treated came up again during the eighteenth century with the problem of cremation. If in the funeral the "rest in Christ" should be represented symbolically as the new status position, then the question must be asked whether burial or cremation more appropriately expresses this symbolism.

Cremation was not performed by Christians, in contrast to, for example, Roman practices. In this they followed not so much theological considerations as they did the Jewish synagogue custom which found its deepest expression in the statement that God himself buried Moses (Deut. 34:6). A great value was placed upon a properly conducted funeral in ancient Israel. If the body were not buried or if it were burned, the dead soul no longer had a home.[3] Originally, cremation had nothing to do with the resurrection of the dead, a doctrine that was contested in the synagogue. Roman officials did, however, occasionally burn the bones of martyrs with the intended polemic of making their resurrection impossible. But this tactic was considered a vain effort by Christians, as Augustine confesses in The City of God (I, 12): "And so there are indeed many bodies of Christians lying unburied; but no one has separated them from heaven, nor from that earth which is all filled with the presence of Him who knows whence He will raise again what He created."

The propagation of cremation during the Enlightenment unfortunately began in connection with a deliberate confrontation with the Christian belief in resurrection. During the French Revolution in 1797, the first great but unsuccessful attempt was made to introduce cremation as an obligatory form of burial.[4] In the nineteenth century cremation found special recommendation among Free Masons, Free Thinkers, and Marxists, but also with liberal Protestants. Particularly vehement opposition against it came from Jewish circles. The Roman Catholic Church on principle also prohibited a church service in connection with cremation in the Canon 1203 CIC. In 1964, a statement of the Holy Office was published to the effect that a Christian funeral can be attached to cremation if this is not carried out with the conscious intention of going against Catholic dogma.[5]

The ideological basis of cremation is the concept of the purifying power of fire, the purification and liberation of the soul, as it is written above the entrance to the crematory in Zurich: "Flames dissolve the mortal and free the immortal."[6] The grave appears as the emblem of peace in the dark; it is the emblem of death. The fire, on the other hand, is the symbol of life, of the upward-striving and creative spirit.[7] Reasons of a more practical nature are sanitary considerations, the increasing expensiveness of land for burial, particularly of municipal property, and partly related to that, the lower costs of cremation. The distribution of the ashes on a reserved piece of lawn within the cemetery can, besides the practical, have also an ideological background: to be reunited with the earth, to integrate in the whole of nature, and to participate in the cycle of life. Semiconscious anxieties of being buried alive and the frightening notion of a slow decay (similar to the idea that a sudden death is preferable to a long suffering) certainly play a role as well. As a result of the increased mobility in modern society, the dead sometimes has to be transported over long distances, which becomes much easier in case of cremation; a separation from the burial place can be avoided by taking along the urn containing the ashes.

Practical objections against cremation, in particular the danger of no longer being able to investigate a homicide attempt, have been removed by legal regulations. More crucial are ideological and therapeutic objections. The grave symbolizes the place of tranquility and peace in expectation of the coming kingdom of God. It is a place of remembrance to which one can always return again (a situation which does not exclude morbid dependencies). More than cremation, which is not performed before the eyes of the survivors, the funeral affirms the reality of the death. This affirmation is also of significance with respect to conducting a service of worship, since the present practice in connection with cremation is to hold a memorial service following cremation in which the body of the deceased is absent. Another reason in favor of a funeral is the fact that an element of brutality clings to cremation; unconscious anxieties about the fire of hell are activated. The aura of having life and death at one's disposal adheres to it, a quality that has found its most pregnant expression in the crematories at Auschwitz. The survivors may also be disturbed because they disposed of the deceased in such a quick way. A marginal problem is the pressure of time under which the service at the crematory frequently is conducted.

In my opinion, primarily therapeutic, and only secondarily, theological, reasons favor the funeral over cremation. This is particularly true with regard to the importance of convincing oneself of the reality of death—the detachment by steps which happens not in a "violent" but in a "natural" way and the grave perceived as a place of memory and peace.

Compared to these therapeutic and theological aspects, the practical motives must recede. Their weight could be diminished through definite procedures: Communalization of the undertaking business presumably could help to lower the costs. The renunciation of selling burying places as a business venture by congregations and municipal communities which do so could facilitate this as well. Cemeteries could be part of the urgently needed "green lungs" for cities and thus prevent the visibility of death in our society from being reduced further.

4.42 The release of the deceased

The ritual at the funeral has the function of making it easier for the mourner to release the deceased and thus of preventing the emotional dependency from simply being transferred from the living to the dead. It serves the purpose of controlling those emotions that inhibit this release. L. Giudice expresses the desire to call back the deceased very clearly, only to retract it immediately:

Our body and our love is a stage that has passed. I often think of it, but do not want to enjoy this happiness again, which may in some future time when God will lead us to undreamt of bliss seem like a soft breeze. To implore back Oki would prolong our way. I am impatient to develop myself towards the end as God wills. We ought to follow someone who passed away and is so much closer to God, and not call him back.[8]

Psychological insight and theological statement point in the same direction. "Christians learn to give up their dead (as well as their own life)."[9]

The idea of wanting to keep the dead is contradicted by the other extreme—the tendency to dispose of the dead rather quickly. Some funerals give the impression that there was a tacit agreement between the minister and all the participants to get this unpleasant matter over quickly. The deceased has to be buried in the ground, and this should be done if possible in a quick and painless manner. The increasing tendency to shorten the funeral ceremony frequently serves such an intention under the cover of a "simple service." The ritual fails in its function to control emotions if it gives the impression that the dead shall be repudiated or that he is not to be released.

4.43 Intercessory prayers for the deceased

A purpose of the ritual is to reduce anxiety. At this point it is first of all anxiety about the "way" of the dead. The question whether something can be done for the dead in order to alleviate the transition for him has been answered positively by the early church as well as the church of the Middle Ages. The baptism for the dead,[10] still meaningful in the time of the early Christian church, nevertheless disappeared later, but prayers for the dead remained undisputed. They were already practiced in the early church, even before a dogmatic idea about the intermediate stage after death had developed. Augustine gave reason for the propriety and meaning of intercessory prayers, while at the same time limiting its effect to specific forms only. His arguments became authoritative for the Roman Catholic Church. Intercessory prayers can, according to Augustine, increase God's mercy, in contrast with a pompous funeral, a large funeral procession, and the erection of huge commemorative stones which, though possibly of some comfort to the living, are of no service to the dead.[11] Out of intercessory prayers and Holy Communion at the graves grew the mass for the dead.

The Reformer fought with all determination against everything that gave the impression of influencing the state of being of the deceased in the world beyond. Together with the doctrine of purgatory, the vigils and masses for the dead and everything related to them were abolished. Luther writes:

Accordingly, we have removed from our churches and completely abolished the popish abominations, such as vigils, masses for the dead, processions, purgatory, and all other hocus-pocus on behalf of the dead. And we do not want our churches to be houses of wailing and places of mourning any longer, but Koemeteria as the old fathers were wont to call them, i.e., dormitories and resting places.[12]

Intercessory prayers for the dead were completely rejected neither by Luther himself nor by his followers. However, the tendency existed of restricting these intercessory prayers to private praying; accordingly, intercessory prayers for the dead are found only in a few Church Orders and liturgies for funerals. According to F. Schulz the phrase in Ps. 31:5, "Into thy hand I commit my spirit," is closely connected with the hour of death in which the persons present verbalize this petition on behalf of the dying, "praying, so to speak, *cum mortuo*, not yet *pro mortuo*."[13]

In late nineteenth-century Lutheranism, intercessory prayer was subject to vehement discussions.[14] The liturgies of the VELKD (United Evangelical-Lutheran Churches of Germany) and EKU (Evangelical Church of the Union) currently in use contain the intercession for preservation from the Last Judgment and for resurrection. Purism, arising out of the original concerns of the reformers not to force upon God the law of action, is probably unnecessary today. Intercessory prayer for others is, nevertheless, justifiable only when it is also used in other crisis situations. It would be wrong to give the impression that whereas in other situations active involvement can make a difference, nothing but prayer will help here. Intercessory prayer presupposes further that the deceased, even as one who is dead, exists in the common expectation of the new society. The idea of vicarious action by the living for the dead also presupposes such a community and can serve as a bridge for an adequate understanding of church activities.

How strong anxieties about the dead are today is hard to estimate. Still, it is remarkable to read what Giudice writes in her journal:

The few passages in the Bible about hell now burned in my soul. As long as one is happy, paradise seems close to the touch and hell very far, one reads only occasionally about it, untouched. . . . We exclude hell from our daily life, just as we exclude death. Yet I only knew that I feared for Oki. Had he died with some guilt—I don't refer to the thousands of venial offences we all commit—had he died with guilt, I no longer could have escaped from the jaws of fear. After the funeral my panic fear yielded. I felt as if Oki had reached his destination, the place provided for him by Jesus. . . . Should we pray for the dead? It was not a question I asked, for I had to pray for Oki. . . . I prayed to God just the way I felt it and thus found a certain peace in my distress. Only later, when I was capable again of thinking, was I bothered by the question of whether I had the right to pray for Oki.[15]

The reduction of anxiety through the ritual very likely was originally related to fear of the dead, although this is no longer recognizable in today's funeral rituals. Numerous customs in simple societies are to be mentioned in this context, such as avoiding saying the name of the dead aloud and not speaking maliciously of him. The nightly watch at the casket is related to this custom. For the same reason, for example, the deceased is taken away through a side entrance or window in some German customs, for fear that the deceased might find his way back. When being passed through the door he is carried feet first, in order to prevent the deceased from looking at the entrance. The cross at the grave serves as sign of preservation and the tombstone as a weight, to keep the dead in his grave. Well-known are the numerous stories about the dead who cannot find peace because a sin he had committed or that was inflicted upon him by others had not been expiated. The peaceful *requiescat in pace* as an epitaph is dubious; concealed in this blessing can also be the inclination to avert the return of the dead.

The conjuring customs have dwindled today, but the anxieties, frequently based on the guilt feelings of the bereaved, remain. The idea of a destroying fire in hell or a painful purification can have a distressing vitality. It is this aspect of anxiety reduction that Neidhardt had called particular attention to. He points out that, through the ceremony,

an event considered threatening for the life cycle has been regulated. It helps the bereaved to return to their daily routine. Many ceremonies have this effect, according to Arnold Gehlen. They satisfy the need for stability in the circle of events. Extraordinary things are perceived as a threat and release anxiety. The ceremonial used in these cases assists in coping with the extraordinary as if it were something regular. The ceremonial thus has the function of promoting relief.[16]

4.44 The new status

The ritual signifies that the new status has been attained, that is, in the case of the funeral, that the deceased actually occupies the status of a dead person. This aspect has been especially emphasized by American pastoral theology[17] in view of the American custom of using cosmetics to give the deceased a youthful appearance from which the traces of death have been obliterated. Such customs correspond to a society in which health, sports, and youth are preeminent values, but they deny that a real status transition has taken place which is irrevocable.

Actually to be confronted with the reality of death is an essential function of the funeral. The separation requires a visible presentation so that every attempt of denial is prevented. Therefore, the presence of the casket during the funeral is important, while the coffin lid should already be closed to signify the irreversibility of the event. The strongest affirmation of death is the immersing of the casket and the first throwing of soil (this impression should not be mitigated by throwing flowers instead of soil on the casket). It is a widespread conviction that children should not participate in a funeral since they supposedly are incapable of bearing the brutality of this event and the heightened emotionality of the immediate family. The more recent literature assumes a different attitude, based on analysis of children.[18] The death cannot remain hidden from the child; in any case he notices the absence of an important person from his environment and is frightened by the unusual behavior of the adults. Adults, as far as they are particularly affected, are too strained emotionally to talk to children in detail about the event. Since children notice this they do not ask questions (to the implicit relief of the adults) or seem to be satisfied with evasive answers ("Grandpa has gone on a long journey"; "Mother is now with Jesus"). However, since they have only vague notions about what death actually is, their fantasies are unlimited. Children often are convinced for many years, based on "child-like" or misleading answers, that the father or mother has abandoned them deliberately or as some kind of punishment. They accuse Jesus of having deprived them of their most beloved one, feeling that "Jesus already has enough angels." Besides allowing children to participate in the funeral, additional and detailed explanation must be given in order that they may have a more realistic picture of death. The more openly adults have spoken about death with a child prior to an actual occurrence of death (which seldoms takes place today because the socialization of death-repression begins in childhood), the easier it is to reduce overpowering fantasies. However, a child should by no means be forced to participate.

4.45 Public recognition

The funeral ritual signifies public recognition of the status transition the dead has gone through. The wish to honor the dead includes a bundle of motivations. The principle *de mortuis nil nisi bene* may originally have been spoken out of fear of revenge of the dead who still dwells invisibly among the living. In praising him, the bereaved also try to shake off guilt feelings. At the same time they want to secure the transition of the dead by making references to his exemplary life. However, it seems that paying respect in public during a status transition plays the essential role. Thereby the church represents the public, substituting for society.

It is obvious that the function of public recognition which, of course, not only refers to the dead but also to his family, cannot be observed efficiently by the church itself. Nevertheless, one should be aware of the fact that the church only symbolizes the public; it by no means *is* the public. The more "public" the deceased is, the more redundant the church becomes for the function of honoring him. If the deceased was an important figure in public life, very quickly it becomes obvious what a limited role the minister has in representing society. He then must share this role with others or stand back completely.

That the church and not the state normally assumes the task of public recognition also has a functional aspect. "Since the church assumes here a publicly relevant task, it saves the state from providing such rituals itself and thus from having to interfere directly in the private sphere. Even without the right for sovereign acts, the church is still public enough to give help without obligations. It therefore makes it possible to protect the ranks of family from direct controls." [19]

From the perspective of social politics, the church finds itself in an extremely precarious situation by taking over the responsibility of the funeral. Chr. Ferber's critical comments on the undertaking business can also be applied to this service of the church: There, the socially unresolved relationship between privacy and publicity is reflected. [20] "Death belongs," so Ferber, "to the very few events in the life of a person by which his existence as a personality becomes a subject of public recognition." [21] While a person takes on and gives up various roles during a lifetime, with the occurrence of death, the person as the bearer of all social roles ceases to exist. Where, however, a society is adjusted to the achievement of specific results, where dissolving of social relations is required in the interest of social change, there is no room for interest in personal matters. The desire of every person to be taken seriously as an individual who strives for meaningful self-realization is pushed aside. "The communication from person to person, even though seldom accomplished in the private circle of life, in the small communities of family, friendship, and small groups is not achieved with the public even in death." [22]

The church is in danger of becoming the servant of a society that takes no interest in the person by acting pseudo-publicly. But it also can make quite clear, in its vicarious honoring of the deceased, the conflicting thesis that even death does not bring the public recognition needed by this person and to which he has a right. To cite Ferber once more: "Not the self-alienation which disposes of itself is revealed in death but rather the lack of a chance for self-realization, the compulsion for privatizing imposed through the social constitution which denied the expression of the total personhood of the deceased." [23] The funeral is the last opportunity to honor the dead and mourn because of the loss.

4.46 The community of the dead with the living

The funeral ritual affirms the existing basic ideas about death in a society; it reminds the participants of the great legion of dead with whom the people present at the grave live together. The ritual renews the attitude that has to be assumed toward the dead. It affirms the community between the living and the dead. "There is a kinship of kind, too," Warner writes; "today's dead are yesterday's living, and today's living are tomorrow's dead. Each is identified with the other's fate. No one escapes."[24]

Nevertheless, the general statement about the status of the dead can never be definite, because the images of death in our society are too variable. Carlin speaks about a fourfold interpretation of death, integrated in the ritual conduct at the funeral: the interpretation of death by the family; the theological interpretation as given in the liturgy and in the minister's sermon; the cultural attitude toward death whose influence nobody escapes; and, finally, the attitude of the person who attends the funeral merely as an observer or because of social obligations.[25] Although liturgy and sermon carry the theological interpretation, how much it determines behavior remains a question.

4.5 The status transition of the bereaved

The funeral ritual not only has the potential function of symbolizing the change in the relations between the deceased and the bereaved, but also between the bereaved and his environment. (1) It constitutes the way he has to go, (2) keeps his emotions under control, (3) reduces his anxiety to cope with the new situations, (4) awards him the new status, (5) proclaims this new status in public, and (6) reassures the bereaved that he will be accepted again in the world of the living and that the intermediate condition of his isolation is not permanent.

The duality of the ritual visible at the funeral is found in all status transitions. Confirmation, for example, signifies not only symbolically how children become adults, are no longer under the influence of the parents, and must find their own way and their own recognition by themselves and by the environment. It also shows how parents, through this coming of age of their children, are left behind as "bereaved" and must cope with a status no longer determined by their children and learn no longer to see in the children the center of their interactions.

4.51 The detachment from the deceased

For the survivor, the funeral ritual symbolizes the method and goal of a gradual detachment from the deceased. The succession of actions, such as putting the body in the casket, the closing of the casket, and its lowering into the grave or the basement of the crematory, are steps that indicate that the way of separation will not be abruptly but gradually accomplished.

4.52 The controlled mourning

The ritual controls the expression of emotions in various ways. It can repress emotional outbreaks as well as intensify them; it determines the moment when the display of feelings must be particularly intensive; it frequently assigns a different behavior according to the differences in sex; and, finally, it is defined in the ritual who, as a person very close to the dead, must show intensive grief, while other people present simply must observe a certain behavior control in their role as mere participants.

By comparing the funeral rituals practiced today in modern Western civilizations with those in less differentiated societies with their loud lamentations and protests, it seems that apathy is the normal behavioral pattern in Western societies, interrupted only by occasional "outbursts," particularly at the lowering of the casket. Already the term "outburst" indicates the strong restraint imposed by the apathetic conduct; the features of suppression without protest prevail.

That in modern Western civilizations the silent, painful acceptance has replaced lamentation and protest is due to the shaping power of Christian tradition. It signifies surrender to the will of God. If the loss is his responsibility, then any protest and lament must appear as lack of confidence, no matter whether one finds comfort in the hope of life after death or not. Besides, a stronger reality awareness may play a role here, according to which it is not admissable and meaningful to protest and mourn for something that is undeniably lost. The will of God and social awareness of reality build a coalition against the expression of feelings.

In the modern funeral ritual the possibility of acting out aggressions toward the deceased and the circumstances of death are omitted. Mercedes B. Concepcion illustrates how the funeral rites in a Roman Catholic village in the Philippines permit at three instances a display of behavior in which the grief stricken are allowed to scream, cry, and accuse the deceased aloud, to throw up their arms in despair, to faint and become stiff, and also to display violent behavior. This happens on the way from the house of mourning to the church, at the closing of the casket after the priest's blessing, and at the lowering of the casket. This is considered a sign of genuine admiration, grief and child-like piety toward the person who is buried.[1] Concepcion cites the report of a priest who observed a funeral there:

Shrieks began coming from the ermita, or cemetery chapel. This was another funeral, the couple concerned being from Barrio Baras. They had lost a child of some 20 months named Domingo. Since I was standing near the gate now and also near the ermita and the woman seemed to have fainted, I moved toward where she was. As I did, the husband was dragged out by two men. He was screaming incoherently and fighting them, but his legs were weak. Suddenly he stiffened. Without any discussion or alarm, the two men picked him up under the elbows like a tamping pole and pounded his feet against the earth, lifting him up each time like a log held vertically between them. Some of the people around began to laugh at this. After some four or five times he unstiffened, began to scream again and fight his helpers. They took him out of the cemetery to the road and then on a few steps to his house in Baras.[2]

It is important for our context to see that such a forced expression is confined to a certain stage limited to a particular time. It cannot spill over into the other, but is replaced by other ritual acts. However, not only the opportunity for acting out aggressions is suppressed in the present rituals, but the expression of other feelings as well, above all, weeping. It is obvious that in the course of this century an increasing de-emotionalizing of the funeral has taken place. The reasons that lead to such a degradation of expressive emotional acts are various: It was believed that only in this way the attention for the word of God could be kept; the relatives in fear of losing control over themselves ask "to make it brief and painless"; the minister himself feels helpless if he is eventually confronted with emotional outbursts. Besides, according to social norms, the expression of feelings in public is unsuitable and is banished into the private sphere. In spite of these partly acceptable and partly questionable arguments, it seems to be necessary to pay more attention to this particular aspect of de-emotionalizing and the abridgment of the funeral ritual connected with it. De-emotionalized and abridged rituals give the embarrassing impression that the dead will be disposed of as quickly as possible.

It is obvious that there is no consensus as to whether public rituals should repress emotions and should keep them in the private sphere, or whether the rituals should facilitate their expression. The bereaved themselves very often are of the opinion that any form of public grief is hard to bear and seems to be like "giving a performance"; private grief in a nonritualized form, on the contrary, is considered as "genuine." Those bereaved who weep a great deal during the funeral and have a breakdown at the grave are considered "hypocritical," although certain mourning reactions are expected; if a close relative appears to be completely unmoved, this will find social disapproval. Therapeutically, such a release of feelings is advocated because it facilitates grief work. Generally the bereaved should be entitled to the freedom of behaving according to their own feelings whether or not they feel any grief, are able to express strong feelings, or want to express their grief publicly.

A minister alone will hardly be able to change the behavior of an entire society which focuses on repression of expressing feelings in public, even if he recognizes the therapeutic value of free expression. He can forgo strengthening this repression and make it clear through explanation and his own reaction to such outbursts that here nothing embarrassing and disreputable is taking place. Therefore, the minister as the leader of the ritual must take care that the liturgy of the funeral and his message set grief reactions free rather than inhibit them, as is mostly the case at the present time. Theologically, not to be allowed to mourn is as much "law" in the negative sense as not to be capable of mourning if guilt feelings and resentments against the deceased are blocking the expression of grief. The minister's action is good news if it releases unrestrained bereavement. To enable this is an essential step toward a new adaptation to the environment. The ritual can contribute to it as far as it does not repress emotions but lets them flow freely and can at the same time absorb the outbursts through the process of the liturgical order.

4.53 Reducing anxiety

We have already spoken of the anxiety that can come from a vindictive dead person and from the concern for the dead. But there is also the anxiety of the survivors who are not able to detach themselves from the dead and who become involved in his death. There is the concern of not being able to cope with the loss and to come out of the condition of disorganization. The future of the family may be threatened financially. Finally, the death of the other unavoidably reveals the threat to one's own existence. One of the functions of the ritual is to reduce the anxiety of the mourner.

To begin with, it is the structure of the ritual itself that contributes to reducing anxiety. By arranging the disruptive and destructive consequences of a death in organized sequences of events, the ritual, with its structure of order, counteracts the inner chaos and the feeling of being lost. It provides a behavior pattern of "small steps," which, however, cannot just be transferred into the daily life of bereavement, yet shows that detaching oneself from the dead without losing him can be accomplished. Because the ritual is limited in time, it indicates that mourning will not last forever.

In addition to that, the ritual refers to a number of possible coping mechanisms. It bears witness to the sustaining love of God and the concern of members of one's community, who provide solidarity when they gather around the bereaved at the grave. It can encourage those in despair to deny the death no longer but to face it fully. It calls to mind the past common life and demands the process of recollection, which contributes to the detachment from the dead. If it can demonstrate that enough meaningful tasks remain for the survivor and that substitution is possible, then the way into the future is open.

The contemporary funeral ceremony could contribute even more to reducing anxieties if it would concern itself also with the guilt feelings of the bereaved, which are often present in the mourner. In studying the liturgies and funeral sermons, it becomes clear that hardly any attention is paid to this aspect of coping with grief. Forgiveness for the survivor also remains only a side issue in the mass for the dead. On the other hand, the funeral rituals of less differentiated societies include a great number of purification rites. The liturgical statements "for we are consumed by thy anger" and "the wages of sin is death" try to explain in general why the deceased, as any person, is under the destiny of death, but fail to provide a meaningful aid to the mourner as to how he should cope with his individual guilt feelings. Guilt and guilt feelings exist unrelated side by side; particularly the emphasis on general sinfulness hinders the bereaved from articulating his own actual guilt feelings. To express forgiveness of sins can help to break down the walls separating the mourner from his social environment.

4.54 The new status

The funeral ceremony not only refers to the way of detachment and readaptation but also bestows already upon the mourner the new status. It refers to a wife who has lost her husband as widow and to her children as orphans. However, it not only symbolizes the external social change of status but also the internal change initiated by the grief process. Especially is this new identity for the bereaved guaranteed by the ritual. He is no longer the one who has loved this particular person who is now lost, but someone who will live without this person, no matter what memories bind him to the deceased. The ritual represents the detachment as a completed one and therefore assists in the liberation from the domination and the image of the dead. Persons are no longer loved only because they resemble the deceased. The ritual can make clear that the mourner has become a different person for whom the deceased sooner or later will be another, a strange person, even though the mourner maintains the deceased within himself and remembers him.

4.55 The publication of the new status

The funeral ritual makes the new status of the bereaved public, provides him special rights, and places him under special protection, just as this function is repeatedly underscored in biblical instruction concerning the public and legal recognition of widows and orphans. The mourner to a certain extent becomes taboo through the ritual in the dual sense peculiar to a taboo. On the one hand, he is met with a certain shyness; on the other hand, society grants him a protected realm.

In the intermediate stage between the occurrence of death and reintegration into the social environment, the bereaved is avoided in a particular way, just as the dead and as the sick, especially the sick with incurable disease. In less differentiated societies, not only the widow but also the next of kin of the deceased are submitted to rigorous restrictions.[3] However, avoidance of the mourner is also found in the Western world.

According to a survey made by G. M. Vernon, only 25 percent of the respondents to the questions would, if they met someone who had lost a loved one through death since their last encounter with this person, mention it; 37 percent would not themselves initiate the subject and 24 percent would prefer that no mention of the death be made by either party, while the rest could give no answer or refused to answer.[4] Clerk describes this avoidance of the bereaved out of his own experience:

An odd byproduct of my loss is that I am aware of being an embarrassment to everyone I meet. At work, at the club, in the street, I see people, as they approach me, trying to make up their minds whether they'll say something about it or not. I hate it if they do and if they don't. Some funk it altogether. R. has been avoiding me for a week. I like best the well-brought-up young men, almost boys, who walk up to me as if I were a dentist, turn very red, get it over, and then edge away to the bar as quickly as they decently can. Perhaps the bereaved ought to be isolated in special settlements like lepers.

To some I am worse than an embarrassment. I am death's head. Whenever I meet a happily married pair I can feel them both thinking "one or other of us must some day be as he is now."[5]

The bereaved is avoided because he is a reminder of the possibility of one's own death. This is especially true if the death was a violent or untimely one and was accompanied by long suffering. Death awakes unadmitted anxieties for the examiner and interpreter himself, which may explain in part why scientific studies until a few years ago dealt little with the subject of death and grief.

Yet the ritual not only isolates the mourner, like the sign of Cain, but at the same time places him under the protection of God. To dress in distinctive mourning clothes is a visible expression of this function of the ritual. L. Giudice tells how much she at first refused to wear a mourning dress.

It had been difficult for me to dress in mourning; it was almost harder to take the black dress off again. By now I liked the black suit in which I had suffered through all stages of agony and did not want to put it aside. In the severe pain I felt ill at ease as in a knight's armor, but it also sometimes provided protection. Wrapped in blackness and grief, I hardly noticed people and things in the city and nobody dared to approach me with trifles. If I felt that I was about to cry while walking the street and could do nothing to stop the flow of tears, I even wished to hide behind a dense widow's veil which I had despised so much before.[6]

In addition to the recognition that the deceased is allotted through the public character of the ritual, it also promotes the recognition of the survivors. For them it transmits the feeling that they, in spite of the loss and change of status, continue to be accepted members of society. Just because grief very often is related to a feeling of self-devaluation, already honoring the deceased can help the bereaved. What Irion called the "service of memories,"[7] the public recognition of shared events and experiences, is a help to the mourner.

Finally, the publication of the new status can cause the bereaved to realize the finality of the death. Since the ritual makes the death public, there is no longer a point of return for the mourner. He cannot cling to the unrealistic hope that everything may be a terrible, unreal dream.

4.56 The community between the bereaved and the living

Finally, the funeral ceremony can have the function of affirming in general that the loss of a person and the mourning for him is not the experience of that mourner alone, but that there were others before him who overcame this burden and that this will continue to happen. The funeral is not the place for a general discussion of what a "trial by God" means and what sense it makes. Rather the experience of pain is generalized; it no longer appears to be the individual problem of this one person, but makes him a member of the group of people who, with the help of the Christian faith and by psychological techniques, have overcome the crisis. Thus the ritual affirms the values generally employed by a society for coping with such a loss.

5. Care giving agents

The term "care giving agents"[1] signifies the circle of people who are also sometimes called "transition technicians."[2] During the crisis of mourning a number of professional agents are called in to take charge. Their function is to assist the mourner in coping with his situation. Among them are the physician in the hospital, the general practitioner, the funeral director, and the minister, together with their personnel (nurses, morticians, drivers of the funeral cars, pallbearers, gravediggers, organist, sexton). In the following pages we shall briefly analyze in what function and at what time they come in contact with the mourner and what help they can provide besides carrying out their special duties.

5.1 The physician in the hospital
Usually it is the task of the doctor in the hospital to inform the family that death has occurred (the following also is true to some extent for the floor nurse if she has been assigned to this task). He is in a professional conflict of roles, which affects his behavior toward the survivors. His professional responsibility is focused on alleviating pain, preventing death, and the realization of the socially recognized right to health. He possesses authority and power. In addition, there is not only the hope and confidence in his ability to heal on the

part of the patient and his family but also the expectations in his magical omnipotence and infallibility. The physician himself may be susceptible to the gratification of being in charge, in control, having power, of being in a superior position in which somebody is dependent on him. Another factor that determines a physician's behavior is the knowledge of having control over death. According to H. Feifel, one of the major reasons certain physicians enter medicine is to overcome their own fears concerning death. He proves this by an investigation he completed about the attitudes of physicians toward death, which indicates that physicians are more afraid of death than patients themselves and a control group of healthy people.[3] All these demands made by others upon him and those he makes upon himself as well are destroyed when death occurs. According to W. M. Easson's observation, a physician reacts to death with angry feelings and finds himself in a constant battle with it the younger he is, while older doctors have coped much better emotionally with the inevitability of death.[4]

Considering this defeat, the physician now faces the fact of having to "confess" it publicly to the family, a task for which he necessarily is highly limited emotionally, and sometimes it may ask too much of him. In addition, his goal in passing on the death notice must be to act most considerately, in order to prevent a general emotional breakdown of the family, if only for the reason that the information frequently has to be given in front of other visitors and patients. Frequently there is no chance to spend more time with the family. Because every death crisis signifies failure and defeat, the physician to a certain degree finds himself in a difficult situation. This urges him to assure the family that everything possible has been done, that dying was not painful for the patient but rather a relief. He may add the comforting remark that the end was anticipated for some time, although he seems to be surprised that it occurred so quickly. Frequently he will describe death as natural and inevitable. But in any case his function is restricted to the stage of shock. An occasional practice in such cases is to call the hospital chaplain to assist with the family.

5.2 The general practitioner

The second of the care giving agents is the general practitioner. He comes into contact with the mourners relatively frequently, even after the stage of control, partly because he is approached for prescribing sleeping pills and tranquilizers; partly because the psychosomatic symptoms provide an officially recognized opportunity to consult a "caring person"; and also, partly because already a kind of routine contact exists, which often was intensified through the illness of the now deceased. C. M. Parkes sees another possible reason that a widow visits her physician more frequently than usual in the support that he provides. "She is in a more dependent frame of mind, and it may be that she is encouraged to attend by a G.P. who sympathizes with her lot and is prepared to devote more time to her care than he would otherwise do."[1] Whatever the reason for consulting a physician may be, it is remarkable that according to the study by Clayton et al. 44 percent of the widows interviewed by him visited a physician.[2]

Increasingly the public is made aware by the professionals of the health problems related to grief. It is an essential presupposition, as demonstrated above, that grief is recognized as an independent disease entity. Physicians confronted with bereaved generally see only the physical restlessness and tension, as well as sleep disturbances, which are treated with tranquilizers and sleeping pills. How much this treatment is of essential help or only inhibits the grief process has not been sufficiently researched so far.

The general difficulties of the general practitioner's are similiar to the minister's, even though the physician may have known the bereaved longer than the minister. For one thing, GPs have little training for approaching the psychological aspects of the disease, although they no doubt can acquire certain experiences in life that can be helpful to the bereaved. On the other hand, they, too, lack the time to deal in more detail with the problems of the bereaved, which may, for instance, result from guilt feelings. A colleagial relationship may prohibit a serious consideration of the accusations made by the bereaved against the physicians in charge. In general it can be said that the role of the GP consists in strengthening and prolonging the controlled stage through medication.

5.3 The funeral director

The funeral director is the care giving agent who, at the present time, has the most intensive contact with the bereaved during the controlled stage of mourning. Usually he is informed sooner than the minister about the death of a member of the congregation and has a decisive influence regarding the funeral procedure. He has the knowledge of how to proceed in the case of a funeral, knows what legal steps are necessary, and he can define what represents a simple, average, or expensive funeral. He may expect to be recognized in this professional know-how of his, and he reacts with displeasure to special demands deviating from the professional routine.

The relative or friend who takes care of the arrangements for the funeral on behalf of the immediately affected hardly has his own standards for what is considered an appropriate funeral. For the family, in most cases, the desire to perform the last honors through what is considered for the norm an appropriate funeral is decisive. However, the outcome of this decision is dependent on the funeral director. An important factor, besides the wish to honor the deceased, are guilt feelings. The embellishment of the funeral is a financial sacrifice in order to atone for neglects in former times. The extraordinary event of death has priority over financial considerations. A decision has to be made immediately; therefore, there is little opportunity to obtain comparative offers. All of this provides a more favorable basis for the undertaker than for the bereaved with respect to negotiations about the funeral.

Nevertheless, an undertaker deals not only on a business level. He understands his profession as "ministry" and considers himself not only the deliverer of the casket and the shroud and the provider of the grave site, embalming, transportation to the cemetery or church, and pallbearers. He takes on emotional functions as well. He has to give the relatives the impression that he will take good care of the corpse; in many cases he will also comfort his clients. For example, a minister reported to the author that an undertaker in a small town had defeated all his competitors within a few years, not because the carrying out of the funeral differed in such a remarkable way from others, but because he showed great sensitivity in counseling with the bereaved. At this point, counseling may also include areas such as financial contributions for the funeral by the community, funds from industries and corporations, insurance money, etc.

There are a number of role conflicts between the tasks of the funeral director and the minister.[1] C. C. Bachmann, after a conference between ministers and funeral directors, formulated the following critical factors observed about some clergy by funeral directors. The funeral directors regret the status consciousness of the minister. They observed stereotyped behavior, as well as words said over and over again without much effect or meaning. Clergymen tend to throw their weight around with families and lack consideration of others' feelings. Finally, the undertakers seem to detect a certain hostility, concealed behind cool aloofness from the whole business, which they would just as soon finish in order to get back to more agreeable tasks.[2]

Such opinions cannot be generalized and also betray some resentment of the minister's higher social status compared with the status of the funeral director.

5.4 The minister

5.41 The social position

The fourth of the care giving agents is the minister. In general, he is informed about the death by relatives or by the funeral director. Even though counseling in case of a death belongs to the official responsibilities of a minister, his professional interaction generally is restricted to a short visit in the house of mourning, during which mainly the forthcoming funeral and its performance is discussed, since he is usually the leader of this ritual. However, under certain circumstances he has to share the leading function with certain social, fraternal, or patriotic groups. He has no influence in their attitude toward the biblical message. In most cases the funeral takes place in the funeral director's funeral home. Often enough the bereaved is not known to the minister, especially if the deceased was not a member of his congregation. All of this is to speak to the point that there are numerous difficulties in the way of the minister's most effective personal counseling of the bereaved.

Just as funeral directors have their complaints about ministers, so pastors are critical of the exaggeration of the decoration with respect to casket, floral decoration, candles, and musical arrangements as set up by the morticians. This in their opinion has a pseudoreligious appearance, opposing the Christian belief in resurrection. They are annoyed that most of the time it is the undertaker who sets the date for the funeral. It is also somewhat common for them to accuse the undertaker of selfish business interests. Ministers are particularly disturbed when funeral directors take over such tasks as counseling and spiritual consolation to the bereaved, which they consider their own legitimate task. The conversations which we conducted in groups of ministers, however, made it obvious that in most cases the pastor had no personal contact with the funeral director and made no attempt to influence him.

In the opinion of M. Bowers et al., the minister's antipathies and resentments toward the funeral director come primarily from two sources. First, the funeral is the only service in which the pastor has to share the limelight with another person. He conducts baptisms, confirmations, weddings, etc., by himself. The second and more significant reason is that, if the minister himself cannot come to terms with death, then "the funeral director is the final affront to the pastor's unresolved fears, and so the object of the resentments and antipathies that cluster about the idea of death as an enemy. If you cannot overcome death, you can at least try to make life miserable for the person who reminds you of your personal failure." [1]

Ministers also sometimes speak disparagingly about funeral participants. They are devaluated because they only wish to glorify the dead. The trouble is that the ministers do not see through the glorification as a function of the defense mechanism. The bereaved are accused of only being interested in what they will inherit, and the quarrel about that begins already at the grave. For them, the funeral does not seem to be an act of Christian faith; rather, all they actually wanted was a beautiful service, overly organized in order to demonstrate their devotion toward the deceased. Worse yet, the term "death cult" may even be applied to this kind of behavior. Pseudoreligiosity is the accusation made against the bereaved, without any reflection on the part of the minister as to what extent sentimentality is the only religious mode of expression available to the bereaved in such a situation. They do not question the legitimacy of their own theology, which causes them to label such a behavior by the bereaved as pseudoreligious.

Such a distortion of the situation of the bereaved and his psychic condition, resulting from the pastor's inability to cope with his own anxieties and predicaments with respect to death, at the same time complicates counseling with the bereaved, which would be an excellent possibility for the pastor, thanks to his social position. It is true that this possible help can be effective only in the regressive and adaptive stages, but the institutionalized activity in the stage of control creates an essential groundwork for effective counseling in the following stages. If the minister succeeds in gaining the trust and confidence of the bereaved during the phase of control, then a road is opened up for helpful ministry later on.

The minister has several advantages: (1) He knows at least some of the families whose members he has to bury. But even if the family was not known to him, first contacts had been made by a visit previous to the funeral in order to discuss the arrangements. The minister had a chance to observe the peculiar reaction by each member of the family to the grief situation.

(2) Very often there still exists for him the unique situation for a professional counselor of visiting members of his congregation at home. The reason this is so important is the fact that grief, normal as well as pathological mourning, is

considered neither a medical nor a social problem that would induce a person to consult a specialist. Grief is also not thought of as a problem of living, such as a marital crisis or alcoholism, for which one seeks help at a counseling office. The opportunity for a personal visit at the house therefore provides an incomparable chance to help.

(3) The minister is an outsider; he is at an emotional distance from the anxieties and tensions within the family. He stands outside the grief situation and can keep an objective position, particularly in view of the irrationality often arising in grief.

(4) The minister is thought of, whether he likes it or not, as the representative of moral values. It may complicate the conversation if the minister cannot make it clear from the beginning (perhaps in the funeral address) that he does not understand himself as a "reinforcer" of expectations by the social environment or societal norms. But he should not deny this general role expectation. This permits him, for example, to raise questions about the relationship between the mourner and the deceased as none of the other care giving agents is able to do. Since reproaches toward the deceased and one's own self are often exaggerated in the emotional excitement of mourning, he can see such reproaches in the right proportions. As far as he has sufficient insight into what the social environment expects from the bereaved (expectations that he, indeed, partially affirms but does not feel able to fulfill himself), the minister can relativize the moral expectations by others and the bereaved himself and release the mourner from the pressure of having to act according to the norms of his environment. If the bereaved cannot feel grief, even though the social environment expects this of him, the minister's assurance that not being able to mourn is not already a sign of irreverence or even unbelief can be of some relief.

(5) The minister, again whether he likes it or not, is a specialist for religious questions. It is true that there are no generally recognized opinions about the fate of the dead or immortality in our society. But a variety of viewpoints exist which are strong enough to bother the mourner constantly, although they are often confused and contradictory, so that

there is a great reluctance to discuss them publicly. The mourner may feel the dead's presence intensely. Magazine stories about spiritualistic séances come to his mind; questions about how to imagine resurrection become important. There is the fear of revenge of the dead; his return at night. One can expect from the minister that he has heard about all of these and can help in clarifying them. He is one of the very few people with whom such questions can be raised, as soon as he is willing to take seriously even the most confused opinion.

(6) The minister can be a "person of general confidence" and no doubt the more so if he does not try to interject specific evangelical goals. Since he does not need to pursue material interests, and he is not commissioned (apart from conducting the funeral) with the professional performance of a certain task for the bereaved, he is freer than other care giving agents for all the problems of the bereaved. He does not have to know all the solutions for these problems, but he can acquire the confidence and the reputation that he knows how to "go about things" and how to bring these problems closer to solution. A position free from the pursuit of material interests, enjoying general confidence and communication, can have very positive results on counseling the bereaved.

(7) Finally, the minister may be someone who, contrary to other professions and thanks to his own professional objectives, has time. To have time for someone is one of the things hard to come by in a society focused on rationality and growing needs. Such a statement may seem to be pure disdain, considering the pressure of time which everyone complains about. But this may be one of the most important goals a reorganization of the ministry should aim for.

5.42 Pastor and funeral

Frequently the participation of the minister in the funeral is seen negatively by him. The word is circulated among ministers that he is needed there only as "master of ceremonies." Expressed in this devaluating judgment is the opinion that the funeral is not an essential task of the church, or that certainly only those who had been active in church life are entitled to it. At the funeral, the minister sees himself confronted with strong expectations from without, which he cannot approve on the basis of his theological viewpoint. Besides, he has the impression, not altogether wrong, that he is needed at the funeral only because no one can celebrate it more appropriately than he. At the bottom of the devaluating judgment, that the minister is only "master of ceremonies" at the funeral, lies a series of misunderstandings which shall be discussed as follows: (1) The fact that the minister is called upon as a transition technician is not a disregard of his profession; it rather derives from a general tendency toward task divisions in our society. (2) A retrospective view of history shows that the church assumed the responsibility for the funeral, allotted to it by society in a very object-oriented way, and built upon it for its own purposes. (3) The minister does not realize the therapeutic function of the ritual and therefore tends to devaluate it; this has been mentioned above already and does not need to be repeated here.

(1) If ministers complain about being called on only as "death agents" and "death specialists," then it has to be pointed out that these also existed in former times when there were fewer specifications of functions in society. This is verified by an institution like the mourning women who formed an official guild in ancient Israel. In the time of the New Testament such a task was obviously assigned to the older widows (I Tim. 5:9). W. Neidhardt has pointed to the contemporary task division and emphasized that the minister's function as a master of ceremonies not be considered negatively: "The service of the master of ceremonies at this event is just as important as the one of the gravedigger or the innkeeper who prepares the meal for the funeral guests."[2] As leader of the ritual, the pastor is first of all a specialist who, just as the mortician or the registrar, is called upon for a special function. To adopt such a functional division of tasks is certainly not humiliating in the eyes of the public. Rather it could be asked whether it is not unbiblical for a minister to think he must dominate the scene, even if it were for the sake of the gospel.

(2) Furthermore, one has to consider whether or not

theology and church themselves have contributed to the fact that increasingly the responsibility for the funeral has devolved upon the minister. Since the Enlightenment, theology has increasingly emphasized death as the last area beyond control in a world dominated by man. This was aimed at a citizenship with an optimistic attitude toward the world by referring evangelistically to death, which makes every chance of turning back impossible, and by characterizing heaven as the true goal of all human endeavor. While the other sciences increasingly turned away from the death issue, theology necessarily became the last discipline that dealt specifically with the questions of death. The same can be said of the practice of the church. We must recall that it was not at all self-evident from the times of the Reformation on that the deceased should be buried with the assistance of the clergy, let alone with a worship service. Rietschel and Graff cautiously mention that the funeral had been "mostly" attended by clergy.[3] Even during the nineteenth century, the funeral with the leadership of a minister was not common.

5.43 The minister's emotional problems in counseling

As much as it may be regretted in theological literature that our society no longer dares to face the fact that every human being is moving toward death, nevertheless, the minister too is part of this society in which the visibility of death is strongly reduced. The death of the other affects him also, and even if he is determined to relinquish the mechanisms of denial, he still faces the anxiety of death as all creatures. Like the physician, he is constantly confronted with the fact of death, and even theological knowledge about the resurrection of Jesus and belief in the resurrection of the dead does not abolish the recognition that death is an inevitable reality. He experiences how people perish lonely and isolated in hospitals and identifies with this loneliness of dying, which at some time may be his own. He sees the despair of a person who has lost his most-beloved and cannot but help compare his behavior with reactions he himself presumably would have if one of his loved ones should die.

As Bowers and her coauthors write, "He seeks to represent

the divine while being human, and would seek to give insight into the mysteries that are ultimately as mysterious to him as to others. He would speak of immortality while deeply aware of his own mortality. He would seek to explain the meaning of death when he has only conjectures and not answers."[4]

Unresolved earlier grief experiences may play an additional role if counseling with the bereaved becomes difficult or impossible for a minister. Bachmann describes the case of a young minister who had a morbid preoccupation with his own death. He had made out a last will and testament with elaborate details about his final disposition. It was to be shrouded in mystery, with no burial in the usual sense. After he had been spirited away from the deathbed there was to be a rough pine box, no ceremony, and everything would be over with quickly. No one was to mourn him. There was to be a simple memorial service afterward. All was to be light and hope and the Christian's promise of immortality. This stemmed from some impression concerning the greedy preoccupation of funeral directors who milk their parishioners. However, conversations revealed that this pastor had had a bad experience, a residual carry-over from the time when his mother died, and he had been unable to resolve the grief in his own situation.[5] A whole series of "ecclesiastical defense syndromes"[6] have been created in order to dissociate oneself from the anxieties of nonexistence. Such defensive attitudes hinder the free and open exchange of thoughts and feelings between the minister and the bereaved and limit the minister's effectiveness for deeper pastoral counseling.

One such defensive syndrome is the guise of being set apart. The act of ordination marks the minister "as a custodian of the sacred mysteries"; he holds an office that grants him extraordinary sacramental powers, which are effective even against death. Bowers believes, based on several cases, that one motivation that underlies the choice of ministry as profession is the search for mastery over death, in a totally different way than other people. "They could perform funerals repeatedly but never be buried themselves. They could stand at the edge of the grave and walk away from it. The repeated symbolic act gave emotional security and the assurance of a power even over death."[7] The special emphasis he exerts on his office permits the minister to be way above the despair of the mourners, because death can do no harm to him.

Another form of defense is the mask of ritualized action. In his conversation with the family, the minister limits himself to explaining the ritual sequences of the funeral. He does not inquire about how they are coping with the loss but rather uses faulty reassurances, such as, "Your husband is better off now," or "He's gone to his eternal rest." Such phrases are attempts to avoid the hard reality of death and tend to cover up rather than release feelings. Bachmann calls this the "silver-cloud approach."[8] A short prayer, abruptly begun, excludes all further questions and enables the minister to save face and leave the house of mourning, perhaps even with a good professional conscience.

The use of special language too can function as such a defense or mask. "Unfamiliar words weighted with traditional use but little personal meaning may be a wall rather than a bridge."[9] This special language frequently is a way to create a distance between the minister and the bereaved.

Bowers et al. refer further to the mask of keeping busy. "Some pastors carefully cultivate the idea that they are terribly busy about a number of important tasks and that they break in upon these many duties to pay the dying patient a quick favor by their short visit." Besides, he gives himself the impression of having fulfilled correctly the various duties of his office. Considering his busy schedule this short visit and an abbreviated ceremony should satisfy the needs of the bereaved.

Not far from this is the behavioral routine. In this case one is convinced he understands the situation at a first glance. "One can mix the variations of the liturgy with the treasure of stored thoughts for sermons as needed. All the stops of orthodox objectivity and friendly humanisms can be pulled."[10] Such a routine can be overcome only by repeatedly taking a new account of the meaning of the ritual of the burial. Conversations with colleagues and occasionally attending other funerals can have a preventative effect.

A frequently used escape is sentimentality, which covers up the emptiness and insecurity. Even highly rational ministers in such situations develop remarkable skills in evoking sentimental feelings by stressing in detail the notion of the deeply caring heart of the father and the never-tiring hands of the mother. Maser says of such sermons, justifiably, that they "make full but do not satisfy." [11] Sentimentality betrays that the minister would very much like to break through his own reserve and that of the people present but does not reach the deeper level of feelings.

Finally, it is necessary that the minister keep in mind that particularly in counseling with the bereaved, libidinal and aggressive feelings are transferred to him, and he not seldom counteracts with another transference to the bereaved. The positive transference builds a necessary bridge between the bereaved and the minister; without it, counseling is not possible. The survivor is deprived of a love object and now transfers affection to a person who offers concern and understanding for him. However, the minister must understand that fundamentally this affection is not meant for him but rather for the deceased, and that he is being used as substitute for the lost love object. If he has no experience with the phenomenon of transference, there is the danger involved that he may exploit the interest shown in him and the church for congregational or missionary purposes. This frequently will result in a mutual disappointment, as soon as the bereaved has overcome the regressive stage and is free again to direct his feelings toward such persons and objects that provide a genuine substitute for him.

In the same manner, a negative transference can occur in the regressive stage. The minister draws the hate feelings upon himself since he represents the reality of the loss and through his action separates the bereaved from his loved one finally and inevitably. If the submission to God's will or God's invisibility makes it impossible for the bereaved to direct his reproaches against God, they then can turn against his representative on earth. By attempting to begin a conversation, a minister may run up against a wall of hostile silence; the bereaved may express some fussy criticism about the conducting of the funeral or about the neglect of the now deceased, even if the family had taken no steps to inform the minister of their desires and needs. The minister very likely is tempted to respond in an inappropriate way, partly because he feels he is being treated unjustly, partly because of self-reproaches that he did not provide care in time for the dying. His reaction shows he is hurt, but he does not realize the projection behind such emotional expressions. However, he will have to take such emotions seriously and search for their origin in a conversation. They could conceal a real faith crisis, but it could just as well be an aggressive transference that is actually meant for the bereaved's own father.

As we already pointed out, the minister himself is constantly in danger of transferring to the bereaved his negative feelings about his ministry at the funeral. The observations cited above are not false in themselves, but often their interpretation is one-sided. Far too often the minister projects his own anxiety and insecurity upon the bereaved and thereby hinders himself in understanding the various forms of coping with grief. An attitude of criticism makes it impossible to discuss how much certain forms of coping with loss are theologically and therapeutically (which presumably should not represent a contrast) legitimate, where they ought to be promoted by the minister or critically corrected.

In summarizing the activity of the care giving agents, one can say, according to the present state of matters, that though they fulfill an essential function for the bereaved, in particular during the stages of shock and control, none of the care giving professions sees its main focus in psychological counseling with the bereaved. To the extent that they pay emotional attention they are not specifically trained for it and, in spite of some normative appeals and protests, consider this a secondary responsibility which serves chiefly the prevention of emotional breakdowns. "Only rarely are questions of clients' mental health or mental health implications of professional procedure made the subject of explicit interest." [12] In other words, we face the situation that the physician in the hospital notifies the bereaved about the final failure of his efforts; the funeral director arranges the funeral and the formalities attached to it; the minister conducts the funeral; and the general practitioner prescribes tranquilizers. Each of these professionals relates himself sympathetically and with understanding, but none feels called, based on his primary professional duties, to take care of the special emotional problems and difficulties. However, at the same time, among all the professions mentioned, there is a concealed suspicion that the others could go beyond their limits and deal with issues that are part of one's own professional field. This is in a particular way true for the minister who disqualifies counseling by the funeral director and the physician, but hardly makes greater efforts himself to spend more time visiting the bereaved after the stage of control.

5.5 Counseling

In looking for the theological rationale with respect to extra pastoral duties, only baptism can be considered a genuine task of the church's. That the funeral has to be conducted by the minister cannot be substantiated either in the New Testament or in tradition. It is a task partly assigned to him by society, partly sought out by himself. Task division seems quite appropriate; the situation at the grave is, to say it pointedly, too serious to allow for dilettantism. This would presumably be the case with church members if they themselves should have to perform this task, considering the fact that they are no longer accustomed to any kind of ritualistic form. Therefore the funeral is not a task that could be pushed aside easily. Because the church has made this task so much its very own, the danger arises that the responsibility of taking care of the deceased shapes the public image of the church to a great extent. This affects even the image of God as it is clearly seen in obituaries with phrases such as "God called into his Kingdom . . . ," which means that the kingdom of God only begins after death and is a kingdom of the dead, not of those living today. Consequently there is the acute danger that a church specialized to such a degree in regard to death no longer has much to say for the living.

Precisely for that reason, so it seems to us, is the church's ministry to the bereaved so important, since it ought to point out at the time of bereavement, how the road of separation through death leads to renewed life. If the ministry of the church ends with the funeral, then the minister implies that he has done his part; if and how life goes on is not his concern. From the perspective of the bereaved there is therefore no difference between the physician in the hospital, the funeral director, and the minister as "death agents"; their task is finished when the dead is buried. That God is not merely a God of the dead but also of the living can under such circumstances not be seen in the conduct of the minister.

Therefore, the ministry of the church in the grief process cannot begin with the occurrence of death, as it is still largely practiced today, and cannot be concluded when the minister leaves the grave with measured strides, as it unfortunately happens often enough. (1) Counseling with the bereaved already begins when in the sermon and within groups in the congregation the issue of death and mourning is discussed. (2) Practical ministry to the bereaved must start when a church member has been ill for some time and a fatal end is anticipated. (3) It is continued in a conversation with the mourner before the funeral. (4) The funeral as well as (5) gatherings of family and friends are further occasions of coming into contact with the bereaved. (6) Finally, a number of conversations can follow, until the minister or some other professional in the church gains the impression that the mourner will cope with his loss without further complications.

The funeral itself, and therefore the conversations prior to it as well, so far have been left to the pastor. We do not at all, however, intend to give the impression that the minister alone has the right to counsel persons who undergo bereavement. Other professionals in the church often have a closer contact to the dying and his family. In restructuring the ministry of the church, long overdue, it should become self-evident that other professionals, for instance psychologists, can take on such responsibilities within the ministry of the church. Apart from his social prestige, the minister has not much advantage over other professionals or co-workers in the church with respect to counseling with the bereaved. He is just as untrained as they in dealing with bereavement. Only an improved education in counseling, which also includes the special situation of the bereaved, can lead to an adequate church ministry. For simplicity's sake we speak only of the minister from here on, but want to make it clear that the following statements apply in the same way to other professionals in the church, as far as they received special training for handling crisis situations.

In counseling with the bereaved it is necessary *to take into consideration the stage of grief the mourner is going through at the time of the conversations.* Counseling has a different objective, a different character, and a different methodological approach, depending upon whether it takes place during the controlled stage, in which the mourner is still under the impression of shock, where he can hardly come to his senses and is taken care of by his family and care giving agents, or in the regressive stage in which the bereaved is particularly preoccupied with his relationship to the deceased, or in the adaptive stage where it becomes possible realistically to estimate the loss and to approach modes of coping with a lasting effect. Something similar is true for the eight tasks mentioned above which the bereaved has to solve; in different stages the solution to certain tasks is preeminent, and the conversational issues are determined by that. In the same way the specific form of contact must be examined with respect to the task for which it can be particularly helpful.

5.51 Training in grief

Sufficient opportunities are given in worship services and various memorial days to talk about death, life after death, and grief. Nevertheless, sermons and discussions must be based very strongly on personal experiences and ideas of the church members. Instead of indoctrination, the first task of a minister is to find out how church members think about these problems and how they imagine coping with a loss. Naturally, a certain communication barrier is to be expected, but it is not an extremely high one. With respect to the mourner, it would be important to explain his situation and his behavioral modes, but also to clarify the meaning of the funeral ritual. It is an essential theological task to thrash out standards and criteria for an appropriate death. Therefore it frequently will be necessary to aim for an increase of the ambivalence tolerance in order to reduce rigid reactions about good and bad, valuable and nonvaluable. In such conversations, the social status of the bereaved can also be discussed, for instance, the question of his being avoided and his social-political demand for exemption from the work process.

5.52 Counseling in the situation of anticipatory grief

In making his pastoral calls at the home of patients, the minister will also meet families who anticipate the death of a loved one. It is important that he is aware of the fact that the grief process has already started here. His concern for the dying should be immediately united with the concern for the family, since in the course of the grief process the family members already detach themselves from the dying and thus reinforce his otherwise strong isolation. This leads to the question of dealing with the dying, which is not the issue of this study. However, it is important to make clear to members of the family who already have started the grief process that their changed behavior is sensed by the dying and increases his feeling of being already cut off and buried.

If the loss does not occur abruptly but can be anticipated, the detachment is effected by steps and mostly without deeper complications. Certainly, nursing can become a burden so that ambivalent feelings against the suffering person can arise, leading to relief at his death, which then often activates guilt feelings. The work of mourning needs greater attention if the fatal disease strikes a child or younger person; here the impact can be particularly great, because the slow deterioration of the condition causes a longer period of suffering which makes parents reach for the most obscure means to save their child. Here the reassurance of having everything done properly and nothing neglected is extremely important.

5.53 The visit prior to the funeral (stage of shock)

Calling on the survivors before the funeral is subject to conflicting judgments. For some ministers it is hardly more than an act of condolence which they want to get over with as quickly as possible; the value of pastoral care is considered extremely low. For others, this is the most essential and frequently only form of personal pastoral care, after which further individual concern for the bereaved is superfluous. Both are extreme positions which miss the real opportunities such a visit provides.

The visit prior to the funeral takes place in the controlled stage of the grief process and has its essential point of reference in the funeral itself. It serves as adequate preparation and should contribute to bringing to bear in the best possible way the spiritual and therapeutic function of the funeral. Beyond that, such a call can explore the necessity for a more attentive counseling and actually lay the groundwork for exactly that. The well-trained observer may notice that the grief process will be loaded with complications. However, the conversation itself should be in touch with reality and exclude deeper underlying factors. That means that intensive use of a nondirective approach is just as inappropriate as explaining psychological and exegetical problems. In regard to timing, the visit should be farther from the stage of shock and closer to the time of the funeral.

If the conversation takes place in the parsonage, it will be primarily person to person. Since, however, the organization of the funeral is generally left to a family member less affected and therefore functioning more effectively, the minister frequently does not talk to the most grief stricken. Besides, the interruptions in the parsonage are of a different nature than the ones in the house of mourning, which result from the coming and going of family members and friends. Compared to parsonage meeting, the visit in the house of mourning has the advantage of gaining some insight into the degree of mourning and the various reactions of individual family members. Since the gist of the visit is not individual pastoral counseling, the minister's visit in the house of mourning is preferable to the family's visiting the parsonage.

The minister has to be aware that the bereaved are depending on him. They desire that the funeral be conducted in an appropriate and satisfying way for all concerned. In most cases the family overestimates his knowledge of the deceased and wish to influence him not to include in his address embarrassing facts about the deceased and their relationships with him. In addition to this, quite frequently there is the need to present the deceased in a good light before God's representative. The family members must satisfy the minister with respect to their insufficient participation in church life. Therefore they tend to be—consciously or unconsciously—all too eager to agree with his ideas and interpretations, even though they think quite differently in individual matters. The minister has to keep in mind that every kind of indoctrination becomes a routine exercise for the family, with which they buy the service of the minister. For that reason he should spend the greater part of his visit in listening. Naturally, the situation will be quite different if he knows the family and is considered practically a friend.

Talking less enables the minister to be more attentive to his environment: how intense the grief reactions of individual members are and how they differ from one another; who is in charge of the general organization; how the presence of the deceased is observable; what is being said about him and what attention is paid to him when the viewing is at the home; whether there are neighbors who take care of the household; these observations can speak louder than statements by the family. Modes of speaking and behaving by the bereaved give further hints to how death was accepted.

It should be recognized that the essential help for or hindrance of the bereaved comes from his immediate environment, that is, his family and other relatives. Therefore, it is necessary for relevant counseling also to have certain information about relatives and friends who are not immediately affected by the death to the same extent. The form of family unity is of importance in the concern for the bereaved. Great tensions within the family are not without influence on the grief process. Family and friends largely set the standards for how the bereaved must behave himself; they have their specific ways of supporting him.

Even within the inner family circle coping with grief is quite different. For example, brothers and sisters will not react in the same way toward their widowed mother, because they have had various relationships with her and are not identically coping with loss. A favorite daughter very likely will mourn her father more than would a son, whose adolescent rebellion has led to repudiation of the father.

Since the temporal process of mourning within a family varies, tensions and conflicts can arise very easily when some family members are already in the adaptive stage of the grief process, while others are still in the regressive stage. The same is true for different coping mechanisms. If one family member indulges in a series of activities in order to cope with his pain, this can lead to great disapproval by other family members, who cope with their grief through other mechanisms.

A good family unity does not automatically ensure adequate help for the most grief stricken. A family may cooperate very well with respect to financial and vocational matters, yet may be completely helpless when emotional problems arise. The conviction of family members that they understand each other extremely well can have a very inhibiting effect on the needs for expressing negative feelings about the dead. In particular, heightened irritability and frequently general distrust along with the rejection of any help and similar unusual behavioral modes of the most grief stricken are often annoying to the rest of the family and are often misunderstood. In this situation, it is indispensible to include the relatives in the circle of persons being counseled.

Furthermore, with respect to family and social environment, "closeness" and "distance" to the deceased are relative terms. It is not always the immediate family that is most affected by the loss. The impact of a grandmother's death on a child whom she had constantly spoiled can be greater than on his parents, who have anticipated her death for a long time. Occasionally it is a friend who loses more with the deceased than the family itself. This is true, for example, when close friendships have developed among older people who scarcely keep social contacts with others. There are older people who assumed a certain father or mother role for the younger, even though these merely lived in the same house; here too it may happen that the loss is felt much more deeply by the person who lost this protection than by family members.

Individuals who are most neglected at a time of death are children. Death is not explained to them and they are put off with clichés. They are sent away to relatives and therefore are unable to gain immediate experiences. They observe that intimate persons behave very irritatingly and are hardly approachable; that their questions are answered defensively and evoke painful emotions. But nobody seems willing to take the time and make the effort to explain the events to the children and so prevent them from developing fantastic ideas. Contrary to the general opinion, children should attend the funeral service to convince themselves of the reality of death, but, of course, not against their own will.

These few references must be sufficient at this point to substantiate that counseling with the bereaved is not only a matter between the most grief stricken and the minister, but must also include the family. It is important to know what help the mourner can expect from the family and how in general a family copes with loss.

The most obvious starting point for a conversation is the story of the process of dying and death. To talk about it already implies therapeutic significance. It is not unimportant for forming a judgment to know how long the suffering process has dragged on and how unexpectedly death occurred. Physical disfigurement, caused by wasting away through disease or accident, generally creates a severe shock. Not infrequently the dying seem to undergo a complete change of personality; they no longer recognize their family, or, even more aggravating, they become strangers full of hostility toward them. Here the minister may have to make certain clarifications, based on his greater experience. This also applies in case the family makes irrational or justified reproaches against itself, of having failed essentially or of having been absent at the time of the death. The reinforcement of the reality should be in a more affirmative vein than in a lecturing tone.

When the conversation moves on to biographical data the minister believes he needs for his sermon, he often will discover that it is rather difficult for the family to compose such a biography based on exact data. It seems more important to inquire about crucial family events, good and bad ones, the dating, marriage, wars and the time of depression, years when the children grew up, particularly eventful vacation times, the golden wedding anniversary, the celebration at the firm after many years of work. All of this is more important for remembering the deceased than precise dates. Human life is divided by crises and successes, not by decades. Such reports can say many things about how love and hate is distributed within the family, and also how a family has coped with its crises. The minister should take notice of high family tensions, if within a short period a series of crises has occurred of which the recent death is only the last one. Posing a question about possible sleeping difficulties might help to bring up the subject of physical symptoms of grief. Under all circumstances the way of informing children and their attendance at the funeral must be discussed.

Another important point of discussion is the conduct of the funeral service itself. The wish for a certain biblical text, such as memory verses from the confirmation day or wedding, the wish for certain hymns or other parts of the liturgy, as well as the formulation of the obituary, can be starting points for a religious conversation in a deeper sense. Ministers, however, should avoid defense reactions if the family equates the relief from long suffering with salvation through Christ, the active love for the family as a sacrifice and guarantee of eternal life, and the will of God with the actual cause of death. Our speech patterns are not rich when it comes to describing such an event; even the minister's is not richer, unless he alludes to biblical expressions. Nevertheless, it is quite possible during such a pastoral call to enter more deeply into the meaning that the bereaved attach to this death, whether they experience it as timely or untimely, as just or unjust, as punishment or relief. The basic rule to be observed here as well is to help the family to express themselves; it is not the time when the minister should be concerned with theological accuracy.

Finally, the last issue is the immediate future. The widowed frequently live in with one of the children for some time; older widowers, if they remain in their own house or apartment, will need somebody to take care of them. Children may be left without parents. A difficult financial situation might arise until social security "comes through." In any case, the conversation should be confined to the immediate future.

Even if the four issues mentioned here, circumstances of death, biography, funeral, and immediate future, do not enter into the deep dynamics of grief, they are nevertheless depressing for the mourner, as certainly as the articulation of them is felt helpful in nearly all cases. The conversation may be interrupted with outbursts of tears and it may be extremely difficult for the mourner to utter a word. A minister frequently feels quite uncomfortable in such a situation, blames it on his own clumsiness, and may be anxious to withdraw discreetly and without giving offense. But tears release the numbness of shock caused by the death and talking, even if troublesome, is better than growing numb with apathy. Whether a minister wants to lay the ground for future pastoral calls or restricts himself to this one conversation, he should in any case make therapeutic recommendations. Some of the most essential aspects are the assurance that weeping and the absence of grief are just as little ground for moral condemnation as the relief felt at the death. He should make it clear that even hostile and reproachful feelings toward the deceased are nothing unusual. Finally, he should encourage the bereaved to free himself if necessary from the expectations of his environment, if he thinks he is not able to fulfill them.

For further conversations certain diagnostic observations may also be essential, even though they cannot be fully explored in this first conversation with its focus on the funeral. For one thing, it may be possible to decide whether further counseling would be at all meaningful. The bereaved may leave the community soon after the funeral. They also may clearly refuse counseling, or at least show their unwillingness for it, interpreting it as an invasion of their privacy. On the other hand, the mourner can count on the quality of help that will be received from relatives and friends. A mother perhaps can comfort her daughter about the loss of a child much better than the minister. Value judgments and expectations of a rural community might prove to be more effective than his own efforts. From this first pastoral call it may be further inferred which coping mechanisms the bereaved will choose. Finally, part of the diagnostic estimate is the evaluation of ego strength in its individual factors, such as adaptability to changed situations, adequacy of reality testing, control of impulses, ability to communicate with other persons, degree of independence, kinetic activity, and perception of psychic conflicts. Nevertheless, here the minister will have to limit himself to individual observations.

This first conversation can not only fulfill diagnostic functions but actually can be a form of treatment. G. Jacobson and his associates observe that, frequently, patients who merely received a diagnostic treatment already were under the impression that they had been helped sufficiently in their problems. The authors therefore recommend considering each session as if this would be the last opportunity for therapy.[1] Indeed, the mere inquiry about the circumstances of death, the history of the lifetime shared, and the immediate future can have cathartic effects; the interest shown by the minister is received as gratification. Nevertheless, we have to be critically aware that in the stage of shock the mourner has not yet become sufficiently conscious of his problems and he has not yet fully entered into the painful process of grief work. Which ways of coping, right or wrong, he will choose is still open for him and therefore also must remain so to some extent for the observer. A matter-of-fact composure toward the event of death may have given way to a total breakdown a week later, full of hostile reproaches and thoughts of suicide. Therefore diagnostic observations should by all means be carefully interpreted.

One major concern of the minister's must be to gain the confidence of the mourner and his openness and willingness for further conversations. Certain behavioral modes and linguistic expressions can block a discourse from the beginning. Very few pastors are aware of how they tend to dominate in their behavior and way of speaking, pass on moral judgments, expect particular reactions, and, without sufficient fundamental reasons for it, interpret those reactions immediately. Confidence, however, can be gained only by identifying with the situation of the mourner and by offering help without request.

For a sympathetic observer, presumably the prayer at the end of the visit would give the best insight into the minister's attitude. Very often it is not easy for him to decide whether a prayer is at all appropriate. A direct question will nearly always find a positive response in view of the authority of the minister associated with his office. It is of importance that a mutual openness has been achieved and is preserved. The prayer should not suggest that the minister is trying to protect himself from embarrassing impressions, that he now draws his efforts to their conclusion, or tries to put down the mourner's necessity for talking. In certain cases, if talking is difficult for the bereaved, prayer can become an important means of communication. It should not summarize the theological theories the minister could not quite get across during the conversation, but should convey more the nature of the lamentation with which the mourner can identify. Difficulties which the mourner will encounter should be mentioned; in this way the prayer gives expression to the mourner's anxieties and reproaches. The prayer should not proclaim God as the unmoved Lord, ruler over life and death, but rather as One who is immersed in the boundless suffering of his creatures.

5.54 The group for whom the funeral is intended (controlled stage)

We have described above what functions the funeral ritual can have and tried to illustrate this with respect to certain issues and various ritual forms. It is obvious to assume and can easily be observed that not all functions mentioned will have the same weight in the practical implementation. We largely had to resign ourselves to examining the funeral liturgies used today and new proposals with respect to which functions they particularly emphasize. Nevertheless, the question has to be raised, To whom is the funeral ritual addressed above all: (1) to the dead; (2) to the participants of the funeral who are less affected by the death; or (3) to the mourner? The minister, of course, can be counted on to establish different points of emphasis than the ones resulting from the liturgy.

(1) The Roman Catholic liturgy for the dead reveals in its very title, pro defunctis, for whom it is meant primarily. The comfort for the mourner is expressed only in an indirect way. By reaffirming in the ritual that the dead person is not lost but rests in God's hands, by emphasizing the expectation of resurrection and reunification, the mourner at the same time is told that he need not to be concerned about the deceased. It is further recommended to him to accept this particular death as fate inflicted upon mankind and as sign of God's will. From honoring the dead the bereaved may also derive certain comfort. He himself and his problems may perhaps become an issue in the sermon and the concerns of relatives, but are not thematically expressed in the liturgy. It seems that theologies oriented toward contemporary liturgical orders also advocate theoretically that the funeral focus on the dead. According to B. Bürki, the funeral is meant "first of all for the deceased. The event for us is not only an opportunity or even a pretext; we perform an eventful action in the strict sense of the word. Our love is directed toward the body and person of the deceased brother, our hope is hope for him."[2] Above all, under the aspect of "honoring," theologians like Dehn advocated the significant role the deceased plays for the funeral. For Dehn it is mere theory to believe that one should address oneself primarily to the bereaved. The deceased is present and makes his demands: "The church renders to the dead what is the dead's. . . . Each funeral ceremony is honoring the deceased and that is also true for the church funeral."[3]

(2) On the other hand, where proclaiming the gospel is highly emphasized, the church ritual focuses primarily on the funeral participants. For Harbsmeier, a funeral in the Christian sense is "nothing else . . . but proclamation of the gospel at the occasion of the death of a member of the congrega-

tion. . . . The deceased is dead. He has gone, God knows where and how."[4] It is "necessary to minimize the difference between the dead and us as much as possible in the funeral and. to make our own image appear in the image of the deceased: This is us!"[5] He presupposes that the death has its deep impact on the participants no matter how close or how distant they had been to the deceased.

In the considerations for the funeral, it tends to be assumed that the people gathered at the funeral are very open to the message of the sermon. Whether this applies to the immediate family must be left undecided; they may be too much occupied with their loss to be able to pay special attention to individual statements in the sermon. Neither can such an impact be assumed among colleagues and club members present, neighbors and friends, since they are often present merely for "pious" reasons. Under special circumstances, for instance, if it is an extremely well-liked colleague, if he died "much too early," if the death was violent or perhaps colleagues shared the responsibility for it, such as in an accident at work, then the impact may go beyond such emotions or pious demands and evoke anxiety about one's own death. This refers in particular to older people, since every death of someone from the same age group raises the inevitable question as to how long one can escape death oneself and for whom, again, a portion of the world is lost. It is this experience that induced S. de Beauvoir to say at the funeral of her mother that she attended a dress rehearsal.[6]

Whether the impact brought on by one's own death anxiety provides the occasion for proclaiming the gospel was answered positively by Asmussen: "At the funeral the minister is primarily the servant of the church, which sends him among the people with the mission of teaching and calling into discipleship."[7] Corresponding to this he has to proclaim death as the wages of sin. Through this testimony death becomes the great call. The teaching focuses in a special way on life after death, whereby it has to be testified that with death, the decision regarding the dual opportunity existing after death has been made. The doctrine of the resurrection is the central theme. H. Flemming stated it even more decisively: "Anyone who at this point does not take the evangelistic approach sins grossly against his Christian ministry . . . the funeral is the outstanding missionary opportunity for the church."[8]

If one tries to counteract the repression of death and point to the seriousness of the decision every death represents, then at the same time the question has to be raised whether there are sufficient therapeutic means available to absorb such an intensification of the existential death anxiety effectively. Just as it is impossible to start depth therapy if there is not enough time available to work through the inevitably arising basic anxieties, neither can death anxiety be provoked if there is no follow-up counseling. The funeral symbolizes a status transition and is an attempt to appease the anxieties awakened by it; it is not the occasion for a conversion. The shock caused by death may become the reason for a fundamentally new orientation, but to exploit it as such systematically is irresponsible pastoral care.

W. Krusche wants to avoid having the funeral assume a missionary-evangelistic aspect. He is not concerned with reminding and warning everyone that they could be just as quickly surprised by death and therefore a return to God is rather urgent. However, he proclaims to all participants the death and resurrection of Christ. In doing so he assumes a basic psychic situation for each of the participants in the funeral: "They are, in each case and under all circumstances, people who are like myself helpless with respect to dying, who are like myself in danger of not recognizing the lifetime given to them as a time of saving grace offered to them. They are, like myself, subject to the promise that whoever believes in Christ should not perish but have eternal life."[9] He wants to bring the situation into focus, not "in order to function as psychotherapist and to 'take away' the sadness from his audience, but rather to be able to say the *message* pointedly."[10] Similar is Harbsmeier's opinion that no preacher knows the labyrinth of a grieving human heart; this is known by God alone. What moves all human souls, however, is the question of death, and the task is to point out how precisely in this perplexity the question of God is implied.[11]

The possibility that the funeral with its sermon should be meant primarily for the most grief stricken is rejected by both authors. Pastoral counseling is important, but the essential opportunity for it is during the conversation prior to the funeral.

(3) The position that the grief sufferer is primarily the center of concern in the funeral has been increasingly adopted in recent years. As one example the thoughts of H.-J. Geischer may be mentioned: "The dead is and remains dead. The question as to what comes afterward and where is inapplicable. At the most the dead 'exists' in memory. What had been the meaning of his life is an obligation for the living." Therefore, the will of God must be formulated in a concrete way for the living. Thanks may be given for the things past, and the statement may be made that God had been strong in all weakness.[12] The funeral should focus completely on the grief stricken by trying to interpret, in part with the help of the past life of the dead, the meaning of life for the survivor. At this point this meaning would have to be defined more specifically as "being in Christ."

We wish to follow this opinion of H.-J. Geischer's to a great extent. The grief sufferer should be the center of attention in the funeral ritual. He is the one who suffers most; he has to be helped to recognize and accept that his relationship to his loved one and to his environment has changed. The funeral must give him support to adjust to the relations between himself and the dead and between himself and the social environment. The undeniable fact that the mourner is very much occupied with himself cannot be used as a pretext for ignoring him in order to evangelize or to proclaim to the other participants the death and resurrection of Christ and its impact on our existence; a ritual has no room for exposition and discussion. The few words and actions that find their way to the grief sufferer have more weight than any form of missionary instruction. In the tense condition of grief, a few distinctive signs are enough, such as the care with which the service is conducted, the tone of the minister's voice, and the mentioning of the full name of the dead, which once more represents fully and completely this unique person. What the message of the gospel is, is expressed in this situation, in how it enables the mourner to cope with this overpowering loss. In order to avoid misunderstandings, this applies to this point in time, not to the coming stages of grief work.

5.55 Postfuneral calls (regressive stage)

If the purpose of the funeral is to make clear that the Christian God is not only a God of the dead but also a God of the living, a God of those who seek to find life, then the ministry of the church cannot end at the grave. Basically at least one postfuneral call should be made. That it frequently never takes place is in our opinion not so much a question of time as a result of the minister's uncertainty about the purpose of such a visit and about his own conduct. Fundamentally, however, it is precisely the time of transition into the regressive stage that is connected with special difficulties for the bereaved. In particular, after the relatives have left the mourner, he faces a great loneliness. Therefore a visit by the minister is especially needed; he is the only one of the care giving agents whose responsibility is not over with the end of the controlled stage, and also the only one who can professionally, on his own initiative, be concerned about the bereaved. Previous calls can help to determine the right time for this visit, and an appointment may be made at that time. Under no circumstances may the minister add to the disappointments of the bereaved by not keeping his promise to call on him, even if this had been a very noncommittal suggestion.

The whole intention of the research presented here aims at the fact that one pastoral call for counseling in a crisis situation is not enough. This applies not only to the time of bereavement but also to other crisis situations characterized by stages similar to those in the grief process. Here, too, the aim in counseling is dependent upon the person concerned, that is, what stage of the coping process he has reached. Still it would signify some progress if at least one postfuneral call became a part of the minister's duties and if he had enough information at his disposal to make such a conversation meaningful.

Should it be impossible for the minister because of lack of time to visit all the members of his congregation after a funeral, he could select the most urgent cases and deal more intensively with those that represent a particular hardship. The criteria for such hardship have been mentioned above (3.8). This is not the place to deal specifically with the techniques of counseling which also are applicable to all cases of crisis ministry. A detailed discussion of it can be found in other works.[13] C. C. Bachmann names a series of principles that must be observed especially in ministering to the grief sufferer.[14] Some of his points seem to be of particular importance.

The essential concern of this call, but also the following calls, is to encourage the grief sufferer to express his hurt and loss. Responsive listening to what the bereaved says allows him to break through his isolation and creates communication in which he is treated as a human being. The minister should not be disturbed by long silences and faltering speech; nor should these cause him to talk too much and to ask too many questions. He must show that those pauses do not make him uncomfortable but are, rather, "natural" according to the situation. Counseling should enable the counselee to release feelings and allow him to say what he wants, knowing that he will be accepted, regardless of whether his feelings are in agreement with the basic premises of society. The minister has to avoid being a "moral policeman" and "enforcement officer" for social norms. Religious questions about death and eternal life have to be considered seriously, since frequently the mourner is bothered by them constantly. The minister as counselor may not act as a theological specialist for whom the confused religious ideas of the counselee are far beneath his own level. Most often at the beginning of the counseling it is not known to which areas conversations will lead. Moral questions can conceal religious problems, or vice versa, guilt feelings can be hidden behind religious discussions. It is important to respect the private world of the counselee. Each person has a right to be himself and to show only that part of his inner self that he wants anyone to know about. He also should not be put on the defensive.

Because of heightened emotionality, the relations of the bereaved to the deceased as well as to his family are tense and difficult. Therefore the counselor is constantly asked, either silently or directly, to take sides in favor of the grief sufferer. The minister should not take sides, at least not before all the facts are in and it has been clarified whether or not guilt feelings or anxieties of an entirely different nature are concealed behind accusations and complaints. The counselor can carefully direct the counselee's attention back to his share in these difficulties and help him to gain a certain distance from them. This is frequently a question of time; with the end of the regressive stage, vulnerability and distrust which had caused difficulties in interactions with the dead and with his family often disappear.

The minister should aim for a postponement of decisions regarding distribution of the inheritance and the future of the bereaved, which can either not be or only under extreme difficulties be canceled in the adaptive stage, in order to prevent a hasty substitution. Another aim should be keeping the social and geographical environment rather constant; if a world has collapsed for the bereaved, he then should not face the additional burden of adjusting to a totally new environment and new people. This is particularly true for children, who frequently are sent to relatives, and also for the elderly for whom readaptation is especially hard. As much as it is the right thing to do, for example, to take a widow to the house of her son or daughter, nevertheless, during the regressive stage she should be able, if possible, to live in the rooms familiar to her and where she can unobstructedly work through her memories. Only in the adaptive stage might moving to a home or living with her children be considered (compare 8.4).

Counseling with the bereaved requires patience precisely because the situation is so undefined and difficult for the bereaved to clarify. The counselor should not attempt to rush things. The bereaved needs time to get hold of his situation. Contrary to other crisis situations, in counseling with the bereaved, it is usually not the disclosure of repressed and supressed experiences that are at stake but rather the process of becoming aware of situations and relationships that have changed. Resisting awareness is in general considerably less than, for example, in the separation experience of someone divorced. The minister can count much more on the self-realization of the bereaved and therefore should be particularly reluctant to make any attempt at interpretation.

Unavoidably, especially in later conversations, the minister is asked for advice in practical matters as well, such as relocation, financial security, etc. In any case it would be preferable that the minister possess certain information about such occurring problems or at least know other professionals to whom he could refer the bereaved. If necessary, the minister himself must take steps to provide practical help.

When to terminate a counseling session with an individual is hard to decide. When we deal with strong resistance in the psychoanalytical sense, to terminate has the function of exercising a certain pressure on the client not to waste his time. In other cases of crisis counseling too, a referral made by the minister will be helpful and often necessary. This can be done in the beginning by the minister's saying that he has only limited time, maybe one hour to spend with him. Generally this also holds true for counseling with the bereaved. However, at the same time it should be kept in mind that in view of the mourner's withdrawal the conversation starts very slowly. What generally appears in the grief process is repeated in the counseling session during the regressive stage: The mourner tells his memories over and over again and the ways in which these memories are told change only slowly. It is often hard for the conversation partner to decide whether this is only (in the Freudian sense) a matter of repetition, or whether progress in working through memories is actually gained.[15] In other counseling sessions the beginning of repetition of issues already discussed is a criterion for breaking off; this criterion does not apply here. Therefore, in grief counseling a certain flexibility is needed. The minister should be responsible for terminating a session but also should be open enough not to stop a conversation, finally on its way, after the appointed time has run out.

In conclusion, we have to state criteria for certain circumstances in which a minister not trained as a therapist should refer his counselee to a professional therapist. These are, on the one hand, formal criteria that help the minister realize that he has reached his limits; on the other hand, they constitute the already described objective criteria that signify a pathological coping with grief (compare 3.8).

The formal reasons[16] for a minister to initiate a referral are: (1) The bereaved is under heavy emotional distress, and the minister lacks the time for a number of counseling sessions with the bereaved. (2) The minister had set up such sessions, but no recognizable progress could be seen after four or five conversations. (3) The counselee's emotional problems cause so much personal distress and uneasiness for the minister that the necessary distance for pastoral care no longer is present.

PART III

The mechanisms of coping

6. The narcissistic coping mechanisms

6.1 Survey

6.11 The defense mechanisms in grief
The mechanisms of coping, as they are called in this study, are generally to be found in psychoanalytical literature under the term *defense mechanisms*. This latter term was appropriate insofar as classical psychoanalytical research concentrated primarily on the inner-psychic conflict situation. It focused especially on the question of the kind of defense mechanisms employed by the ego in order to defend itself against the pressure from the id and the demands of the superego. Only in his later years, S. Freud saw in the defense mechanisms forms of mediation between the inner-psychic apparatus and the external world. Thus he writes in *Analysis terminable and interminable* (1937):

From the very outset the ego has to try to fulfill its task of acting as an intermediary between the id and the external world in the service of the pleasure principle, to protect the id from the dangers of the external world. If, while thus endeavouring, the ego learns to adopt a defensive attitude towards its own id and to treat the instinctual demands of the latter like external dangers, this is at any rate partly because it understands that later action of instinct would lead to conflicts with the external world. Under the influence of upbringing, the child's ego accustoms itself to shift the scene of the battle from outside to inside and to master the inner danger before it becomes external. Probably it is generally right in so doing. In this battle on two fronts—later there is a third front as well—the ego makes use of various methods of fulfilling its task, i.e., to put it in general terms, of avoiding danger, anxiety, and unpleasure. We call these devices "defensive mechanisms."[1]

Above all, the study of children and stress research focused increasingly on the question of how the ego reacts to conflicts with the external world and copes with them. For example, Lazarus, as a stress researcher, speaks of "coping-reaction patterns."[2] In the following pages, *defense mechanisms, defensive mechanisms, and coping mechanisms are used synonymously in order to characterize the entire process of grief work.* There is no consensus in literature with respect to the number, identification, and classification of defense mechanisms. A comprehensive representation of the mechanisms used in coping with grief has not yet been published. G. Krupp offers the most detailed specification: he names searching for the lost object, annoyance, denial, substitution, and identification.[3] Based on observations in the available material, eleven defensive mechanisms are mentioned here: (1) breakdown of reality testing; (2) denial and repression; (3) searching; (4) mania; (5) protest; (6) search for the guilty; (7) identification with the aggressor; (8) helplessness; (9) recollection; (10) incorporation; (11) substitution.

Following a suggestion by E. Bibring,[4] the defensive mechanisms are to be distinguished according to the instinctual needs they oppose. Thus breakdown of reality testing, denial and repression, searching, and mania belong to the *narcissistic* coping mechanisms; protest, search for the culprit, and identification with the aggressor are *aggressive* coping mechanisms; and helplessness, recollection, incorporation, and substitution belong to the *object-libidinal* coping mechanisms.

All the coping mechanisms mentioned here have various functions, depending upon whether they serve to support the position to which the psychic organization has regressed or whether they help to create a basis for establishing new relationships and achieving restoration of the former functionality. Those of the first group, to speak with Miller and

Swanson, are simpler, result in severe distortion of reality, are less goal-oriented, and create social difficulties. In the second group, the coping mechanisms are rather complex, distort less of the perceptual field, are applicable only to specific kinds of problems, and gain social approval more easily.[5] Each of the defense mechanisms that plays an important role in coping with grief can have either *more regressive or more adpative characteristics*, depending on the function it fulfills.

What is meant by that shall be explained with two of the coping mechanisms, recollection and substitution. Recollection as a regressive mechanism concentrates entirely on remembering the deceased. The survivor is completely occupied with him. His efforts are focused on the reassurance that the loved one is not dead, only absent and can be brought back at any time by compulsive repetition of every memory connected with the dead. At the same time, the memory is very distorted; mostly the positive features are recalled; the deceased is glorified. Recollection as adaptive mechanism results in an image of the deceased adequate to reality, with all its merits and disadvantages. Essential and unimportant memories are separated, and the bereaved no longer links his memories to the deceased only and is freed from compulsive repetition.

If the bereaved uses the mechanism of substitution in a regressive way, then he tries with great intensity to find a substitute for the lost love object. He can quickly remarry merely because the new partner has a faint resemblance to the former spouse, or he can engage himself in intense nursing of other people, after he no longer is able to nurse the love object. The adaptive mechanism of substitution is no longer determined by the compulsion to replace this lost person but sets one free to see the potential new marital partner in realistic perspectives and in his peculiarity and uniqueness. The bereaved may perhaps discover that it is quite different to nurse other people, compared with taking care of a particular beloved person. He then will search for other more appropriate and suitable activities as substitution.

At the beginning, the narcissistic coping mechanisms prevail in the grief process, since they are primarily focused on the support of one's own ego, even though this can only be achieved through almost total isolation from the social environment. The aggressive coping mechanisms presuppose a certain interaction between the ego, the lost love object, and the social group. In the last stage of the grief process, however, the object-libidinal defense mechanisms dominate the picture; they are more strongly aimed at the use of the social environment and the lost love object in order to start the restoration of the psychic organization.

Regressive coping mechanisms primarily have the function of relief. They permit postponement of the full emotional recognition of the object-loss that took place. It is possible to escape for some time from the nagging problem of feeling guilty about the death by blaming the physician who treated the patient. Glorification of the dead allows for a postponement of working through the hostile feelings the bereaved harbored toward the deceased until a time when the ego is capable of realistic judgment and can accept the negative as well as the positive features of the deceased as part of his humanness. The denial of death allows the full recognition of what is lost to come about only gradually.

Caruso's statement about the inner psychic defense mechanisms also applies to the defense character of regressions occurring with the loss of the love object: "By trying to suppress or to avoid conflicts, the defense mechanisms are working *as much against* the instinctual demand *as for* it, *as much against* the demand of the external world *as also for* it. They are fundamentally ambivalent; they serve the eros *and* the thantos; the individual and the social demand."[6]

All of this has yet to be discussed in detail; at this point only one aspect is important, namely, that the regressive mechanisms as we have distinguished them here, can delay the regression of the psychic organization by their irrationality and deficient recognition of reality. However, the price for this is the isolation of the bereaved from his social environment. The bereaved cannot count on his regressive behavior finding social approval over a longer period. Someone who denies recognized realities, who does not accept a clear distinction between an internal and external world, who defers psychic energies all too much, and, besides, concentrates on an "egocentric" way only in his own suffering, must expect that in the long run he will be characterized as a pathological case and treated accordingly. Even in the immediate grief period, such modes of behaving and experiencing defined by society as irrational are often not recognized as legitimate. This makes communication with the bereaved extremely difficult. In anticipation of general disapproval he fears the risk of talking about experiences, which frequently are even for himself of a disturbing nature.

It is not surprising that there is much more material available on the regressive stage than on the adaptive. The behavior of the bereaved during the regressive stage differs much more from ordinary, "normal" conduct and is therefore so much more conspicuous. Besides, the observations frequently are based on patients who did not succeed in going beyond the regressive stage, and for whom, therefore, regressive behavior became persistent. The cautious steps taken by the bereaved in trying out how well he can bear the full reality of the loss, the first new contacts made in order to substitute for the loss, the gradual restoration of his own inner-psychic organization, and the incorporation of the deceased are essentially more unobtrusive and their success is less endangered.

Therefore, on the basis of the material available we will deal in the following three chapters primarily with the description of regressive behavioral modes, largely neglecting the adaptive devices. This is of importance for two reasons. First, in this way it can be explained in detail which positive functions regressive reactions can have; an understanding of them in society cannot be assumed. On the other hand, it can be pointed out with greater emphasis, and this is a crucial therapeutic aspect, how pathological grief develops from regressive grief reaction.

6.12 *Social promotion and inhibition of grief work*

The social surroundings of the bereaved (family, friends, colleagues) play an important role in grief work, no less than the norms and behavior patterns of the entire society. They can either facilitate or hamper the regressive and adaptive forms of the coping mechanisms employed by the individual. The social environment can confront the bereaved with expectations which he feels he cannot fulfill in the regressive stage. To recommend remarrying to a widowed person is of help in the adaptive stage; yet in the regressive stage, in which the bereaved has not yet sufficiently detached himself from his former spouse, this must seem to him an exacting demand and a betrayal of the deceased. Or, the family can constantly take care of the bereaved and in this way prevent him from reassuming responsibility for his actions. With the end of the controlled stage, the grief process is structured very little. The existing general rules are felt as a burden by the bereaved if they are enforced by the social surroundings. By assuming the viewpoint that everyone knows best what is good for himself, however, the social environment can deny any support, which again is not necessarily helpful for the bereaved.

In general, it is safe to say, that society as a whole, but especially the occupational sector, has little regard for the psychic condition of the bereaved. That the bereaved is incapable of concentrating on work and cannot pay full attention in dangerous situations at work or in traffic is hardly taken into consideration. The close connection between accident and grief has not been systematically researched so far; yet such a careful study as that by R. Silverman[7] illustrates, with a series of case studies, how individuals are pushed into neurotic behavior disorders through the coincidence of stressful working conditions and the additional preoccupation with grief.

From here on, each of the coping mechanisms to be dealt with will be examined in a special paragraph with respect to how much norms, ideas, and practice of the social environment and the entire society support or hinder it.

6.13 The threefold direction of eschatological statements

The development of defense mechanisms is closely linked to the shaping of religious ideas. While so far only the joint genesis has been stressed, in the following three chapters the attempt shall be made, with respect to each of the coping mechanisms dealt with, to work out how theology and church practice refer to the mechanisms employed by the individual and either supported or hindered by society. What difficulties created by a theology that has concerned itself little with specific psychic and social defense reactions becomes particularly conspicuous at this point. There is no research available about how much the practice of the church recognizes these defense mechanisms in the funeral sermon, liturgy, and counseling and makes them subject to theological criteria.

It is largely undecided which eschatological testimonies are to be held theologically legitimate, in particular if the individual's death, destiny, and the relation between the dead and the living are at stake. We consider here only such eschatological statements that meet a threefold statement of direction: (1) They must contain one aspect indicating the coming of the kingdom of God; (2) they must critically oppose certain repressive social conditions and religious ideas that justify, excuse, or disguise them; (3) they must motivate change in the ideologies and behavior patterns of society recognized as untenable, as well as the religious beliefs and practice of the church supporting them.

(1) Often Christian eschatology has been accused, and frequently with justice, of limiting itself to feeding the suffering with hopes for a better world to come and thus stabilizing the earthly power structures. The "kingdom of God" can be so characterized and painted in bright colors that the believer is induced to disloyalty to this world. Or he can, in an exaggerated salvation-egoism, focus entirely on gaining access to heaven, without regard to the suffering in this world or the joy that can be found on earth. A particular eschatological symbol, however, is legitimate only if it not merely describes precisely the negative dimensions of existence, but also motivates to take action against them.

(2) Eschatological statements, on the other hand, cannot limit themselves to describing negative dimensions of existtence critically without making eschatological and practicable statements about how existing negative social power

structures can be overcome. It does not matter whether this negative aspect of existence is described as radical unbelief or total social alienation. In any case a miracle is expected, because human misery is so great that only God can bring about a revolutionary change. As long as eschatological testimony restricts its utopian aspect to the declaration that everything will be entirely different, and the motivating aspect fails to state its goal and call for spontaneous interpersonal help, then the corresponding eschatological declaration cannot be recognized as a theological one.

(3) An eschatological statement is also insufficient if it is restricted to the motivation to improve the world through love and humanity. When the specific power structures cannot be attacked critically, and at the same time there is no utopian objective developed, the motivation is left up in the air. If no "new society" is expected, "the builders work in vain," that is, the comprehensive character of the kingdom of God is no longer effective. Short-term actions have to cover up particular objectives; there is the danger of giving in to ostensible technical demands which permit no excess of hopes.

In addition, one-sided emphasis on the motivating aspect of the eschatological testimony can result in not taking seriously enough the negative dimensions of existence, whether rebellion against God or alienation of society. The implementation of changes may be overestimated and mythemes left uncriticized, which raises to a pitch the undeniably necessary changes that bring on a total upheaval.

Eschatological statements must prove themselves in the three statements of direction outlined here: *utopia, criticism,* and *motivation.* Specific statements must be tested as to how much this threefold aspect is guaranteed and to what extent corrections are necessary and possible, for there are eschatological symbols which cannot be preserved. A good example of a complete eschatological statement in every one of these aspects is given by E. Jüngel in the symbol of equality. As a critical statement it points out the inequality and alienation of human society. It motivates implementation of equality in the social process. It sets a utopian goal which opposes critically those who consider equality an impracticable goal as well as those who see this equality already realized.[8]

In this as well as in the following two chapters, in eleven sections, the attempt is made to analyze at first a specific coping mechanism of individual grief in its regressive and adaptive stages. In a second step, social factors are featured which can facilitate or inhibit this defense mechanism, often depending on which stage of the grief process the bereaved is going through. Value judgments and behavior patterns of other family members, of the social environment, and of society are also looked into. Finally, in a third step, Christian theory and practice are set in relation to the respective mechanisms, social norms, and behavioral modes. In this confrontation, criticism of Christian theory and practice must begin at the point where they fail to meet the threefold aspects of eschatology and overlook or stress in a one-sided manner individual aspects.

6.2 The mechanism: breakdown of reality testing

6.21 Psychological aspects

The coping mechanism breakdown of reality testing could be just as well classified under the mechanism of denial. However, breakdown of reality testing is dealt with separately in order to stress the specific character of perceptual disorders which occur: (1) visual hallucinations, (2) auditory hallucinations, and (3) sensations that the deceased is present. It is appropriate to list here also (4) dreams about the deceased which become possible because reality testing is greatly reduced in sleep.

Perceptual disorders in the context of loss of the love object are part of the derealization experiences related to the grief process. The world in which the bereaved lives with the deceased seems not yet dead, but it has lost some of its reality. Distortion of reality represents an attempt to keep the dead in the common world.

The disorder of perception during grief can take place without the dead's seeming to return to life; at times objects and people appear either smaller or bigger than they actually are.[1] Von Gebsattel reports the experience of a patient (although clearly depressed), which is occasionally also made by the bereaved:

I do not see the faces of people plastically—this is somehow a disturbance of mental visuality—they are so strange to me, as flat as a pancake, just as flat as the boards on the wall where the glasses stand, they actually ought to fall down. . . . The boards are merely lines, the bed is the same, if I look at it—it has neither length nor depth. . . . People, even though I still notice them—I still have retained my knowledge about people—are, however, like air, going in and out, ghostly—phantom-like.[2]

It happens rather frequently that the bereaved begin activities for the deceased before they realize that he is no longer alive, such as, for example, setting the table for two persons. A young widow told Marris: "I used to put the kettle on and make tea for him. Or when I'd come home and find him not there, I'd think he'd just gone out—he used to go out a lot in the evening . . . —and at work, when the girls got talking, I used to think 'I'll tell Harry that when I get home.'"[3] It is the very time of returning home which gives reason for daydreaming: The grief sufferer hears the steps of the deceased on the stairway, hears the sand crunch in front of the house, and believes that the door opens: "I saw Kay standing just inside the front door, looking as he always had coming home from work. He smiled and I ran into his outstretched arms as I always had and leaned against his chest. I opened my eyes, the image was gone."[4] A mother who has lost a baby may hear it cry while she is half asleep and rush to his bed before realizing that all of this was only a desire.

Almost half the widows in a group interviewed by C. M. Parkes, reported that they had, particularly in the first few months after the death, repeatedly misidentified persons and recognized in them their deceased husbands. In many cases they believed they saw his face among the crowd on the street or in a passing car. A young woman from Nigeria said, "Everywhere I looked I saw his picture. Rather common things could bear his features."[5]

Mina Curtiss writes:

THE NARCISSISTIC COPING MECHANISMS

At first I had the fantasy that you were in the other room, that you had just accidentally left it when I came in. Then I used to expect to meet you in the street. . . . At another time, Alice and I were in a delicatessen store when a man came in who walked like you, who had your figure, your skin coloration, your kind of clothes, even in the style of your coat, to buy a box of chocolate. I would have talked to him immediately, if it had not been for the tired, disappointed look in his eyes, so different from your alertness and liveliness. "Jack has just come back," I said, "death has made him tired. He does not know me, but I must talk to him immediately."[6]

Shortly afterward she fell in love with a man who looked like her deceased husband, until she finally realized that her husband was actually dead.

For a year or so I fantasized myself into a love relationship, because there was something in the tone of his voice, in his gestures that reminded me of you. But intonation and gestures are no test for the heart and spirit. It was you whom I loved, not him, and now that I suddenly know that you are dead, my freedom to love you, you yourself and not someone else, has been restored.[7]

Daydreams are hard to distinguish in these reports from actual hallucinations. Wretmark reports a case of inhibited grief. A twenty-one-year-old woman had lost her nine-month-old son. At first she could act controlled and resumed her work at the factory after three days.

The first manifestations of grief [a lump in the throat, a feeling of emptiness and heaviness, and severe pain in hands and feet] nevertheless were replaced by an apathetic attitude. She found it increasingly difficult to do her work. Jobs she previously could do very easily and almost automatically now seemed to be much more difficult. It was observed that she refused to remove the child's bed. Clothes and toys remained in the same place. She became increasingly quiet, began to avoid other people, and gave up her job a few months later. In the meantime she had lost ten pounds and was physically exhausted. After admittance to the hospital she reported that she saw the boy in his bed every night, but as soon as she stretched out her arms toward him he disappeared. Sometimes she had the definite feeling of holding him in her arms. As soon as she was not occupied in one way or another, her thoughts immediately went back to the child.[8]

Children who have lost their father or mother very often tell in illustrative ways how their parents sit at the edge of the bed and talk to them.[9] Almost half the patients Parkes examined told about similar visual disturbances. Often shadows are perceived as visions of the deceased.

(2) Not infrequent are auditory hallucinations; a creak at night or a sound at the door is interpreted as the husband moving about the house or coming home. One patient of Parkes's reported that she, while sitting in a chair, has the feeling the deceased caresses her ear and whispers that she should rest.[10] In another study, widows reported that they hear their husband cough or call out at night. (3) Besides visual and auditory hallucinations, the feeling that the dead person is present is an even more common phenomenon.[11] Some of the widows told Parkes: "I still have the feeling he is near and there is something I ought to be doing for him or telling him. . . . He is with me all the time, I hear him and see him, although I know it's only imagination"; "When I am washing my hair I have the feeling he is there to protect me in case someone comes in through the door." For some, the presence of the dead is particularly strong at his grave. In a novel by J. Agee, such an appearance of the husband who was killed in a car accident is described:

It began to seem to Mary [the widow], as to Hannah [an aunt], that there was someone in the house other than themselves. She thought of the children; they might have waked up. Yet listening as intently as she could, she was not at all sure that there was any sound; and whoever or whatever it might be, she became sure that it was no child, for she felt in it a terrible forcefulness, and concern, and restiveness, which were no part of any child.

"There is something," Andrew [an uncle] whispered.

Whatever it might be, it was never for an instant at rest in one place. It was in the next room; it was in the kitchen; it was in the dining room. . . .

When she [Mary] came through the door of the children's room she could feel his presence as strongly throughout the room as if she had opened a furnace door: the presence of his strength, of virility, of helplessness, and of pure calm. She fell down on her knees in the middle of the floor and whispered, "Jay. My dear. My dear one.

You're all right now, darling. You're not troubled any more, are you, my darling? Not any more. Not ever any more, dearest. I can feel how it is with you. I know, my dearest. It's terrible to go. You don't want to. Of course you don't. But you have got to. And you know they're going to be all right. Everything is going to be all right, my darling. God take you. God keep you, my own beloved. God make his light to shine upon you." And even while she whispered, his presence became faint, and in a moment of terrible dread she cried out "Jay!" and hurried to her daughter's crib. "Stay with me one minute," she whispered, "just one minute, my dearest"; and in some force he did return; she felt him with her, watching his child. . . .

"Be with us all you can," she whispered. "This is good-bye." And again she went to her knees. Good-bye, she said again, within herself; but she was unable to feel much of anything. "God help me to *realize* it," she whispered and clasped her hands before her face; but she could realize only that he was fading, and that it was indeed good-bye, and that she was at that moment unable to be particularly sensitive to the fact.

And now he was gone entirely from the room, from the house, and from this world.[12]

(4) To the category of breakdown of reality testing to prevent the loss belong the dreams about the deceased. In the investigation by Gorer, about 40 percent of the interviewed recalled such dreams of the person they were mourning. Widows are by far the most regular dreamers about the lost person compared to the rest in the interviewed group of bereaved.[13] Freud frequently pointed out the series of dreams by which conflicts are indicated and overcome.[14] In the dream of the mourner a remarkable compromise is made between the desire that the deceased be alive again and the acceptance of the reality that he is lost.

For the psychoanalytically trained, the bereaved's dreams are important information about the process of grief. A constant repetition of the same dream can indicate that for some unknown reason the grief process is inhibited and cannot progress further. Dreams in which the deceased appears in a frightening, threatening, or distorted form signify, in general, ambivalence conflicts between the deceased and the bereaved. Subsequent dreams that bring back the deceased in a friendly figure give reason to hope that the hostility begins to dissolve in favor of a positive feeling and that the grief process is coming to a positive close.

Ch. Anderson describes the series of dreams by a man who had lost his wife during the blitz in England. His pathological grief reactions made hospitalization necessary. During his recovery he had the following series of dreams.

During the initial part of his illness his wife appeared injured, covered with debris and rebuked him constantly for his dilatoriness in joining her; she accused him unendingly of having killed her. What was peculiar was that all the other objects whom he cherished in his household appeared injured, diseased, or revengeful. His four children, all actually in good health, appeared in his dreams in various states of reduction. His eldest son, whom he knew to be well, appeared often in his nightmares, drowning, maimed, or afflicted/ crippled and inflicted with a wasting disease. ... Even the household dog to whom my patient was greatly attached and who was in good health, appeared diseased, mangy, wasting, and malevolent. Gradually and over the course of months these dreams changed in content and affect. His wife became well and friendly and both children and dog lost their malevolent appearance. With this my patient became well once more.[15]

Ch. Anderson divides the dreams of mourners into two groups. In the one, the dead person is again alive and healthy and the past happy experiences can be repeated. In the other group, the dead appears hurt and hurting, persecuted or haunting; he wears the shroud and shows the signs of his disease or injury. He intends to destroy the dreamer, or the dreamer does the most horrible things to the already injured. Anderson believes he can conclude from this that, in the first case, a basically harmonious relationship existed between the deceased and the survivor and the grief process takes its proper course, while the grief work in the second group of dreamers obviously is aggravated by the ambivalence conflict and the outcome is uncertain.[16]

The absence of dreams after a death is also a certain sign that since the loss is so grave the grief process is delayed; the mourner behaves in his dream as if nothing happened. Thus, according to Gorer, none of the six parents who had lost a growing child ever had any dreams.[17] Even children, in spite of their otherwise various dream activity, often after the death of the most important loved one have a dreamless sleep. Occasionally the repressed dreams lead to frightening experiences, as Gorer reports of a shopkeeper who never dreamt of his wife after her death:

I couldn't sleep in there after the wife died. I was upstairs after the wife died and I was watching television for the first time after she died; and all of a sudden I could see my wife as plain as anything, sitting in one of those chairs. I flew downstairs and never went in that room again. . . . It was very frightening. It's a lovely room.[18]

Furthermore, it can happen that the denial of death is opposed in an agonizing way through destructive dreams. The dreams can present the death repeatedly in an aggressive manner, while the seemingly nondeceased show themselves with external injuries or are killed in accidents. Not only the actual burial, but other funerals as well are dreamt of again and again. The dream expresses the desire to let the dead die, so to speak, and give him his peace which is denied to him through the denial of his death.[19] The reality of death can be recognized in various ways in this dream reported by G. R. Krupp:

Mrs. C, age forty, was married to a man much older, but was quite happy in the marriage. Her husband died suddenly. She was very grief-stricken in the beginning. Within forty-eight hours of the death she dreamed: "He appears and I have hurt my tooth. I told him. He was solicitous, like a father. I pointed in the back as if something there could be repaired." The patient woke up extremely disappointed when she realized that it was only a dream.[20]

In this case, the reality of death is emphasized through the awakening; what Freud said about the anxiety dream applies here: "We tend to interrupt the sleep before the repressed wish of the dream has achieved its fulfillment over and against the censorship."[21] Even though the dream work has failed in its purpose, nevertheless it is a proper dream: It has renounced nothing of its essential nature. In another case, according to G. R. Krupp, a similar dream is repeated several times, interrupted by awakening and accompanied by considerable disappointment.[22] The sleeper is awakened as if by a night watchman if a disorder of perception threatens, which cannot be fought off by the dream censorship only.

Other forms of reality acceptance are manifested in dreams in the fact that the deceased appears feeble and ill. Occasionally the dreamer knows that the person appearing in the dream is actually dead, but he feels sorry that the deceased obviously does not yet know it. Sometimes, however, the deceased seems to be alive but in some strange way not approachable and as if he were absent.[23]

In general these dreams fulfill, as Gorer has observed, their positive function as coping mechanisms. In almost all cases the dreams were consoling (negative dreams in several cases were directed toward dead parents). Mostly the deceased was recalled as much younger than he was at the time of his death. Pleasant talks are recalled and joint activities remembered. Gorer relates the comments of a seventy-one-year-old wife of a pensioned bricklayer talking about her loved younger sister:

I dream about her too, she often comes to me, you know; we have a laugh and that; we're always together and working in my dreams, you see. Because we worked together sometimes on the land years ago and we used to have a wonderful laugh and game out in the fields; and I can always see her in that field, you know, and the games we used to have.[24]

How the dream can provide consolation for the mourners, bring the deceased back to life, and reunite him with the bereaved, all these motives are summarized in the last verse of the famous poem by Edgar Allan Poe of the "beautiful Annabel Lee," who was taken from her lover:

> For the moon never beams without bringing me dreams
> Of the beautiful ANNABEL LEE;
> And the stars never rise but I see the bright eyes
> Of the beautiful ANNABEL LEE;
> And so, all the night-tide, I lie down by the side
> Of my darling, my darling, my life and my bride,
> In her sepulchre there by the sea—
> In her tomb by the side of the sea.[25]

Visual and auditory hallucinations as well as the sensation of the presence of the deceased and the dreams about him mainly belong to the regressive stage of coping with grief. As Caruso says, "the beloved is replaced by an *image* of the beloved—a faint image, an image increased in its value but at the same time a devaluated image because it is no longer an actual living one." [26] In a similar way, Clerk complains of not being able to recall the face of his deceased wife. Nevertheless he explains it like this:

We have seen the faces of those we know best so variously from so many angles, in so many lights, with so many expressions—waking, sleeping, laughing, crying, eating, talking, thinking—that all the impressions crowd into our memory together and cancel out into a mere blur. [27]

Something similar can be said of the dream process. At the beginning the dreams are vivid and clear but become increasingly more pale and more indistinct. [28]

6.22 Sociological implications

In D. W. Rees's opinion, a surprisingly large number of mourners "see" their dead relatives after they have been buried or cremated. Visions of this kind are not unusual for survivors who are otherwise coping with their grief in a "normal" way. But it is an experience the bereaved will talk about only if asked. Rees confesses that he did not notice this phenomenon during the first decade of his medical practice, since such experiences are not revealed spontaneously either to the physician or the minister or to relatives or friends. One will have to agree with Rees that what we find here is a coping mechanism hardly known but of help and support to many bereaved: "The climate of opinion in modern Western civilization is obviously such that many people feel that they are unable to disclose to others one of the most interesting and important experiences of their life." [29] Social standards do not allow one to draw full support from this repressive mechanism since it isolates the individual and in addition gives him the aggravating impression of having socially unacceptable experiences. Such visual disturbances are a vivid example of the fact that they are considered psychiatric illnesses only because they are not known in public and not known to be as widespread as they are.

Contrary to this, in less differentiated societies it is conceded that the "soul" of the deceased at first cannot leave its original dwelling place and needs time actually to separate itself from its family and tribe. W. L. Warner, to mention only one example from the extensive ethnological material, gives a detailed description of the rituals of the Murgins, all of which serve the purpose of gradually dissolving the relationships between the deceased and the living. As a soul, the dead must be treated with great caution. The ceremonies move in two directions. For one thing, they serve to complete the separation and, on the other hand, to reconcile the spirit and to suggest to him that he travel quietly to his fountain of the dead and not hurt and disturb the living. The forms of ceremonies focusing on the second function are manifold and take more time, as if the living were unwilling to release the soul of the deceased. In the hymns sung during the funeral ceremonies not only the anger of the deceased ancestors is expressed, because the deceased has not received the appropriate treatment, but also the complaint that the female members of the family are not willing to give up the bones of the dead.[30] The Murgins clearly assume an intermediate stage in which the deceased is still present for the bereaved, while our society denies the bereaved the recognition of the experience of perceiving the deceased. Even though this is, at least for the regressive stage, the actual experience.

6.23 Image, or "night of the loss of images"

In the course of the grief work, as Caruso and Clerk have noticed, it becomes more difficult to imagine the face of the deceased. The fading of his image is for the bereaved often a frightening experience; no longer to be able to imagine the deceased signifies betrayal and unbearable loss. It would be more appropriate to say that the deceased is merged into the world the bereaved experienced together with him and could experience only with him. The dead and the living are united in the *images of happiness of days past;* the evening walks together, a pleasant and relaxed evening somewhere out in the country, the moment of reunion after a long and painful separation. There are certain gestures and movements, so familiar to the bereaved; reconciliation after a severe argument, an irrational but pleasant habit. It is the gesture of breaking the bread by which the disciples of Emmaus recognize the risen Lord; it is the daily meal with bread and fish in which his new life is retained. The memory of the dead is not kept alive in individual features, words, and actions. Images are more likely the vessels in which the essence of his character is kept and preserved.

What is valid for past happiness also holds true for future salvation. The character of the kingdom of God and the rule of Christ can be expressed only in images. Only in malleable images is saving grace present; only seeing, contrary to believing and hoping, expresses the fulfillment of what is believed and hoped for. The Old and New Testaments are not afraid to describe in numerous images the "new society"; the parables of the kingdom of God are not told only for the sake of comparison, but rather the listener is promised and awarded the message of the parable as well the telling of the story. In spite of this, a strong rejection of all images has succeeded in theology. E. Hirsch speaks of the "night of the loss of images"[31] that has overcome us and which he considers positive. Bultmann's comment is expressed in the now famous statement "Christian hope knows that it hopes but does not know what it hopes for."[32] Recently he underscored once more that the transition from this world into eternity cannot be imagined as life analogical to the earthly, but rather represents itself *totaliter aliter*. This transition can be experienced only in border situations in which we perceive our life not as real but as one marked by death.[33] Karl Barth spoke of the things to come as the "beyond of God"[34] and thus has dismissed the question of the content of hope.

Hirsch argues for the positive evaluation of the lack of images with the opinion that it is necessary "to counteract the modern confusion of belief in eternity and fantasies of primitive times."[35]

However, abstract eschatological terms, such as "God's beyond for men" and "to be with Christ," even though they fulfill the utopian function of eschatological statements, largely lack a motivating power. One would also have to ask whether or not the critical impulse of eschatological declarations already is cut out, since the criticism of the power structure has to be so radical that it no longer attacks anything specific.

Two "vivid" eschatological images can be pointed out which neither fall under privacy, as characteristic of the eschatology of family, nor rise to such a degree of abstractness as the "kingdom of God" and the "new society." The one image is the "city," the other the "garden."

In the Old and New Testaments the city is the symbol of a fulfilled life. To regain and to see again Jerusalem has been an aspiration for centuries; to forget it means to forget one's own self and thus to die. John's apocalypse sees the new Jerusalem descending from heaven; the city becomes the visible sign of the divine kingdom. Then, as much as today, the city was attractive. Just like the secular city, the heavenly Zion is decorated with splendid walls, streets, and buildings. Here the exchange of goods and knowledge takes place; here is the center of power when the kings move to Zion.

H. Cox deserves special credit for having made us once again conscious of the comprehensive significance of the eschatological symbol of the city, no matter how one reacts to his thesis of secularization.[36] He has made theologians aware of the immense possibilities and hopes the image of the city implies. The symbol of the city for him has also a critical function. He points out how life becomes impoverished by withdrawing to the suburbs and falls victim to an idealization of the family with all the attendant psychic difficulties. He restores the negative counterimage, the anticity, as Babel and Rome had been for the Bible. Cox referred to the kind of activity and amount of fantasy that had been set free in order to reach the pragmatic goal of city renewal. The satellite city, as ugly as it may be in details, cannot be understood without the prophetic hope promised the city according to the biblical message, as much as technical and economic forces lead to neglect of the human communality factor. Cox saw precisely in the criticism and correction of such hopes one of the most significant tasks of the church. Just as the symbol of the city has critical and motivating effects, it also sets a utopian goal theologically, aimed at a city full of life and interaction, full of beauty and the removal of loneliness. The goal is "the joyful communication of everyone, free of all hardship, distress, and anxiety and enjoying one another; in the joyful seeing of God they are not isolated from one another but better and more than ever united." [37]

Against this background the message is valid at the grave of people who died in loneliness, deprived of communication; it applies to the bereaved who dread their loneliness by making clear to them the promise of the secular city with all its possibilities of communality and by referring to the utopian city with its abundance of fulfilled life.

The second eschatological symbol, the symbol of the "garden" seems to contradict the one of the "city." Is the city not the horrifying image we want to escape by all means, even if this means curtailing our opportunities? The image of the garden also has a solid biblical tradition. The restoration of the Garden of Eden with its effortless way of making a living, the absence of pain and death, and the daily natural encounter with God has been a hope, projected not only into the world beyond but also activating human striving. In contrast to the image of wilderness and jungle, the image of the garden depicts the reconciliation of human labor with nature's conditions, which perhaps has never been expressed more fully than in an English park, which attempts to give the impression that, in spite of all human efforts, this garden in its variety, its views, lakes, and buildings is "natural," created without human interference. It is "pacified nature," awakening images of tranquility, relaxation, and melancholy about the mortality of life. This is the reason cemeteries try more and more to adopt this symbol of the garden and become parks. This may be characterized as denial of death, yet it seems that precisely in this way the symbol of pacified nature finds its realization.

This is not to say it is known what "garden" and "pacified

nature" really are. But to place the garden only in the world beyond, as it happens in many church hymns, destroys the eschatological validity of this symbol. We know in the meantime how nature can be exploited and ravished in all pride to conquer the world. And it is the critical declaration of direction of this eschatological symbol that fights such attempts. To turn the world into a garden is difficult for us to learn. We have not yet sufficiently understood that the city as such is not a countersymbol to "pacified nature," but only that city in which nature is buried under concrete, and in which private interests ban the green areas. Just as we still have to learn not to consider our gardens as exclusively "my garden." The neat hedges around individual graves, the borders of the grave, the family burial place reflect the present social structure that the eschatological symbol of the "garden" and "pacified nature" opposes.

6.3 The mechanism: denial/repression

6.31 Psychological aspects

In the literature on grief work the mechanism of denial is considered one of the most important coping mechanisms. As G. Krupp has pointed out, "the denial defense may well preserve the individual from complete disintegration under the full impact of the blow."[1] In general, however, psychoanalysis talks about denial as a mental device if an event in the outside world with unpleasant consequences for the ego either is completely blotted out, not recognized, or devaluated in its significance.[2]

However, in the case of denial of a death, we are dealing not only with the negation of external realities but also with the denial of now unsatisfied instinctual demands of the id. That process is generally identified as repression. Denial of external realities and repression of instinctual demands are closely related in grief; whereas, depending upon the individual, either the coping mechanism of denial or the coping mechanism of repression is more strongly employed.

Denial and repression are so universal in grief that they are implicitly present in all coping mechanisms dealt with here, particularly in the narcissistic. Inadequacy of vision control can be identified as a denial of reality, as far as it is perceived through the senses of seeing, hearing, touching. The defense mechanisms we have to deal with at this point are, with respect to definition, limited to the cognitive and emotional function of the psychic organization. Far more than the inadequacy of vision control, the death is intellectually accepted but repressed and denied in its emotional significance or vice versa. The following combinations of repression and denial are observable in grief. (1) *Avoidance:* The bereaved can only further deny the reality of death by avoiding everything that could remind him of the loss. (2) *Mummification:* Death is accepted, but it is denied that this results in a change of the environment; the dead is "mummified." (3) *Cognitive denial:* Death is not accepted intellectually; however, a sadness appears whose origin does not become conscious. (4) *Emotional repression:* Death is recognized intellectually, but the survivor is incapable of feeling any pain. (5) *Displacement:* The loss is intellectually accepted, but coping with it emotionally is impossible and is therefore displaced by secondary grief symptoms (including those of a somatic nature). (6) *Denial in fantasy:* Even though death is accepted intellectually and partially emotionally, at the same time a wild fantasy develops that death did not occur. (7) *Ego splitting:* Death is fully accepted but denied in a dissociated part of the psychic organization; the deceased is largely isolated from it.

(1) *Avoidance:* If the defense mechanism of denial mainly takes the form of avoidance, then this signifies an attempt on the part of the bereaved to avoid everything that could remind him of the loss. He dispenses with seeing the deceased once more and demands that the funeral be kept rather short. He attempts to avoid contact with the minister and the doctor since they represent death for him, and he must apprehend that they will talk about the deceased. He withdraws from his family and his social environment as soon as the deceased is mentioned in the conversation. In an extreme case he might forbid talking about the deceased at all.

While in the regressive stage, avoidance can be a meaningful behavior in order to absorb the impact of the shock of death; during the adaptive stage it leads to a behavior inappropriate and strange in the opinion of relatives. The bereaved does not visit the grave. G. Wretmark reports a young girl who refused to believe in the death of her mother, for she never saw her in the casket. If she visited the cemetery she passed by the grave of her mother as if it had nothing to do with her and placed flowers on the grave of her grandparents, not far from it.[3] In a seminar with ministers the story was reported of an older widower who, even though he accompanied his family in the car whenever they visited the grave of his wife, waited in front of the cemetery for their return. Pollock reports further cases of such an avoidance in situations in which a parent had died before the patient reached the age of six. In each of these cases the patients never visited the cemetery where their father or mother was buried. In addition, they had experienced amnesia lasting several months after the notification of death.[4]

(2) *Mummification*: It is also denial if death is accepted, but, at the same time, the environment in which the deceased lived is kept unchanged, and partially even behavior patterns are still carried on as if he had not died. Gorer terms this "mummification" in a metaphorical sense.[5] The house and every object in it is kept precisely as the deceased had left it, as if it were a shrine that would be reanimated at any moment. The most notorious example of mummification in recent English history is Queen Victoria, who not only preserved every object as Prince Albert had arranged it, but continued the daily ritual of having his clothes laid out, his shaving water brought, and the table set for two.[6]

A typical case of "mummification" is reported by Jackson. Two elderly ladies had lived together all their lives. When one of the sisters, who had assumed the male role, died, the surviving sister could not be convinced of the death:

She went through the activities of the funeral and the next few days with a smile and a cheerful word for everyone. Again and again the pastor heard her say to friends: "Ruth isn't really dead. My faith wouldn't let her die. I believe she is still here with me even though I can't see her. Why should I be sad? We will always be together."

As time went along the pattern of her life became clear. She was keeping up the play upon her sister's presence with complete sincerity and candor. Two places were always set at the table, and though no food was served the dead sister, she explained, "In the spirit body we don't need food. We just don't want to be ignored." Flowers were kept in her sister's bedroom. Her clothes were left hanging in the closet untouched except for an occasional cleaning. As much as it could be acted out, the presence of the sister as a spiritual being was accepted. When guests came, she would say, "I know Ruth would want me to thank you for coming." When Christmas gifts or cards were mailed, they were signed "Minnie and Ruth." [7]

Throughout the regressive stage of grief work, it is valuable for therapeutic reasons not to change the surroundings too much. The ego of the bereaved has to make so many adaptations that it represents relief if the immediate environment remains constant. This is above all true with children, who are even more upset by being sent off to friends or relatives during the first period of mourning. It also refers to the aged, whose adapting abilities are diminished. For them a relocation can increase their mortality rate significantly. [8] In the adaptive stage, on the other hand, the recognition must prevail that the environment too has changed, and not only the relationship to the deceased.

(3) *Cognitive denial:* Death can be denied by not accepting it intellectually. The bereaved feels a deep sadness but cannot explain its cause. That conflicts from childhood are being repressed when the patient cannot remember anything is a device well known in psychoanalytic practice. Often a patient might remember a great part of his childhood rather vividly and in great detail during an analytic session, while he suffers a total amnesia with respect to others, in particular pathogenic periods and times of conflict. [9]

Helene Deutsch reports on a patient in her middle years who, for no obvious reason, shed hot tears at the beginning of every analytical session. Her weeping was not compulsive but quiet and soft, yet without reference. In situations where sadness could be expected, however, she behaved extremely controlled and expressionless. She was quite willing to share her sad experiences with others and could sink into deep depression if some of her friends suffered a misfortune. She reacted with intense concern and sympathy, particularly in cases of sickness or death within her circle of friends. During treatment this sadness was traced back to a grief experience in her youth; even though it was the divorce of her parents rather than death that was the traumatic event. For her, however, this had no connection with her feelings. Deutsch considers the behavior of this girl extreme but believes such a reaction to a significant loss in a milder form occurs quite frequently.[10]

(4) *Repression of emotions:* A more far-reaching denial of death is the case if the bereaved recognizes the reality of death rationally, and acts accordingly, but represses the death emotionally and therefore experiences no sadness. The subject matter remains conscious, but the effect related to it or the significance of this threat is repressed.[11]

What W. Schulte identifies as a nucleus of melancholic experiences applies also in certain cases to the bereaved: a not-being-able-to-grieve. Schulte describes a depressed man whose son had committed suicide. The physician's attempt to express his condolence is warded off by the man's saying that this was precisely the most terrible thing—he could not feel anything. Only when the depressive stage abated could the bereaved cry and express grief similar to a bereaved (for whom this is only possible in the adaptive stage), when his emotional recognition was no longer separated from his rational recognition.[12] It is the "failure to fulfill, as it were, an emotional quota," which is felt so agonizingly.[13] In this example as well as in similar cases, the grief process remained inhibited over a longer period. The grief work was not set in motion for reasons that can only be presumed in the report just mentioned.

(5) *Displacement:* The negation of death and the inability to mourn may express themselves only in psychosomatic symptoms or a disease as manifestation of grief.[14] This has been observed by Karl Stern *et al.* in older people. Stern writes: "Under certain circumstances the older person is more

ready to 'channel' material that would produce overt emotional conflict into somatic illness."[15]

Nevertheless, his argument is not coherent at this point. He sees the reason for such a displacement in the assumption that the aging person's ego is too weak to carry out the work of mourning. According to this argument, the weakening of the ego would set in motion denial, allowing grief reactions only as illness. On the other hand, Stern *et al.* consider it a subject for special study to decide whether these somatic illnesses represent a tendency toward self-punishment or an identification with the deceased.[16] However, it is safe to assume that the aging person uses defense mechanisms other than denial.[17]

(6) *Denial in fantasy:* In particular with children in whom reality testing has not yet fully developed, it can happen that even though reality is perceived, it is negated in fantasy.[18] S. Freud formulates this device in "Formulations Regarding the Two Principles in Mental Functioning" (1911): "With the introduction of the reality principle one mode of thought activity was split off; it was kept free from reality testing and remained subordinated to the pleasure principle alone. This is the act of fantasy-making, which begins already in the games of children, and later, continued as daydreaming, abandons its dependence on real objects."[19]

(7) *Ego splitting:* Freud, in his fragmentary manuscripts "The Splitting of the Ego in the Defensive Process" (1938) and "Outline of Psychoanalysis" (1938), indicated the process of denial through ego splitting.[20] He illustrates with the case of a child how the ego can solve a conflict between the demand of the instinct and the command of reality: "He replies to the conflict with two contrary reactions, both of which are valid and effective. On the one hand, with the help of certain mechanisms he rejects reality and refuses to accept any prohibition; on the other hand, in the same breath he recognizes the danger of reality."[21] Both of the parties obtain their share. But this success is achieved at the price of a rift in the ego. The partial denial of reality Freud demonstrates especially in fetishism, but points them out also in grief reactions. He mentions the case of an obsessional neurotic who in every situation in life oscillated between two

assumptions—"on the one, his father was still alive and hindered him from action; on the other, his father was dead and he had the right to regard himself as his successor."[22]

Particularly in the defensive mechanism of "searching," which we will discuss below,[23] this splitting of the ego becomes obvious. The deceased is isolated from the remaining psychic organization and leads his own life, hardly connected with the other thinking and feeling. Contrary to "mummification," such isolation of the dead does not require unchanged environment; life seems to go on undisturbed, while the bereaved keeps the deceased "to himself."

6.32 Sociological implications

As we have already explained, the denial of loss in many cases can have a positive function by shielding the bereaved person from the full implications of his grief. It can become a device through which the implications of the loss can be increasingly accepted. Even in the adaptive stage it must not lead to a behavior considered morbid by the social environment. It may, however, result in considerable conflicts with the environment.

H. H. Brewster describes the case of a married woman who is unable to accept the death of her brother and carries on a vivid imaginary relationship with him. This resulted in considerable difficulties with her husband and children.[24] As Helene Deutsch explains, the effort to keep the dead alive can absorb so much energy that the gratification gained from it is lost again in the weakening of the ego.[25] Increased irritability and distrust in the environment which does not share the conviction of the bereaved can drive him into social isolation. Somatic illnesses that at first represented only a displacement become chronic.

It ought not to be the case necessarily, but the denial of death frequently remains unrecognized within neurotic disorders. There are cases of schizoid personalities who can keep the existence of the deceased so much to themselves that it is not conspicious even to the family. Relatives may notice certain farcical forms of behavior without feeling the necessity to intervene. The bereaved person decides to have long conversations at the grave every Sunday or to keep his own house just as it used to be when the deceased was still alive.

The mechanism of denial is socially supported by the fact that there are no uniform ideas in modern Western civilizations about what death actually is. Ideas that life continues are widespread. Very often they go together with the belief in the existence of God, but even without believing in God, belief in immortality is retained. Neither spiritism nor the dogma of rebirth depend on the belief in God. Neither is there any social consensus about whether death means really the end, waiting for a general resurrection of the dead, or a transition to a form of existence free of the body. The dead have, metaphorically speaking, no place where they can be found, whether in Hades or in heaven, or a "place of rest, in the expectation of the coming of the Kingdom." That neither death as finality, nor the resurrection, nor the eternal life in heaven can be "proven" is only a sign of the fact that no social consensus can be reached about these issues.

6.33 The reality of death

Theology frequently has contributed to the denial of death. We particularly have to talk about the denial of death in theology if death is postulated as an event without any specific meaning and content and as a transition without problems into a special world. Denial of death in the practice of the church can consist of expecting either highly controlled, emotionless grief reactions from the bereaved, or even an expression of joy. This might be conceivable if such demands correspond to the inner experience of the bereaved. However, if they become repressive, they come close to a philosophical world view like the stoic's, which denies the significance of death and suppresses any kind of grief reaction.

Bachmann relates a case study about a minister's wife who had lost her father several years ago. The father had represented security, but also he wanted her to be independent, on her own. He as well as her mother had not wanted her to cry or to show feeling. This attitude was reinforced by her husband who told her that she had "to bear loss with a smile on your face or else you belie your faith." She had been listening to her husband's sermons on death, which led her to believe that she had no right to cry. After the death of her father she had become increasingly irascible, easily hurt and insecure in her relationships. It was not until she had had several interviews with a counselor that she was able to accept the death and to express fully her grief about the loss. From then on her relationship with her family improved and became normal.[26]

Minimizing death marks the modern sects of spiritualism and Christian Science. They dogmatically deny the "existence of death"; consequently, convinced adherents of these sects would be going against their tenets if they admitted mourning. These represent perceptions in which old religious ideas are sustained with "scientific proofs" which can under such conditions again secure the stability of belief in immortality, frequently lost in traditional faith. A spiritualist stated in a conversation with Gorer:

You've got the loss, but it's only the physical loss. [You don't feel sadness] because we look at it and treat it in a different way, what we call a more normal way. . . . The knowledge—and I say knowledge, it isn't a belief—the knowledge which I have today counts so much in life that it displaces fear and doubt and—as you would term it—grief, and they just become nothingness.[27]

As far as the church has preserved the dimension of future in hope, it has not been spared the accusation that religion contributes to the denial of death or in any case does not recognize it fully. This criticism is correct, especially in cases where, for example, eschatology has taken over from philosophy a dogma of immortality of the soul without reflection and where, being neither affirmed nor rejected through the practice of the church, a number of customs and habits have invaded the church, amounting to a cultic glorification of the dead. It ought to be said here, however, that it is often hard to draw the line between respect and reverence for the deceased and a death cult.

A basic change took place with the new approach of Protestant theology in the twenties. In contrast to the transcendence of God, the nothingness of human life and death is stressed; death becomes the final and fundamental decision for or against Christ. The thesis of the modern repression of death, presumably today largely a common part of theological understanding, has a specific ideological function. It preserves the unbearable dimension and acuteness of death in order to make man aware that his utopian and reforming ideas must fail, and that a possible solution must aim not at repression but at acceptance of death as the final limit to human efforts.

The emphasis on the reality and inevitability of death accentuates the experience of death anxiety and considers this experience as something deeply human. Thus theology wants to keep this experience open for man and not leave him under the compulsion of having to deny this fear of death. The reality of man's finality shall not be hidden from him. Theology maintains that only in facing this reality will those forces become effective which secure the courage to overcome this death anxiety, never to be repressed anyway.

Accordingly, those elements in the image of Jesus that show his anxiety of dying have been stressed more, linking him to all creatures. "I have a baptism to be baptized with; and how I am constrained until it is accomplished!" Jesus says according to Luke (12:50). The scene in Gethsemane recalls for the Christian tradition that death is not simply a phenomenon that can be skipped with quiet certainty since it is only the gateway to eternity. The death of Jesus "is not the 'death as friend.' This is death in its entire horrible atrocity. This is really 'the last enemy of God.'" It would have been feasible to obliterate these features of the death anxiety of Jesus in the first gospel in the history of tradition, as it happened with John and the rest of the New Testament (disregarding Hebrews 5:7 where Jesus is seen as one who "in the days of his flesh . . . offered up prayers and supplications, with loud cries and tears, to him who was able to save him from death"). Jesus' death anxiety certainly is not reported as the basis for a methodological principle to frighten man at his last hour, but is rather the deepest expression of his humanity.

It seems to be a specific theological contribution not to

appease the bereaved's awareness of death, but rather to deepen it and to bring it fully to consciousness. D. K. Switzer comments:

It is not unexpected that practitioners and writers in the field of pastoral care would be more prone to perceive a sense of emptiness and meaninglessness and the question of one's own death and to develop an interpretation of these factors in relation to anxiety with more frequency than others. Certainly to do so is more in keeping with a theological orientation than it is with the behavioristic-experimental approach of much of contemporary academic psychology.[28]

Two of the central contributions from the theological side will be cited.

J. Berger assumes that man is shocked by the experience of death. The walls of human understanding of death are loosened or destroyed; he is thrown into the healthy restlessness of the reassessment of all values. The power of the impact is so great that it even penetrates the center of human consciousness. The sermon at the grave must, according to Berger, aim at the collapse of all human defensive efforts. Berger employs an immensely aggressive language to describe the task of proclaiming the gospel. It is charged with the responsibility "to storm the walls of such human understanding of death." The resistance arising again and again must "be broken." "Overcoming and breaking man's opposition to the confrontation with the reality of death through the proclamation of the gospel at the grave"[29] takes place by enforcing a reversal of all human thinking about death, by destroying all illusions about death, and by undermining all humanly possible attitudes toward death.[30]

According to Manfred Mezger, proclamation and faith do not lead around death but help one to endure it: "The decisive first and last lesson of life is that man's death is not caused by illness or accident but by the will of God, that is, non-mythologically speaking, that man is freed of himself through the gospel and willing to accept death as his death."[31] The task of the sermon is a new "actualization of the historicity, that is, volatility and mortality of human existence, which is irreversible in its direction and cannot be lived on trial."[32] It is of no significance at this point whether the mourner admits this to himself or not; the human situation remains the same. "The explicit or implicit inquiry addressed to *all* living has preference in any case: whether we pay only a moment's reverence to death, the destiny for all of us, or whether we implicate death constantly in our considerations."[33]

We can assume of these authors that their primary concern is to help the bereaved. They proceed from his existential state of feeling threatened, intend to help him to reach full realization of it and to prevent him from employing defense mechanisms offered by society. The full, unobstructed realization that man's destiny is to die should create an open situation in which effective comfort can be given through the message of Jesus' death. This is first of all a coherent conception, even if it is questionable whether a short address at the funeral can actually achieve all this with a penetrating effect.

What seems to be doubtful, however, is the pedagogical objective of Berger and Mezger, namely, that the bereaved ought to be reminded that there are irreversible decisions and irreparable behavioral modes. For Berger, the deceased is a vicarious figure for the living; he testifies to the decision that became sealed and irretrievable through his end. The proclaiming of the gospel will remind the bereaved of that irrevocability in order to appeal to him to make a decision for or against God.[34] Mezger is less concerned with such traditional decisions of faith than with decisions concerning attitudes and behavior. However, he too demands: "Less pious emotions at the grave, more seriousness about death and its irretrievability! Not so much apocalyptical vocabulary, rather some investigation of behavior! Here applies, with due distinction, what the scripture says: 'Weep not for me, the dead, but weep for yourselves.'"[35] Here the deceased becomes a deterrent and an admonition for the bereaved by referring to the fact that human actions are irrevocable. Beyond that, the dead gains no positive function for the bereaved himself, as can be the case with the coping mechanisms of recollection and incorporation.

Nevertheless, it would be overestimating the possibility of a funeral address to attempt in those five or ten minutes available to interpret the reality of death for the survivors, and at the same time to announce the consolation of the gospel. The entire ritual of the funeral must focus on this reality of death. P. E. Irion, for example, considers the funeral as helpful "insofar as it enables mourners to confront realistically the crisis in which they exist."[36] Only the bereaved person who accepts the reality of death is able to understand fully his feelings of emptiness, his resentfulness of other people, and his desire to be left in peace. "The separation from the body of the deceased by burial or cremation further affirms . . . that the relationship as it has been known has really been broken."[37] Jackson states it similarly: "The funeral is a time for facing reality rather than denying it."[38] Reality cannot be ignored or avoided without disrupting moral practice and social responsibility. "The Christian faith," he writes, "is geared to even the most distressing aspects of reality, and its message becomes triumphantly relevant only when all of life is accepted without illusion or limitation."[39] On this basis he affirms the American custom that has developed in the last decades of viewing the corpse at the funeral home.[40]

Theologically, it appears legitimate neither to deny death and to discuss it to a point of nonexistence nor to ascribe a role to it that supercedes all other human crises in terms of significance, which also initiates anxiety.

To reveal this existing reality of death, and thus the attendant anxiety, and to make the mourner more conscious of it are essential tasks. From a counseling viewpoint, it is certainly also right to deal with the openly expressed anxiety in a case of death; nevertheless, Tillich's warning is valid: "Certainly the anxiety of death overshadows all concrete anxieties and gives them their ultimate seriousness. They have, however, a certain independence, and, ordinarily, a more immediate impact than the anxiety of death."[41] Considering this aspect, it certainly would be wrong, particularly at this point, to stress the threat and vanity of human life in a demonstrative and pedagogical way and thus give death almost a demonic dimension. The sufferings of society are great enough without having to state an example of human powerlessness with respect to death.

Therefore it seems more sensible in counseling with the bereaved not to underscore so much the reality of death as the reality of loss, even though one might say that every failure and every loss represents a certain death experience. And death is one of the essential symbols in which failure and loss are conveyed. The eschatological view would then have to speak at best of the "reality of suffering." In the "new society," suffering and death are overcome. However, a life would not be fulfilled if it did not harbor the memory of past sufferings and past losses. The marks of the nails which the resurrected Christ bears when he appears, according to the Gospel of John, are a vivid expression of the suffering and the disease leading to death, but they promise that in a future life the suffering of past generations has not vanished.

In its critical function the eschatological concept "reality of suffering, of loss, of death" opposes the repression of death, whether it is motivated socially, as a world view, or religiously. To say it with the words of Caruso: "Death must be recognized so that it can be fought";[42] one is not permitted to leap over.

The reality of death must be fully accepted; a clear separation between what signifies reality in our society and what we hope for, no matter on what basis, must be established.

6.4 The mechanism: searching

6.41 Psychological aspects

The defensive mechanism of searching implies a separation, but this separation is not considered final. In the assumption of the bereaved the love object is only temporarily absent. He is still motivated by waiting for the return of the lost or by unconsciously or half consciously pursuing the active search for him.

J. Bowlby became aware of this coping mechanism through his investigation of separation reactions of children. When the absence of the mother begins to make the child anxious, he starts searching for her.[1] Bowlby believes he can prove that the child's response to separation from a significant person is reactivated in adults.

There are three main forms of reactions expressing the search for the lost object: (1) seemingly aimless hyperactivity, (2) calling for the deceased, and (3) roaming around in the hope of meeting him.

(1) One of the most remarkable changes Lindemann observed in bereaved persons is seen in the activity throughout the day: "There is no retardation of action and speech; quite to the contrary, there is a rush of speech, especially when talking about the deceased. There is restlessness, inability to sit still, moving about in an aimless fashion, continually searching for something to do. There is, however, at the same time, a painful lack of capacity to initiate and maintain organized patterns of activity."[2] In neuropsychiatric studies as well, instead of an apathetic and depressive behavior, which might be expected, frequently an increased activity is observed.[3]

This behavior might be partially traced back to the "vacuum activities,"[4] already previously described. As Parkes rightly contends, the searching behavior of the bereaved is not at all, as Lindemann believes, aimless. It only seems so because the bereaved with all his activity does not accomplish what he wants, namely, to find the lost person.[5] The bereaved is not always conscious of the goal of this hypermotility. However, Parkes also quotes in his study, statements by the bereaved themselves which affirm his contentions. As one widow said, "I can't help looking for him everywhere. . . . I walk around searching for him. . . . I felt that if I could have come somewhere I could have found him"; and another, "I go to the grave . . . but he's not there."[6]

(2) Quite common is the calling for the deceased, especially in the stage of shock but also later on. "Dwight, where are you? I need you so much," wrote Frances Beck in her *Diary of a Widow*.[7] Such calling for the lost person is, as with

children, often connected with crying, but crying here is not an expression of helplessness but rather, if one accepts the interpretation by Bowlby, an "instrumental" weeping aimed at compelling the deceased to return.

(3) Finally, there is the active searching for the deceased; the bereaved visits places associated with the lost person. Some return to the hospital where the loved one died only to realize that he is no longer there. For a long time the unexpressed and only vaguely realized hope is kept alive of meeting the lost person in the street. This often creates a conflict with the desire to avoid everything that reminds one of the dead person. It might happen that the bereaved visits and walks around the various places where they used to go together to find the deceased there. But the memory of previous times of happiness there often are so painful that he flees rapidly. Occasionally the bereaved returns repeatedly to the place where he had seen the dead person for the last time. A psychologist, known to the author, hiked again and again in the Odenwald [area in Germany] where her father had been denounced and arrested because of his political convictions during a vacation almost thirty years ago. He had disappeared forever and presumably lost his life in a concentration camp.

Searching for the lost object is typical for the regressive stage and recedes during the adaptive. Nevertheless, the defense mechanism can become resistant in its regressive form. In several studies, E. Stengel investigated the psychopathology of compulsive wandering,[8] which he describes as an irresistible impulse to leave the house and wander around aimlessly.

This condition, usually accompanied by a change in the mental facilities, can last for hours or even days. Usually the mood attached to it is depression, sometimes mania. The appetite is low and there is little need for sleep.[9] Stengel believes he can prove that with such persons "usually the relation to one parent or the parents generally was either completely lacking or was never developed fully,"[10] because they had died early or were separated from the child. In some patients the desire to find the dead parents again was very strong.[11] Stengel could observe that this yearning arose immediately before and after the flight. They perceived the idea that the dead husband was not really dead but alive and that he could perhaps be found by wandering around.[12]

The coping mechanism of searching is particularly observed in case studies of children. This is understandable, since for a young child's mind the separation from a loved one is not much different from death, especially if there is no chance for him personally to experience the reality of death (for example, by attending the funeral). Edith Jacobsen provides very descriptive case studies, one of which shows clearly how waiting for the return of the deceased mother extended into adult life.

Robert, a married man in his thirties, had lost his mother in childbirth toward the end of the oedipal period. The newborn child, a boy, also died on the same day. When the tragic event occurred, the child was completely ignored. He knew that his mother had left for the hospital to have a baby, but nobody informed him about what had happened. The next day he was taken to relatives, where he stayed for some time. Placed in a new environment with grieving adults, the little boy went through a period of helpless confusion, and then a deep loneliness and depression, with feelings of self-estrangement. Neither his father nor his relatives ever gave Robert an explanation of his mother's disappearance. Later on whenever he asked his father what had happened to his mother, the only answer would be: "Your mother was an angel." Unsatisfactory though it was, this answer helped the child to create an utterly glorified, rather mystical picture of his lost "angelic" mother.

Robert moved into his grandmother's house. His conflicts increased when his father took a city apartment, where he would spend his evenings with various mistresses. During this time the lonely child began to develop a family romance. It revolved around fantasies of being the son of an aristocratic British family. In his family romance, a mother figure did not play a particular role. It is of interest that these fantasies had a considerable influence on his appearance, bearing, and behavior, which suggested a British upper-class background.

When Robert lost his father in his early twenties, he immediately married a well-bred intelligent girl, who came from a family socially higher than his own.

Robert had come for treatment because of his recurring states of depression and depersonalization. Their analysis revealed an intensely cathected sado-masochistic fantasy life, which had its origin in violent primal-scene fantasies, aroused by his mother's pregnancy and death. The analytic material showed that these fantasies were linked up with unconscious suspicions that his father might have killed mother and child in the sexual act. These fantasies were so unacceptable that they had to be warded off by a denial of his mother's death. The secrecy that surrounded his mother's sudden disappearance could be explained just as well by the assumption that mother had left his father because of his immorality and worthlessness. How firmly Robert believed this story became clear when [he reported] that every morning he would run down to the mailbox, expecting to get a "special" letter. Each time he would return very much disappointed that again "the letter" had not arrived. The mysterious letter, for the arrival of which he had stubbornly waited as long as he could remember, was a letter from his mother and brother who, as he suspected, lived somewhere in a faraway place, and would one day write and return to him.[13]

As Edith Jacobsen observed, almost all her patients who were orphaned as children or at least had lost one parent, developed a blooming family romance that the parents would return rich, gifted, or of noble birth. From these parents they once had been separated and with them they would be reunited. Those fantasies frequently were the motivation, as in the case of Robert, to search for families and persons who met their imaginations.[14] Such fantasies about a special childhood, where "Heaven lay about us in infancy" (Wordsworth), are frequently also found in young adolescents who are in transition of separation from their parents, as Martha Wolfenstein points out. They develop a nostalgia for the lost childhood which is overestimated in view of the inevitable separation. Wolfenstein contends that in the grief of adults, the nostalgia for the lost paradise of childhood is revived, and yearning and searching is begun to regain this lost state.[15]

6.42 The "new society" as home
An examination of sixteenth- and seventeenth-century hymns concerning death and dying will reveal the various ways in which yearning, searching, and the journey to the

home beyond is expressed. "I wish I were at home and away from the comforts of this world," for example, speaks of the search for a home far exceeding all the comfort this world can provide. Others speak of the pain of separation and to the superelevated land of childhood, dominated by fathers and protected by fathers. The "departure" (Bloch) to a future country is hardly to be found anymore in popular ideology. Many lands are used up, such as the fatherland and motherland, and even the attractiveness of the golden West has ceased. Hope is reduced to the yearning of finding the way back to the common "home." Only among people who have actually lost their homeland, such as refugees, does home still remain a desirous goal that takes on all the more glorious forms the less a fulfillment of the desire is conceivable.

E. Bloch has collected and analyzed the "geographical utopias" under the title "Eldorado and Eden." One of the most important "outlines of a better world" is the Promised Land; "it is waiting behind the desert in a promised yet unexplored splendor." [16] It is the second Eden, after the first was lost. But the Promised Land, which repeatedly has occupied fantasy, even to the time of the Crusades, has a messianic dimension: Only at the end of history will Canaan appear in its full glory. The belief that the earthly paradise could be found somewhere was, according to Bloch, always alive in the Middle Ages and the early Industrial Age. "Even though the *entrance is forbidden, the search for its location, living in its outer vicinity* are permitted and biblical." [17] When this paradise could not be found on earth, the yearnings were aimed at other planets; first at the moon, whose craters J. Kepler still took for huge, walled cities; then at Mars, whose "channels" led to the assumption of a more advanced civilization than ours. This may be one of the reasons the geographical utopias have died; the universes that still represent promise are unattainable in the lifetime of a human being. It is precisely the exhaustion of these geographical utopias that leads to taking only the present earth seriously and, instead of searching for a paradise, striving for a "reconstruction of nature." The geographical utopia is transformed into a temporal one. However, the intention strived for in the idea of the Promised Land is sustained when it is united with the hopes for this world.

Bloch's exposition will have to be taken seriously when we turn to the theologically explicit eschatology. In the search for the coming the geographical component is essential. It cannot be dispensed with as it is in the concept of salvation's coming to realization only in the moment of I-Thou relationship, in mere futurity, or in a transformation of all existing conditions. When hope no longer can speak of a path[18] and eschatology of a home that is also meant geographically, then it is in danger of becoming "disloyal to this earth."

J. Moltmann has included this geographical aspect in his theology of hope under the term "exodus church." That "here we have no lasting city, but we seek the city which is to come" (Heb. 13:14) is a text often chosen for funeral orations, but our life as a "journey" is often understood in this context merely in an individualistic sense and has been all too spiritualized in its symbolic power. Although Moltmann predominantly sees the kingdom of God in sociological relations and therefore defines "salvation" as "realization of the eschatological hope of justice, the humanizing of man, the socializing of humanity, peace for all creation,"[19] he also makes statements in which the geographical world of man receives such eschatological promises: "The expectation of the promised future of the kingdom of God which is coming to man and the world to set them right and create life, makes us ready to expend ourselves unrestrainedly and unreservedly in love and in the work of the reconciliation of the world with God and his future."[20] Nevertheless, Moltmann wants to understand "the home of reconciliation" only in "new creation out of nothing."

Whether the eschatological symbol of home still can be retained in spite of its misuse through ideologies has yet to be examined. It would be regrettable if this symbol were restricted only to the home of the family and thus to merely personal relations. It is an important function to regain the aspect of future which permits "home" then to become an eschatological declaration. Theology and psychology share the common goal of ceasing to seek the "home" in the past. When psychology undertakes the difficult process of making conscious the unconscious search for the home from the past, in which the "world was still in order" since there was a father and a mother present, it at the same time tries to make the patient recognize that there can be no return to this "land of childhood." What is searched for with "home" cannot lie in the past. Theology has the same intention; it too must make clear that there can be no return to the *status integritatis*. Psychoanalysis and theology aim at bringing the finality of separation to recognition in grief: in spite of all the searching the deceased who represented "home" is lost. If he were to return, the unreality of a ghost would cling to him, because the estrangement between him and the survivor has already begun.

The critical aspect of "home" also directs itself against any attempt that evokes the hope for returning "home" after a separation of many years. The place once representing "home" has changed so radically that it makes the returning person a stranger; it disappoints because it matches neither the memories nor the glorifications that have developed from these memories. Even if this place with its people had never changed, the person coming home is no longer the same and therefore a home of a different nature, not with the quality of the old, would be necessary. If a lost home is made an absolute goal, theology must develop all its critical power to oppose effectively all illusions and inevitable disappointments.

However, the criticism implied in the eschatological statement "home" cannot be made at the expense of its motivating power. It is not enough to criticize returning to the home as ideology if these desires and yearnings are not directed toward the search for a "new home" where these illusory ideas do not have to be lost and suppressed but can be pressed for their realization. Everything positive contained in the old home must be retrieved in the new home. If home on principle exists only as something past, then the return to it can be understood only as a worldless return to a place no longer existing. If, on the other hand, the concept "home" develops future hopes, then it can keep the "loyalty to the earth." If, on the contrary, the searching component of the eschatological idea is taken away, the yearning inherent in all future-oriented activities, then every new home is condemned to contain from the beginning the element of being lost. Only the searching for a home promises its final fulfillment.

6.5 The mechanism: mania

6.51 Psychological aspects

Usually we refer to mania in the context of manic-depressive behavior disorders. Like depression, mania characterizes a syndrome and is not simply identical with euphoria or elation. This syndrome may occur in a wide variety of disorders but is found in its purest form in manic-depressive behavior disorders.

The basic affect of mania is euphoria; the patient feels happy and unconcerned; even heavy strokes of fate do not affect him. Some patients entertain extraordinary notions about their power and importance which enable them to involve themselves in senseless and risky enterprises. Frequently the euphoric mood is accompanied by troublesome irritability. Contrary to depressed patients, manic persons are extremely self-confident. With such feelings of magical omnipotence and supreme self-esteem goes an extraordinary lack of guilt and shame, and often even a denial of realistic danger or actual loss. Accompanying the euphoric, expansive, and irritable mood of manics is the accelerated pace of psychomotor activity. Frequently the increase of verbal production is striking, with logorrhea and its counterpart in thinking, a flight of ideas.

Melanie Klein, based on some statements by Freud to be discussed later, identifies mania as a defense mechanism against depression. In her opinion, the basic affect of mania is omnipotence, which is linked with the mechanism of denial. Mania gives the ego the impression that it can punish the lost object by killing it; this is the most extreme expression of disparaging the significance of the loss.[1] The special form of denial consists in the fact that the ego denies the emotional significance of an external event: "Even though it would admit that a death occurred, the ego defends the notion that this is of no significance."[2]

In grief, the defensive mechanism of mania can be traced in three different forms. The first two belong more to the regressive stage, while the third is more obvious in the adaptive stage. S. Freud has underscored the first two forms, even though not specifically in grief. According to him, mania, for one thing, is a temporary triumph of the ego over the aggressive superego; secondly, it is a happy merger of the two. The later notion was especially emphasized by Lewin. K. Abraham has indicated above all the adaptive form of mania in the form of joy in having finally overcome the painful separation.[3]

(1) In order to understand the first aspect of mania, the *feeling of triumph*, we have to go back to *Totem and Taboo*, which here too plays a key role in the analysis of grief. There Freud has pointed out that at the act of sacrificing the totem animal, the murdered animal is bewailed and lamented. But soon after this mourning there follows loud festival gaity. Freud then gives an insight into the nature of the holiday:

A holiday is a permitted, or rather a prescribed excess, a solemn violation of a prohibition. People do not commit the excesses, which at all times have characterized holidays, as a result of an order to be in a holiday mood, but because in the very nature of a holiday there is excess; the holiday mood is brought about by the release of what is otherwise forbidden.[4]

Those celebrations owed their origin to the mythological event of triumph over the primal father whose murder is repeated in the sacrificial act of the totem animal.[5]

In "Mourning and Melancholia" this triumphant feeling over the father is now internalized and turns into mania. From Freud's psychoanalytic point of view the content of mania is no different from that of melancholia; both the disorders are wrestling with the same "father complex," only in melancholia the ego has succumbed to it, whereas in mania it has mastered the complex or thrust it aside. This state of triumph and relief lasts until remorse and reproaches return again, just as after the murder of the primal father. Freud compares mania with the feelings of "some poor devil" who, "by winning a large sum of money, is suddenly relieved from perpetual anxiety about his daily bread."[6] "When mania supervenes, the ego must have surmounted the loss of the object (or the mourning over the loss, or perhaps the object itself)."[7] "Whereupon the whole amount of anticathexis which the painful suffering of melancholia drew from the ego and 'bound' has become available. Besides this, the maniac plainly shows us that he has become free from the object by whom his suffering was caused, for he runs after new object-cathexes, like a starving man after bread."[8]

Freud was of the opinion that no such form of mania can be detected in grief itself. The reason for this, he believed, lies in the fact that recognition of the death's occurrence is enacted in steps, and thus the experience of loss is not so agonizing that the regressive mechanism of mania would have to be exerted.[9] Melanie Klein's experiences, however, indicated that "feelings of triumph are inevitably tied even to normal grief, and the result is a slowing down of the work of mourning, or rather they contribute to the difficulties and pain the bereaved experiences."[10] Since mania represents flight from a breakdown, it can inhibit the work of mourning. Generally speaking, however, it is rather an active mechanism.

Just as it is not possible to maintain this condition of release and relief all the time in a manic-depressive disorder, neither is it possible in the grief process. Mostly the condition alternates between depressive and joyful moods. C. M. Parkes describes the case of a widow who constantly oscillates between agonized searching for the deceased and a temporarily joyful finding.[11] The following case illustration by Fulcomer depicts this manic state of a bereaved:

A young executive of a publishing company, thirty-four years of age, was the bereaved man in this case. Immediately following the burial service he assisted relatives from out of town in getting to the railroad station and catching their train. When he returned to his apartment, his mother-in-law had prepared dinner, but the bereaved man ate very lightly. He was up from the table early and proceeded to prepare both of his children for bed. His father-in-law left for his own home and the bereaved husband walked to the street with him and talked with him until he had departed. Afterward he just sat around not seeming to know what to do with himself.

The next morning the bereaved man was up at his regular time, cheerful and active. He insisted that he make the breakfast and that he prepare the children's food "just as D. (his deceased wife) would have done." And he said to his mother-in-law, "Mom, I'm going back to work right this morning. That will surprise them, but the more quickly I get back to normal the better." He breezed into the office and acted as if nothing had happened. His colleagues noticed that he was trying to keep busy and stay away from them. He talked only about business. Naturally they tried to act as if they expected him to be back at work already. This behavior was continued for the remainder of the morning. The bereaved husband left for lunch a few minutes before the others, and he returned early. After lunch he appeared to have lost the energy that he had possessed that morning. He would call the secretary, dictate a letter (having a hard time keeping his mind on it), and then decide to leave other dictation until later.

Shortly after 4:00 P.M. he changed completely. He dictated seven letters and worked like a trojan until quitting time. On the way out of the office he asked someone to ride with him. While driving home he spoke about bowling at a regular Friday-night session. All the way to his home he appeared cheerful. When he arrived at his apartment, the bereaved man played with his children, insisted that he be allowed to help prepare the evening meal, and ate heartily of it.

After the meal was completed, he helped prepare the children for the night, aided with the dishes, called his father-in-law on the telephone and visited a storage concern to make arrangements for moving his deceased wife's parents. His mother-in-law thought that it was harder for her than it was for him.

In the morning the bereaved husband was up at his usual time. He helped with the children but ate little breakfast. He spoke little and appeared depressed. As he left the apartment he said: "I'll be all right, Mom. But sometimes it is hard to see how I can get along without D." . . .

During the entire morning, the bereaved man appeared depressed to his associates in the office. He did his work, but he was not up to his normal ability in either efficiency or speed. He spoke only when necessary. Later he approached the desk of a friend and said, "Would you mind if we ate lunch together? I have been feeling discouraged all morning. Maybe what I need is company." These two men, plus two more intimate friends, ate lunch together and had a jolly time. The bereaved husband seemed to have forgotten the gloomy aspects of his situation. All that afternoon he appeared cheerful, worked rapidly, and went out of his way to chat with people.

But by the time he had reached his apartment, the bereaved man was again depressed and definitely showed it. Before the evening meal was ready, he picked up his violin and tried to play but soon laid it down in discouragement. He drummed on the piano for a few minutes. Next he tried to play with the children, but even that appeared unnatural. Suddenly he stood up and said to no one in particular, "D. I have to get over this somehow." He stood by the window a few minutes and his mother-in-law noticed him wipe his eyes.

When dinner was served, however, he again seemed cheerful and active. He discussed his children and their future. The next morning the bereaved man awoke in good spirits and at the breakfast table he informed his mother-in-law that he had had his first good sleep. Only for a short period before noon did his associates in the office observe him to be depressed. At lunch he sat at a table with a group of young men and women and seemed to enjoy himself thoroughly. The remainder of the day, both at the office and at his home, he maintained his cheerful appearance. The next day too, the bereaved man was depressed for only a short time. As he relaxed after the evening meal, his mother-in-law noted a definite appearance of depression.

During the next two weeks, the bereaved husband experienced brief periods of deep depression; but after the first few days, they did not come every day. He kept busy and remained cheerful. He attempted to resume all of his former activities, but was not able to enjoy them as before.[12]

This case illustration demonstrates, besides the alternating response of depressive and manic behavior, a hypermotility during the manic stage. It confirms the generally recognized observation that manic persons are characterized by the ambitious undertakings shown in their daily routine; they overload themselves with unrelated activities, only to let them drop abruptly with a sudden loss of interest.

At the same time, the case study mentioned above reveals that manic disorder can be the reason the work of mourning is not carried out appropriately. It is true that periods of

depression gradually become shorter and occur less frequently. This, however, is obviously achieved only through
compulsively repressing all memories of the dead: the
apologies of the bereaved made to the dead for his behavior,
since this seemed to him the only way to cope with the loss,
indicates how much the bereaved is aware of the violence in
his behavior. The deceased is repudiated, not integrated.

(2) In *Group Psychology and the Analysis of the Ego*
(1922), Freud understood mania as suppression of the
ego-ideal,[13] but in addition had extended this interpretation:
"It results always in an experience of triumph if something in
the ego coincides with the ego-ideal";[14] that opens the door to
understanding mania as the *merger of ego and superego*. S.
Radó interprets this fusion by explaining it as a repetition of
the baby's early experience at his mother's breast: He becomes
one with the good object, represented by the mother. Just as
self-punishment in depression yields reconciliation with the
love object, so hunger is followed by the elation of satisfaction. The ego regains its self-confidence by repeating in the
fantasies of mania the infantile sequence of anxiety, hunger,
and satisfaction at the breast of the love object.[15]

This merger of ego and mother, which for Radó and Lewin
represents a substitute for the ego-ideal and any love object, is
divided into an "oral triad" by Lewin. The oral triad consists
of the wish to incorporate the love object, the wish to be
consumated by it, and certain forms of sleep.[16] The first two
mechanisms need not occupy us at this point; they will be
considered subsequently under the coping mechanism of
incorporation.[17] At this point, it is important to take a closer
look at the connection between mania and sleep as observed
by Lewin.

Already in *Group Psychology and the Analysis of the Ego*
(1922), Freud referred to the connection between mania and
sleep, both of which have in common that ego and superego
coincide almost fully.[18] Lewin sees the genesis of this merger
in the deep and, as he assumes, dreamless sleep into which
the infant falls after oral satisfaction. Only with the increasing
perception of the environment and added desires is the
"satiated" sleep superseded by a sleep in which the memories

of the day and repressed desires make themselves conspicuous.[19] Adults, even in the regressive state of mania, will hardly experience such a sleep of dreamless satisfaction, but nevertheless, dreams of a cheerful mood with a lot of playing as in "innocent" childhood will occur. Corresponding to the flight of ideas during the day is a "dream flight" at night, in which many scenes supersede one another rather quickly.[20]

A "good" sleep as result of satisfaction can in the regressive stage of mania provoke the desire to be reunited with the lost love object through dying. Just as there is a "good" sleep, there is also a "good" death, which is considered a state of nirvana and a place of pacified tranquility.[21]

As in a "good" sleep, ego and superego, ego and lost love object are reunited in a "good" death. As Bibring writes, the suicide fantasies about the "good" death are without signs of aggression and self-destruction. "'The ego let itself die.' Death represents sleep and peace, a kind of nirvana. Dying is identical with the need to be no more an 'ego'; but it is not the need to destroy one's own self brutally or to punish it. A young man wanted to go to sleep and freeze to death in the ice and snow of his beloved mountains; another desired to swim way out in a lake until he was exhausted and then go down tired and peacefully. A young girl, every time she was in a depressed mood, had the fantasy of drowning in the sea and her body dissolving in the ocean and of being 'absorbed' by it."[22] In Bibring's understanding this is the unconscious desire to return to the mother's womb and to let one's own ego be consummated by an omnipotent medium.

Martha Wolfenstein describes the reaction of a fifteen-year-old girl to the sudden death of her mother, who died of a brain hemorrhage. Coping with her death was extremely difficult for the girl because at that time she appeared to be in an incipient phase of adolescent detachment from and devaluation of the mother. This double separation triggered a reversal of the adolescent process of detachment from the mother. There was instead an intensified cathexis of the image of the mother with a strong regressive pull toward a more childish and dependent relation. On the eve of her birthday, the girl went for a long ramble by herself through springtime fields and experienced a dreamy euphoria, a kind of oceanic feeling. Wolfenstein interprets this feeling of oneness with nature as a symbolic realization of the wish to be reunited with the mother. She concludes this from the heavy disappointment on the girl's return. Being confronted at home with her still grieving father precipitated the feeling that the wish was not coming true.[23]

Additional cases where death was understood as reunion are reported by others. For example, one twenty-nine-year-old man wished to die, partly as the wish to go to sleep, partly as the necessity to be united with his dead brother and his (still living) mother.[24] Among the more or less conscious reasons Moss and Hamilton identified as motivations for suicide, hope for a greater future satisfaction, including a lasting reunion with the lost love object was one of the most important.[25] In the theological paragraph we will indicate how religious ideas can intensify the wish for reunion through suicide or "letting-oneself-die."

(3) The third form of mania emerging, besides the temporary surmounting of a hostile superego and the merger of ego and ego-ideal, is the *feeling of relief* if the bereaved has the impression of having largely overcome the loss. Where the death had a lesser impact on the bereaved it appears as unadmitted satisfaction "to have gotten off the hook" once more and escaped death, as a satisfying sensation which not only older persons gain from obituaries and from attending funerals. The bereaved too may have such experiences. However, for him the actual feeling of relief is experienced only when he has the impression that by and large he has coped with the loss. When mania is mentioned in stress research, it always refers to this variation of mania, the experience of having gone through a stressful event and having survived.

Abraham, who appears to be very much influenced by Freud in his study of pathological mania, has underscored exclusively the relief experienced in successful adaptation in grief.

Namely, it can be observed that the mourner who, with the help of the "work of mourning," gradually detaches his libido from the deceased feels at the same time that he succeeds in this detachment an *increased sexual desire.* This is also expressed in a more sublimated form in a heightened adventurous spirit, expansion of the spiritual circle of interests, etc. The increase of the libidinous desire can, depending on the individual course of the work of mourning, start after a shorter or a longer period following the object-loss.[26]

6.52 Sociological implications

All three forms of coping with grief through the mechanism of mania are also in a certain way socially promoted.

(1) Even though our society does not know the ritual laughter demanded in particular in less differentiated societies, nevertheless, the funeral ceremony in part serves the purpose of evoking euphoria and of *repressing grief in this way for a short period.* It is true that since the last century the customs of the death watch, which were mostly connected with a great alcohol consumption, have disappeared. But the use of alcohol to repress agonizing memories is still a half-legitimate form used to create a temporary mania. Just like the "saturated sleep," intoxication through alcohol is a means to becoming like the deceased and uniting with him.

As the study by Clayton *et al.* maintains, an increased alcohol intake in the year following bereavement was mentioned by about 50 percent of the interviewed widows.[27] The possibility cannot be excluded that as the limit of social acceptability is exceeded, the result might be called a pathological drinking pattern with some similarities to mania.

Another type of mania that provides a temporary release from stress is something generally called "black humor." As Jackson observes, sometimes at the gathering of the bereaved in funeral homes or cemeteries, there is a use of humor that at first seems inappropriate.[28] Martha Wolfenstein in her study of humor indicates (what Freud already had observed in some notes) that humor is used to disguise a painful reality, and bring it down to size so that a large and painful experience can be handled.[29]

(2) The individual ideas of reuniting with the mother, the

merger between ego and love object, are socially supported at the grave, especially the family burial place. W. Fuchs indicates that casket and grave represent maternal symbols. The grave not only symbolizes the return to the mother's womb, but beyond that the enclosure in the maternal body of nature. The family burial plot intensifies this symbolism, because it further indicates the return to the elemental family organization. "Such a return to the midst of the family through a reunion with the ancestors is a widespread motive of all religions and is part of the most important consolation mechanisms."[30]

(3) Finally, the adaptive aspect of mania is socially regulated through rules, according to which a bereaved can participate again in joyful celebrations, in a wedding or a party, at what is considered the appropriate time. Here too the formerly strict conventions have been diminished; it is left to the individual mourner to decide when he feels the need for such activity after such an event. This means also that the regulations have become invalid which prevented the bereaved from throwing himself all too soon into a variety of social activities which serve only to repress his almost unbearable experiences. On the other hand, even today social conventions implying at what time a bereaved should no longer exclude himself from such social activities are in existence.

6.53 Joy

The early church attempted to understand death as a joyful event, contrary to the death customs of the Greek and Roman cultures, and to express this in its practice. The ambivalence of such a practice can be detected in the description by St. Augustine, cited above,[31] of his own exemplary behavior at the grave—not showing any sign of grief in public, while privately making every effort to initiate the process of grief. Only two examples of the early church's effort to identify death as a joyful event will be mentioned here.

In Greek and Roman cultures the actual memorial day for the dead was the birthday of the deceased. The remembrance frequently was celebrated with an offering at the graveside.

Christian practice changed this custom. Here the day of death became the actual *dies natalis* and, like a birthday, was celebrated as a joyful event. Presumably, the bases for this practice were the celebration of memorial days for martyrs as holidays as well as passages from the New Testament, primarily from the Gospel of John, in which death and rebirth are closely connected.[32]

The pagan practice, customary everywhere, in which the procession to the grave was accompanied by wailing and musical instruments, was replaced step by step. In the Christian funeral ceremony increasingly the dirge and lamentation, and also the musical instruments, were thrust aside. The Apostolic Constitutions, which represented the practice in the Eastern Roman Empire in the middle of the fourth century, recommended instead the singing of psalms. Several authors of that time report a psalm-singing, alternating between monks and men on the one side and women and girls on the other. From the West as well the use of psalms at funerals is reported, especially after the persecution had ceased and public funerals for Christians were possible. We have proof of the use of Psalm 23 ("The Lord is my shepherd"), Psalm 32 (forgiveness of sins), Psalm 115 (praise of the Lord), and Psalm 116 (thanksgiving for recovery and vows). These are not psalms of wailing, as we see; they rather express mainly thanks and joy.[33]

The hymns referring to death and dying found in our hymnbooks are full of the disparagement of this world and filled with hope for a fulfilled and blessed life in the world beyond. Since some of the hymns from the sixteenth century are still part of the Protestant hymnbook for the church, they might be considered an official representation of theological doctrine still relevant today. The most distinct expression of this notion is the interpretation of the word by Paul that "for me to live is Christ, and to die is gain" (Phil. 1:21), a passage found in a number of hymns referring to death and eternal life. But what constituted for Paul strength for the present life now becomes fundamental for a future existence. What for him meant renunciation of his previous aim in life is understood in these hymns as physical death.

Hymns in which death is interpreted as a transition into a better existence and the world is painted in dark colors must cause misunderstandings today, since they express a confidence and faith in which neither death nor the Last Judgment are considered threatening. They witness to a deep trust in the help of Christ, in contrast to which the forces of destruction and guilt no longer have any weight. Today such a notion is hardly understood in its depth, and thus the transition appears to be a passage into a better world without any problems. However, to understand this transition as a joyful event would far exceed the belief and perception of death of the average church member.

In dealing with the psychological aspects of mania we came across two images in which, for the bereaved, death is regarded as fulfillment and joy if it is understood as reunion or as sleep. We shall now pursue these two statements theologically.

(1) Describing death as union, as the ego's being caught up in a comprehensive unity, resembles the mystical union with God. The release from the confinement of one's own existence and the yearning to be permeated by an all-encompassing power is a manic experience. What can be only temporarily accomplished in this manic union is promised as a permanent condition by death.

The merger of the ego with the supreme superego or the ego-ideal was described by M. Wolfenstein in the case of the nineteen-year-old girl who had lost her mother as an "oceanic feeling." Freud thought of religious experience as such a feeling, but attempted to explain it as the result of the child's helplessness and longing for the father.[34] He described this merger of ego and love object in the love experience and compared it with the way the ego can identify with the Christ figure (as in religion) or with the general in command (as in an army).[35] But since he saw the influence of the father as the constant element, not at all subject to historical change, rather than making it clear that the behavioral mode of the father is shaped by society and religion, he did not pursue the question of the theological significance of the ego-superego fusion any further.

A second form of the merging of ego and all-encompassing unity has not yet been recognized sufficiently theologically. The question could be raised whether the death instinct ought not to be considered precisely in this context: as the ego's renunciation of staying alive, and, instead, making the attempt to return to an all-encompassing unconscious condition. What speaks for the close bond between "oceanic feeling" and death instinct is the fact that Freud originally identified the death instinct as the "nirvana principle." This is a notion that expresses in a particular way the absorption of the ego by an immaterial nil, though not without quality, which equates with the experience mystics have described as "annihilation."

The allergic attitude assumed by dialectical theology toward mysticism[36] has, as far as it can be observed, prevented a discussion between theology and psychoanalysis about the religious elements in the "oceanic feeling," the "state of nirvana," and the "death instinct." We cannot make up for it at this point. Nevertheless, we should indicate the aspect of union, since we deal here in particular with the assessment of a notion of death that is rather often advocated. Summarizing, it can be described as the absorption by a greater, all-encompassing unity, whether it is God, nature, or matter. At least the positive element of such a notion shall be mentioned: Here the separated and isolated individual is incorporated into a greater abundance and released from his privatized circumstances.

Brunner especially has concerned himself with the aspects of release and joy in eschatological statements. For him the goal of world history also includes the "realization of the human desire for happiness and life."[37] Hence the perfected end of creation is represented by the symbol of a marriage or a festive meal. Brunner underscores that "this joy consists not merely in the negation of negations, in deliverance from death and sorrow, but includes also the sense of fulfillment of life."[38] He reacts negatively only to the interpretation of the symbol of marriage along erotic lines, without the fellowship of persons in mutual encounter (just as the Old Testament protests against the association of cult and eros, and the New Testament does not at all feature erotic symbols. Besides, "the erotic is in its very essence a mystery of the individual and private universe—something withdrawn from public and social life").[39] Even though the somewhat aseptic image of the eschatological marriage needs certain corrections, we will have to agree with Brunner that the image of joy and (marriage) feast is an essential part of the eschatological images. That there are critical judgments to be made can be seen in some theological publications attacking our ability to celebrate.[40]

In this context, Paul Tillich has to be named; he thought it legitimate to apply the term "blessed" (*makarios, beatus*) to God and to the believer. He defends the thesis: "The Divine Life is the eternal conquest of the negative; this is its blessedness. Eternal blessedness is not a state of immovable perfection—the philosophers of becoming are right in rejecting such a concept. But the Divine Life is blessedness through fight and victory."[41] This is precisely the nature of mania—that it can only be fully understood against the background of overcoming suffering and guilt.

(2) Just as the early Christians could celebrate death as they did the joyous event of birth, they also spoke without hesitation of death as sleep. Even Luther could write ingenuously in a hymn: "Death has become my sleep."[42] A particular sleep is thought of here, the "sleep of the just," not disturbed by nightmares, a sleep not disturbed by anxieties of punishment, a sleep one could wish the sick neighbor as well. To rest in peace is a blessing not self-evident and initiated by the experience of the dead who cannot find peace.

If we follow the presentation by Althaus, then the Lutheran Orthodoxy, under the influence of Calvin, has not sustained the notions of death as sleep. It has rather, like Calvin, advocated a separation of body and soul, in which it could rely on isolated statements by Luther. In general it was spoken of as an eternal life of the soul, even if the soul did not yet live in the full presence of God and its fulfillment. Orthodoxy expresses itself in this respect much more cautiously than many church hymns of that time. They very much yield to an individual eschatology which promises the individual a state of grace immediately after death.[43]

THE NARCISSISTIC COPING MECHANISMS

If one speaks today of an intermediate state between death and general resurrection as a "sleep" of the dead, then most likely this sleep could be understood as analogous to manic conditions. It could be compared to a kind of intoxication in which a number of pleasant images appear without the possibility of stopping the rapid sequences of imaginings and reaching a sense of reality. The close connection between joy and sleep could explain best the state of being between death and realization of the "new society."

7. The aggressive coping mechanisms

The coping mechanisms in which aggression represents a rather strong component include the following: (1) the protest against death and the lament over it which easily can turn into accusation of the dead person; (2) the defensive mechanism of searching for the person who is to be blamed for the death or at least has not prevented it; and, finally, (3) the defense mechanism by which the mourner identifies with the deceased and accuses himself of being partially responsible for the death.

It is contested in scientific discussion as to how adequate it is to speak of aggression in grief. That ambivalence and hence aggression toward the dead person exists has not been clearly answered by S. Freud, as we saw earlier, even though he perceives them in the mourning rites of "primitive" tribes.[1] E. Jacobsen, who equates grief with sad mood, formulates somewhat vaguely: "Angry and sad mood . . . commonly exclude each other, although it frequently happens that aggression is used as a defense against the painful experience of sadness."[2] Presumably it is more accurate with respect to the role of aggression in grief to speak with Parkes of feelings of anger and resentment, which normally are nothing more than a general irritation and frustration accompanied by reproaches against everyone and everything that does not have to suffer such a loss. However, it seems that in order to master this general irritation and frustration, the bereaved employs the device of aggression, which then is directed toward specific persons, such as the dead, "death agents," relatives, or the bereaved himself.

With respect to the frequency of self-reproaches and accusations of others there is little data available. In an unidentified sample, Marris found, among 15 percent of the widows, resentments toward the dead; among 13 percent, accusations of others; and among 11 percent, guilt feelings.[3] In the study by Clayton et al., 13 percent of the interviewed suffered from self-reproaches.[4] A. H. Kutscher mentions in an interview of a social group, not identified, that about 40 percent of the survivors reported guilt feelings.[5]

Among psychiatric patients who suffered a loss through death, the percentage is considerably higher. Forty-three percent of Parkes's patients accused others, and 79 percent condemned themselves.[6] E. Lindemann found hostile feelings among 50 percent of the bereaved who were able to cope with their loss without further complications; in pathological cases of grief, however, the percentage was 63 percent.[7] Although Marris could not detect essential differences with respect to proportions of accusations toward the dead person, other persons, or oneself, it is quite conceivable that the aggression toward the dead is weaker than toward others or one's own self because one is obliged to love and devotion toward the deceased.[8] Yet, it just as well could be said that now the latent aggressiveness toward the departed is expressed much more overtly, as is frequently the case at the separation of two people in love.[9]

The studies mentioned above, as well as a number of ethnological findings, make it seem undoubted that aggressions occur in grief, even if they are not acted out in such a violent form as is frequently the case in less self-controlled societies. We have to agree with Bowlby when he contends that aggression alone does not make grief pathological: "One of the main characteristics of pathological grief is nothing less than the incapability of expressing openly the effort to find the lost object again and to scold at it."[10]

7.1 The mechanisms: protest and lamentation

7.11 Psychological aspects

If the bereaved see the cause for their present painful condition primarily in the deceased, and therefore bring reproaches against him, this is, according to Bowlby's theory, a reactivation of separation anxiety. The abandoned child primarily sees in the absent mother the cause for his loneliness. He cries to bring back the mother; he develops hostile feelings; he reacts angrily to the returning mother in order to prevent her from leaving him again.[11] The purpose of all these reproaches and accusations is, as Bowlby writes: "Let us find the guilty; they seem to run away; let us set right what is wrong, let us restore what had been lost, let us make sure that it is never repeated."[12]

The protest reaction to loss, the vehement attempt to regain the object, represents an important therapeutic step in coping with grief. The more intensive the efforts, the more certain it is that the bereaved realizes that the love object is irretrievably lost. While, for instance, the mechanism of searching still purposely assumes the lost object must be found again, the protest without result forces the inevitable realization that the lost love object cannot be regained. The emergence of painful yearning is an essential step toward reality testing and the willingness to give up the love object.[13]

A case study by Fulcomer can exemplify how a general attitude of protest is combined with accusations of the dead:

The bereaved person was the young wife, aged twenty-nine, of a sporting goods salesman. In the immediate stage she had made a lachrymose response (the steady-weeping, nonspeaking variety). After this she was taken by a brother to her home where her parents, another brother, and a sister-in-law awaited her. While driving to her home she did not weep or utter a word. When she arrived at her home, the other brother came out to the car to meet her. Immediately she began weeping violently, crying, "It isn't right. He was only thirty-two years old and was just getting started in business. I can't live without him." She wept so violently while making these protests that much of what she said could not be understood. She continued this violent weeping and protesting for over forty minutes. By this time she no longer had the physical energy to continue her energetic weeping, and relatively quiet sobbing replaced it.

After her brother had told her: "You must get control of yourself," soon the weeping ceased and the wife remained quiet. She did remark to her sister-in-law: "You are lucky, you still have your husband."

When the meal was ready, they tried to persuade the bereaved woman to eat something. This immediately brought on another scene of loud weeping and protests. She again accused her husband's employer of allowing him to use gasoline for cleaning, she accused herself of previously discouraging her husband from taking the position as manager of a store. This had continued for twenty minutes when the father insisted that a doctor be called to help to quiet her. When the doctor came she threw an awful fit and cried that she wasn't going to take any dope to make her forget her husband. By the time the doctor had gone she was quite exhausted and willing to eat some food.

Soon after that the minister came and then she let herself go again. She cried and cried, blaming herself and just about everyone else for her husband's being killed. Without her knowing it, someone dissolved one of the pills the doctor left into a glass of water and she drank that. Soon afterward she went to bed.

The next morning she appeared to be extremely despondent. Her two brothers and she drove to the funeral director's parlor. The bereaved wife indulged in another scene of violent weeping and protesting as soon as they arrived at the funeral home. It became necessary for the brothers to return her to the house. Twice that morning, both times when friends called, the bereaved wife burst into violent weeping and protesting. And four times that afternoon, as well as twice the same evening, she repreated her periods of energetic weeping and protesting. During the periods in betweeen she appeared extremely gloomy and dejected. The following day, too, was marked by fits of weeping and protesting and periods of complete despondency. Twice during the funeral service and once during the burial service, the bereaved wife wept violently. Further periods of violent weeping and protesting occurred when she returned to her home.[14]

Such waves of pain, despair, and protest may last until complete physical exhaustion sets in. They emerge especially frequently during the first time of bereavement and become increasingly rare. Each mentioning of the loss can trigger them again. This is one of the reasons the bereaved often refuses to talk about the death or to accept any kind of consolation. If family members and the minister are capable of understanding this need for immediate avoidance of pain, then this might reduce their helplessness and prevent their withdrawing from the bereaved. They will be able to sit quietly with him to share his grief. Words at such a time are less important than supportive presence.[15] Before Job's friends began to commiserate with him and comfort him, "they sat with him on the ground seven days and seven nights, and no one spoke a word to him, for they saw that his suffering was very great" (Job 2:13).

Beyond protest and complaint, the complaint can turn into accusation. The bereaved is full of resentments, "because he left me alone, precisely now when I need him most." The death is felt as a personal insult; it seems as if the deceased had left purposely with the intention of abandoning his family. Such emotions about abandonment and deprivation and resentment are more frequent on an unconscious level, as can be inferred from the answers of bereaved persons.[16]

Other examples for the accusation that the dead person has acted malevolently were found by Parkes. He reports on a widow, the second wife of the deceased's, who felt offended by his death: "He looked so happy in his death that it made me think that he was united with her [the first wife]."[17] As Anne Philipe wrote in her journal:

Sometimes I resent the fact that you have died. You have deserted, you have abandoned me. Because of you I can no longer bear the gray skies, the November rains, the last golden leaves, and the black, bare trees, in which I used to see the promise of spring.[18]

As Caruso noted, the aggression in the reproach "How could you leave me" can also express itself in the attempt to devalue the deceased.[19] He is disparaged in his importance for the bereaved. He is treated as if he were totally unimportant for the survivor. This can be made explicit in some outwardly demonstrated indifference; just as a child punishes the bad object, so the bereaved punishes the deceased by ignoring him. He purposely neglects the embellishment of the funeral and the care for the casket in order to retaliate against him for his disloyalty. The bereaved might give away or sell belongings of the deceased to take revenge on him in this way.

7.12 Sociological implications

Protest and complaint in view of death are quite customary in less differentiated societies. Goody, to mention only one example for ethnological material, describes in his report about the mourning customs among the Lodagaa, a West African tribe, the announcement of the death that occurred. The moment of death is announced with a loud plaintive cry by the female relatives. Soon afterward xylophones are played to inform people living further away. The sound of the xylophones is heard until the end of the funeral. The loud laments last throughout the entire funeral ceremony; they are full of hostility toward the dead who has left his family.[20]

The world of the Old and New Testaments also knows the lamentation for the dead. It constitutes loud shouting (in Mic. 1:8, the prophet's grief, depicted as mourning for the dead, is compared with the lamentation of the jackals and the mourning of the ostriches) and weeping, both of which are then replaced by a song of lamentation for the dead, as David lamented Abner when he was buried (II Sam. 3:32). The lamentation before the corpse in the house of mourning seems to have been the original practice; it started immediately after the death occurred. The lamentation is performed either standing or lying in front of the bier. The second form takes place in front of the house, on the street. If we read in Eccl. 12:5, "because man goes to his eternal home, and the mourners go about the streets," we presumably have to picture a rhythmic circling of the bier, a pattern that can still be traced today in Arabic customs.

The third form is the lamentation on the way to the grave and at the grave itself. This is described for us in the Old Testament at the funeral of Abner (II Sam. 3:31-34). The mourners walk in front of the bier on the way to the grave. David follows the bier and only at the grave he acts as singer and sings his lamentation in the immediate proximity of the grave. As David's wailing and mourning for Saul, Jonathan, and the other warriors who died in the battle of Gilboa demonstrates, lamentations also can be held far from the deceased.

If we want to imagine vividly the *situation of the lamentation*, naturally we must then *call to mind* the ceremonies with which we became familiar at the beginning; they in part have become gestures of pain accompanying the rites. Then we see the wailing and weeping women barefoot, wrapped in rough clothes, with streaming hair, rushing into the death chamber. Frequently they are described in an entirely different way: they enter in deep silence, as if they did not yet know of the death and only at the sight of the corpse they utter a terrible cry. Then the ghastly lamentation begins: they cower down on the floor in dull pain and cast dust on their head, or they swing in a passionate dance around the bier, pulling their hair and beating their chests and cheeks. The sound of wild cries of lamentation are heard until the waves of excitement are calmed; deep silence falls, and in a sudden inspiration one of the women rises and begins the song of lamentation. How much is pose in these expressions of pain, how much intoxication produced by the power of the hour, cannot be determined.[21]

Lamentations for the dead form a special literary style, which must be distinguished from the songs of lamentation. It is preserved only in a few fragments in its original form (lamentation for Abner, II Sam. 3:33-34; for Zedekiah, Jer. 38:22; David's lamentation for the fallen warriors of Gilboa, II Sam. 1:19-27; the song of the "reaper death," Jer. 9:20-21). It is also found with regard to the political realm as lamentation about Israel and Jerusalem and used as song of derision by Isaiah and Ezekiel.

The mourning of the dead in ancient Israel was not a part of the Jahweh cult, for death represents the final, irrevocable termination of life. The underworld (sheol) to which the deceased descends does not belong to the kingdom of Jahweh.[22] It is possible neither to remember Jahweh in death, nor to call his name in prayer. Hence the mourner would not be able to turn to Jahweh and ask him to have mercy upon the deceased. Accordingly, the lamentations lack any mention of the name of God and any expression of hope. The deceased is praised for his distinct qualities; the kind of death he suffered is described; and the feelings mentioned that bind the mourner to the lost person.

Contrary to this, our culture knows hardly an opportunity for protest, lamentation, and for an active "acting out." If the outbursts are too violent, a doctor is called (as the case illustration by Fulcomer proves), and some sedatives are administered. The reason such an acting out does not take place is to be seen less in the fact that love and devotion for the deceased forbid public reproaches and other ambivalent expressions against the dead than in the cultural attitude that death is natural and final.

Nevertheless, it cannot be said in general that death is accepted in Western societies without complaint and protest, and that no reproaches are made against the dead person. Such a protest can be detected most likely in children and adolescents, as J. Bowlby and M. Wolfenstein have shown.[23] For children and young persons, the deceased continues to exist, and death is not a natural, but rather a fortuitous event. Something similar is exemplified by Italo-Americans. For them death is a tragic event, inflicted by some religious power, yet with which free communication takes place, just as the general way of conduct is highly expressive. No one is needed for reproaches; one does not even have to blame oneself for having failed the dead person. The deceased continues to live, and in all the pain there is at least someone who can be mourned.[24] Therefore, an actual acting out of the protest reaction against the dead, who maliciously deserted his loved ones, becomes possible in this ethnic minority.[25]

7.13 The question of natural death

The public protest against death, as it was demonstrated in examples of lamentations from the Old Testament, has been silenced. It is true that there are here and there voices regretting the disappearance of lamentation. Some liturgies contain psalms of mourning from the Old Testament for readings (originally those did not oppose death), but today, the selection of psalms offered by the liturgies are aimed at the finality of human life and stress the will of God rather than expressing protest.

The question to which we must address ourselves in this section is the justification of lamenting and protesting death. If death is nothing else but the result of sin, either the original sin of Adam or the sin committed anew by every person, then death is not to be lamented but must be accepted as punishment. If death, on the contrary, represents a hostile power, opposing the divine, then lament and protest make sense. If man has to blame himself for death as consequence of his fall from and rebellion against God, then the protest is completely inappropriate. It only convicts man of what he always has been doing in rebellion and protest against God. Understanding death, as the last enemy to be overcome, however, makes the battle and protest against it an eschatological task.

The senselessness of a passionate protest against the steel will of God was formulated by Elizabeth Barrett Browning in her poem "Grief":

> I tell you, hopeless grief is passionless;
> That only men incredulous of despair
> Half-taught in anguish, through the midnight air
> Beat upward to God's throne in loud access,
> Of shrieking and reproach. Full desertness,
> In soul as countries, lieth silent-bare
> Under the blanching, vertical eye glare
> Of the absolute heavens.

K. Barth in his *Dogmatics* attempted to travel a middle road. For him, a Christian has been crucified and is dead and therefore lives with Christ. This is confirmed in baptism; thus man has been delivered from the overhanging curse, that is, death. However, this does not mean immortality; as the life of Jesus demonstrates, there is a positive connection between man being God's creation and mortality. To be finite is the form of existence of all human life. As Barth says: "It *also* belongs to human nature, and is determined and ordered by God's good creation and to that extent right and good, that man's being in time should be *finite* and man himself mortal. . . . Death is not in itself the judgment. It is not in itself and as such the sign of God's judgment. It is so only de facto."[26]

In the same way, Barth speaks of a death free of curse: "Man is freed from unnatural death. But this obviously means that, as he is freed for eternal life, he is also freed for natural death."[27] With the concept of natural death the meaning of death as part of God's creation becomes obvious again, which otherwise cannot be seen clearly as long as man is not saved but is in the bondage of sin. Barth terms it the "merciful death" and recalls the peculiarly calm statements in the New Testament about those who have "fallen asleep."[28]

E. Jüngel follows Barth's train of thought and actualizes it at the same time. For him there are two forms of death anxiety. In one form, the ego threatens itself by setting itself as absolute and thus exclusively seeking itself. It remains fixed upon itself and misses this lifetime as the place for historical encounter. A Christian anticipates the finitude of his life and does not set his hope "in his life, with the dignity of his good and the burden of his bad works, but in God alone. With this hope also a disempowering of death takes place in his life, which we can term a spiritual scoffing at death."[29]

The other form of death anxiety is the "threat of an untimely or unnatural death."[30] According to God's creation man has a right to a natural death at the end of his biologically determined lifetime. It belongs to the duties of the Christian faith to enforce this right. Jesus himself, so Jüngel, in his untimely death has underscored the obligation to take care for a natural death, which today is neither politically nor socially nor medically realized. As long as there is war and a death penalty this natural death is not yet realized.

Jüngel refers here explicitly to W. Fuchs's Todesbilder (Images of Death). The central purpose of this book is to create the image of a natural death and to analyze the various factors that inhibit the realization of natural death as well as the idea of a natural death. Natural death is the biologically given boundary of life. This is not realized as long as untimely and violent death exists and ideas that interpret death as punishment and fortuity continue to dominate.[31] Jüngel can go along fully with Fuchs's social-political demands, since he too defends natural death and assigns the right to bring about the final death, namely the death of curse and punishment, to God alone. By being selective with regard to Fuchs's writings, Jüngel conceals the fact that he absolutely adheres to a death inflicted upon man by God because of sin, that is, he continues to adjudge God the right to inflict a "violent" death by denying resurrection to that person who is not on positive terms with him.

Doubts about whether death really must be understood as a biological necessity or an order of God's creation have been expressed by several authors whose ideas are not determined by theology. H. Plessner proceeds from the widespread thesis that man is the only one among all living creatures who knows death is inevitable and makes no exceptions. Nevertheless, for him it is beyond comprehension that this is bound to be so.[32]

Freud stated, "Biology has not yet been able to decide whether death is the inevitable fate of every living being or whether it is only a regular but yet perhaps avoidable event in life. It is true that the proposition 'All men are mortal' is paraded in textbooks of logic as an example of generalization, but no human being really grasps it, and our unconscious has as little use now as ever for the idea of its own mortality."[33] At another point he writes: "Our habit is to lay stress on the fortuitous causation of the death-accident—disease, infection, advanced age; in this way we betray our endeavor to modify the significance of death from a necessity to an accident."[34]

If death is accidental, however, this signifies that perhaps it has an avoidable cause, in any case a cause brought about individually. Instead of submitting to a remorseless law of nature, to the inevitable, we can not only protest against death but also inquire about its cause. As Freud himself realized, it may be that belief in the internal necessity of dying is yet another illusion, "which we have created 'to bear the burden of existence.'"[35] As Caruso remarks, Freud for a brief moment had the thought that "death perhaps might not be an inevitable fate and ought not to be endured by man,"[36] that it is an accident and sets free the question for its cause.

THE AGGRESSIVE COPING MECHANISMS

From a theological point of view there are four objections to be made against the notion of natural death. (1) This idea presupposes a finite number of experiences which can be lived through in the course of a lifetime, in order to die at the end "satisfied with life." However, the options for shaping one's life attractively have increased so much that any life, even if it reaches a "biblical" age, must seem too short and its end "unnaturally early."

(2) H. Gollwitzer indicates that the experience of happiness and a fulfilled life by no means makes departure easier for us. Happiness may even sharpen the pain of separation to the utmost. "If in a changing society man no longer finds his wealth in the possession of property and power, but rather in his fellow men, then it is a perfect illusion to think, because he recognizes this as his true happiness, that therefore his own death and the death of others will become more tolerable for him." [37]

(3) And yet not only the opposition to parting with a happy and fulfilled life but also the experience of old age creeping up on us is an argument against the concept of natural death. Precisely the circumstances of natural death, the ailments of old age, the lack of mobility and receptivity, the anticipatory death in social isolation, all of this makes it hard to see in it only signs of a natural end. It is precisely the expansion of medical knowledge, which allows the extension of the process of aging and dying, that mediates the experience of a slow decay over a considerably longer period than ever before. Hence it challenges much more intensively the whole question of meaning. [38] In addition, the numerous medical interventions, still on the increase, confront us ever more urgently with the question of what can still be considered natural and what not; whether "friendly methods of dying" do not make death "all too natural." [39]

(4) Jüngel as well as Fuchs understands "natural" death as a social-political demand to employ all means of medicine to prevent the premature death. It is a question whether in the long run this notion is sufficient motivation for the fight against death. If death at the age of seventy is already considered natural, then the difference of the twenty or thirty

years of life an individual still could have lived based on mere biological facts is considered irrelevant. Even without that, there is the danger that our society offers the person who is no longer gainfully employed only the prospect of waiting for death. It can happen all too easily that the physical and mental decline is considered natural. This is certainly an essential reason that geriatrics and geriopsychiatry are only gradually being recognized as important tasks in our society. Frequently social factors that help to determine the aging process are overlooked.

Fuchs concedes that in order to avert this repressive element in the notion of natural death, actually the utopia of a final victory over death is needed. He refers to the book by R. C. Ettinger, *Aussicht auf Unsterblichkeit* (Prospects of Immortality), in which he discusses the possibility of delaying decomposition through cryogenics with, according to Fuchs, "a certainty presented with the zeal of a sectarian" that some day medicine will be able to remove any cause of death. Fuchs terms this a "negative utopia,"[40] for it assumes only a change in medicine; the social conditions are supposed to remain constant. This criticism is correct but misses the question, namely, what significance does this utopia accomplish by the overcoming of the death possess?

In contrast to this, Paul Althaus has pointed out: "All serious and joyous struggle against illness, as carried out by our physicians, is based on the belief, perhaps unconscious, that we are called to overcome death completely."[41] In the fight against deadly forces, according to Althaus, lies a promise and a symbol far exceeding any result achieved so far, and without which the painstaking process of therapy and the dying person's joy over gaining a few more days would become meaningless. "In this respect the physician's profession and all services dealing with sickness have an eschatological meaning."[42]

The four reasons mentioned here make it clear that the statement about the "natural death" cannot be an eschatological notion. It is true that it fulfills a critical function by eliciting a polemic against the untimely and violent death. It also has motivating power, even though here the danger arises of equating "normal" and "natural"; yet it has no utopian function since it does not include the conquest of death.

The recognition of scientifically approved reality and the theological statement, as is found in Barth and Jüngel, form a union which a catholic philosopher like J. Pieper, terrified as he is by this, can only identify as a union of theology with ideological materialism.[43] The theological doctrine of complete death admittedly has the legitimate intention of emphasizing the absolute sovereignty of God with respect to the revival of the dead and a new creation. But the question is whether this is not advocating an image of God that, under the aspect of hope of conquering death, is insufficient.

Hedinger, in one paragraph of his book *Hoffnung zwischen Kreuz und Reich* (Hope Between Cross and Kingdom), spoke of "hope as arguing with God,"[44] and thus opposed an idea of God in which God is beyond all justice and is always right. For Hedinger, God's right is not something to be pushed aside at any time by his omnipotence, but is part of his nature. The opinion that God is always right could dangerously overstress man's capability and provoke the idea that "the suffering person must and can prove himself before God by an excess of enduring generosity."[45] When a man argues with God and protests against him, this does not indicate being alone and only in the right against God; rather the believer is protesting with the God of the future against the God of the present. This is exemplified in the parable of the "arguing widow" (Luke 18:1-8a), who protests against the judge who ignores the injustice she has suffered and does not vindicate her. How much more is the protest against God justified if the conquest of death is at stake.

7.2 The mechanism: the search for the guilty

7.21 Psychological aspects

Besides protest and complaint, the search for the guilty constitutes an aggressive defense mechanism. It is experienced as helpful and consoling to know who caused the death or who has contributed to it.

The question of the laws of causality is one of the earliest interests of the child's, as Rochlin has stressed again and again: "The child's interest in the search for explanations of phenomena and experiences begins very early in life. The answers that he seems to prefer, whether his own or those furnished by others, tend to have certain common characteristics. They are outside of logic and are not testable. They are often dependent upon the power of wishes and magic. To the child all is governed by law and ruled by a higher authority or force, whose favor needs to be courted." [1] The child conceives of the world as directed by forces that are subject to persuasion. The conflict thus lies between the governing power of wishes and the laws of causality. The child, according to Rochlin, finds the two best reconciled in religion, where both hold sway, but in which explanations or causes are intimately related to wishes. [2] Next to the infantile investigations about sex the young child's discovery of death has an equally singular effect in Rochlin's opinion. [3] Death is seen in the same context in which other causality problems are solved.

Regression in grief involves reactivating some of such infantile notions about the laws of causality. The craving for acceptable explanations can lead the bereaved to ask repeatedly for a detailed description of all the counter measurements undertaken by the physician. [4] As David Sudnow has observed, frequently the first question asked by a family member following the doctor's death notification is: "What caused the death, doctor?" This question is asked even if the doctor has already explained the development of the case. The physician then continues to inquire about previous symptoms of the disease, even though they no longer can be of importance for the treatment; no notes are taken. The doctor's inquiries as well as the relatives' questions merely serve the purpose of helping the grief-stricken to get over the impact of shock. [5] In the same way, the circumstances that lead to a fatal accident are often discussed again and again. A mother, known to the author, lost her only son in an accident. He was run over by a car at night, but the exact circumstances were never found out since the driver escaped. There were no eyewitnesses. Even weeks after the accident the mother still had the wish that the police would get hold of the driver, not primarily to bring him to trial, but to learn in detail what caused the accident. Repeatedly she would combine the details she had received from the police to find the proper "explanation."

The "craving for explanation"[6] makes it possible in the regressive stage to make a shift in the range of causes with regard to their significance. A short-term delay in medical help, which has nothing to do with the fatal outcome, can be raised to the actual cause of death by the bereaved. A belated visit at the deathbed where the father is found no longer alive might lead to heavy self-reproaches, unsuitable to the cause. During the regressive stage it can be more important in some cases to let the mourner find a helpful or conceivable cause than to insist on the objective reasons which led to the death.

Arthur and Kemme make an important point in their discussion of infantile concepts of death. They observe that children were much less interested in the question of *what* had caused the death of their parent than knowing *who* was to blame for it. Sometimes such reproaches were made against a distant relative, but most frequently the child blamed the surviving parent for the death. According to Arthur and Kemme the tendency throughout was to blame a real or imagined person for the death and to replace the explanation within the scope of physical causalities with an explanation from the scope of personal responsibilities.[7]

An investigation about the assassination of President Kennedy confirms this observation: Children mainly conceived Oswald as the murderer, while adults tended to see a right-wing extremist or Communist plot at work.[8]

Nevertheless, there also seems to be a tendency among adults, at least in the regressive stage of grief or in other crisis situations, to direct these reproaches against a concrete person rather than against abstract social conditions or an incomprehensible divine order. It is easier to blame the unfortunate driver involved in the accident than the insufficient facilities for traffic safety; easier to attack the doctor in charge than the deficient hospital equipment; and less difficult to get excited about the minister than about the injustice of God. Interviews during the bombing attacks on England in World War II revealed that the English people were filled with reproaches against their own authorities much more than against the Germans.[9] Smelser reports a similar observation:

After the fire in the Coconut Grove Bar during World War II the public was fixed on several scapegoats following one another—the busboy who actually caused the fire when he attempted to replace the lightbulb, someone who removed this lightbulb as a joke, public officials who obviously were too lazy to check the safety of the club's building, and the owner of the club. Such blaming characterizes the attempt to make someone personally responsible for the tragedy.[10]

One important reason that not only children but adults as well tend to insist so strongly on personal responsibility for the death in the question of causation is the fact that there is no objective definition for death, that death presents itself as subjective continuum on various levels.[11] Biological death is not identical with physical death; nor is psychic death identical with the death of interaction with the social environment, nor social death with the religious death. Death has a different cause on each level; besides this, levels are not strictly separated, but overlap. Hence it is quite possible to place the weight of the question on a particular level and also to shift from one level to another.

Frequently, blaming a third party is observable. Almost 30 percent of the widows interviewed by Marris blamed the doctor, minister, God, or fate.[12] Another widow had attacked the doctor rather violently and later apologized for it when she regretted her behavior: "'I just went berserk. Poor Dr. Roberts got a good hiding.' She added, 'afterwards depression set in and I lost interest.'" It was, as Marris notes, as if her anger, at least as long as it lasted, had given her courage and sustained her.[13] Unclarified hostility toward the doctor or surgeon can, as a case study by Lindemann illustrates, under certain conditions lead to depressive behavior disorder.[14] Since the physician in our society symbolizes the essential defense force against death, it is feasible to see in him the actual cause for the death, as soon as there is the slightest suspicion of false diagnosis or maltreatment. Particularly if the patients belong to the lower social class, the suspicion might arise rather quickly that the doctor has not used all means as he does with his private patients. Hostility may also be transferred from one person to another.

Janis describes a similar case of a woman after the stress of an operation.

Mrs. Blake's postoperative sessions provide numerous examples of excessive aggressiveness in response to nonprovocative actions on the part of parent-surrogates, and her reactions seem to involve a reactivation of childhood resentments and protests. Her conception of the surgeon as a dangerous sadist first occurred when she discovered that the area of her surgical wound was larger than he had told her it would be. . . . The same exaggerated misconception of the surgeon recurred about ten days later, at which time the only basis for her suspicions was the fact that she was currently suffering much more pain and discomfort than she had expected. . . . From the beginning of her analysis, she had repeatedly complained about the analyst's adherence to the standard rules of psychoanalytic treatment; but in the postoperative sessions the complaints were blown up into accusations that the analyst had no intention of helping her, was taking no cognizance of her suffering, was ignoring her efforts to be a "good girl," and wanted only to get rid of her as soon as possible.[15]

Hostile feelings can also be directed against ministers who are the visible agents of an unmerciful God or an incomprehensible destiny. In one case described to the author, the friendly concern of the minister was seen in contrast to the conduct of the one he represents: "One could talk to the minister much better than with anyone else. . . . Yet one just cannot avoid asking: 'Why did it have to be him?' since there are so many young men who treat their wives in a terrible way, so many bad fathers. It is so unfair, it just cannot be possible."

Such comparisons on the basis of moral judgments are quite common. For instance, a young girl told the author of her last visit with her mother in the hospital: "She is in a room together with an eighty-year-old grandmother who had already been hospitalized three times. She says that soon she will be released and yet my mother must die; that is simply unfair." In all these cases, either God or destiny is accused of not having observed certain rules, such as the bad person has to die before the good or the old before the young. "Religion has to give an answer to that," demands a widow who refuses to go to church since the death of her husband.[16]

7.22 Sociological implications

The search for the guilty can initiate an extensive ritual in less differentiated societies.

As soon as an adult dies among the Lodagaa, not only are the respective funeral rites set in motion, but other rituals are performed as well. Their goal is to find the one who caused the death. With the exception of the death of infants and old people, death is treated as a case of murder.

The cause of death is seen on three levels: The immediate cause is the disease, the snake bite, or magic powers. The conveyer of death is to be found among the members of the tribe itself. And finally, an ancestor or spirit, who is worshipped at various altars, has induced the death. The conveyers of death are identified by medicine men. The spirit of the dead is asked to appear in the dream of that person who has to give the funeral address and tell him who is to be held responsible for the death. The magician, by using certain methods, can identify a number of possible persons from scattered items that belong to the property of the deceased. He can cast shells which, depending on their position, can give further information. Other devices are used for examining the widow and children to ascertain whether they are guilty of being accomplices. One custom, largely dispensed with, consisted of dividing the clothes of the deceased into two bundles and carrying them on the head while circling around the maternal clan. The person in front of whom the bundle dropped was guilty.

The essential ritual to establish the cause of death, however, takes place approximately three weeks after the funeral on the occasion of an event called "beer of the magician." This consists of an interview carried out by one of the oldest members of the family and secondly of a prediction, a task assigned to another tribe. Here again a selection is made with the help of certain techniques from the shell money and smaller items formerly owned by the deceased. Each of these items identifies someone who could be responsible for the dead. Then the shell money is cast, whereby the individual family class, the earth altar, the ancestors, and the protective spirits are called upon. When the right name is mentioned, the shells fall in the right order, one upward and one downward. A sacrificial drink is poured on the earth altar and another drinking vessel with beer is available for the participants. A feast at the house of the dead person concludes the ceremony.

During this action no specific name is mentioned, only those supernatural powers decisive for the death are identified. It might be announced that magic had been employed and a certain related tribe was responsible for it. The specific person who induced the death, a magician or a witch is only an agent who conveys death.[17]

It would be meaningless in this case to wonder about the success of such a ritual; as frequently in the bereaved's quest for the cause of death, the purpose is not a genuine investigation, but rather the search for the guilty, which exhausts its function in succeeding as defense mechanism. Even though our devices for establishing death are more appropriate, such as the death certificate, stating the cause of death, autopsies where the cause is in question, etc., their complexity alone indicates that they too serve the latent function of reducing the anxiety about death in society. Certainly rational arguments for such extensive regulations with regard to establishing the cause of death can be given. The practical implementation, however, often is no less ritual than the device of the Lodagaa.

The practice in less differentiated societies also differs essentially by allowing for an aggressive acting out. There is an abundance of ethnological material in which the acting out is immediately aiming neither at the deceased nor at one's own self. Thus the destruction of the entire property of the deceased is such a way of acting out among Indian tribes and elsewhere,[18] as is the breaking of vessels and other objects reported at funeral rites from Greece and Great Britain.[19] Nevertheless, the acting out can also take on aggressive forms and attack other people. Durkheim reports on the mourning rites in Australian tribes:

They are to be seen throwing themselves upon one another and trying to wound each other. Sometimes the attack is real; sometimes it is only pretended. There are even cases when these peculiar combats are organized. Among the Kaitish, the hair of the deceased passes by right to his son-in-law. But he in return must go, in company with some of his relatives and friends, and provoke a quarrel with one of his tribal brothers, that is, with a man belonging to the same matrimonial class as himself and one who might therefore have married the daughter of the dead man. This provocation cannot be refused and the two combatants inflict serious wounds upon each other's shoulders and thighs. When the duel is terminated, the challenger passes on to his adversary the hair which he had temporarily inherited. This latter then provokes and fights with another of his tribal brothers, to whom the precious relic is next transmitted, but only provisionally; thus it passes from hand to hand and circulates from group to group.[20]

Durkheim sees here a strong similarity with the vendetta that is closely related to mourning. Where this custom once existed or has continued today, the period of mourning ends when vengeance is taken on the offender, either the tribe or the family who is held responsible for the death.

Our funeral rites, in contrast to "more primitive" societies, offer almost no opportunity for acting out hostile feelings against a third party. This is still an option for children by playing funeral where aggressive actions can be carried out. The adult frequently has only the choice of turning his hostility against doctors, ministers, and relatives. The Christian attitude manifests itself in bearing such displaced, one-sided, and exaggerated reproaches in the discipleship of Christ, knowing that human beings under the impact of death have no alternative but to turn their hostility against others. That minister who is willing to bear such accusations tacitly is acting more in accordance with the gospel than someone who tries to defend God and therefore also himself. To endure the pain of not having any helpful answer to the question of God's guilt means perhaps much more than the assurance of a cosmically structured justice of balance.

7.23 Death as penalty

In a case of death we have to anticipate that occasionally the bereaved sees the ultimate cause of his loss in God himself. He may protest and accuse God of allowing dying and death at all. The bereaved might accuse him of having acted unjustly with this death by not observing certain principles. He may be called unjust for letting the good die and the bad live, or because he does not observe the rule that the older must die before the younger, the person nobody loves before the one more important to the bereaved, the mentally retarded before the genius. Vice versa, death also can be perceived and accepted as punishment by God because the bereaved has committed an offense that can be expiated only through the death of a loved one.

As already mentioned above, the regressive phase makes it easy to establish an immediate connection between a self-committed offense and the death of a loved one. St. B. Friedman et al. discovered that the majority of parents of children who suffered from leukemia indulged in self-reproaches for not having the children treated well enough. Some parents went as far as interpreting this disease as God's penalty inflicted upon them for this neglect and other sins.[21]

E. Jackson describes the case of a pilot in a heavy-bomber squadron who flew many bombing missions over Japan during World War II. During one of his visits to the United States on leave, he married and became the father of a son. Although he participated conscientiously in his military assignment, part of his mind remained unconvinced. He started going to the chapel regularly and expressed feelings of guilt about the ruthless destruction of aerial warfare. He was supposed to be brought to trial, but because the war was ending at that time the interest in his case diminished. A few months after returning to civilian status, his son, then sixteen months old, was killed in an accident. He remained dry-eyed and coldly efficient and made all the arrangements for the funeral. After the funeral he talked rather incoherently to his parents and friends about the price he had to pay for ruthless destruction universally. He said: "I did this to a thousand parents. I can never live long enough to undo the damage I have done. I have had to pay so little." He began to visit a pastor with whom he spent hours discussing involved problems dealing with love, hate, forgiveness, and restitution.[22]

In the autobiographical illustrations of L. Giudice, a split in the image of God can be seen, of the kind a minister presumably is confronted with quite often, precisely by people who are familiar with the Christian faith. Giudice writes: "Since Oki's death I clearly distinguished between my prayers to God and to Jesus. Death, hell—in front of these stood God, of whom I was terrified; but God had sent Jesus to us so that we would not be destroyed by him."[23] And at another point she writes: "Where Jesus had wept, I was allowed to suffer; he who became a human being knew how I suffered.... At this point I consciously prayed to Jesus, I could implore him for mitigation. To God I only dared to say: 'Thy will be done.'"[24]

The connection between God's justice and God's love is one of the fundamental issues theology has struggled with since its existence and presumably will be engaged in as long as theology exists. Death repeatedly gave reason to define this question more precisely and there is no hope of giving an adequate answer in a few pages. We can only point in the direction in which to search for probable answers.

The theological attempt to interpret the merciless death in the full meaning of the word is represented in the dogma about the Fall and the further developing estrangement from God described as original sin. The positive function of this statement is first of all that the individual human misbehavior toward God is collectivized. The close connection between illness and sudden death as punishment for individual offenses against God, as still dominant in the Old Testament, is broken. This also means that sins of omission can never be raised into offenses that justify such punishment.

Punishment by a "merciless" death thus is, as it were, imposed upon the entire human race in all its generations; the social structures create the alienation and compel God's penalty as death sentence.

Besides, especially the newer Protestant theology increasingly interprets sin no longer in terms of moral acts as offenses against God's law, but rather as the individual's general attitude toward God. Sin is generalized to a relation to God that failed, out of which then sins as misconduct in interactions with others only grow. As E. Brunner writes: "For what is sin? It is the revolt of the human 'I' against its creator, the rebellion of the defendant, one who deems that he must and can win his freedom."[25] E. Jüngel formulates sin in a similar way, demonstrating it from the Old Testament. Sin is "rebellion against God, who is related to man in all circumstances of human life; sin leads into a state of nonrelatedness."[26]

Even if sin is described primarily as attitude toward God, this, however, can be implemented only in social categories. If one tries to describe the relationship with God as merely a personal I-Thou relation, then it becomes impossible to speak of a "kingdom of God." At the same time, it becomes difficult to bring up the theological intention that man's sin primarily consists in his attempt to take God's place and thus to try to level the distance existing between God and man.[27] In order to express this displacement of God, theology intentionally or without intention frequently uses a social terminology, such as rebellion and revolt. Nevertheless, these terms suggest specific associations and presume the social-political positions of those who conceive sin in such terms.

There is only one way, according to the presently dominating theological opinion, in which the rebellion can be punished and atoned for through God, namely, by death. In this context, the death penalty has been interpreted theologically in various ways as God's judgment already implemented during life on earth: By giving up his full relationship and proper distance from God, man himself makes his life irrelevant. The biological end merely reveals the vanity of a life that has already died the "death curse" of irrelevance, a result of the "curse for the bad deed which makes everything irrelevant and thus indeed continuously must beget evil until it finally gives birth to death which reveals the vanity of an irrelevant life by destroying it."[28] More traditional is the concept of a resurrection for the purpose of judgment, where then the final death or an eternal punishment is inflicted.

The alternative to inflicting the death penalty to which God is entitled is pardoning, based on and depending on Jesus' death. No matter how his death is understood, it still has the impact of recognizing the full justification of the death penalty, of abolishing rebellion and mediating a new relationship to God which will outlast biological death and is focused on its total eradication.

We shall have to discuss further Jesus' power to overcome guilt. At this point, we are urged to ask what theology gains by holding on to a criminal law for guilt that inflicts as the highest expiation the death penalty. This concept presupposes that God, and the law representing him, is never at fault but always right. Against such a God all forms of protest, complaint, and accusation are meaningless and represent only an increased disregard for the judge. We have already rejected such an image of God with reference to the hope that argues and advocates a concept of "convincing" God.

A further question arises as to whether expiation is at all possible. Paul Althaus asks the question whether one can ever make good or "pay back" for omissions. No expiation can undo the invasion into another life; it has become history. Expiation "is a nonthought, whether we think of the immediacy of our acts to God or of their history-shaping power."[29] Expiation is imaginable only as a new beginning, not as retaliation or settlement of accounts.[30]

If the thought of expiation becomes problematic at all, then the question arises as to whether one can continue to defend theologically that it is God who inflicts the death penalty upon man. Does God not take on "inhuman" features if modern society increasingly attempts to abolish capital punishment, while God is still looked upon as the one who inflicts the death penalty upon mankind? K. Barth and his school have emphatically contested the legitimacy of the death penalty pronounced by man. They have claimed that with the death of Christ, the curse of the death penalty upon mankind is abolished and no man has the right any longer to take the life of another human being through a violent and therefore unnatural death, not even on the basis of the legal code. Even though solemn power to inflict death is given to God alone, the question remains whether the divine superiority could not also be formulated in such a way that no "inhuman" features invade the image of God.

It must be more clearly emphasized, as this is the case so far in contemporary theology, that God does not seek the death of the godless but rather the life of the righteous. That may be difficult for a community of believers who derive their identity from such a traumatic event as the crucifixion of Jesus. This would demand deriving from the fact of the "merciless" death of Jesus the definite statement that God does not want death and therefore theology too cannot but protest against death and must seek to motivate its conquest.[31]

At this point we will follow K. Rahner's train of thought in the attempt to clarify what we have said above. Rahner speaks of the "hiddenness" and "darkness"[32] of death and with this concept he deliberately wants to keep open the existential experience of whether death is truly the ruin, "the pure end" of man, or a pure perfection. No human experience will ever be able to reveal whether "the concrete death of man is either salvation or damnation, punishment for sin or an act of faith."[33] What can be judged theologically, however, according to Rahner, is the attitude toward the darkness of death. Man can deny explicitly and existentially the radical problem and the questionableness of death as a mystery. This again may happen in two ways. The denial may be enacted in despair, or man may try to explain its final sense through a positive existential understanding of his own essence. To be more precise, such an explaining of its final sense in any case takes place if death is understood as mere transformation to the state of free spirit, that is to say, through death, the spiritual principle is freed from the confines of matter and corporeal existence; if death is conceived as pure subjectivity; or, finally, if death is regarded as a return to the eternal cycles of biological life.[34]

It remains a mystery for man whether death has any connection with God; that question cannot be answered. Theological criteria have only exclusive characteristics; they merely exclude certain interpretations of meaning and contest at least that one interpretation can claim to be absolute and autonomous. It would be necessary to examine beyond Rahner whether the coherence of death and conciliating punishment belongs to the "hiddenness and darkness" of death and whether such a connection can be considered at all in a theologically legitimate way.[35]

7.3 The mechanism: identification with the aggressor

7.31 Psychological aspects

Identification with the aggressor represents a defense mechanism which, as Anna Freud has pointed out, not only contributes to the development of the superego, helping it to cope with undesired instincts, but also constitutes "one of the most significant means in the confrontation with anxiety-producing objects of the external world."[1] With some examples from child therapy she illustrates how children assimilate some features of the anxiety-producing person, play the role of this person, and thus cope with past or anticipated danger. In the development of a superego this mechanism plays an important role, because in this way the ego assumes the value judgments of these authority figures "in the fight with the authority figures, that is, in the confrontation with its anxiety-objects."[2]

This superego is for Freud at first represented by the father: "In the course of development through childhood, which brings about an ever-increasing severance from the parents, this personal significance for the superego recedes. To the imagos they leave behind are then linked on the influences of teachers, authorities, of self-chosen models and heroes venerated by society; these persons need no longer be introjected by the ego, which has now become much more resistant. The last figure in the series beginning with the parents is that dark supremacy of Fate, which only the fewest among us are able to conceive of impersonally."[3] It is quite conceivable that a relation between the superego and the ego is formed, whereby "the superego, the conscience at work in it can then become harsh, cruel, and inexorable against the ego which is in its charge."[4] It may be that the ego then subjects itself to the heightened sadism of the superego. But it can also be the case that the masochism in the ego itself seeks punishment, whether from the superego within or from parental authorities without. In both cases there is a craving which is satisfied by punishment and suffering.[5]

In "Mourning and Melancholia" Freud has illustrated this identification with the aggressor in the behavior of a melancholiac who had suffered real injury and disappointment from the love object. But instead of abandoning it completely, the ego identifies with the disappointing object; thus the negative features of the object fall upon the ego of the melancholiac.[6] In the same way as it conceives the disloyal object the ego now treats itself; its criticism and animosity relating to an insulting object are launched against itself in the course of identification. The ego is criticized, disparaged, must suffer, and derives a masochistic satisfaction from this suffering.[7]

The defense mechanism of identification with the aggressor, however, is not only to be found in a child or depressed person, but can also be traced in "normal" grief. In contrast to the aggressive defense mechanisms we have dealt with so far, in mourning the aggression is not directed against the dead or other persons and powers, but against one's own self.

The range of defense mechanisms also includes another coping mechanism which, like the mechanism of identification with the aggressor, is focused on the restitution of the lost object within the psychic organization.[8] We identify it as the coping mechanism of incorporation.[9] These two defensive mechanisms of introjection differ in that in identification with the aggressor, the aggressive part of this relation is significantly higher than in incorporation, where also aggressive instinctual drives exist, but the libidinal prevail. Eduardo Weiss summarized this as follows:

A similar transformation can be observed in a person who has lost someone he loves. At first helpless to control his id-cathected longing for the lost one, he engages in the "mourning work" in a process of bodily identification with the deceased, at the end of which he loves, instead of the actual person, the egotized, autoplastic restoration of that person within himself. Only to the extent to which the deceased person can actually be substituted by such an internalization does the ego feel emotionally free from the lost love object. . . . The process leads to self-hate and self-reproach when the person incorporated is the object of ambivalent feelings of mixed hate and love.[10]

When aggression is directed toward one's own self in grief, then the lost object continues its dominance of influence over the survivor uninterrupted, through an act of incorporation into the psychic organization. This is particularly the case when the survivor (marriage partner or child) had been sublimated to the deceased. The dead person therefore had inhibited the development of the superego in functioning as the dominating figure shaping the life of his dependent. The father— or mother—proportion of the superego prevailed over those parts of the superego shaped by society and religion. Father or mother constitute even for the adult the greater part of his conscience.

Even if the individual always had submitted to his situation of dependency, the death of the dominating subject can, as D. Switzer has correctly observed,[11] set free the repressed hostile feelings, and the mechanism of regression can be reactivated. It is quite conceivable that the bereaved experiences a sudden relief and liberation. There are spontaneous remissions by depressive or schizoid patients at the death of the domineering love object.[12]

This release of hostility toward a person who before has been looked upon with respect and admiration must be a terrifying experience for the bereaved. This can be seen in the difficulty of articulating these ambivalent feelings in front of the therapist or minister. In fact, the experience of relief can be so shocking that it is not sustained for very long. At least in the regressive stage very quickly the fallen spouse or parent is restored to his former domineering position, lest the bereaved miss the protection and care, even though he has suffered by it. The fallen and restored love object, however, is now, in the fantasies of the bereaved, apt to take revenge on the revolting survivor. Therefore he has no choice but to turn the released aggressions toward his own self. Accusations by the domineering superego unite with the bereaved's self-reproaches at having wished and even welcomed the death. However, it seems still better to him to take the blame and in this way to preserve the protection of the superego, rather than free himself from the conjugal or parental principles governing the superego.

Grinberg made a rather satisfying distinction when he distinguished persecutory and depressive guilt in grief. The persecutory guilt, stemming from the persecutory object, is introjected in the superego and perceived as threat and punishment, as against the depressive guilt, deriving from the ego-ideal, that is, the ideal image the ego makes about himself.[13] This distinction is not unimportant. Aggression against the dependent child or the dependent conjugal partner can take on various forms. We not only have to consider it an aggression when the dominance becomes absolutely obvious and is enforced with every means of physical and psychic brutality. There are also hidden ways of domineering; a mother, for instance, may be overprotective toward her child, only to prevent him from becoming independent. One conjugal partner may impose his will upon the other by his constant needs, requiring help and care and thus binding the other to himself, or by showing such overwhelming kindness that the other must feel worthless. Guilt feelings will develop not only in cases where the survivor feels disobedient toward the domineering power of the lost object, but also where he was overwhelmed by attentive care and affection, to which he felt unequal and which he could not match with something equally valuable. Therefore it is meaningful to speak with Grinberg of two sources of guilt feelings; one is the superego, the other the ego-ideal.

Guilt feelings can be divided into four categories according to the sequence of their intensity. The most short-term is guilt arising from relief felt when the relationship was ambivalent; at least in the regressive stage, this is taken back rather quickly. In the second place are guilt feelings resulting from certain neglects. Greater weight is attached to guilt feelings that the mourner links to death wishes. Particularly aggravating, however, can be the guilt feeling of having survived.

(1) One source of self-reproach is the relief felt by the bereaved, relief to be freed from a heavy burden. In a case illustration by Marris, one widow expressed such feelings of relief: "I felt relaxed. There is nothing wrong in feeling relieved. I was completely exhausted and absorbed by sorrow and the rush back from the hospital every morning to prepare a meal for my girl." But at the same time she has to defend herself against the reproaches, not yet expressed, that such a feeling of relief is not proper.[14] When the relief is experienced subsequent to a suppressed death wish guilt feelings can be particularly intense.

(2) The bereaved may accuse himself of not having observed carefully enough the signs of the disease and of hesitating much too long before calling a doctor. He may feel guilty for not having consulted several and better medical authorities who might have suggested a better therapy. The bereaved also may reproach himself for having followed the wish of the dying to be taken home from the hospital; the same may occur in the opposite case, if for the same reasons the dying patient was not taken to a hospital. Other reproaches originate from the all too few visits; many examples could be given of reproaches for not having cared sufficiently for the dying. They can be reinforced by other survivors, when, for example, a widower says of his daughter:

Her mother was having treatment in the hospital and she moved her out. She took her away to her home in T'm. I as good as accused her of killing her. She actually murdered her mother; I kept telling her the doctors were not as good in T'm.[15]

Particularly violent and quite common are the guilt feelings of parents at the death of a child. B. Friedman *et al.* report the behavior of parents on the hospital floor for children with leukemia. Almost without exception they all blamed themselves for not having been attentive enough to notice the first symptoms of the disease.[16] These self-accusations usually vanished quickly, particularly if the physician reassured them that even an earlier diagnosis could not have changed the fatal course of the disease. Among a minority of parents, however, the self-reproaches remained insurmountable or were then related to failure to have been more receptive to the child or to having been too strict with him. Such self-reproaches could not be removed in shorter conversations, since here, as the displacement shows, more deeply rooted guilt feelings were reactivated.[17]

Besides neglecting the patient, sometimes disagreements previous to the death may also cause self-reproaches. Autton reports a married couple's quarrel about an unimportant matter at breakfast. On the way to work the husband suffered a cardiac thrombosis and died before reaching the hospital.[18] The widow's guilt feelings and remorse were extraordinarily severe, because the last words they had exchanged were arguments.

The assurance by some authority that nothing of importance was wronged plays an important role. The recognition on the part of the doctor that the wife had gone through so much trouble that "she almost became a victim of death herself" is of great help with respect to the frequent self-reproach of not having cared sufficiently. The bereaved often tends to praise himself for his great concern and care for the dying. This serves likewise as a defense against unexpressed reproaches and becomes effective only when others affirm it fully.

(3) Long periods of nursing frequently may stress the patience of the survivor to the limit; they not only cause unpleasant reactions but may lead to the sudden desire, immediately repressed, that the patient may die soon.

Freud saw in the fulfilled death wish against the father the original sin of mankind, "the main source of the sense of guilt,"[19] in which all individual death wishes participate. Though this is just as much a mythological expression as the doctrine of original sin committed by the first human being, nevertheless, it points to the universality of the death wish. It can also be seen in the bereaved.

(4) Guilt feelings are very pronounced in case of some "competition for survival"[20] as Lifton termed it, as it took place, for example, in concentration camps. Any attempt to escape the selection process meant at the same time the death of another person, as in the case of decimation, where the weaker was forced to take the number that inevitably meant a death sentence, or in "chumming up" with the guards and the SS in order perhaps to have one's own name replaced by another on the death lists.

The writer E. Wiesel was fifteen years old when he was taken to Auschwitz. He also took care of his father in the concentration camps in Buna and Buchenwald. When his father died he observed "in the recesses of my weakened conscience" a feeling of being "free at last." He describes how he therefore feels ashamed of himself forever and has guilt feelings. The impact of this experience was so tremendous that, after his liberation and during an illness, he thought while looking in a mirror "a corpse gazed back at me. The look in his eyes as they stared into mine, has never left me."[21]

The stereotype phrase used by patients with war neuroses, "The bullet actually was meant for me, not him," is not a meaningless cliché but expresses the deep conviction that the survivor has no right to be alive. It implies an intense feeling of one's own wickedness; the survivor feels guilt-ridden and is convinced of his complete worthlessness.

Any dying person can convey experiences comparable with the guilt of survival. Any survivor, no less than the doctor, "must cope with the guilt the inquiring look of the dying evokes, behind which lies the question 'Why should I die while you live?'"[22] It is precisely this staring, accusing look that helped shape the custom of closing the eyes of the deceased to create the impression of peaceful sleeping rather than of reproach.

Similar guilt feelings were detected among the survivors of

Hiroshima, especially if parents survived their children, who therefore died an "untimely" death, that is, a death that in the normal course of events would have occurred only after their own. The survivors of Hiroshima characterize these guilt feelings as "living hell." Lifton writes:

And from these extreme experiences we come to realize that no one's emotions about death and survival are ever experienced entirely as individual matters; that images of dying are bound up with inner questions about who and what will survive, and images of surviving with who (and what) has died in one's place.[23]

For the Hiroshima survivors, also, the internalized picture of the accusing eyes of the dead were of great significance. It was hard for them to free themselves from it, particularly since they live in a culture where—much more than in the Protestant-Christian world—the value of the individual is primarily determined by the value judgments of others, in particular the parents. This cultural determination forces one to identify oneself with the dead and to look at oneself with the eyes of the dead.[24] Lifton speaks in this context of "identification guilt," the guilt of having stolen the life of the other and actually to have to die in his place.[25]

It is a plausible need of the bereaved's to be freed from the guilt feelings toward the aggressive deceased. He will attempt to atone for the offenses he committed. In many cases, however, in particular if the bereaved is in the regressive phase, there is a strong compulsion to carry out the atonement on the level of a primitive world order. As a result, many means of expiation available in daily life or in church rituals for forgiveness of sins become ineffective since they do not attain this primitive world order and value judgment.

The regressive character of guilt and expiation shows up (just as in the mechanism of searching for the guilty) in a strong personalization. The bereaved "feels an irrational and persistent guilt about the death, as if he were to blame for it or at least had contributed to it through his errors."[26] On the other hand, preoccupation with the dead person leads to making this guilt a matter exclusively between the deceased and the survivor. All other people and factors are eliminated.

Finally, the penance must equate the guilt of the bereaved. A person who has caused the death of another must die himself. Guilt as well as forgiveness cannot be generalized and spread out over the entirety of mankind; therefore, devices of Christian forgiveness are usually ineffective.

Bereavement features a number of means of penance. (1) The *ius talionis* demands that the survivor himself suffer death; he commits suicide or follows the deceased into death. In most cases, however, he implements death only symbolically. He reaches the border of psychic disintegration in his grief, but through sacrifices pays his way out of death. Identification and therefore the paying of the penalty is executed as partial self-denial and sacrifice of possessions. The symbolic character of the act is recognizable in the existence of a clear relation between death and death substitute. Besides the total identification reaction, other types of internalization mechanisms, patterned after the classification suggested by G. K. Krupp,[27] can be identified: (2) Long and intensive nursing may ease guilt feelings. (3) The bereaved may conceive the grave as a place where he receives orientation from the dead, and through great sacrifices in furnishing the funeral and burial place, as well as through the trouble of regular visits to the grave, he pays for his guilt. (4) The mourner may identify with the deceased by killing himself symbolically, by hurting himself and sacrificing parts of his body, such as hair. He also may assume the symptoms of the illness of the deceased; his becoming sick then represents his penalty for his guilt. (5) The mourner may through the color of his clothes announce that he actually belongs to the dead and impose other devices of self-denial and self-isolation. (6) The mourner may identify with the personality of the dead by adopting certain mannerisms, traits, and characteristics stemming from the aggressive arsenal of the deceased. (7) He may feel so strongly obligated to the deceased that he takes on the business interests and other activities of the loved one; nevertheless, in this case it frequently is difficult to distinguish precisely between a more libidinal introjection and a substitution. Whether identification with the aggressor is predominant can then be recognized above all by the symptom of compulsion.

(1) *Suicide:* Cobb and Lindemann give an example of a young man who had received minor burns in the Coconut Grove fire. He was treated at the hospital and on the fifth day he learned that his wife had died. He seemed to be unusually well-controlled during the following short period after his stay in the hospital. Shortly afterward he was returned to the hospital by his family because he exhibited an increased irritability and hypermotility. With great effort it was possible to establish enough rapport to carry on interviews. He felt extremely tense, unable to breathe, exhausted, and lived in a frantic fear that something terrible was going to happen.

"I am destined to live in insanity or I must die. I know that is God's will. I have this awful feeling of guilt." With intense morbid guilt feelings, he reviewed incessantly the events of the fire. His wife had stayed behind. When he tried to pull her out, he had fainted and was shoved out by the crowd. She was burned while he was saved. "I should have saved her or I should have died too." He complained about being filled with an incredible violence and did not know what to do about it. The rapport established with him lasted for only brief periods of time. He then would fall back into his state of intense agitation and muttering. He slept poorly, even with large sedation. In the course of four days he became somewhat more composed, had longer periods of contact with the psychiatrist, and seemed to feel that he was being understood and might be able to cope with his morbid feelings of guilt and violent impulses. On the sixth day of his hospital stay, however, after skillfully distracting the attention of his special nurse, he jumped through a closed window to a violent death.[28]

Suicide and suicidal thoughts are not uncommon among mourners. Sometimes such bereaved persons draw attention through their behavior and are hospitalized. Wretmark reports that eighteen out of twenty-eight bereaved who were under his psychiatric care, showed intensive guilt feelings and eight thought definitely of suicide; three actually made an attempt.[29] Yet more frequently suicidal persons are not conspicuous to their environment, because of their general withdrawal. Often their statements referring to this are not taken seriously. There are also passive forms of "letting-oneself-die," which are in part aggressions turned inwardly.

(2) *Nursing:* An observation by de Beauvoir can certainly be generalized: A long nursing period represents a discharge from guilt feelings the bereaved harbor toward the deceased:

There is certainly something good in this delay for us: It saved us from remorse. If a loved one leaves us, we pay for the guilt of surviving with a thousand agonizing expressions of re-morse. . . . Since one can never—not even within (contestable) limits one sets for oneself—do the utmost for somebody, still many self-reproaches are left for us. We became guilty in recent years with respect to mother particularly of neglect, failures, and carelessness. Through the days devoted to her, the peace she found in our presence and through the victories over fear and pain, we had—at least it seemed to us—made up for all of it. Without our persistent alertness she would have had to suffer much more.[30]

(3) *Funeral and burial arrangements:* No doubt the funeral is an occasion when feelings of guilt toward the dead are satisfied to a large extent by the purchase of a fine funeral. J. Mitford cites an article from the *National Funeral Service Journal,* in which this function of the funeral is clearly recognized and recommended for exploitation in the sales approach:

A funeral is not an occasion for a display of cheapness. It is, in fact, an opportunity for the display of a status symbol which, by bolstering family pride, does much to assuage grief. . . . It seems highly probable that the most satisfactory funeral service for the average family is one in which the cost has necessitated some degree of sacrifice. This permits the survivors to atone for any real or fancied neglect of the deceased prior to his death.[31]

With respect to taking care of the grave, a considerable display is observable. It seems that essential changes have taken place since the last century. While in former times cemeteries were left largely uncared for and were also avoided because of fear of the dead, today the grave is constantly looked after. This may reflect a certain prosperity, which manifests itself also in the care of gardens. This also signifies that the burial place becomes a location where the survivor performs certain obligations toward the departed. The neglect of graves is interpreted by society as a lack of piety for the dead. Quite the opposite is true in case of unusual devotion and care which finds special social approval, as Jackson illustrates in the following case:

A little Italian lady in a small New England industrial town . . . lost a child in the early school years. She made a sacred vow that she would visit his grave every day. Each day she trudged up the hill to the village cemetery, rain or shine, summer or winter. The years have come and gone. Her other children have grown and she has many grandchildren. She will never go to visit them if it involves being away so long that she cannot make her daily pilgrimage up the hill to the cemetery. She has so completely identified herself with that grave that she is willing to kill off much of the other experience of her life. She is completely enslaved by an unbreakable emotional tie. In her simple way she explains a bargain that she must keep, for it is a sacred pledge. But the vow made under the pressure of acute grief has about itself the element of enslavement that appears when an identification is carried on so long that the normal life of the bereaved person is seriously handicapped. What her neighbors take for unusual devotion and faithfulness is more nearly described as the irrational behavior that is the product of an unfortunate state of unresolved emotional disturbance.[32]

The grave can become a permanent place of encounter with the dead person. The archaic fear of the cemetery grows out of the symbolic power of the location: Here it can be experienced in a concentrated form that the deceased has not yet released the living. The pilgrimage to the grave on Sundays and the conversation there with the deceased is a custom in our big cities more common than usually assumed. This as well as observing the day of the death, betrays the constantly felt demand of the dead person. Jackson summarizes this experience in the pregnant point, "Too many cemeteries become the burial place of the living as well as the dead."[33] Also, caring for and frequent visiting of the grave are recognized as a sign of great piety and a truly religious attitude, less in the view of the official church than in the eyes of those who adhere to a certain general religiosity.

A further device for atonement are the donations and contributions to local churches and community helping agencies. They serve to some extent to keep the memory of the dead alive; frequently, however, they represent some degree of sacrifice for the dead and create the conditions to carry on his work. This is, of course, only a possibility for atonement open to people with certain financial means.

(4) *Injury and illness:* Less differentiated societies express the symbolic identification with the dead and the partial atonement toward him frequently in self-inflicted injuries and in cutting off the hair. The bereaved today demonstrate the same by assuming the symptoms of the illness the deceased had suffered from. For self-injuries and cutting of the hair and beard, numerous examples are found, for example, in the Old Testament. They also reveal that both acts were not merely understood as mourning rites but were also recognized as sacrifice for the dead.

Even though self-inflicted injuries are forbidden in Lev. 19:28 ("You shall not make any cuttings in your flesh on account of the dead or tattoo any marks upon you") as well as in Deut. 14:1 ("You shall not cut yourselves or make any baldness on your foreheads for the dead"), it seems that this repeated commandment had not been effective, for, at least in Jer. 16:6, the prophet pictures the total destruction of the people of Israel by saying that nobody will be left for mourning: "Both great and small shall die in this land; they shall not be buried, and no one shall lament for them or cut himself or make himself bald for them." The shedding of blood is, as customs of other people show, most essential; it is considered, for example in Lev. 17:11 ("For the life of the flesh is in the blood"), as the location of life itself. Self-infliction is a means of identifying with the deceased. The prohibitions in Leviticus and Deuteronomy assume that this sacrifice was attached to the death cult and communion with the dead person, which presumably also was practiced at first in Israel as it was in the surrounding tribes. Attempts were made repeatedly to suppress it. That cutting oneself also was considered a sacrifice is indicated in the story in I Kings 18, in which the prophets of Baal tried through such practices to force their God to intervene. A sublimation of self-infliction is apparent in the importance of red as a color of mourning in ancient Rome.

Though self-mutilations in this form occur rather seldom today with respect to atonement, nevertheless, in the *Psychopathology of Everyday Life*, S. Freud has indicated that many apparently accidental injuries happening to neurotic patients, but also to children and healthy adults, are really self-inflicted, brought about by self-reproach. Such a person punishes himself by skillfully making use of an external situation: "The required external situation may accidentally present itself or the punishment tendency may assist it until the way is open for the desired injurious effect."[34]

Even though the cutting off of hair is forbidden in Lev. 19:27 and Deut. 14:1, presumably for the same reasons as self-inflicted injuries are forbidden, it is reported in Jer. 16:6; Amos 8:10; and Ezek. 7:18. In some cases not all hair was cut off, only some on the forehead, as Deut. 14:1 seems to indicate. The shaving of the beard is mentioned in Israel only on the occasion of a ritual for a public disaster (Isa. 15:2; Jer. 41:5; 48:37), but is testified to from the vicinity as an individual mourning rite. Since hair signifies masculine strength, particularly if it is thick, in this ritual, too, the symbolic identification with the powerless dead becomes obvious.

In some phrases and customs the identification with the dead through the sacrifice of hair is still preserved. It is still frequently customary to put a lock of the bereaved's hair in the casket. "To pull out one's hair" even today is a form of acting out on the occasion of a loss and that a bereaved "lets himself go" is often noticed in the neglect of hair (and clothes).

While self-inflicted injuries and the sacrifice of hair connect the possibility of acting out with the atonement, today the atonement is enacted through illness as a form of partial "following-into-death" and by assuming symptoms of the deceased's illness. This conforms to the contemporary tendency of acting out grief passively rather than actively. The connection between disease and physical suffering and the task of atonement was observed by Lifton among isolated survivors in Hiroshima who "adopted a masochistic post-A-bomb life-pattern, through which they derived a certain amount of satisfaction in suffering, death anxiety and death guilt tended to remain prominent, and were often converted into bodily complaints."[35] Physical suffering, however, can be helpful only as long as the guilt to be expiated is limited, because, otherwise, the only possibility left is to bring about sufficient atonement for the sin committed through one's own death.

Illness manifested as the need for self-punishment with respect to the deceased was pointed out by S. Freud in Dostoevski.[36] The temporary cure of depressive patients as soon as they became inmates of concentration camps is well known. The depression returned as the possibility of expiation was taken away from them by their release.[37] It is also a familiar experience, which Lindemann could also observe in depressive mourners,[38] that patients were cured through electroconvulsive therapy, since this is a way of paying for guilt.

Identification with the aggressor by taking on symptoms of his illness has mostly been observed in neurotic patients. Among the patients Lindemann examined 25 percent manifested this form of identification; among Parkes's patients 20 percent did. Naturally, such numbers mean little, since it remains unknown how many of the bereaved consult a doctor because of such symptoms and how many doctors are capable of diagnosing the underlying psychosomatic dynamics.[39]

That a mourner can acquire symptoms resembling those suffered by the dead person during his last illness is, of course, already well documented. Krupp describes the case of a twenty-three-year-old student who entered psychotherapeutic treatment following severe depression and anxiety that occurred three months after his mother's death. The mother had been very domineering, both rejecting and possessive. Periodically the patient would reach out for independence, but he always returned home. After his graduation his mother died of cancer following a short illness. He had no significant reaction. He thought this absence of emotion was to be expected since he had been fighting with her all his life and "hated her." Soon afterward he met a nurse and they became engaged. Throughout the courtship he was involved not only with the girl but also with her mother. Some time later, after renting an apartment for himself and his future bride, he suddenly developed severe symptoms which forced him to return home. Like his mother, he complained of stomach pains which radiated to his back, and when severely depressed he would, like her, retreat into bed and remain under the blanket.[40]

Parkes reports a forty-two-year-old man who in his own words had "modeled" himself entirely according to the image of his father. After his father's death from coronary thrombosis he remained in a depressive mood for three months. Following a few signs of improvement he developed chest pains on his left side and was convinced that, like his father, he suffered from coronary thrombosis. The patient entered analysis and his condition improved slightly. After a tooth extraction, however, he felt pain in his groin and suspected that he had a thrombosis in the same place where his father also had had another thrombosis.[41]

(5) *Clothes:* Identification with the aggressive dead person is displayed also in the change of clothes which symbolizes the transformation of identity.[42] Not only the transition from a pagan to a Christian existence is indicated by a change of clothes, but resurrection as well, where the deceased are dressed in new garments. To rend one's clothes and put on sackcloth is one of the most frequently reported mourning rites from the Old Testament world (see, for example, Gen. 37:34; I Kings 21:27). Yet it is not always clear whether the "sackcloth" should be imagined as rent clothes or as a special garment (such as in I Kings 21:27; II Kings 19:1, yet here on the occasion of public mourning; compare also Gen. 37:34). It has not been completely clarified whether the basic condition is nakedness (indicated in Isa. 32:11 and Micah 1:8) and the rent clothes and the generally ordered bare feet represent only a mitigation.[43] The statement by Paul "so that . . . we may not be found naked" (II Cor. 5:3) at the day of resurrection might

indicate the analogy of being unclothed and dead. From all these customs only the wearing of mourning clothes is preserved until the present time, and even this sign of mourning is abandoned more and more.

(6) *Behavioral modes and characteristics:* Frequently, identification with the dead person occurs in assuming the moral behavior, features, and gestures of the love object. Breuer recorded of Anna O. that when she looked into a mirror after her father's death, it was not herself she saw but her father.[44] Under the term "Return of the Repressed" S. Freud depicts the history of development of a young man who as a child had identified himself very much with his aggressive father, but remained passive for fear of the father and at the same time clung to his mother. After the death of his father, however, he displayed characteristics that were a carbon copy of his father's. He developed an absolutely selfish, despotic, and brutal personality that obviously felt the need to oppress and hurt others. The repressed identification with the aggressor was now reactivated with the death.[45]

Another case illustration is the identification process of a thirty-four-year-old businessman who was hospitalized because of severe anxiety attacks, weight loss, and chest pains with anticipation of heart thrombosis. These attacks first occurred two days after the death of his father.

Like father, the son experienced pericardial pain; dyspnoea, with a need for oxygen; and anticipation of death by heart attack. He began mumbling while going over papers at work, his speech became so indistinct that no one could understand him; he began sighing and saying, "Oh, oh, oh!" with a sad expression on his face that made the resemblance even more striking. He began being abrupt with salesmen and other people, in sharp contrast to his usual pleasant manner; and he used his father's stock phrases, such as "Come on, let's get going"; "Okay, spit it out"; "Can't you do it yourself?" Like father, he began compulsively arranging the office: replacing light bulbs, reorganizing samples, sweeping the floor. He returned home from work seeking grievances—inspecting the house and garage for things to complain about; began wearing a dark raincoat with the collar turned up and pulling the brim of his hat over his eyes; indulged in temper tantrums: breaking a radio, overturning a lamp, kicking a lawn mower. And like father, he experienced lack of sexual desire and occasional impotence.[46]

Even though this may be an extreme and pathological case, elements of such a behavioral response are not unusual. The survivor is obsessed by the thought of what the dead person might do in a given situation if he were still alive. One widow said: "I am deliberately seeing things in the way my husband would have if he were still alive. I was surprised myself that I could face things and cope with them as I had never been able before."[47]

As in the child's behavior the authority of the living parent is taken over, so likewise is the authority of the dead husband. Emancipation from deceased parents is in most cases more difficult than emancipation from the living; this is particularly true with children who have never seen their parents but are always confronted with the idealized picture painted by others. Since they cannot check it out in their daily interactions with the parents and thus cannot detect any deficiencies which could offer a chance for liberating criticism, the dead parents always remain superior.

(7) *Assumption of responsibilities:* Finally, the identification with the lost object can also take place when the survivor assumes some of the tasks the dead person had performed or left unfinished. An archaic form of such identification is the vendetta in which the avenger acts vicariously for the dead. As a result he takes the risk of suffering the same fate as the deceased. Today such identification occurs in taking over the public office he held or the management of the business of the deceased. The case of Mr. and Mrs. L., Jackson reports, illustrates this form of identification:

Mrs. L. was an active, energetic little woman, very much involved in church and community affairs. She was even elected to the school board in town and was quite a figure in the community because of her vigorous stand on public issues. On the other hand, Mr. L. was retiring. While he never interfered with the affairs, he seldom participated. . . . He was seldom seen at public meetings and never attended church though his wife seldom missed a Sunday. He preferred to work around the house and in the garden, which was his pride and joy.

The Sunday after Mrs. L. died, her husband came to church and sat in the place that she usually occupied. It was assumed that this was an act of devotion toward her memory, but no one expected to see him there again for some time. However, in the two years that have elapsed since her death, he has missed the regular service of worship only during vacation time and when he was away on business. Not only that, he indicated that he would like to serve his wife's unexpired term on the school board. . . . He continued to move into other community activities. . . . At the same time the garden and the property showed signs of neglect. He did not devote the time or interest there as he had formerly done. In many respects he was a different person. Though he had not shown any marked signs of grief at his wife's death, there was evidence that his life had been profoundly changed by that emotional experience.[48]

Nevertheless the result is ambiguous: While Mr. L. followed entirely in the footsteps of his dead wife with respect to his activity, some people smilingly remarked that at last he was able to possess his own soul and speak his own mind.

Already when the emotional chaos is calmed down with the help of regressive mechanisms, many of the accusations can no longer be justified. The bereaved gradually finds himself in a position where he is able to evaluate realistically the significance of his offense. What before seemed to be a crime committed by the doctor proves to be a bad incident in the adaptive stage. To this extent the bereaved has the right to forget these reproaches against himself and others. Particularly in case of recriminations for having neglected the dying, forgetting the guilt is a positive adaptive mechanism.

The second form of adaptive behavior by self-reproaches is articulation. Relatively simple therapeutic help may cause the reproaches and self-accusations to collapse. Talking it over enables a person to get into proportion these exaggerated dimensions; the primitive cosmic view about a direct connection between guilt and death and criteria for an appropriate age for dying can be corrected. We should give special consideration to examining why our funeral liturgies do not include explicit forms of forgiveness. It is true that the mass for the dead is an expiating rite, including the survivor as well. To forgive the dead, the others, and one's own self is the essential goal in the adaptive stage.

The content of the adaptive stage is strongly determined by what is seen as the goal of the identification process. The defense mechanism of identification with the aggressor presupposes the domineering position of the dead person. This predominance can be rooted in social superiority, in exemplary ethical qualities, or in an aggressive superiority over the living. Jackson is right in pointing out that the dependency of the woman in our society makes it important for widows in particular to continue this relationship of dependency by identifying with her dead husband.[49]

Freud, who in his patriarchal view presupposes the authority of the father and even concedes sadistic features as a natural consequence of this authority, considered the mourner's identification with the dead as the most essential mechanism besides recollection in coping with grief. Many of his students followed him at this point, even if they, according to the North American family structure, de facto replaced the father with the mother, since she dominates there in the emotional area.

One can make distinctions, as Siggins does, between a number of forms of identification with the dominating love object: It may be "morbid" identification with the lost person's illness or death when the mourner takes on his symptoms, or a more positive identification with the vital and satisfying aspects of the relationship when the mourner develops personality traits of the lost person as continuous submission to the dead person or to carry on responsibilities in the "name" of the deceased.[50] Nevertheless, it is a serious question whether a deceased should impose his will upon the survivor, even if this represents for him some form of staying alive, and whether even the most outstanding ethical accomplishment survivors might achieve on behalf of the deceased give the right to hinder the emancipation of the survivor. Can a theory about grief take over such a value judgment without reflection?

The question arises whether the adaptive stage is not a unique opportunity to work through the relationship with the deceased and attain an attitude in which, symbolically speaking, the bereaved liberates himself from the dead without deserting him, and in which he introjects the lost object in such a form that his image no longer is distorted by hate and submission (or by it's compensation in an "overpowering" love). In the case mentioned above, Mr. L. seems to have succeeded in finding some balance between his own emancipation and the introjection of his dead wife. He now can admit to himself the feelings of relief and release without having to develop guilt feelings. It is certainly an important task in counseling with the bereaved to strengthen these feelings of relief which they might experience after a death and which run so contrary to the social conventions. It is necessary to help a positive development of such feelings, so that the deceased will neither be abandoned nor continue his dominance, but can for the first time become a "partner" of the survivor. The numerous attempts to do penance by the bereaved, but also the Christian concept of forgiveness, has to be judged by whether the primary intention of expiation and forgiveness lies in the reparation of an actual or fantasized guilt or in enabling the bereaved to fully recognize his relationship with the dead and to effect a constructive change in himself. If ultimately his guilt feelings and attempts at expiation serve only to bind him even closer to the deceased and under his dominance, then this is in a theological understanding of human interactions not legitimate.

In theological tradition the death of the neighbor is generally characterized as "temptation." The bereaved's belief in a loving God and a trustworthy earth is destroyed. The deceased may have been master and protector, but may have also fulfilled the need to dominate and to care for. The "temptation" of grief provides the possibility, theologically speaking, of changing the relationship to the deceased fundamentally; instead of seeing in him a master and protector (who, nevertheless, neither proved to be master over death nor offered protection against it), the bereaved can perceive in him the brother. Instead of having a subordinate who is used for satisfying the desire to rule or made dependent for the rest of his life by overpowering devotion, he can be recognized as one's equal.

He can be perceived in the same way God perceives us, as symbolized in the day of judgment, namely, as a victim of social structures. Seen and accepted in this manner, the deceased and the bereaved remain united in the expectation of the coming kingdom of God.

7.32 Sociological implications

In contrast to older societies, the modern world in fact has no socially approved forms for acting out aggressive feelings in grief, nor for expressing these verbally and paying a penalty for the guilt resulting from it. "Following-in-death," as it was a social duty among the Suti, at least for the upper classes, can be brought about actively only by committing suicide. Instead of wailing, self-inflicted injury, sacrifice of hair and rending of clothes, there is only the short-term consolation of having given the dead a wonderful funeral. The social duty today is to praise the deceased and to speak well of him. This is a form of reparation not to be pushed aside too easily; when Jackson identifies idealization of the dead as the best and easiest way to solve guilt feelings,[51] admittedly this is a possibility, but the negative sides of the deceased then must still be turned against the mourner himself in form of aggressions.

Instead of providing possibilities for expiation, social norms about the correct behavior in mourning are an additional source for self-recrimination. The social role of the bereaved demands the display of tears and to be severely grief-stricken, but precisely the ambivalent feelings toward the deceased can inhibit the overt demonstration of grief.[52] Not to feel or express grief will inevitably evoke the disapproval of family members and social environment. The wish not to go along with the local funeral arrangements is considered a neglect of the dead and results in social disapproval.[53] The survivor may recover more quickly from the loss and his grief than is permitted by public standards for an appropriate mourning period.[54] This may make him feel guilty of not honoring the deceased in the right way and of having loved him less than he admits to himself.

In a case study, Jackson reports an orthodox Jew who felt a

strong sense of obligation to both the national and religious traditions of the Jewish people. His son David S. did not share his father's interest; in fact, he felt that too active an interest in Jewish matters was detrimental to the life of individuals. In what might be considered overt rebellion, he married a Protestant girl. It brought on a vigorous argument between father and son. Things went on for years, with a rather difficult adjustment having been achieved by both sides, that is, they carefully avoided any further discussion of such matters. After the father's death the son and his family were not able to participate fully in the traditional funeral rites, but did what they could. David S. developed strong feelings of guilt and went to see the rabbi, who admonished him severely and indicated that there was no freedom from guilt for him until he had fulfilled the demands of his father and his father's father. This he could not do in good conscience. When he became ill a few months later and the pastor called on him, David's first remark was: "Is this also a punishment for my sins?"[55] The Jewish tradition that imposes a strong obligation upon the son toward the father, particularly regarding his funeral, had caused an insolvable conflict with the son's negative attitude toward ritual forms.

In a culture where "the family of God is the family,"[56] where ancestor worship is therefore a socially accepted form of the relationship with the dead person, this can be a great help for the bereaved. J. Yamamoto et al. drew an interesting comparison between the mourning behavior of widows interviewed by Marris in London and a small sample in Tokyo.[57] Both groups felt the physical presence of the dead person, but in contrast to 90 percent of the widows in Tokyo who experienced this presence, there were only 50 percent in the London group. Yamamoto et al. see the reason for this difference in the fact that the widows in Tokyo observe a socially approved and promoted behavior pattern. They burn incense at least once a day; the photograph of the departed, the urn with the ashes, flowers, water, rice, and other offerings are dedicated to the ancestor. The widow can ring a bell at the house altar, burn incense, and talk about her happy and sad feelings with the ancestor. It is remarkable that none of the Japanese widows showed any kind of self-recrimination, yet 60 percent reproached others.

Fuchs critically pointed out the remainders of social control that the deceased continues to exercise in our society, even with public approval. "That the dead grandmother or another relative looks down from heaven, checks the behavior, and can do all kinds of things certainly most people have learned in their childhood. . . . As a result of the failed liberation from the parents during adolescence and continuous over-identification, father or mother or conjugal partner even in death still function primarily as agents of behavior control in their role as interaction partners." [58] Some authors consider the fictive social relation as standard: "Interpersonal relations do not cease with death; the deceased may continue to influence the survivor for many years." [59]

An individual possesses actual legal possibilities beyond his death in various ways. He can determine his style of funeral (such as cremation against the will of the family). He continues to have legal status. In his last will he can exert control beyond his death by stipulating that the handing over of the inheritance be bound by attaining a certain status or age. The family members can gain social approval in continuing the deceased's "life work" or completing it and raising the children in his "spirit."

It becomes clear that even society in its present form does not permit taking away from the deceased his dominant position. It is left to the individual to cope with aggressions against the unjustified dominance and turn them against himself. Freud in his patriarchal attitude advocated submission to the father, since it is always the bereaved who evokes the father's reproach and punishment with his death wishes, even though Freud himself suffered under this father image, as his constant preoccupation with this issue reveals. He also recognized the consequences of such an attitude, namely, melancholia. With or without intention, this places him in one line with certain Christian traditions, which know only the unconditional submission under God and advise the individual to seek the cause of aggression and the resulting guilt by themselves. *Ihr laßt den Armen schuldig werden und überlaßt ihn dann Pein* ("You let the poor become guilty and then leave him alone with his pain"—Goethe) is still the consequence of the public attitude, as far as it supports the individual coping mechanism of identification with the aggressor. This calls for a decisive new approach of theology.

7.33 The universal redemption

It is a generally recognized fact that nowhere in the Christian funeral is the contradiction between a biblical theology and the funeral ritual so evident as in the problem of the Last Judgment. While the New Testament statements together with the theology prevailing since the twenties with reference to the Reformation speak with some clarity of a judgment (even though this judgment may be interpreted existentially as the decision which man receives upon the judgment of his life), neither the liturgies nor the funeral orations give appropriate recognition to the judgment and final damnation.

There are more deeply rooted reasons for this fact. The notion of total death and general resurrection at the beginning of the "new society," for instance, has succeeded over liberal traditions even in the funeral practice. That, on the other hand, judgment is hardly mentioned certainly has various causes; some of the most important are mentioned here in a rather brief way.

(1) The upheaval in Protestant theology in the twenties yielded a basic rejection to expressing faith in moral categories. This de-moralization of theology, which is quite positive in itself, makes God's judgment dependent upon whether that person believes in him, trusts in him, and is in contact with him. These are all categories of inner attitudes which do not express themselves in external actions and therefore cannot be judged in terms of their sincerity or insincerity. If sin is collectivized as misconduct and rebellion against God, then this is hardly to be gathered from the individual's interpersonal behavior.

(2) The extreme privatizing of individual behavior, without that conception of sin, makes it extremely difficult to establish

general categories of moral misconduct. Neither in terms of certain forms of Christian behavior, for example, church attendance, nor in terms of ethical issues, such as sexual morals, has such a uniform social consensus been reached that a minister could refer to it in his funeral sermon. In addition to this, he frequently does not even want to, since he does not understand his role as reinforcer of contemporary moral standards, but rather sees himself as someone who protects discriminated minorities against moral rigidity.

(3) A deeper insight into the fact that individual actions are socially conditioned has shaken the moral judgment even where it was clear-cut previously, such as with respect to suicides, criminals, mothers of illegitimate children, and sexual assailants. It becomes much more obvious, at least in scientific research, how social mechanisms single out certain people and force them into the role of one who inevitably will fall victim to moral condemnation. There are many precipitating factors from as far back as early childhood, of which the strength of a person's own decision-making ability is only one, which lead to such actions disapproved of by society on the basis of a broad consensus.

If so far in the systematic considerations the notion of judgment has nevertheless been retained, then three viewpoints were operative, which, however, are not convincing to the extent that it may seem at first.

(1) The majority of the passages in the New Testament relevant here speak of a coming judgment. Nevertheless, there are also a few passages that assure salvation for all human beings. According to Rom. 5:18, Jesus' act of righteousness leads to acquittal and life for all men; Rom. 11:26, 32 speak of God's mercy upon all men (see also Eph. 1:10 and Col. 1:16, 20). According to I Cor. 15:25 ff., all things shall be subjected to Christ and God will be everything to everyone.

(2) The threat of "death away from eternity" belongs to the ethical-educational type of thinking and occurred repeatedly as one of the attitudes of the churches', as Tillich points out.[60] The churches were afraid that the teaching of universal redemption would destroy the seriousness of religious and ethical decisions. It is hard to say how much the threat of

punishment with eternal death actually still has a preventive effect today. Frequently the concept of responsibility, for example, is so emptied and secularized that it is doubtful whether it can still be understood as a statement about God's judgment which everyone must face who feels responsible for himself.

(3) Finally, it is indicated that whoever indicts man recognizes him as committer of his deeds and as a responsible being. Thus it is conceded to this human being that he is not only under biological or societal determination, but a person who decides for himself. The guilt of society is my guilt as well. H. Gollwitzer insists on this viewpoint, but identifies it as a utopian viewpoint, possible to make only if based on God's reconciliation with man already consummated in Christ. In the last analysis the purpose of judgment is not punishment but recognition of failure. If one refers to an eschatological judgment then it cannot be a judgment that animates unconscious and neurotic anxieties, but rather a verdict comprehensible to the indicted and one that changes his actions.[61] The judge is replaced by the doctor, as Gollwitzer says; actually it would be more precise to say by the therapist, whose intention is primarily to help a person recognize a particular misconduct. Through this process he helps the one who has failed and done wrong to others to a change in his attitude. It is the decisive theological intention that the symbol of the eschatological judgment does not lead to an earthly or heavenly expiation, but to the often painful recognition of failure, and results in a behavioral change. The primary intention is not reparation, which is never possible in the full sense, as we have shown above. If this is understood, then we must ask whether the symbol of eschatological "judgment" should not be more clearly subordinated to the eschatological statement of the "universal redemption" than is now the case in systematic considerations. Only the full revelation and development of the "new society" can bring forth the will of God clearly, namely, that God desires life not death. However, for one who recognizes this will of God in the words and deeds of Jesus, the educational, personal, or

punishing aspects the symbol of eschatological judgment represents can only be of secondary importance.

The vast majority of currently available presentations of eschatology leave judgment and universal redemption unreconciled. For Brunner, both aspects "remain juxtaposed in their harsh incompatibility. . . . Our answer is: both voices are the Word of God." [62] God's holiness and his love remain parallel to one another and incompatible: "We must listen to the voice that speaks of world judgment as to the voice of God himself in order that we may love him. Only through this indissoluble duality do we grasp the duality of God's being." [63] Künneth demands besides responsibility "another, a second necessary realization" in order to express the consummation of the goal of history. [64] Kreck leaves the question open: "To what extent a person actually abides or can abide finally in opposition to Christ is beyond my judgment. It is, in spite of all intruding negative phenomena, out of my reach and exceeds my competencies. As little as we dare try to upset the proposition that the belief in Christ alone saves and disbelief condemns, and as certainly as it must be proclaimed that this will be revealed before the very eyes of everyone on the day of the Last Judgment, just so little can I judge what possibilities God has, who—as we have seen—fulfills his promises in his own way, loyal to himself and yet also in royal freedom, putting us to shame, in order to lead men to the realization of the truth." [65]

Karl Barth without doubt defends universal redemption most clearly. This for him is rooted in the doctrine of predestination, according to which the free grace of election is the divine determination of man, demonstrated on the cross where Christ is rejected himself in order to save us all. This is the positive decision, described by Barth as follows: "the kingdom of Heaven opened and hell closed; God vindicated and Satan overcome; life triumphant and death destroyed; belief in the promise the only possibility and disbelief in it the excluded possibility." [66] The difference between those who believe and those who reject remains, but this difference consists only in that some testify, accept, proclaim, in order to make evident what the others do not yet recognize. [67]

Looked upon from the central eschatological symbol of the "new society," the symbol of "universal redemption" definitely has the preference over the one of "judgment." The theological intention can only be to make the "new society" sensible and convincing. But theology cannot threaten that the rejection of this realization perhaps will be decisive for time and eternity. Theology cannot assume that the individual already is a "person" responsible for all his actions and to be held responsible for them, but aims at creating conditions in which the individual no longer falls victim to the social structure, but which actually enable him to act sensibly and responsibly.

As a criticism of the power structure the eschatological symbol of "universal redemption" turns against any form of trial that proves incapable of making the delinquent recognize his faulty actions. It criticizes a system that is content if the guilty submits and recognizes law and order without changing or being able to change his own attitude. It condemns a criminal procedure in which even the best therapeutic efforts are effective enough only to neutralize the harmful influence of the prison atmosphere. "Universal redemption" attacks critically a society that believes itself to be able to remove the evil of society by inflicting physical and social death, instead of realizing how much it is to be blamed for the misbehavior of the individual.

The eschatological notion of "universal redemption" motivates not condemnation of the other but rather the effort to convey to him an insight into his actions that will transform him. It calls for more detailed inquiry and research of the factors to which a person's guilt is attributable. It is a driving force for finding ways of living by bringing to the surface the nucleus of failure with respect to the deceased and taking it seriously. It makes us realize that not always is the ideal-typical (Freudian or Christian) "father" right as against the ideal-typical "child" and subordinate. "Universal redemption" transmits the capability of bearing hate and meanness, since the offender does not know what he does and is being forgiven beforehand. The concrete effort is not governed by eradication but reintegration (which nevertheless must not be achieved exclusively at the cost of the one to be integrated).

The "new society" realized with the Messiah is introduced as a constitution of persons in which repressive compulsions are no longer necessary. Severity and gravity are attached to it, which is characteristic of the overcoming of failures and exploitations of all kinds; the costs of the victories are not forgotten, yet are forgiven.

8. The object-libidinal coping mechanisms

8.1 The mechanism: helplessness

8.11 Psychological aspects

In his contribution to *Das Problem der Depression* (Problem of Depression), and he regards grief as part of it, E. Bibring identifies the general feeling of helplessness of the depressive as "the core of all types of depression."[1] Depression can involve the additional component of aggression as well as strong regression to oral behavior, but the central issue in depression is a feeling of helplessness: "Depression in its character is not the result of warding off aggression but a way, peculiar to man, of reacting to failure and disappointment, as often as the ego finds itself in a condition of real or imagined helplessness against overpowering difficulties."[2] Whatever it might be that causes defeat, upsets self-respect, and destroys hope, "the result remains the same: The individual will feel helpless in his loneliness, isolation, weakness, inferiority, viciousness, or guilt."[3] At the same time Bibring refers to the "secondary profit," as he calls it, which many patients gain from their depression: "By demonstrating their self-imposed sufferings, the patients attempt to attain important narcissistic ideals."[4]

In all manifestations of helplessness, the dual aspect peculiar to all defensive mechanisms becomes very conspicuous. Helplessness is the awareness of one's inability to carry on and therefore to give up. The helpless individual no longer exerts control over himself and his environment. This brings him to the edge of dying himself. Many manifestations of helplessness, exhaustion, apathy, muteness, but also the older custom of walking in "sackcloth and ashes," indicate a symbolic death. At the same time, helplessness is a gesture of submission and appeal, not to obtain any profit or triumph from the defeat of suffering the loss. As Radó puts it, it "hopes to win love."[5] It is the plea to God for ending the suffering and to the social environment to accept the bereaved again in the community of the living. In a case study for the "attention-getting response" Fulcomer illustrates such behavior of helplessness:

This woman, thirty-eight years of age and the wife of an insurance adjuster, made a collapse response in the immediate stage and a protestive response in the post-immediate stage. Immediately following the burial service, two brothers and her mother accompanied the bereaved wife to her home. (A new home into which the couple had moved less than four months before the death of the husband.) Before they had reached the driveway of the house, the bereaved woman began weeping violently. This continued until ten or fifteen minutes after she was in the house. Her mother and brothers tried to console her, but she accused them of attempting to make her forget her husband and became so violent that they ceased their efforts and allowed her to continue weeping.

When she had become less violent and was sobbing quietly, she threw her arms about her mother and pleaded with her not to leave. "I am so alone now," she sobbed. A few minutes later she went to her bedroom and flopped across the bed, remaining there for more than half an hour. On the next day she came out to the kitchen. There she sat and watched her mother and began telling her all the terrible fortune she was experiencing. She went into the minutest detail so that her mother could hardly stand to listen to her. Finally she went into the living room where she counted and arranged all the messages that had come in. When they were ready to eat, she would only drink a glass of tomato juice. And during the entire time the others were eating she did not say a word.

As one of her brothers was departing after the meal, the bereaved wife threw her arms around him and wept violently. "Thank you for helping me," she cried. "Without you I could not have stood it. Be good to B. You don't know how lucky you are to still have her. Here I am still so young and left alone." She continued to weep until after he had gone.

Later in the evening she insisted upon doing something, but after fifteen or twenty minutes she appeared to become despondent and sat speechless in a chair. Her mother insisted that she go to bed. At this request the bereaved wife wept vehemently and accused her mother of not realizing what a loss had been inflicted upon her. This behavior continued until her mother had helped her get into bed.

On the following morning the bereaved wife was up early and appeared extremely depressed. According to her mother she moved around looking as if the whole world were coming to an end. She spoke only when spoken to. Later on her mother found her weeping. She cried: "Oh, Mother, I feel so lonesome without him. I just can't believe he is really dead. What can I do! What can I do!" Shortly after she had recovered from this, a friend called and a scene of weeping followed. She related all her troubles to this friend and told her how fortunate she was to still have a husband. The bereaved woman had dressed herself in one of her black dresses that morning. She insisted that the mourning sign be left on the door for a month, and she purchased some black material so that another black dress could be made. During the afternoon she had a period of despondency and several instances of violent weeping.

On the following day, several scenes of weeping occurred, once when a lawyer called to arrange settlement of the estate, once when the pastor called, and once when two friends called. To each visitor and to those who called on the telephone she seemed anxious to speak and tell her troubles. The fifth day after the funeral, the mother of the bereaved wrote: "It is very difficult to lose a husband but she is making a fool of herself. Others of us have gone through the same thing without inflicting our grief upon everyone else. She has been improving slightly during the last few days, thank goodness. But if, within the next few days, she doesn't entirely stop making a display of her emotions when people call, I shall tell her what she ought to be told."

However, the bereaved woman did gradually put an end to her periods of weeping and complaining. Gradually, too, the periods of despondency disappeared. She insisted upon wearing black dresses until the fourteenth day after the funeral.[6]

This case illustration describes vividly how the widow attempts to secure attention and support from family and friends. It reveals, too, the lack of understanding in the reaction of the social environment which makes it actually impossible for the bereaved in their helplessness and pleading for help to cope with their grief.

Visible signs of helplessness are general exhaustion, apathy, and weeping. The bereaved prefers to risk the disapproval of his social environment than to repress and hide his suffering and pain. Each summoning to "pulling oneself together" counteracts everything helplessness aims for in the regressive stage, precisely to let oneself go, not to cling to the dead person in a violent and compulsive way, and not to give the impression through a controlled behavior that nothing has happened.

(1) Physical exhaustion the bereaved generally experiences accounts for the impression of helplessness.[7] Bowlby tried to explain this state of exhaustion as a result of the protest against separation and the attempt to regain the lost object; this phase of protest leads to the stage of depressive mood, following a complete breakdown of all resistance. However, we will have to agree with J. A. Averill that this depression of grief cannot explain the mere physical or mental exhaustion.[8] The effort to dissolve the tie to the deceased may also use up energy.[9] Finally, the fact that the bereaved uses his entire energy for maintaining his psychic organization may account for the exhaustion.

(2) In addition to exhaustion, the symptoms that give the impression of helplessness also include apathy and lack of self-initiated activity. This represents a great similarity to depressive behavior. Diminished physical activity, however, cannot be made accountable for the appearance of apathy. Ekman and Friesen[10] were able to prove with films about the behavior of the depressed that during an interview situation the patients are not distinguishable from normal persons undergoing the test with respect to the total number of their movements. However, the mode of their motions clearly give the impression of helplessness and impoverishment of movements.

(3) The inability to speak is also a sign of apathy and helplessness. In *The Theme of the Three Caskets* (1913) Freud points out that dumbness in a dream represents death. Though dead persons do appear, they are distinguished from the living by their inability to speak. In fairy tales, too, dumbness frequently is a condition a person has to go through

in order to restore a beloved one to life, that is, by identifying with death itself.[11] It can be observed frequently that the bereaved during the first period of grief respond only if spoken to. Job's friends waited for seven days and seven nights before they began to speak to him (Job 2:13). At the same time, the bereaved can feel great need to talk about their experiences, sometimes to the point of exhaustion once the ban of silence is lifted. Talking also serves the purpose of activating the sympathy and help of others.

(4) Helplessness is expressed in non-Western societies by the use of soil and dust. Here, too, the dual relation between partial identity with death and the appeal to the sympathy of others occurs. Soil and dust symbolize being buried, the vanity of one's own self. Dust is an element of the dead. In Isa. 26:19 they are identified as the "dwellers of the dust."

In the Israel of the Old Testament mourners strew dirt, dust, and ashes upon their head. Some passages, such as Jer. 6:26, suggest that the mourners also rolled in ashes. The enhancement of this behavior is seen when the mourner or penitent sits among the ashes, as this is reported in Job 2:8. This custom is also found in Jon. 3:6 where the people of Nineveh covered themselves with sackcloth and held a fast following Jonah's call for repentance, while the king sat in ashes as a symbol of his repentance. The meaning of ashes (the word is often used as identical terminology for "dust") is largely unknown. It could refer to the ashes of the deceased and also to the remainders of a totem animal dedicated to the dead or the gods. In a diminished sense, this meaning is still preserved in daily speech when one refers to exhaustion by saying that one feels "completely burned out."

(5) The most vivid expression of helplessness, however, is weeping. It can exhibit various emotions. We can cry at the happy ending of a hardship. Anger and madness can bring tears to the eyes of the bereaved, since the lost object cannot be recovered. Phyllis Greenacre defines the aggressive significance of such weeping more precisely as a coincidence "of the beginning change from hostile aggression to the use of its energy in a positive and non-destructive way."[12] Weeping leads from the stage of shock and disbelief through the stage

of control to regression (the giving up of oneself) and adaptation (appeal to the help of others).

At this point the expressive aspect of weeping comes to the foreground and becomes dominant. Tears no longer flow because the bereaved sees himself confined and depressed, but because he experiences relief. He changes from a state of tension to a relaxed attitude, from being up-tight to relaxation, from despair to hope. Weeping is no longer the expression of resistance, but has become a unity with the entire person. The awareness of one's own powerlessness is now also understood emotionally. The impact on the mourner is so great that it results in an act of inner abandonment.

Apart from the fact that tears contribute to the total pattern of helplessness, they also can be made accountable for a number of symbolic meanings of which some are also significant for the grief process. According to Melanie Klein, tears signify the expulsion of the bad object who has died and deserted the bereaved.[13] On the other hand, according to Jackson, they symbolize a kind of "washing away" of irritations. Just as the eyeball responds with increased secretion to remove a disturbing particle of dirt as quickly as possible, so tears symbolically can serve to wash away pain and other irritants of life.[14] Finally, and this Greenacre has stressed, weeping stays in a symbolic connection with looking and yet not seeing. The eye is the most important organ for the affirmation of the loss. The eye searches for the lost person, yet cannot see him. Tears symbolize this interchange of seeing as it happens within the grief period by recognizing the deceased in other persons, and not-seeing, since the loss of the deceased is final.[15]

The free flow of tears is an important sign that a loss is recognized fully and the bereaved opens himself completely to the loss. The words by Goethe *Die Träne quillt, die Erde hat mich wieder* ("The tears well to my eyes, I have been given back to earth again") is an expressive formulation of this fact. The inability to weep can be a sign of inhibited grief and possibly lead to pathological consequences if the transfixed, dry-eyed pain cannot be dissolved.

The group of symptoms expressing helplessness as a

defensive mechanism includes mainly exhaustion, apathy, dumbness, and weeping in which not only the shedding of tears but also sighing and sobbing have to be thought of. The wringing of hands belongs to it as an expression for not being able to act. This defensive mechanism of helplessness very likely suggests escaping into a physical disease, since this will secure attention and care that one could not receive merely as mourner.

Arthur H. Schmale, in an empirical study, researched the connection between loss and the onset of an illness. He discovered that the affect of helplessness is the most frequently experienced antecedent of disease onset, for example, 50 percent more frequently than anger and about 70 percent more than fear and shame.[16]

The results of this and other research caused Engel and Schmale, as well as their associates, to speak of a "complex of ego giving up," implemented by desperation, depression, grief and other sufferings of loss.[17] It represents a nonspecific condition for the beginning and intensification of both somatic and psychiatric diseases. Engel and Schmale circumscribe this process with the following characteristics:[18] (1) The patient describes his experience in phrases such as "it is simply too much"; "it is of no use"; "I cannot stand it any longer"; "I give up." This expresses both helplessness and hopelessness. Engel and Schmale speak of helplessness if the reason for the ego's "giving up" is its awareness of its inability to defend itself against a loss of autonomy; they term it hopelessness if the loss of autonomy is combined with a feeling of despair coming from the patient's awareness of his own inability to provide himself with gratification.[19] (2) The patient is aware that he is less and less capable of self-control and uncertain whether he is still behaving normally. (3) The relationship to the love object is severely disturbed. (4) The outside world is conceived of as so totally changed that former expectations no longer have a chance to be fulfilled in the same manner as before. (5) The patient feels the loss of continuity between past and future and his own incapability of looking to the future with hope and confidence. Therefore the future seems less attractive. (6) There is a tendency to reactivate feelings, memories, and behavioral modes from the past with similar negative implications.

Grief does not necessarily lead to the complex of ego giving up. Schmale observes in his investigation that all wives of men with terminal cancer reflected manifestations of grief, but only slightly more than half were so helpless and without hope with respect to the impending loss[20] that somatic and psychic disorders occurred. Generally, according to Schmale, physical symptoms occur as a consequence of the ego giving up when the actual loss was preceded by more or less severe somatic or other disorders in previous years.[21] Schmale states only vaguely the direction in which a specific illness could develop from the mechanism of giving up and hardly goes beyond some early observations by Freud.[22] Helplessness primarily affects, according to Schmale, the general ability of resistance in a negative way, the immunity against infection and organic disfunctions.[23] Through his own research he discovered a possible correlation between helplessness and hopelessness and the development of cancer.[24] How much psychosomatic effects of loss in grief, as described above in a summarizing way, are attributable to the mechanism of giving up, either completely or in part is—as far as this can be judged—just as unsettled as the physiological interaction between ego giving up and disease onset.

8.12 Sociological implications

Among the various forms in which helplessness expresses itself, weeping in particular is socially demanded, even though with clear restrictions. H. v. Hug-Hellmuth cites the conversation with a child:

"You know, Grandma," Toni said one day, "when you die I will cry."—"Yes, but why?"—"Well, that's what one does, isn't it?"[25]

The child's response reflects the social expectation just as the question asked by a Bavarian farmer's wife, which K. Meuli quotes: "What is the custom here, dear cousin, where do you start crying, while still at the house or when you get to the cemetery?"[26] It is not always easy to decide how much crying is exclusively a social norm or how much this norm serves the intensification of the individual experience. Durkheim sees in weeping not at all a natural reaction to the impact of the loss; according to his observation this is a social duty imposed upon the bereaved by the social environment: "One weeps, not simply because one is sad, but because one is forced to weep."[27] In Meuli's opinion the social character of weeping is recognizable in that it is artificial, too prolonged, and public. The artificial character can be proven, he says, with some known folk customs in which onions and pepper are used to stimulate the flow of tears. In addition, weeping is continued for more than a half year. Unquestionably there is a socially demanded "public" weeping which displays the bereaved's affection and is easily elicited as group phenomenon, for instance, where in the church special pews for the bereaved are customary. Sitting there they can demonstrate weeping during the service every Sunday anew. Or another example is the custom of the women of the village visiting the cemetery before dawn where they cry and weep at the graves of their loved ones. But weeping is also a spontaneous, individual response.

Nevertheless, there are also quite opposite expectations demanding controlled behavior. While adults are more likely to cry in case of death than children, this is less a result of social norm than the general inability of children to cry under such a shock. Yet already by about the age of twelve, the social control is noticeable: Male members of society consider it unworthy to shed tears and declare this a female matter.

Among the persons interviewed by Clayton et al., 79 percent mentioned having wept on the occasion of death.[28] Social-cultural influences are clearly seen here, known from other investigations: Only 56 percent of the men, but almost 96 percent of the women said they had wept[29] (naturally this statistic is questionable since there are social norms about weeping and nonweeping that tempt the interviewed to conform to these norms in their answers). Insofar as weeping is a means of relief and an unmistakable appeal to the help of the social group, that is, it has a therapeutic function, men are excluded from this opportunity as well as adherents of certain religious convictions which together with the feeling of grief also forbid its expression.

That weeping evokes the support of family and relatives is observable in the outburst of tears during a conversation prior to the funeral and at the open grave. This induces the attention of relatives, the same they would give a weeping child. They use comforting words in which affirmative remarks are repeated; they take the weeping person in their arms, show other signs of affection, and give him something to eat or to drink. Such comforting gestures are mainly displayed by women, seldom by men, perhaps with the exception of the husband. Men mostly have only certain gestures available, such as patting on the shoulder or back.

The death of a family member is the most radical event within a family, as can be inferred from the participation even of distant relatives in the funeral ceremonies. On no other occasion is the help offered so spontaneous and are such sacrifices made (for instance in high travel expenses) as in case of death. This demonstrates that in extremely severe crisis situations a relatively strong tie is still effective within the family network and is reactivated on such an occasion. Frequently relatives meet at the funeral for the first time.

In general, it is expected of the family members that in view of the obvious helplessness of the most grief stricken they provide support for a certain period, especially in the controlled and the regressive stages of mourning, by making the necessary arrangements for the funeral and running certain errands for the bereaved. At this point complications may arise if certain conflicts already existed and are now occasionally intensified, considering the heightened emotionality of the entire situation (such as the often cited quarrels about the inheritance, beginning even at the grave). When the deceased had been a very domineering personality who by no means had anticipated his death, it can become rather difficult to take his place temporarily and provide the help needed. Finally, it is important how the family has handled difficulties and disagreements before. Families may be efficient and well-organized with respect to financial or professional matters, but completely ineffective in catering to the emotional needs of their members.[30]

Neighbors and friends mostly are of great help, not only in the village but also in those city districts with an older settlement. The assistance of neighbors and friends may be limited to a condolence call but can also include other more active help. According to Gorer, more than 60 percent of the bereaved had received their neighbors' and friends' expressions of sympathy.[31] Condolence calls are often rather difficult, since there is no established social code of communication between the bereaved and the visitor. Should the person who calls speak of the loss, or would this provoke an outburst of weeping in the mourner which might prove contagious? Besides, as an outsider one never knows how tragically the loss has affected the mourner. An antique dealer describes the situation right to the point:

People are a little embarrassed to talk about these things, even if they feel quite sorry. One doesn't know quite what to do. Quite a well-known figure in [this town] who died about a week ago—well, his son who I know fairly well, I didn't quite know whether to go in his shop and say, "Well, I'm sorry about your father" or not. He has probably got plenty to think about, and plenty of closer friends. . . . I've found it a little bit awkward when people came in and spoke about my father, because I had to repeat the same thing over and over again, till I was tired of repeating it really.[32]

Approximately half of the mourners who had received condolence calls felt, so the report by Gorer, that they had received comfort and support from them; less than half said that they had found them painful in various degrees. On the other hand, those who had not received sympathy were resentful.[33] It seems a fair generalization to say that whether the family's and neighbors' sympathy and condolence is of some comfort and help depends significantly on the mourner's ability to accept help offered to him. If he can cope with his loss only by withdrawal, then condolence calls can become a heavy burden. The more the work of mourning is internalized, the less comfort is to be found in those calls by the bereaved, if one may infer this from the data collected by

Gorer. The better they are adjusted socially and psychologically in their communities, the more they are able to experience comfort and support from such calls.

The support of the family and social surrounding may not help the bereaved at all, and, in fact, may impose a burden on him if he is still in the regressive stage, while the family assumes that it is time to interfere and the bereaved should start with active problem-solving. They may impose activities on him for which he is not yet ready, such as attending parties or beginning to search for a new marriage partner. Even though he may be grateful for some suggestions, at this point he may find himself strained and not capable of meeting such expectations.

In view of the alternating desire to withdraw and the need to seek the company of others to be strengthened and comforted by them, it is often hard for the family and social group to adjust in the right way to the bereaved. The bereaved fluctuate in their emotions, especially in the regressive stage. They refuse to talk because it reminds them too much of their loss, and because they think they have no right to impose their problem on others. At the same time they feel left alone if nobody cares. The role of the comforter is therefore less than rewarding, which can cause resentments in him if he ceases to realize what the mourner is going through and interprets a momentary rejection as proof that the bereaved basically objects to his help.

The apparent "egocentricity" of the bereaved, his despondency manifested in the attitude that "there is no grief like my grief" make the family members helpless, not knowing what to say to the bereaved when the condolence formulations of the social code are already quite hard to say. The bereaved seems to be unable to listen to these words and to accept them, even if he senses their good intention and is grateful. Particularly for children who have lost one parent, the withdrawal of the mourning conjugal partner, who is in no way able to interpret and explain the situation, represents to some extent a double loss and thus a double burden.

The social environment often misunderstands the distrust exhibited by the bereaved toward them and takes it for a personal offense, even though this distrust aims at a world that no longer proves to be trustworthy. A reproach, such as "don't let yourself go," betrays all too easily to the bereaved that family and friends, in spite of their well-meant encouragement, are not only helpless, considering the "egocentricity" of the bereaved, but also have the suspicion that he wants to exploit them.

As Autton points out, it is a significant responsibility of friends and relatives to keep the bereaved in contact with the outside world, not in order to divert him but to facilitate his return and to prevent the bereaved from isolating himself socially. It can be quite meaningful to encourage him to new activities and social contacts in the adaptive phase.[34] With the gradual onset of this stage, the bereaved's attitude of helplessness and the desire to secure attention and care diminish and gradually disappear. Nevertheless, regular visits should be retained, especially on the birthday of the deceased and the anniversary of his death, because the bereaved feels more sharply the loss he had suffered on such days.

8.13 Hope and courage

That there is hope of coping with particular crises appearing in the course of every human life is not at all self-evident. Considering what a heavy impact death can represent, verified means of coping may fail. Every successful solving of a crisis, however, intensifies the hope of being able to cope with a new crisis just as well. Paul, too, clings to the conviction that endurance intensifies hope (Rom. 5:5). His experience is expressed theologically in the confidence in God's faithfulness; he will not let the individual perish but sustains and supports him. The attitude corresponding with God's faithfulness is best identified with the two ideas hope and courage.

Even though hope belongs to the Pauline triad, faith, hope, and love of I Cor. 13:13, it hardly played a role in theological discussion until the sixties. "Hope belongs to the original forces of human existence and accompanies [man] as a driving force during his entire life. And yet philosophers and theologians rarely mention it."[35] Hope surfaces in Künneth occasionally as hope for personal resurrection;[36] it appears in the later editions of Althaus' *Letzte Dinge* (Last Things) in a scarcely integrated final paragraph as "attitude and action."[37] Hope is regarded as being existential in G. Marcel[38] and H. Kimmerle.[39] There, Christian hope is distinguished from common human hope by promising more precisely futurity to man and assuring him that he will not be destroyed by things past. On the other hand, the "theologians of hope," like Moltmann, Sauter, and Hedinger, to mention only the main exponents, take the structures of hope from the Old Testament, even though the resurrection of Jesus Christ is understood as the final reason for all hope.

Sauter, for instance, gains what constitutes statements of hope from texts from the Old Testament.[40] According to those, hope signifies first of all anchorage in the future. It is hoped for that a carefully prepared vineyard will produce a good harvest in that the winegrower finds himself relying upon the things to come in his entire effort. "Hope therefore is never aimless, and is also not actually endangered by error of recognition (deception), but, owing to its nature, by 'disappointment,' which dissolves the goal."[41] Hope is, further, "confidence, elasticity, support." It is not kindled by an accidental deficiency; "instead, it focuses on a constitutive 'not-yet,' an openness, an 'outstanding' of reality."[42] This gives it the element of elasticity, endurance, and perseverance. "Hope does not stand for itself. God's action is in the best sense its presupposition."[43] Therefore, and this is to be said as a third aspect, hope is at the same time testimony, which can be abbreviated as "hope for Jahweh," as it is found as a typical element in the lamentations. Hope finally is "visioning called for"[44] which can express itself in images and symbolic actions.

The ground of hope is rooted in the promise; it "grants man *its* future. It affects us as the Word of God, creating future and giving access to it."[45] It announces, according to Moltmann, "a reality that has not yet appeared."[46] The word of promise has not yet received its reimbursement in reality and stands in contrast to the immediately evident present reality. It is still searching for its fulfillment which, however, is not the revival of something past, but descends toward something to come. It cannot be finally defined since it has not yet come to its conclusion. Any fulfillment of the promise can only call attention to the fact that the fulfillment is not perfect, that there is still a "peculiar surplus of promise,"[47] which becomes the occasion for a new announcement of things to come.

While the statements about hope grow out of an analysis of the existential situation and from the history of promise of both Testaments, Tillich begins with the analysis of courage, in order to do justice to something that can be identified as the "faithfulness of God." Instead of faithfulness he uses the term acceptance, a notion from the psychoanalytical field. There it is the therapist who conveys this courage to the patient, and in the last analysis only he can convey it because he participates in the same ontological structure out of which his patient in all his alienation lives too.

For Tillich, the popular belief in immortality is a mixture of courage and escape. It is an expression of maintaining one's self-affirmation even in the face of one's having to die. One could also say with Bloch that the desires for immortality would "provide the self with a lamp for the grave, decay-free and enlightening even the strangest night; they have deceived death several times, yet they also have shined upon death."[48] But the desires for immortality and one's own courage were only capable of doing this by continuing one's finitude, that is, one's having to die, infinitely, so that the actual death never will occur.[49] This however, is an illusion and logically speaking a contradiction in itself. It makes endless what, by definition, must come to an end.

What constitutes the "courage of despair," which, for Tillich, conquers the anxiety of fate and death? For him this courage to face despair is an expression of faith on the boundary line of the courage to be. In this situation the meaning of life is reduced to despair about the meaning of life. But as long as this despair is an act of life it is positive in its negativity. "Religiously speaking, one would say that one accepts oneself as accepted in spite of one's despair about the meaning of this acceptance." Even in the moments when we are overcome by anxiety and despair about meaning, being affirms itself through us. "The act of accepting meaningless-ness is in itself a meaningful act. It is an act of faith."[50] The faith that creates the courage to take the anxieties of fate and guilt into itself has no special content, since everything defined is dissolved by doubt and meaninglessness. Neverthe-less, even this faith is not an eruption of subjective emotions or a mood without objective foundation. According to Tillich this faith reveals various elements. The first element is the experience of the power of being which is present even in face of the most radical manifestation of nonbeing. The second element is "the dependence of the experience of nonbeing on the experience of being."[51] The third element of faith is the acceptance of being accepted. In the religious answer of faith this element of acceptance is emphasized in a particular way. "To accept this power of acceptance consciously is the religious answer of absolute faith, of a faith which has been deprived by doubt of any concrete content, which neverthe-less is faith and the source of the most paradoxical manifesta-tion of the courage to be."[52]

8.2 The mechanism: recollection

8.21 Psychological aspects

The classical theory of mourning worked out by Freud has as its basic element the conflict between an object-libidinal attachment and the reality principle. The reality principle prevails over the libidinal ties with the deceased. The mourner recognizes step by step that the love object no longer exists, gradually dissolves the individual ties, and invests the libido in other relationships. This takes place through the process of remembering; every time he remembers an individual feature of the deceased or a happy day spent together the mourner becomes conscious of the fact that this has passed forever and there is no way of repeating it with this beloved person.

The mechanism of recollection plays an important role in

the grief process. Mourners in most cases are extremely occupied with recollections of the deceased; at first the memories concentrate very much on the last days and then gradually stretch out over a longer period.[1] Even though very often there is a great need to talk about the deceased, nevertheless, this at the same time provokes memories, painful and hurting. These feelings can be so overpowering that the mourner breaks off the conversation, often abruptly, or seeks to avoid it completely in anticipation of the stress. But there is no escape from the pain; there are too many things, places, and people who awaken the memory and thus the experience that all of this is irretrievably lost.

In most cases the recollections take a somewhat jerky course; they are often set off by minimal analogies, following one another in rather free associations. The quick change of subjects often is initiated by the bereaved because he does not want to persist for too long on one memory, for the pain would be too great if he drew out this particular memory in all its consequences. At the same time, he returns, as if drawn by magical power, again and again to the same memories. He thus tests anew whether he now can cope better with these recollections. Most autobiographies of mourners exhibit a swift change between distant and more recent memories and are characterized by flashbacks as far as childhood. This reflects the real experiences of the bereaved, in particular where authentic diaries are concerned, even though dispensing with linear techniques in modern literature influences such a style.

S. Freud distinguished terminologically between "recollection" and "repetition" in carrying out analysis. In his short paper "Recollection, Repetition and Working Through" (1914) he writes: "We may say that (here) the patient *remembers* nothing of what is forgotten and repressed, but that he expresses it in *action*. He reproduces it not in his memory but in his behavior; he *repeats* it, without of course knowing that he is repeating it."[2] The same can be said about mourners. It happens that though they remember their life together with the deceased, this recollection represents no solution and no step forward in their perception. They repeat and strike again and again against the traumatic event, but shrink back from admitting that this remembering cannot bring back the deceased.

The commonality that exists between the work necessary in analysis and grief work has been investigated by Caruso. What he states about recollection in the process of analysis is also true in many respects for working through grief with the mechanism of recollection. The compulsion to repeat is in itself ambiguous and ambivalent. It contains life and death instincts still entangled. The bereaved is forced to go back again and again to earlier memories; he is apt to understand the thoughts about the life together with the deceased as "repetition" (in the Freudian sense). But this "repetition" can never be adequate, as Caruso points out, since the situation has changed in which the compulsion to repeat takes place. Even pathological repetition cannot force time to stand still; the bereaved carries the dead within him, without actually being able to bring him back to life.[3]

The regression of the compulsion to repeat also includes, as any other defense mechanism, some adaptive core which saves the mourner from identifying with the conservative death principle and with a past snatched up by death. The adaptive aspect of recourse to the past can fulfill its therapeutic function only if it is focused on future things, something that actually has not yet come into being. "The past is actualized, it is 'brought back' to bring in it something into being that has 'not yet taken on shape,' that is, . . . to bring it into play 'toward the future.'"[4] Repetition in psychoanalysis as well as in grief is the bringing back of the past into its future potentiality: "The past becomes 'new,' a resurrection of something that is no more takes place, insofar as it is not yet what it will become. The repressed that we drag along—like a decomposed body—is resurrected to a new life."[5]

The close connection between the process of analysis and grief is a result of the fact that in grief, not only do memories cling to the person of the deceased, but simultaneously the world of the bereaved collapses and earlier solutions to problems are questioned.[6] This means that in grief, too, conflicts of childhood and adolescence are reactivated. E. Weiss indicates that there is often a reversion to the feeling structure that existed in the distant past, especially as it related to parents:

After the loss of father or mother, or any figure of similar importance in one's early development, there is frequently a re-cathexis of an early ego state. The memory of the lost love object as he appeared, often many years previously, frequently seems to replace entirely the actual person as he was at the time of death, and the mourner's early emotions, feelings and affects are intensely re-experienced in the mourning work.[7]

According to E. v. Gebsattel three types of recollections can be elicited at such a revival of past memories. One can distinguish between (1) the adequate experience of psychic matters never experienced, but only lived through, partly from the past, partly from the present; (2) the adequate reexperiencing of psychic matters, previously experienced but inadequately lived through at the time; (3) the adequate reexperiencing of experienced psychic matters that can no longer be remembered (amnestic contents).[8] Every one of these types of recollection is connected with special difficulties not to be discussed in detail at this point. Nevertheless, if it comes to adequate reexperiencing, then this not only has the cathectic effect of acting out feelings, but is accompanied by a correction, expansion, and the laying open of self-knowledge. In addition, the adequate revival can help to reveal the disorders between the individual and his environment, often stemming from early childhood. In this way hate and love feelings are set free to a high degree. The positive effect derives from the fact that negative affects are given up, which disturb a human relationship as soon as they become conscious, "because evil as a conscious attitude is not in accordance with most people," and, secondly, that "precisely after the living through of these affects, the original positive element everywhere, the underlying tendency to love, trust, and devotion" breaks through again.[9] Finally, the adequate revival of memories can contribute to making conscious the world orientation and value structure in effect at the present time. The individual awakes and experiences, in developing a new orientation and a new system, some kind of revival. *"If awakening and revival coincide in the psyche, self-knowledge has reached its level of adequacy."* [10]

In the encounter with bereaved persons it is important to keep in mind that in every one of their recollections, not only are memories of the dead recollected, but these represent at the same time their own conflicts and the breakdown of their social relationships. The process of recollection sets free a number of emotions which would overpower the bereaved if he did not select particular memories. [11]

The basis for this selectivity is frequently the ambivalence that had existed between the deceased and the survivor. This is the denial of repressed aversion which had never been worked through realistically. The fear of aggression consequently forces one to emphasize the positive feelings toward the deceased and cast aside every shadow from him. Even the attempt to depict a realistic picture of the deceased, weighing his weaknesses and strengths, appears to be an insult of the dead person.

The one-sided positive selection of the recollection can be explained by still other aspects besides compensation of guilt feelings due to ambivalence. It can be argued that with the occurrence of death, the hostile feelings reached their goal and can now turn to the positive sides of the deceased without restraint. [12] Glorification can also be understood as an act of becoming aware of the great personal gains received through the deceased which were taken for granted before. [13] The negative features may lose some of their weight in view of death. [14] Glorification may also be the result of the desire to honor the deceased publicly, whereby the consideration of debatable points can be abolished because of the powerlessness of the deceased. Carlin has pointed out that with the death of a family member incestuous desires toward him are set free and may find their uninhibited expression in glorification. [15] In front of the minister the family members may emphasize only the positive aspects of the deceased, because they want to prevent negative remarks in the funeral sermon. To the extent that the minister is for them God's representative, they also attempt to recommend the dead person to him and at the same time to God. The deceased will appear before God in the best light, and he at least will know that the survivors are reconciled to the deceased and do not harbor any feelings of revenge or desires of retaliation. Finally, his idealization has the function, at least as far as the dead person is still unconsciously perceived as dangerous, "of dispensing with him through praise" and appeasing him.[16] All of these may be motives influencing the selectivity of recollection.

In addition, the one-sided selection of positive memories has the function of helping the bereaved himself. The statement that the deceased had been an ideal husband or the assurance of not having exchanged one single bad word with one another during the last twenty years issues from ambivalent feelings. Moreover, such positive ascertainments, even if they do not entirely correspond with reality also help the self-esteem of the bereaved, just as do the compliments of the social environment.[17] To be able to be proud of the deceased sustains the security of the weakened ego. Accordingly, M. Klein sees in idealization the reactivation of infantile behavior through overevaluation to protect his good objects within himself, to reestablish them as protection for the ego and defense against destructive forces.[18] "The inner support the ego receives from its friendly relation to a real, good object increases again the confidence in the internalized objects. Thus the ego—by making use of ambivalence—alternately takes refuge in the external and internal good objects."[19]

The idealization is threatened by three dangers. The more the lost object is reevaluated, naturally the greater is the loss suffered by his death. The more the dead is praised and what he had meant for the community and society is pointed out, the more the survivor must become aware of what he has lost. For example, when in the case of a man killed in battle his sacrifice and service for his country is praised, his widow may ask whether this participation can actually make up for her personal loss.

The second danger of idealization lies in the tendency to

make the lost person into a deity or at least a semideity. The ego is weakened through an overcathexis of the lost object and by considering it an absolute ideal. It may gain certain support from it, but it remains bound to the idolized object. The vow "I shall never forget you" elevates the dead person beyond the relativity of existence. Glorification in the long run turns into an unbearable burden that might lead to a symbolic self-killing (through ego impoverishment) or even suicide. Caruso perceives this danger as particularly strong in women, "because the alienation of the woman in our civilization is deeper than that of man and she therefore expects salvation through him." [20]

There is also the danger attached to idealization of directing the libidinous ties toward the deceased in case of a strongly ambivalent relation while the aggressive ties are displaced to others. This is particularly observable in children who tend to glorify the parent who died or from whom they are separated (the information that father or mother is now an angel may facilitate this) and to divert all aggressive feelings toward the surviving parent or toward the stepfather or stepmother; a mechanism well-known from fairy tales.

It should be pointed out that there is not only a positive selection of memories toward the dead person, but that there can be also a negative one. Wherever the negative feelings toward the deceased dominate, the survivor can no longer remember him intensively and may even actively strive to forget him.[21] He can symbolically remove his name from all memorials, kill the bearers of his name, as this actually happened in earlier times; he can leave his grave uncared for and never visit it. Forgetting is a punishment and contempt, just as B. Brecht states it in the poem "On a Drowned Girl."

When her pale body had rotted in the water
It happened—very slowly—that God gradually forgot her:
First her face, then her hands, and last of all her hair.
Then she became carrion floating in currents with other carrion.[22]

The transition from the compulsion to repeat to what Freud identifies as "recollection" is mostly fluid. Particularly in the regressive phase the observer has the impression that the bereaved would recall again and again the same experiences and events with the dead person without a noticeable change. The more the reality principle can assert itself, the more can be seen of the successful continuous attempt to test the memory again and again in terms of whether one can bear the pain of its unrepeatability. As long as "repetition" governs the bereaved's way of acting, there is the danger that he binds people to himself and performs rituals only because they are analogous to earlier experiences and events. Only if he has convinced himself of the reality of the loss through recollection does he become free for new commitments.

In the "normal" grief process, glorification is gradually reduced during the adaptive stage. "Only gradually, as in normal grief the bereaved regains confidence in external objects and values of all kinds, is he able to strengthen his trust in the lost loved person. That enables him to bear the fact that his object is not perfect, without losing his confidence and love for him, and he no longer has to fear revenge."[23] He is again able to work through the ambivalence toward the dead person. The grief work of the bereaved gradually focuses "on one's own self while learning to leave the deceased the way he is, hearing his silent call to be oneself in his particularity, with a certain gratitude. The task from now on is gradually to withdraw the projections upon the present deceased, stemming from the past shared with the dead person and to honor the secret of the deceased ever more purely."[24] The deceased now can be judged in a fairer and more honest way and the common world be restored within the bereaved on the basis of mutual reconciliation.[25] Successful recollection and a glorification that failed are both combined in a case illustration by Lindemann:

One of our patients who had lost his wife of only a few weeks in the great fire (in the Coconut Grove bar), after his release from the hospital visited quite frequently the former girl friends of his late wife in order to talk with them about her, for example, how these friends had met his wife for the first time or how he had met her. He traveled to the Bermudas and tried somehow to reconstruct their common past. His mother-in-law was very upset about this and his apparent hardheartedness, because he discussed all these things with other people. She could imagine her daughter only as an angel with a palm branch in her hand. She considered it a profanation to think of her, for example, in the kitchen doing common housework. This seemed to her incompatible with the glorified image of the deceased, this being the only way to remember her from now on.

However, it became obvious that the mother's grief process was much lengthier and for some time showed all the symptoms of a morbid reaction, while the young man coped much better with the situation.[26]

This also shows clearly the goal at which the defensive mechanism of recollection aims: not at forgetting, not a "repetition" of the past, but a process-like and productive coping in which the deceased is incorporated in the ego. The process of recollection prepares for the incorporation of the deceased, which will be the subject of the next section.

8.22 Sociological implications

It could be said that "recollection" is the form of coping with grief that represents the smallest denominator of the general attitude toward a future life. One cannot be sure that the bereaved believes in life after death and therefore cannot approach him on this subject at a condolence call. The reassurance, however, that one will not forget the dead but remember him always in general is socially acceptable, even if the bereaved or other listeners have doubts as to whether this will actually happen or even is at all possible. That the dead person remains unforgettable to his colleagues, his political party, or his family, and continues to live in their memory is hardly more believable than the pastoral assurance that he now lives with God; however, it is more socially acceptable.

How the recollection of the deceased develops is essentially determined by (1) what role memory plays at all in a society and (2) how great the general degree of ambivalence tolerance is. (1) It is understandable that in more static societies recollection plays a considerably more important role than in societies where traditions have become uncertain and the social organizations change quickly, even if recollection is always needed to a certain extent for sustaining continuity and for legitimating and motivating the new.

Thus, recollection can have a genuine function in nonliterary societies. This allocates an important task to the aged, because they convey experiences, knowledge, and skills of former generations. Simmons describes the function of the aged in such a society as entertaining, teaching, and reminding.[27] Today, when all these tasks are no longer needed, aging persons along with their recollection have lost their function; they are no longer means of communication with the social environment. Thus the older person remains bound to the past and can use the mechanism of recollection only in the (Freudian) sense of "repeating."[28] Reminiscing as a therapeutic process is here almost impossible. Recollections are overcathected libidinally, the past is glorified; they become a secondary substitute since no primary substitution is possible for the aging.

The more mobile a society, probably the smaller will be its collective memory into which the individual deceased can enter. Where in general traditions no longer are remembered, for the most part individual recollection gives no guarantee to be of lasting significance. Knowledge about the dead person is much easier to recall today; it is much simpler to reconstruct the life of a person than was the case in former times. This "knowledge," however, can mostly rely upon written data and no longer needs any "recollection" that cannot be tested.

Precisely because the collective assurance of remembering the dead person became so uncertain, as well as the religious assurance, the recollection by the family now carries all the more weight. The grave and its care are only examples of this. What is more essential is the social institutionalizing of the private remembrance of the dead.

(2) Essential for the selectivity of collective and individual recollection is also the ambivalence-tolerance found within the social group and society. The more the social environment thinks in categories of good and evil and succumbs to a friend/foe dichotomy, the more difficult it becomes in normal grief as well to avoid a one-sided idealization. When the environment insists that the deceased ought to be either good

or evil and has no tolerance for integrating positive and negative features of the deceased in a total appreciation, then glorification (or condemnation) of the dead person becomes all the more compulsive.

A good indicator in this context is the treatment of one who committed suicide in societies where killing oneself (except in case of the loss of honor) is considered condemnable. The greater the willingness to recognize the factors that can drive a person to commit suicide, or at least to stick to the principle that there is no right to judge, the more likely it is he will be granted an "honest" funeral and the public recognition of his status transition. Clergymen who lament the glorification of the dead and complain of being urged into it by the family should first ask themselves how much they have contributed in their entire ministry to the expansion of ambivalence-tolerance. Since this is often very low in public and also in a family, the survivors have no choice but to insist on idealization.

8.23 Commemoration and recollection

Even though of all coping mechanisms in grief that of recollection undoubtedly enjoys the highest social recognition, it is, nevertheless, not difficult to make this form of coping a subject of theological criticism. Already the speaker at the grave is suspicious of it, otherwise no such pathos would be needed in delivering the commemoration address. The bereaved himself is soon to experience how short the memory of colleagues and former friends proves to be and react with bitterness. War memorials would not be so monumental and overly decorated if it were not so easy to forget the victims of the war. The collective memory of society, of a church, or of a political party may incorporate some important dead people in their memory, such as famous politicians, martyrs, reformers, prominent victims of a later victorious movement in which the deadly fate of the individual is embedded. But even this memory does not reach beyond the existence of this social organization itself.

Even though the motive of remembrance in church and theology plays an important role—one only has to refer to the words of Holy Communion, "Do this in remembrance of me," there are four important theological points to be made that help to see the defense mechanism of recollection also in a critical way. These concern (1) glorification of the dead; (2) the motivation for recollection as seen in the achievement of the deceased; (3) recollection being arrested in the past; (4) the transitoriness of the social group that holds and keeps the memory.

(1) *Glorification of the deceased:* The various motives underlying the glorification of the dead person already have been dealt with above. Ambivalence conflict and protection of the social status with their numerous ramifications are the most important among them, yet not the only motives. Frequently at this point ministers are confronted with their own theological tradition, even if in a distorted and secularized form. How much during the Orthodoxy and until the days of Enlightenment the references to the life of the deceased served the purpose of pointing out the mercy of God in the life of the bereaved is well known. The Lüneburg Church Order of 1643 reads as follows: The funeral address should concern itself with death and resurrection. In addition to that, "the faith and testimony or the good moral conduct of the deceased may be mentioned briefly, so that other people are induced to follow their Christian example; but as far as worldly pride, luxury, and ambition are concerned, these should be omitted and ignored as best as possible."[29] In isolated cases it is also advocated today to include the biography in the funeral oration. This recommendation of including the biography in the funeral sermon is critically restricted by H.-J. Geischer: "To trace the *vestigia dei* in the life of the deceased can only mean: to show that God's power is made perfect in weakness (II Cor. 12:9). 'Guidance,' gifts, engagement, endurance in suffering, love—all of these stemmed from this power."[30]

It would be an essential theological aid to the bereaved to explain to him (and to the minister himself) why he is so interested in the excessive honoring of the dead. There are a number of reasons that should not come under theological criticism: The love may seem exaggerated, since the bereaved only now experiences what he has lost. It may be that he attempts to make up in this way for what he has neglected, the "secret goal of hatred [may have been] reached and the hate, as it were, also passed away."[31] A reconciliation is accomplished. We have emphasized above that from a social viewpoint this "last honor" frequently is the only one ever bestowed upon this individual. It might be necessary to protect him from unjustified suspicions and moralisms (for example, if alcoholism and suicide are considered by society to be strictly acts of personal responsibility).

Nevertheless, the goal should be to see the dead person not as what he was, but to perceive him in the way God will look at him. What love and life can represent under the eschatological aspect can be described only as this person was seen by Jesus Christ for whom "forgiven and forgotten" were the same, while for human beings forgiving is not necessarily followed by forgetting. To encourage characterizing the deceased under these criteria and honoring him is theologically legitimate. To judge him not according to what he was, but according to what he will be after all ambiguities disappear which overshadow every human life is the theological task. This is, without doubt, even under the therapeutical aspect, the right task.

(2) *Recollection and achievement:* The problem of recollection and exaltation is more aggravated today since in most cases the survivors and the minister have different notions of what is to be respected in a life and what will remain. To the extent that statements in obituaries can be equated with the survivors' own value judgments, the criteria are a life of hard work, the untiring care for the family, and the untiring devotion to a task. They gave the life its dignity. On the other hand, the minister tends to base his judgment with respect to the value of life on whether the deceased was a follower of Christ. If already such a moral judgment of the minister's appears hypocritical to the community of mourners, how much more so a judgment of faith. The minister is denied the right to judge even more when it comes to faith, because this is God's privilege alone.

The situation in big cities creates even more difficulties

because the minister frequently does not know the individual members of the congregation he has to bury. These difficulties together constitute a temptation to forgo almost entirely reference to the deceased and merely to preach a sermon on faith without any judgment and comment about the deceased.

If it should come to a judgment with respect to the value of a life then it should be rather from the aspect of criticism of what constitutes a fulfilled life. Can it be theologically justified that a mother is praised because she knew nothing but her family, or has she not been sacrificed to the desires and expectations of this family? The norms of a society oriented only according to performance and production would have to be questioned when they cause the death of a man in his middle years by a heart attack, and by no means is it theologically more legitimate if it is a minister who suddenly dies under such conditions, even if this then is called "tireless service in the name of the Lord." On the other hand, such professional activity or care for the family should not be devaluated with regard to the deceased individual. What other opportunities for a somewhat meaningful and creative life did the person have anyway, considering the social structure?

The traditional phraseology with which this past life is praised in obituaries and funeral addresses has its origin not only in the frequency of an individual's concealment of his life even from family members, but it also reveals that nothing worth remembering can be said socially about this life. It would be acting against the gospel to disparage exactly that which is left to such an anonymous life, the "faithful performance of his duty."

(3) *Dependence on the past:* Not only psychologically but also theologically seen is the danger that recollection keeps a person arrested in the past, makes him subject to this past because he refuses to see that remembering is a process leading to the realization of what is going to be. Theologically speaking it is crucial how Christ is remembered; the structure of recollection for remembering Christ determines at the same time the structure for remembering a deceased. K. Barth attempted to make this plain in his criticism of the irreversible

succession of past, present, and future by opposing a "time of remembrance" with a "time of expectation," both summarized under the "est" of the divine revelation.[32] "*Before* this date of revelation there is not only looking ahead but also a retrospective view, just as *afterward* hope could be absorbed by remembrance."[33]

Metz has spoken of the *memoria Jesu Christi*. It "shows itself not as a memory that falsely relieves one from the risks of the future of freedom. Perhaps it is not a middle-class counterfigure to hope, but holds precisely a certain anticipation of the future of freedom, a dangerously liberating memory . . . , which forces us to change constantly under its impact, if we ourselves do not want to lose it forever."[34] Faith is neither consent to dogmas nor an experienced existential decision, but an attitude "in which a person remembers given promises and the hope lived in view of these promises and ties himself to these memories in a life-determining way."[35] The essential content of these memories is that the power over people was broken and Jesus took the side of the insignificant people, the outcasts and oppressed. Remembrance is not glorification of the past, but recalls past horrors as well as past hopes.

The theological thought forms by Sauter and Metz exhibit a strong structural relationship to the psychoanalytical ones by Freud and Caruso. Remembering the past serves the purpose of activating liberating forces and taking up again broken off promises and developments. In faith, as in analysis, the point is not to let memory become blurred in a glorified past, but rather to make visible and conscious the promise and unfulfillment in a human life in order to find a new approach through the application of specific memories.

(4) *Memory and the social group:* Theologically speaking, only in connection with God can we speak of a lasting memory; every human promise never to forget the deceased, every endeavor to set oneself an indestructable memorial monument, must remain illusions. Human remembering does not secure immortality. At the present time it is hardly necessary to make church and theology aware of this; but they should be reminded of the fact that the assurance of remembering the

deceased has a positive function. It must, however, remain within the boundaries of what is humanly possible, that is, remembering should be spoken of only in cases where the deceased in fact has impressed others and influenced them in a positive way. The promise to remain faithful to the deceased forever and never forget him, on the other hand, must sooner or later result in guilt feelings, repressions, and bitterness since this is beyond the humanly possible.

It is more realistic to speak of, as Psalm 88:12 does, the realm of the dead as a "land of forgetfulness." As an eschatological symbol remembrance is, to use E. Jüngel's phrase, "a saved past." It is "past in the presence of God, it is past . . . glorified and represented by God himself."[36] For Tillich, eternal memory is the living preservation of the remembered event. "With a bold metaphor one could say that the temporal, in a continuous process, becomes 'eternal memory.'" Quite on the contrary, the negative is not remembered at all. It is acknowledged for what it is, nonbeing. Nevertheless, it is present in the "eternal memory" as that which is conquered.[37]

8.3 The mechanism: incorporation

8.31 Psychological aspects

As already mentioned above, in theories of grief the terms "introjection," "identification," "incorporation," and "internalization" are employed differently and not clearly distinguished from one another. We have decided to identify with the term "introjection" the reconstruction of the deceased along with his ideas and desires within the mourner. If this introjection is mainly determined by the aggressive ties between the dead and the living we speak of "identification with the aggressor," that is, of an "aggressive identification"; when these relations are mostly object-libidinal, we speak of "incorporation." However, they frequently overlap.

The term "incorporation" indicates that in this coping mechanism the deceased is accepted in his entire personality, not only in his aggressive or glorified features. Anne Philipe describes what is at stake here:

I have loved you too much to accept that your body disappears and to proclaim that your soul is enough and continues to live. And how should one go about it to separate them from one another and to say: this is his soul and this is his body? Your smile and look, the way you walked and your voice, were they matter or spirit? Both, yet inseparable.[1]

H. W. Loewald has described in more detail the process of incorporation (which he calls internalization) in the grief process and compared it with separation incidents taking place in the introjection of the superego in a child and at the conclusion of an analysis. He discovered here a great similarity.[2] He terms introjection a "particular process of transformation, through which relations and interactions between the individual psychic apparatus and its environment are transformed into internal relations and interactions within the psychic apparatus. Thus an internal world is set up which then in turn can entertain relations and interactions with the external world."[3] Loewald stresses that by no means has this detachment only a negative effect, but that incorporation can mean emancipation.[4] In the mourning work "the transformation of an object-cathexis into a narcissistic cathexis within certain limits is a repetition of an earlier experience, of giving up the Oedipal relations and of restoring them in the ego."[5] Grief's most significant difference from this earlier form of separation Loewald sees primarily as the fact that there are no parents who actively facilitate and support this process of detachment. If the process of Oedipal detachment is carried out in a positive way, then the subject will be in a position to cope with loss without intensive help from outside later on in life.[6]

It can also be stated, in the language of Melanie Klein, that the good inner objects, which the child very early had introjected in the form of his parents, mourn with him and thus comfort the mourner at the same time. "According to his feelings they (the good objects) share his grief in the same manner good parents would. The poet tells us: 'nature mourns with the mourners.' I believe that 'nature' in this context represents the internal good mother."[7]

Just as any of the defensive mechanisms dealt with here, incorporation, too, has stronger regressive and stronger adaptive aspects. The regressive stage is marked by an obvious change in eating habits. The reaction to loss can result in loss of appetite and therefore decrease of weight, whereby the derealization symptoms are not limited only to seeing, but affect taste as well: food tastes like "sand" or like "chaff and sawdust"; if this is the case, anorexia corresponds to apathy. Not to eat after the death of a person may have an obligatory meaning for the bereaved. It signifies, like fasting, that one observes a special obligation. Among "primitive" tribes this is often prescribed for the widow and close relatives of a deceased.[8] It is in full accordance with the symbolic meaning "to have died to the world," and thus has the same meaning as fasting during penance, in which also separation from the world is enacted. Here again is the double meaning of dying on the one hand and gaining a new world on the other.

The unembarrassed participation in the funeral service and the return of a normal appetite are, on the contrary, signs of adaptive coping. A case study can demonstrate the regressive behavior (that became persistent) in incorporation after the occurrence of death:

One patient, a woman aged thirty-nine, whose mother had committed suicide fourteen years earlier, portrays an example of overeating. The father was separated; there were a slightly younger sister, and an eighteen-year-old brother. In the eighteen hours that followed the loss, the patient showed no emotion, but set about informing the father of the loss (shielding him from the knowledge of the suicide), rehousing the children, arranging the funeral, etc. At the end of the eighteen hours, at noon, just before the funeral, the patient felt a sudden craving for a chocolate bar, a rare experience for her. In the ten months following the death, she gained fifteen pounds gradually and almost unaware; she had never been overweight before. Further analysis revealed that the mother had been withdrawn since the patient's infancy, had rejected her, had involutional melancholia and was paranoid. There had apparently been great ambivalence hidden beneath the patient's emotionless exterior. The patient observed that since her mother's death, tension produced bulimia—to achieve relaxation through a distended stomach; or self-punishment when feeling self-hatred; or as an expression of hostility to consume ("chew out") her "enemies." At the same time, the bulimia permitted the incorporating, and prevention of withdrawal, of the sweet-breasted mother who was so longed for in moments of helplessness.[9]

One ought not to make too hasty an interpretation of organic symptoms. Even though each physical reaction as experienced by the bereaved has its symbolic and psychic meaning, still it is frequently only this interpretation that determines the further coping with grief. Symptoms that can be connected with regressive and adaptive forms of incorporation may indicate older conflicts and forms of coping acquired later; they are not necessarily linked to the death. Frequently they apply likewise to all experiences of loss. Loss of appetite and emaciation resulting from it does not necessarily mean one wants to follow the dead by dying, but may express a general lack of willingness (as, for example, in adolescence) to give up a love object in spite of the demand of the reality principle.

The significance of eating generally and of certain food for the bereaved is crucial. As W. W. Hamburger has pointed out, appetite can have various symbolic meanings. Dreams of food usually reveal a craving that has nothing to do with acute satisfaction of hunger, but rather reveal a need for interpersonal gratification or sexual satisfaction or are signs of hostility (biting, chewing) and slow self-destruction.[10]

Charlotte G. Babcock has underscored three adaptive functions of food with which the patient's symptoms in the case study above can be interpreted. Food can remove anxiety and tension; it can give the feeling of being loved and accepted, as it can in reverse lead to influencing others, to conquering and to calming them.[11]

As far as food performs such a helping and supporting function for the bereaved, it can in its actual and figurative form help to facilitate the incorporation of the dead person. To treat oneself to something good or to be treated to it affirms, to speak in the language of Melanie Klein, that the good objects have not died, but can be revived in their practical and symbolical meaning through food and be restored within one's self. It manifests that communication with the world is not broken off, but is, together with the deceased, restored within the bereaved.

8.32 Sociological implications

That the funeral is followed by a common meal is still an almost universal custom in many places today represents in our society the most obvious continuity between "primitive" mourning rites and contemporary practices. The "bread for the mourner" and "the cup of consolation" are mentioned in Jer. 16:7 as a custom of the Israelites' at the lamentation about the destruction of the people of Israel, when nobody will be left to comfort: "No one shall break bread for the mourner, to comfort him for the dead; nor shall any one give him the cup of consolation to drink for his father or his mother." Presumably relatives and friends brought bread and drinks for the mourner, since probably cooking was not permitted in the house of mourning, so that no deadly substance could penetrate the food. In II Sam. 3:35, "all the people came to persuade David to eat bread while it was yet day; but David swore, saying, 'God do so to me and more also, if I taste bread or anything else till the sun goes down!'" Frequently the custom is found of forcing the mourner to eat something.

In funeral meals, no doubt communion with the deceased and the offering for him play an essential role.[12] In ancient Israel offerings for the dead obviously were performed yet were officially suppressed. Thus, according to Hos. 9:4, the mourner's bread was considered defiled and "all who eat of it shall be defiled; for their bread shall be for their hunger only; it shall not come to the house of the Lord." Deut. 26:14 obliges the Israelite to swear by handing over his tithe which was determined for the Levite, the sojourner, the orphan, and the widow: "I have not eaten of the tithe while I was mourning, or removed any of it while I was unclean, or offered any of it to the dead." The uncleanness of the mourner's bread and the offering to the dead are closely related here. Their connection reveals how much the funeral meal, in addition to consolation and help for the mourner, has had the meaning of offering to the dead. The environment of Israel testifies to this custom, but as a cult for the dead it had to clash with the official solemn worship of Jahweh. In addition, they placed food and drinks next to the grave (Sir. 30:18), a custom still found among Bedouins who gather for the funeral meal right at the grave.[13]

The bread for the mourner and the cup of consolation are certainly formulas only for the official funeral meal which is certified for late Israel. Josephus remarks in his report about the costly funeral meal Archelaus arranged for all the people at the death of his father Herod, and he says that already at that time the custom was practiced to such an extent that many Jews made themselves poor, for it was considered irreverent to omit it. It seems to have been an obligation to see that there was plenty of food.[14]

The funeral meal is found just the same in the German folk customs and in contemporary bereavement. The bereaved, together with the people who express their sympathy, usually gather in a restaurant near the cemetery (in a small town frequently the rule observed by everybody is to visit all the restaurants in due course), where coffee and cake, sandwiches or a full dinner are offered, and alcohol and beer quickly lift the spirit. In former times these celebrations often were quite turbulent.

8.33 Corporeality

Viewed theologically, the coping mechanism of incorporation has two points of significance. Firstly, the common meal is a symbol of the coming aeon; secondly, together with the theological interpretation of the eschatological meal, the question of the present and future corporeality of man arises.

In the Gospel of Matthew we find the word of Jesus that many will come from east and west to sit at table with Abraham, Isaac, and Jacob in the coming kingdom (Matt. 8:11). Another traditional word of Jesus speaks of the day when he will enjoy again the fruit of the vine after his death

(Matt. 26:29). The parables characterize the meal as the fulfillment of all expectations and hopes, such as in the parable of the wise and foolish maidens or the invitation to the marriage feast, and as the consummation of reconciliation in the parable of the prodigal son. That Jesus is called a "glutton and drunkard" (Matt. 11:19) shows how little he considered asceticism as a characteristic of eschatological preparation.

The appearances following the Resurrection also find their climax in the common meal. The appearance of the resurrected Lord at dawn by the Sea of Tiberias is introduced with the question "Children have you any fish?" (John 21:5). The disciples at Emmaus recognize in the mode of breaking the bread that it is Jesus who sat at table with them to share their supper (Luke 24). Eating and drinking may serve the purpose of revealing most impressively the reality of the resurrected Lord and averting all objections that this was only the imagination of the disciples. More important, however, is their function of characterizing the eschatological community not as a community of spiritual beings, but as a community of corporeal persons. It averts any theological spiritualization that rejects satisfaction of bodily needs as too materialistic.

The eschatological statement about the common meal secures and interprets what is meant by corporeal resurrection. To interpret corporeality without connection to the meal threatens to take away the realistic character of the promise of the "new society." For instance, this danger exists with Bultmann when, in agreement with Paul, he ascribes corporeality to man "as far as he is having a relation to himself" and thus makes himself the object of his own actions or experiences himself as the subject of something that he suffers.[15] Sauter has rightfully criticized such an anthropological approach that says our identity is, to speak with the letter to the Colossians, "hid with Christ in God" (Col: 3:3).[16] Moltmann expresses his criticism of Bultmann in a similar way: The thing man views as his corporeality is not his self but is rather the very thing from which he succeeds in differentiating himself. His corporeal, physical, and social existence is not identical with "existence" in the sense of the relation to himself as determined by Bultmann. Man achieves neither complete distinction and objectivity in regard to himself nor complete identity in contrast to the world. "If the promise of justification gives him a prospect of reconciliation and identity, then it cannot mean only the reconciliation of man with himself, but must also mean the redemption of his corporeality and of the world that has become to him a world of objects." [17]

The meal, which in a crucial manner expresses what is meant by corporeality, is one of the most important symbolizations of the "new society." The eschatological meal has as its content the multiple symbolic relations given with eating and drinking as an essential human need. It means the self-preservation of life, warmth, and protection. It refers to the serene and relaxed interpersonal relationship among persons. In its content, aggression can come to light, as expressed in the breaking and chewing of the bread. It is comprehensive because it promises narcissistic, aggressive, as well as object-libidinal coping with anxiety and guilt.

The meal speaks critically against an understanding of man in which his corporeality is without significance. Through the promise of corporeality and the meal, "our entire life, including eating and drinking, including vitality and sexuality, including the private and public areas in which hunger, the quest for power, and ultimately killing, rules, is placed under the rule of God." [18] The motivating statement amounts to satisfying the basic human needs in a sufficient manner, not only with respect to their physical aspects but also in terms of all the things attached to the meal of promise: protection, recognition, reconciliation.

The funeral meal and Holy Communion are closely related. An essential aspect of Holy Communion is the remembrance and incorporation of a dead person. This connection has been repeatedly recognized in the course of church history, above all in the early church. The custom of offering to the dead and of performing a meal at the grave in memory of the deceased had at first been taken over without embarrassment by Christians from their religious environment. Step by step the church tried to transform this custom, by way of performing a funeral meal at the graves of martyrs, into a mass for the dead in which the incorporation of the dead was accomplished through incorporation into the body of Christ, where the living and the dead are united. In Protestantism the connections between Holy Communion and the funeral service have been dissolved. In the Roman Catholic Church, also, the liturgy for the dead was so formalized that there no longer exists a living connection between Holy Communion and the service for the dead.

It is not an overstatement if the common celebration after the funeral is said to be under the same sign as the Holy Communion, and it receives its criticism, motivation, and limitation from the symbol of the eschatological feast even though no explicit reference is made to the Messiah. It legitimates itself by reconciling the survivors to themselves and to the dead person. It ought to contribute to ending the reproaches against the deceased and to helping the family and relatives to abate the mutual accusations because of reputed neglect, jealousy about who best took care of the deceased, and the imputation of selfish interests. It is not disturbing if here also particular forms of aggressions are acted out. The funeral meal is supposed to provide an occasion to remember the deceased with all his weaknesses and strengths. It may be cheerful, even though for the bereaved in particular such cheerfulness is short-lived. The function it has through diversion, consolation, and demonstration of family solidarity is quite legitimate. There is no reason to disparage such ceremonies, since this meal is under the expectation of the future.

8.4 The mechanism: substitution

8.41 Psychological aspects

The last of the defense mechanisms important for grief work is the mechanism of substitution.[1] It too serves the purpose of coping with the impact of the loss of an emotionally significant object. The lost love object is replaced by another which offers a comparable gratification, which, however, is usually less valuable than the lost object. Nevertheless, in order to make such a transference possible, it often must display a certain similarity to the lost object.[2] Dissolving the libidinal and aggressive ties to a lost object is, as S. Freud remarks at some points, no easy task, which in addition is connected with great psychic pain. "But anyone who knows anything of the mental life of human beings is aware that hardly anything is more difficult for them than to give up a pleasure they have once tasted. Really we never can relinquish anything; we only exchange one thing for something else. When we appear to give something up, all we really do is adopt a substitute."[3] In a similarly pessimistic way he stated in a letter to L. Binswanger in 1929, "One knows that the acute grief will disappear after such loss, but one remains uncomforted, without ever finding a substitute. Anything that takes its place and possibly even fills the void completely, will still remain something different. And actually this is quite all right. It is the only way to continue the love one does not want to give up."[4] Nevertheless, in "Vergänglichkeit" (Transitoriness) and in "Mourning and Melancholia" we find statements speaking of liberation and a new investment of the libido.[5]

Substitution can take place in various ways: (1) substitution of a lost love object through another person; (2) substitution through an activity that represents caring for others in some special way; (3) substitution through new activities; (4) substitution by oral gratification. Particularly in the coping mechanism of substitution special stress is to be layed on the distinction between the regressive and the adaptive stages.

(1) Among widowed persons, in particular if they still have a chance of remarrying, a strong desire and also some real efforts to find a new spouse become evident in the regressive stage. However, at this time there is the danger of transference. The survivor is still so distinctly occupied with the lost object that he cannot do justice to a new marriage partner and transfers the characteristics of the deceased to the substitute; in the adaptive stage this might turn out to be a deception, perhaps very difficult to eliminate. Jackson gives such an example:

When Mrs. T. died, Mr. T., who had been very dependent upon her, seemed to be lost and disorganized. Mrs. W., a widowed friend of his wife, moved into the emotional vacuum and soon he had transferred much of his dependency feeling toward her. In a few weeks he was sure that he was in love with her. Although there were marked differences in background, religious training, and temperament, he was willing to make any adjustment to fulfill his emotional needs. It seemed that everyone but Mr. T. himself understood the mechanism at work in his emotional transfer. Friends tried politely to caution Mr. T. against an unwise step, but he was not open to suggestion. He had invested another and quite different personality with the ideas and feelings he had toward his deceased wife, and he married his wife's friend, only to find that his idea and the reality were quite different. The person toward whom he had adopted a dependency attitude soon became a dictator, and his life was bound by an unbreakable tie to one who had capitalized on his emotional need at a time when he seemed helpless to interpret his own feelings.[6]

Such phenomena of transference are frequently found in the regressive stage and involve very often, as we shall have to show below, physicians and pastors.

A minister who participated in one of the seminars for pastors reported a variation of such a substitution. While extinguishing a fire, a young man, a member of the local fire brigade, lost his life. He left a twenty-three-year-old widow who considered it some kind of bequest to build a house in that town. Though this had been planned for some time, no concrete steps were taken toward its realization. The widow herself was a complete stranger in the town and had no relatives there. The other members of the fire brigade supported her plan by promising their help in building the house. For the people from the fire brigade this was an active device to cope with this shock and also to overcome their guilt feelings resulting from the insufficient observance of safety measures. The minister attempted, unfortunately unsuccessfully, to prevent a hasty decision. He realized that this kind of substitution would make it extremely difficult for the young widow to dissolve her ties to her deceased husband, particularly if the entire town participated in the building of this "memorial place" and financial liabilities were incurred for many years.

Special attention must be paid to cases in which children become substitutes for lost love objects. This can happen when a child dies and is replaced by a new one, if a child is begotten while facing the certain death of the husband, or if father or mother seek comfort in a child at the loss of the conjugal partner. Particularly the latter case creates extreme pressure for children because they not only have to cope with the loss of a parent themselves, but in addition must comfort the adult.

Albert C. and Barbara S. Cain have demonstrated with some extreme cases what kind of pressures a child faces if it is chosen as substitute for a lost love object.[7] Their research group consisted of severely disturbed children who had been conceived at a time when another child was diagnosed as having leukemia and presumably would not live much longer. The disorders of these substitute children were largely the result of the fact that they were not up to the pressure of being a substitute. The authors specify several factors in such pressure, also appearing in less intensive form in children who have lost a sibling or a parent.

Frequently such children grow up in an atmosphere filled with the memory of the dead child. His photograph is displayed in a particularly striking place; the mother talks constantly about him, and his grave is visited frequently. The substitute child must fulfill the expectations the parents had attached to the dead child, in particular with respect to his looks and his accomplishments in school. He is again and again compared with the dead child, and the results of such a comparison must be negative most of the time.

The substitute child is particularly carefully guarded and overprotected. Every crossing of the street and climbing a tree are looked upon as potential causes for a new catastrophe. With every cough and skin abrasion the parents and the child himself are confronted with the question of whether this is not a sign of impending death. Even more tension is present if the question of guilt is added. The substitute child frequently will assume that his predecessor was penalized by death for some kind of offense, the more so when parents reinforce this interpretation with threats of punishment. The parents may also unconsciously entertain the thought that this child replaced the deceased and therefore in some way is responsible for the death the other suffered.

(2) The "care for others" represents an essential form of substitution to which we have referred above in the context of inhibited grief.[8] W. A. Greene, who concerned himself in particular with this phenomenon, speaks of a proxy mechanism.[9] The individual who is taken care of is usually found within the family but is definitely weaker than the actually grief stricken. It is a child, a younger brother, a younger sister, or someone who is ill and in particular despair. E. Lindemann reports a girl who lost both parents and her boyfriend in the Coconut Grove fire. At first she seemed not to be severely affected and assumed the role of parent for her two younger siblings. This griefless acceptance continued for the next two months. Not until the household was dispersed and her younger siblings were placed in other homes did she begin to show a true state of grief.[10]

Occasionally more distant relatives also can become substitutes for the care taking, such as grandparents or grandchildren; sometimes, in particular with children, even an animal. The vicarious object usually has suffered the same loss as the most grief stricken. He then is not mourning his own loss but rather the loss experienced by this proxy. A mother who has lost her husband may vividly feel sorry for her children who have to suffer such a severe loss and care for them in particular. The expression of one's own helplessness, which the affected person assumes is not heard by the social environment, is projected on the proxy who then at least has found someone who is helping him. The grief stricken "feels and behaves as if nobody was there who could hear him besides himself."[11]

As far as a chronic disease that has led to death after a long period of nursing is concerned, it is obvious to continue the "caring for others" and to transfer it to other objects of care. A bereaved may decide to become a nurse or to assume the nursing of a sick person in the neighborhood. It has proved to be quite helpful for mothers when they were allowed to participate in the nursing of their hospitalized children suffering from leukemia.[12] Nevertheless, according to an observation by Mary E. Bozeman et al., the voluntary cooperation of the mothers can also inhibit the full realization of the grief work.[13] In a case study reported by Greene, a widow concentrated entirely on the caring for her children, without going through a full grief process. Only when many years later one of her daughters married and her son went to college, did the inhibited grief occur because of the loss of the vicarious objects and manifest itself in inexplicable exhaustion and apathy.[14] Therefore careful attention must be paid, in this "substitution therapy" suggested by E. Lindemann,[15] that grief reach its full expression and that this therapy does not begin in the regressive stage.

That in the regressive phase the "care for others" reaction amounts to dissociating oneself from the loss and pain by placing an object which also suffered a loss in between can also be traced in the reaction to the death notice. Sudnow observed: "With regard to most persons one can detect at a certain point that the impact of the loss suffered by the death changes its character for those who receive the notice. A loss experienced by the receivers of the death notice turns into a loss they feel for others."[16] While the immediately affected persons speak of the loss suffered by themselves or their mother, the more distant relatives and friends express their regret felt for the grief stricken and his mother. What Sudnow demonstrates here in the process of social communication shows that in the device of proxy mechanism, the care for others is based on the effect of dissociating. Whoever cares for others instead of suffering himself reacts to the loss in the same dissociated manner as more distant relatives and friends.

This does not at all mean that the "care for others" would not have positive results in the adaptive stage. Ina May Greer reports the case of a woman who lost her mother, whom she had nursed through a long illness. The grief process came to a stop and left her in a depression. However, after talking a few times to a psychiatrist she took the initiative to find a job. At first she tried to become a nurse's aid and was turned away. Finally she obtained a job much like her old one and at the same time became ardently protective of an elderly neighbor.[17] In this case, after working through the regressive phase the mechanism of "caring for others" evidently had led to adaption.

(3) The substitution of the lost love object by hastily assuming new activities in the regressive stage may involve the danger of inhibiting the grief process and preventing the full recognition of the loss. A case illustration by Edith Jacobsen makes this clear.

Mrs. C. had lost her sister a year and a half ago with whom she was extremely close. Since that time she abided in a depressive mood from which she could not recover. Her emotional expression was extremely controlled, her behavior reserved. Her entire inner life seemed to be empty and she could take no interest in anything, not even her work. At the same time she was very restless, tried to avoid friends, and preferred to spend her time at parties or visits engaging in small talk only. Mrs. C. avoided in every way possible the contact with people and things which could remind her of the loss. She was full of guilt feelings toward everyone except her deceased sister. This obviously was a projection of hostile feelings she entertained toward her sister but could not express. To a great extent they were based on infantile rivalry conflicts. Her restless and aimless activity concealed the anxiety and pain she would experience with the beginning of the grief work. Thus not only reality testing was inhibited but the sister remained lost, because she could not, in spite of all her love, incorporate her. Even two years after the death her behavior was unchanged.[18]

Here, too, a hasty substitution sets in before the grief work has gone through the regressive phase. The warning not to precipitate substitution does not mean that the bereaved must constantly think of his loss and may not seek temporary distraction in activities and other substitutions. The essential point is that these distractions are short-termed, just as denial also should be employed only in a limited way in order not to inhibit the realization of the death and the detachment from the deceased.

(4) Finally, the special significance of oral substitutes

should be kept in mind. Hamburger states that "the development of symptoms of over- and undereating in relation to underlying emotional conflicts is understandable in terms of *substitutive adaptive mechanisms.*" [19] In a case study, Martha Wolfenstein describes a child who was insatiably hungry for some time after his mother's death. He consumed great amounts of food and was particularly greedy for sweets.[20] The increased use of medicaments and alcohol observed by several researchers[21] must also be seen in the context of oral substitutes, as well as the frequently observable smoking. While oral substitution can be quite helpful in the regressive stage, a constant oral substitution, for instance in the form of alcoholism, indicates unsolved conflicts forcing a person to persevere in this stage.

The coping mechanism of substitution makes it particularly obvious how important it is to distinguish between the regressive and adaptive stages in the grief process. As long as the bereaved is still preoccupied with the image of the deceased, as long as he repeatedly discovers in other people only the features of the deceased, as far as he compulsively takes care of others and keeps himself fully occupied with activities in order not to face the pain of recognition, short-termed substitutions might be of quite some positive value. They are often necessary in order to begin the grief work with more dissociated forms, until the full recognition of the loss and the necessity of a new orientation have succeeded. Therefore it should be a rule not to engage in any liabilities and commitments during this time which can either never be solved or only with additional difficulties. The same advice applies here which S. Freud gave patients for the time of analysis, namely: "to form no important decisions affecting his life during the course of the treatment, for instance, choice of a profession or of a permanent love object, but to postpone all such projects until after recovery."[22]

8.42 Sociological implications

The coping mechanism of substitution meets to a great extent the societal expectations of not reacting passively and submitting to a disturbing event, but rather opposing it actively and coping with it through decisive actions. These expectations are frequently internalized by the bereaved and motivate him to throw himself quickly into new activities and to seek a substitute for the lost love object. These demands are represented from the beginning of mourning by relatives and friends, at first with the advice "not to let himself go" or "to pull himself together." They soon build up to the pressure that the bereaved must form important decisions, such as those regarding the deceased's property or the bereaved's own future place to live, and must seek new areas of activities and new friends. The bereaved himself does not yet feel ready to make decisions and finds disagreements about the inheritance a desecration of the memory of the dead person. The urge to remarry can be conceived of as betrayal of the deceased. Maddison and Walker report in their study of Boston widows that this expectation was related very soon to these widows by their relatives. Without doubt this was meant in most cases as consolation and encouragement but the widows often perceived this as an imposition, as if a relationship like the former one to the deceased could be replaced right away.[23] The conventional consolation that "one still has the children" or that one "is still young enough to certainly find another husband" pushes the bereaved into activities that may have the connotation of disloyalty. Besides, they very often would have disastrous consequences for him and his social environment if he did give in to this pressure.

The mechanism of substitution raises the question of the replaceability of a person. If an entrepreneur at the grave of a top manager speaks of his irreplaceability, then this must sound like scorn to the bereaved who knows that already one of the persons attending the funeral is designated for the deceased's position. If, on the contrary, the widow speaks of the irreplaceability of this person, then this is much more believable. This calls attention to the fact that in the public arena the meaning of replaceability has a meaning diametrically opposed to that in the private sphere.

In the universalistic sectors of society the individual is a very small unit and his replacement is made certain almost completely even as far as the very top positions in the power structure are concerned. For instance, the institution of retirement guarantees not only the continuity of intense productivity, but also prevents the disorder that might be caused by death in an age phase characterized by an increasing mortality rate. Clearly defined promotion and succession regulations assure that the individual can be replaced immediately; a few hours after the assassination of a president his successor is already being sworn in. Nevertheless, we should not succumb to romantic notions as if in former pre-industrial times a human being was less replaceable. Life then was generally less precious (not to speak of barbaric interim conditions in modern society) and still remains so today where industrialization has not yet succeeded. Death could, as far as leading power figures in society were concerned, cause greater disorders in the total social systems, such as crises of succession, but the replaceability of a person was, generally speaking, rather greater than it is today.

On the other hand, the private relations in the thoroughly rationalized industrial societies have an essentially higher emotional cathexis and are more individualized than in former times. This applies above all to relations between husband and wife and between parents and children. To exaggerate, family relations today can be so heavily emotionally charged because they are based on the indeed very high probability that no child will die before his parents and both parents will reach an appropriate old age. The more intense, the longer, and the more definite a libidinal investment has taken place, the more difficult it is to replace the deceased individual. This is true both for the death of one member of a married couple which has led a truly "happy" marriage over several decades as well as for the death of a child growing up.

This can be explicated on the already mentioned bereavement behavior of the Ifaluk people observed by Spiro. When a family member dies, the immediate survivors display considerable pain and distress. However, as soon as the funeral is over, the bereaved are able to laugh, smile, and behave as if they had suffered no loss at all. Spiro offers the following analysis: Among the Ifaluk the developing child forms no exclusive emotional attachment to any single family member, but rather has diffused and dispersed his emotional ties among many persons. Therefore their family system is such as to develop selves which are initially less vulnerable, yet also in which feelings and conditions of love, ambivalence, hostility, identification, and dependence are relatively weak insofar as a partner or any other given person is concerned. Accordingly, the other is not valued by the self as a unique and necessary personality in self-other relations among the Ifaluk.[24] It has been observed that children in Kibbutzim have formed similarly diffused ties with various persons and therefore the vulnerability to loss is smaller than in an average middle-class family in an industrial society. Our social system, by comparison, ties emotionality extraordinarily to the family sector and therefore increases considerably the vulnerability of members of the family system. Volkart and Michael point out that "basically the culture creates conditions in which the deceased is irreplaceable because he cannot ever really be duplicated. The social role cannot contain a provision for 'automatic replacement' because all our patterns of interpersonal relationships militate against such replacement."[25]

What Volkart and Michael indeed do not consider is the connection between high instinctual cathexis of family relations on the one hand and the increasing totally rational organizing of the whole social system on the other.[26] Coping with the death of a love object is closely linked to the organization of the social network. An economy that focuses on making a person into a freely available and replaceable matter; that on principle questions emotional ties to the place of employment and the group of fellow workers under the rubric of increased efficiency; and that disposes of self-determination as uneconomical must inevitably make the family relationship the only place of individuation and emotionalism. This makes an excessive demand upon the family not only in regard to coping with death. All the family ideology and all the family unity together can at best produce a private individuality which falls victim to the seemingly rigid power structures in society; but they can achieve the irreplaceability of the person only through a long-lasting deprivation and, in addition, guarantee the individual's future life only in the memory of the family but not of society.

Within this separation, generally holding true for modern society, between the rational world of employment, where an individual is replaceable at any time, and the family network, where high emotional attachments make replacement extremely difficult, the possible replacement can also depend upon the internal form of the family network. On the presupposition of a continuum, as used by Elizabeth Bott for her studies of London families, the two extremes would have to be described as "segregated conjugal role-relationship" on the one hand and "joint conjugal relationship" on the other. According to her investigations, a segregated conjugal role-relationship corresponds to the traditional family form. Both conjugal partners have established roles with little overlapping. The husband has close ties to the male members of both families, in particular his own, while the wife keeps strong contacts to the female members. The conjugal relationship hardly needs a higher emotional cathexis than exists also with the rest of the family members. Where, in the other extreme, the joint conjugal relationship dominates, the role difference between husband and wife is nearly completely removed; the husband takes over responsibilities which in a traditional family are considered female, as the wife takes on traditionally male roles. The relations between the conjugal partners are very intense, while only loose contacts are kept to the larger family. Bott observes that usually the wife's ties to her family are particularly intense, while for the husband the network of relationships includes to a greater extent other male friends.[27]

If one applies this systematic to the anticipated reactions at the death of the husband, one might assume that the emotional impact on a partner-like conjugal relationship will be more aggravating than in a marriage with a segregated conjugal role-relationship. In the latter family form, the death of the wife's parents perhaps initiates more psychic complications for her than the death of her husband, because she is less prepared to build up an independent and self-reliant way of life. She will depend much more on her parents' family, and if circumstances require it, have considerably greater difficulties adapting to the male role of earning money. A widow of a joint conjugal relationship presumably will experience strong emotional distress considering the marked mental intimacy in this family form. But she also is more likely to be able to assume important parts of the male role.

The question of whether a segregated conjugal role-relationship or a joint conjugal one is better qualified for coping with the crisis of separation through the death of the conjugal partner can certainly not be answered one way or the other. Neither the traditional family system nor the nuclear family appears to be more flexible for coping with crises, but rather what Sussman and Burchinal have identified as a "developing urban familialism."[28] They state that increasingly a family structure is forming which is characterized by a nucleus family with autonomous functioning, forming its decisions independently and taking full responsibility. In addition there is a kin family network which, even though it attempts to influence the decisions of the nuclear families, does not decide as a unit itself. The kin family above all supports the nuclear family in word and deed and is the one place to which the conjugal partners of the nuclear family turn before appealing to other resorts, and on which they can count to receive emotional and financial support in case of crises such as death. This help will be rendered on the generative level as well as between siblings.

Apart from the emotional tie to the deceased that makes substitution difficult, it can be questioned how much the social organization actually allows for substitution. This is particularly obvious in the possibility of remarriage. In our society, for example, the chances for remarrying are much more favorable for men than for women. The higher mortality rate for men means that, depending on the age group, there are five to ten widows compared to one widower. In addition, according to social rules, a man is supposed to marry a younger woman while a woman must find a husband her age or even older. Thus the small chances for a woman's remarrying are further reduced. Since a man frequently has his social ties outside the family, especially through associates and club members, he need not lay stress on psychic intimacy to the same degree in choosing a new conjugal partner as a woman, who in a society in which the role of the mother is heavily emphasized has only her husband as an intimate partner. She must also take care that the new marriage partner accepts the children she often has from the first marriage. Finally, for the man, social position and financial income play a considerably smaller role as considerations for remarriage than for a woman, whose social status is very much dependent upon her husband's, and who also must be mindful of keeping her present financial standard of living.

Moreover, the environment also recognizes and promotes much more the remarriage of a widower than of a widow, in particular if she is provided for through a pension and life insurance. According to the current common opinion a man cannot take care of himself, much less of children, while it is expected of widows that they respect the memory of their husband and wait an appropriate time before thinking of remarrying. This accounts for the fact that remarriage of a widower is much more frequent than of a widow. According to an American study, five years after the death of the conjugal partner half of the men but only 25 percent of the women had remarried.[29] Based on numbers Marris gives for England and Wales in 1951, in the age group 20-24, 17 percent of the widows remarried; in the age group of 30-34 there were 11 percent; while between the ages of 40-49 there were only 4 percent who remarried. Later on in life remarriage no longer occurs in a statistically significant scale.

Wherever a widow seeks substitution for her loss, disadvantages arise. In case of remarriage she may find a man who assumes no responsibility for her children and the ambivalence of his roles of stepfather, father, and nonfather make an excessive demand on him. If she depends upon her family she may often be exposed to a humiliating dependency. The children's affection and the sympathy and attention of relatives cannot replace the emotional relationship between husband and wife. "So most widows resign themselves to a lonelier life, being both mother and father to their children, and keeping their own company."[30] The tasks remain which the author of the First Letter to Timothy assigned to them:

If a widow has children or grandchildren, let them first learn their religious duty to their own family and make some return to their parents; for this is acceptable in the sight of God. She who is a real widow, and is left all alone, has set her hope on God and continues in supplications and prayers night and day. . . . Let a widow be enrolled if she is not less than sixty years of age (that is, for support by the community), having been the wife of one husband; and she must be well attested for her good deeds, as one who has brought up children, shown hospitality, washed the feet of the saints, relieved the afflicted, and devoted herself to doing good in every way. (I Tim. 5:4-10)[31]

It is also extremely difficult for older people to find a substitute for the deceased marriage partner. A long life together has strengthened interpersonal relations to such a degree that not only the libidinal detachment becomes difficult, but expectations and demands are made on a substitute which make it hard to find such a person, particularly since older persons have much fewer possibilities of contact. Social prejudices render even more difficulties: To remarry after a long marriage is considered a disregard of the deceased. That older people also have a right not only to intimacy and social contact but sexual relations as well is not recognized. Marriage-like unions in homes for the aged and elsewhere or remarriage are strongly disapproved of by the public. To replace the lost conjugal partner with other meaningful activities is just as difficult in older age since neither a professional nor a voluntary activity is welcome. Poor physical and mental flexibility reinforces the lack of possibilities of substitution by a new occupation. Often for older people, the only outlet left is the emotional overcathexis of memories of the past or escape into illness, which allows for gaining a certain attention.

8.43 Representation and substitution

In the paragraph on sociological implications of substitution, we elicited the basic contradiction of our present society which finds its sharpest accentuation in the problem of death. It is absolutely clear that for our social organization the death of a person is practically insignificant. Though there are a number of authorities trying to explain the cause of death and concern themselves with the dead and basing the legitimation of their actions on the fact that death exists, nevertheless, the social structure is in itself "immortal," because it is always capable of replacing the deceased. The death of the individual never means a serious jeopardy. An essential part of our present experience of this world's meaninglessness is related to the fact that within the social network the individual is replaceable at any time.

In contrast to this is a small circle of people, mostly only the immediate family, for whom the deceased is to a great extent irreplaceable. Wherever the relations are not universalistic, functional specific, and affective neutral, but rather particular, functional diffuse, and affective,[32] death causes great shock, because here the deceased cannot be replaced. Only where he is not judged on the basis of his achievements but rather is loved as a person does a genuine loss occur for which compensation is difficult. Only in the close circle of family is his uniqueness and the fact that he is noninterchangeable recognized.

This deep polarization between social replaceability and familial irreplaceability results in the family's frequently being unable to cope with the loss, since it cannot promise the deceased his individuality and irreplaceability without sacrificing itself and without resisting the attempt to replace the lost love object at least partially through other people and new activities. The deceased can be remembered and, in solidarity with the living, incorporated and restored within the bereaved. However, the survivors cannot guarantee his noninterchangeable identity without submitting themselves to the deceased at all costs.

One of the most original theological contributions in recent years used this far-reaching conflict between the unlimited replaceability and individual uniqueness as a point of departure. In her study *Christ the Representative*, Dorothy Sölle made the attempt to introduce anew the concept of representation, which had been neglected in theological discussion and to define it against the concept of substitution.[33] To represent someone means to take responsibility for him temporarily. It is regarded as a temporary expedient and limited to certain areas. A representative does not put himself in the other person's place completely and absolutely. He appears and makes it clear that he appears on behalf of and in the name of the other person.[34] "The capacity to remember is essential to representation as a temporary, conditional, and incomplete act. It is substitution, rather, which demands oblivion. Anyone who replaces me treats me as dead."[35] The replacement represents the other person completely and unconditionally. He acts in his own name, not in the name of the one he replaces. What is replaced is a thing no longer to be remembered.[36]

Representation, however, is possible only if the person who is to be represented does not perceive himself as irreplaceable. The general manager, for instance, considers himself irreplaceable. He feels that even to be represented is tantamount to death. "Unwilling to be unavailable, incapable or dead, he makes himself available everywhere and at all times, makes himself ceaselessly, and, as it were, unsleepingly alive."[37] He denies that our life is not possible without being dependent and in need of others, and he forgets that genuine work and achievement is constituted in being deeply engrossed in the task to be performed. Man needs representation.[38]

On the other hand, representation presupposes the confidence that the representative does not become the replacement and is not anxious to push away the person who is represented. "Any act of representation can turn into substitution if the place of the one who is represented is no longer held open but is seized by the representative for himself."[39] Whoever has to be represented takes the risk of being replaced.

The contradiction between the idealistic thesis "the individual is irreplaceable" and the antithesis "every one is replaceable" cannot, according to Sölle, be resolved by choosing between them. The idealistic thesis represents an ideological disguise of reality, the antithesis hypostatizes the existing structures as if they were the only ones possible and unalterable. This contradiction must be endured and mediated in another, third thesis. The concept of representation as described above appears suited to achieve this. "The synthesis of assertion and counter-assertion, . . . therefore reads: the individual man is irreplaceable *yet* representable."[40]

D. Sölle attempts to verify this model with the Christology of the New Testament and to give it its inner determination from this perspective. She sees here four motives characteristic of the Christian understanding: historicity, universalization, voluntariness, and suffering. (1) "Representation was first radically conceived when it was inseparably attached to a definite person accessible to *historical knowledge*."[41] In the Christian view not any victim can achieve representation, but only Jesus Christ, whose "action and suffering . . . fulfilled in advance all subsequent as well as all previous, all actual and all potential action and suffering by other persons."[42] (2) The universalization of Christ's representation means it does not merely apply to particular groups but now becomes effective for the world, for every world. However, Christ represents us, for the time being, according to the structure of representation, till finally the essence of man out of the not-yet being has found its identity. (3) The representation of Christ takes place voluntarily. It is not a deed out of obligation; nor is it to be regarded as completed all at once. His representation is an unfinished and continuing relationship. (4) This representation is characterized by suffering. The despised Messiah of the Christians, however, proves himself to be the representative of man and God precisely by his suffering.[43]

If one accepts this concept in D. Sölle's sense, then the christologically verified concept takes on an important function with respect to substitution for the dead person as well as for the substitute that takes his place. D. Sölle herself mentioned at one point in her book what representation means for the dead: "There is a vindication of the dead in the truth they affirmed and sought in their lives and even in the truth for which they were killed and betrayed. This representative, commemorative identification with the truth sought (for the most part in vain) by the dead, is decisive for the present and the future of those now living. At the same time, it also leaves room for a future for the dead themselves."[44] It must be said, beyond D. Sölle, that the bereaved can stand up for the dead person, suffer from his defeats, defend him against the social group, represent him in his irreplaceability, and thus assume a christological function. He denies this representation if he deprives the dead person of his historicity, sets himself as representative for an absolute, does not assume the role of representative voluntarily, and avoids suffering which characterizes Christian representation.

The same is true for the person who takes the place of the deceased. He should not represent an ideal image for the bereaved, but must himself be noninterchangeably himself. He should not have the intention of pushing aside the dead person and replacing him. He would not only do injustice to the deceased but also to the bereaved, who wants to keep this person with him rather than to repudiate him. He must take on the representation voluntarily, that is, knowing fully that the bereaved remembers the deceased and has incorporated him. Voluntariness also above all means that a child should never be a substitute for the deceased, since he cannot decide for himself whether he will accept the role of representative, and neither should he be manipulated in this direction by parents. Representation finally implicates suffering, for instance, a second husband's suffering because the widowed wife frequently will not love him with the same intensity with which she loved her first spouse, even though she needs and demands the affection and care of the new husband.

It is essential that both the bereaved and the person who takes the place of the love object are conscious of the fact that they represent the irreplaceability of the deceased and accept this as the christological interpretation of representation in order to avoid mutual miscalculations and disappointments.

9. Epilogue: the death of Jesus and the grief of the disciples (John 16)

In the so-called farewell discourses in the Gospel of John (chs. 14–17), beginning in chapter 14 and particularly in chapter 16, a striking number of ideas and notions from the field of grief are included. Jesus announces his departure from the disciples and promises his return; he will not leave them "desolate" (John 14:18). The announcement of his departure leaves their hearts filled with sorrow (John 16:6); they "will weep and lament," but their "sorrow will turn into joy" (John 16:20). Jesus concludes by saying: "So you have sorrow now, but I will see you again and your hearts will rejoice, and no one will take your joy from you" (John 16:22). The evangelist equates the return of Jesus with the coming of the paraclete, an embodiment of the spirit of Pentecost (John 14:16).[1] Bultmann translated paraclete with "supporter" or "helper,"[2] while the Latin tradition, certainly not without being influenced by the farewell alluded to in this chapter, at this point gives preference to the term "Counselor." On the whole, the farewell discourses, above all in chapter 16, offer a model for coping with grief, which so far has hardly been a subject of consideration.

In chapter 16, the Jesus of John's gospel attempts to give a reason for his departure. The meaning of his death is at stake. In the words of Bultmann: "Their λυπη cannot however be soothed away artificially; they can only master it by coming to understand the necessity of their being left alone."[3] Five viewpoints can be elicited from the text with which the

343

evangelist features the departure of Jesus as meaningful, namely, (1) only in this way can a full comprehension of the words of Jesus be attained; (2) only the spirit taking his place can bring about the constant separation between the world and "his own"; (3) that, through the spirit, the "glorification" and "remembrance" of the first Revealer is guaranteed; (4) that the departure secures meeting Jesus again under qualitatively different conditions; and (5) that only with the departure and return of Jesus is the full eschatological joy experienced. These individual points will be pursued at first following Bultmann's commentary.

(1) *Full comprehension of the words of Jesus:* In John 14:18-20, it is stated that Jesus will not leave his disciples "desolate" but will come back: "In that day you will know that I am in my father, and you in me, and I in you," a statement that is equated with the coming of the spirit (John 16:13): "When the spirit of truth comes, he will guide you into all the truth." That means, according to Bultmann: "In mythological language we are told that the revelation, which took place in Jesus' work, only retains its significance as the real absolute revelation when it retains the element of futurity."[4] Jesus remains the decisive Revealer only if he also remains it in the future, if he is not pinned down to the words and actions of an earthly existence.[5] It is not the recollection and the exact recording of a being historically past that secures full comprehension of the work of Jesus, but rather the coming of the spirit through which revelation is kept at present. Only thus does Christian belief not remain dependent upon a past event; only thus is it possible that a text fixed in writing can open new dimensions of proclamation.

(2) *The judgment of the world:* The promised spirit, however, is in its coming a critical spirit. "And when he comes, he will convince the world of sin and righteousness and judgment: concerning sin, because they do not believe in me; concerning righteousness, because I go to the Father, and you will see me no more; concerning judgment, because the ruler of this world is judged" (John 16:8-11). These statements, not exactly easy to interpret, nevertheless emphasize that the spirit referred to here distinguishes between those

who belong to the Revealer and those who are under the control of the ruler of this world. The coming of the spirit prevents the immobilizing of the critical function observed by Jesus of Nazareth in a very specific historical situation and its fixation on a historical opponent. But he also prevents criticism from becoming an institution. The judgment is passed on in a threefold way, which at this point is not understood as the Last Judgment in some future time, but as a sentence effective in this time and age: "The judgment that takes place in the revelation consists in disclosing the true meaning of the standards and values current in the world. But this means at the same time disclosing who is the sinner, who is the victor, and who it is that is judged."[6]

(3) *The glorification of Jesus by the spirit:* "He will not speak on his own authority, but whatever he hears he will speak, and he will declare to you the things that are to come. He will glorify me, for he will take what is mine and declare it to you" (John 16:13b-14). This at first is a statement that the spirit does not displace or surpass the word of Jesus, as if it were something new. He will "bring to . . . remembrance" (John 14:26) the words of Jesus. "The spirit will not bring new illumination, or disclose new mysteries; on the contrary, in the proclamation effected by him, the word that Jesus spoke continues to be efficacious."[7] Precisely by doing so he "glorifies" Jesus and features him as the decisive Revealer. "It retains the old in the continual newness that arises from the speaking of the word in the present."[8]

(4) *The reunion with Jesus:* The reunion with Jesus appears to be a paradoxical reason for Jesus' departure. But it is obvious that the Jesus who is coming again is of a different quality than the one departing. An illustration given in John 16:21 makes plain that with this "seeing again" a significant change will take place. Nevertheless, the idea of this reunion is not resurrection or Parousia in the apocalyptic sense. This "seeing," as John 14:18 and 19 shows, expresses the same thing as the coming of Jesus to his disciples whom he does not want to leave desolate.[9] Yet he comes back in such a manner that it is not visible to the world. Should Parousia happen in the apocalyptic sense, the disciples would not constantly

have difficulties comprehending what is meant by the Parousia of Christ. Moreover, this refers to a kind of faith described by Bultmann as follows: "The believer is based on the past only in that he was called to the eschatological existence then, an existence that is continually directed toward the future." [10] The believer remains with Christ only so far as he does not hold fast to the past words of Jesus as if clinging to some possession, but keeps himself constantly open to hear the word anew. "The believer always has to catch up with this anticipatory existence, which is peculiar to the word; in catching up with it, he is, however, always at the end of time; his existence stands under the ὄψομαι ὑμᾶσ." [11]

(5) *The eschatological joy:* The departure of Jesus becomes the reason for eschatological joy. The evangelist at this point gives up the comparison between grief and the completion of faith in existence; obviously for him death and joy do not correspond clearly enough. He instead employs the illustration of a mother in travail, whose anguish is followed by joy. Joy makes one forget all the questions and pain of separation. Jesus no longer is an enigma to his disciples. "The believers' existence . . . is joy which no one can take away, because it is not dependent on a cause which can be surrendered to the world and is thus without care or question. . . . Their existence has become transparent to them; they have become 'sons of light' (John 12:36)." [12]

Bultmann succeeds very well in making plausible the words of the Johannine Jesus in John 16 as an interpretation of human existence in its being bound to the divine word as well as in its extension into the past and the future, both coinciding in an "instant." [13] Nevertheless, it seems that an essential element does not come into its own, namely, the interpretation of faith in the concept of a grief process. The existential interpretation as carried out here by Bultmann[14] forces one to consider the numerous concepts from bereavement as basically nonessential, instead of recognizing that here, by means of the grief process, faith is clarified and made understandable. What the disciples, as the examples of believers, experience in the departure and return of Jesus relates closely to the experiences of the bereaved. The two must be held together: The completion of faith cannot merely be explained with the grief process, just as the completion of faith alone does not determine the course of a grief process guided by the spirit. However, what the believer loses with the earthly Jesus and gains with the heavenly is closely related to what he experiences when he loses and regains a loved one in whom he can recognize Christ. This can be explicated with the five most significant statements we have brought into focus for John 16.

(1) *Comprehension:* Only the death of a beloved person makes it possible to comprehend fully what he had meant for the now "desolated" survivor. While the immediate personal presence often prevents the separation of the important and the unimportant, the delightful and the annoying, grief gives the opportunity to see the deceased in his full humanity. The deceased can become a model, but not in the sense that the bereaved anxiously has to ask himself at every decision what the deceased might have said to it. The bereaved becomes emancipated from the literal presence of this dominating person, free to act instead in "his spirit," perhaps precisely because he only now comprehends fully the intentions and aspirations of the deceased.

(2) *Judgment:* If the bereaved shall really become free to "glorify" and "remember" the deceased, he must recognize to what extent his own behavior makes it impossible to form a deeper relation to the deceased and where guilt feelings have inhibited the full comprehension of the character of the deceased. At the same time, he will have to change his judgment in a direction that sees him much more as a victim of the "ruler of this world." He must learn that many things which made the dead person less lovable and incomprehensible to him were actually reactions to pressures from the outside. He must gain the insight that he himself has judged the deceased according to the standards of this world and thus has reinforced the compulsion and pressure weighing on him.

(3) *Glorification:* Precisely the compilation of "remembering" and "glorifying" illustrates that the idea is not the "glorification" of the deceased. On the contrary, the intention is to prevent falsifying the memory of the deceased, either in a

negative or a positive sense. The recollection should not change the deceased's words and actions; he should be loved without hate and guilt feelings, but not adorned with the halo of a saint by which his humanity is denied.

(4) *Seeing again:* Just as Christ should not be abandoned or forgotten, neither should the dead person. But the form of his presence has changed; it no longer is bound to his personal appearance, which dissolves in the memory just as does his body. He becomes a possession, never to be lost, by being restored within the bereaved. This revival of the deceased in the bereaved, which we have described as incorporation, removes the feeling of loneliness and defenselessness. He does not remain "desolated" but gains the deceased as a presence never to be lost again.

(5) *Joy:* That a grief process, like the death of Jesus, can end in joy appears hardly comprehensible to the person suffering the loss; it can only be described as a result understood later. Bultmann considers it such a result when the existence of the believer becomes more transparent to him. Similar statements could be made about the bereaved. Grief can become an experience that leaves a human life not more deprived but enriched and can result in a deeper understanding of the deceased and the bereaved.

If one attempts to understand the death of a close person as a trial of the believer, then the relationship to Christ is tested as well. A false understanding of faith can also block the comprehension of what takes place in the grief process. If the attitude of faith insists on depriving Christ of the element of futurity and holds him fast to the earthly Jesus; if the power structures are not recognized which made Christ a victim; if he is so glorified that his humanity disappears; if he is treated as an object of the past and is not entrusted with the power to help the bereaved to a deeper comprehension of his own existential fulfillment, then the danger may arise that the person once loved and now deceased will be seen in false dimensions and the grief work may end in a negative result. Nevertheless, this is just as true in reverse if the deceased is attributed quasi-divine status and locked into the past.

10. Additional Literature

Abraham, K. Ansätze zur psychoanalytischen Erforschung und Behandlung des manisch-depressiven Irreseins und verwandter Zustände (1912), in Psychoanalytische Studien II (Conditio humana). Frankfurt, 1971, 146-62.

———. A Short Study of the Development of the Libido, Viewed in the Light of Mental Disorders. Selected Papers on Psychoanalysis. London, 1927.

Aldrich, C. K. An Introduction to Dynamic Psychiatry. New York, 1966.

Aldrich, C., Knight, M., and Nighswonger, C. A Pastoral Counseling Casebook. Philadelphia, 1968.

Althaus, P. Die letzten Dinge, Lehrbuch der Eschatologie (1922). Gütersloh, 1961.

———. Retraktionen zur Eschatologie. Theologische Literaturzeitung, 1950, Sp. 253-60.

Bachmann, C. Ministering to the Grief Sufferer. Englewood Cliffs, N.J., 1964.

Barth, K. Church Dogmatics, vols. I/2, II/2, III/2. Edinburgh, 1936.

Beauvoir, S. de. Ein sanfter Tod. Reinbek, 1965.

Berger, P. and Lieban, R. Kulturelle Wertstruktur und Bestattungspraktiken in den Vereinigten Staaten. Kölner Zeitschrift für Soziologie und Sozialpsychologie 12 (1960), 224-36.

Bibring, E. Das Problem der Depression. Psyche 6 (1952), 81-101.

349

Bloch, E. Das Prinzip Hoffnung (The Principle of Hope). 3 vols. Berlin, 1954; 1955; 1959.

Bohren, R. Unsere Kasualpraxis—eine missionarische Gelegenheit? (Theologische Existenz heute NF H.147). Munich, 1968[4].

Bowers, Margaretta et al. Counseling the Dying. New York, 1964.

Bowlby, J. Grief and Mourning in Infancy and Early Childhood. Psychoanalytic Study of the Child 15 (1960), 9-52.

―――. Pathological Mourning and Childhood Mourning. Journal of the American Psychoanalytic Association 11 (1963), 500-541.

―――. Processes of Mourning. International Journal of Psycho-Analysis 42 (1961), 317-40.

―――. Separation Anxiety. International Journal of Psycho-Analysis 41 (1960), 89-113.

Bowman, L. The American Funeral: A Study in Guilt, Extravagance, and Sublimity. Washington, D.C., 1959.

Brunner, E. Eternal Hope. London, 1954.

Bürki, B. Im Herrn entschlafen: Eine historisch-pastoraltheologische Studie zur Liturgie des Sterbens und des Begräbnisses (Beiträge zur praktischen Theologie, vol. 6). Heidelberg, 1969.

Bultmann, R. The Gospel of John: A Commentary. Philadelphia, 1971.

Caplan, G. Principles of Preventive Psychiatry. New York, 1964.

Carlin, J. N. Grief Work and Pastoral Care of Baptist Ministers. Theological dissertation, Southern Baptist Theological Seminary, Louisville, Ky., 1962.

Caruso, I. A., Die Trennung der Liebenden. Stuttgart-Bern, 1968.

Clayton, P., Desmarais, L., and Winokur, G. A Study of Normal Bereavement. American Journal of Psychiatry 125 (1968), 168-78.

Clerk, N. N. (pseudonym for C. St. Lewis). A Grief Observed. London, 1961.

Clinebell, H. J. Basic Types of Pastoral Counseling. Nashville, 1966.

Cobb, St. and Lindemann, E. Neuropsychiatric Observations. Annals of Surgery 117 (1943), 814-24.

Deutsch, H. Absence of Grief. Psychoanalytic Quarterly 6 (1937), 12-22.

ADDITIONAL LITERATURE

Engel, G. L. Anxiety and Depression-Withdrawal: The Primary Affect of Unpleasure. International Journal of Psycho-Analysis 43 (1962), 89-97.

———. Is Grief a Disease? Psychosomatic Medicine 23 (1961), 18-22.

———. Psychological Development in Health and Disease. Philadelphia, 1962.

Feifel, H., ed. The Meaning of Death. New York, 1959.

Fenichel, O. The Psychoanalytic Theory of Neurosis. New York, 1945.

Ferber, Ch. v. Soziologische Aspekte des Todes. Zeitschrift für Evangelische Ethik 7 (1963), 338-60.

———. Der Tod: Ein unbewältigtes Problem für Mediziner und Soziologen. Kölner Zeitschrift für Soziologie und Sozialpsychologie 22 (1970), 237-50.

Freud, S. The Problem of Anxiety. New York, 1936.

———. Thoughts for the Times on War and Death (1915). Collected Papers, vol. 4. New York, 1959, 288-317.

———. Totem and Taboo. The Basic Writings of S. Freud, trans. A. A. Brill. New York, 1938, 807-930.

———. Mourning and Melancholia (1917). Collected Papers, vol. 4. New York, 1959, 152-70.

Geischer, H. J. Tod und Leben. Volksfrömmigkeit im Spiegel von Todesanzeigen. Theologia Practica 6 (1971), 254-71.

Gennep, A. van. The Rites of Passage. London, 1960.

Giudice, L. Ohne meinen Mann. Aufzeichnungen einer Witwe. Stuttgart, 1971.

Gollwitzer, H. Krummes Holz-aufrechter Gang. Zur Frage nach dem Sinn des Lebens. Munich, 1970.

———. Versöhnung, Schuld, Krankheit, in H. Horn and H. Kittle, eds., Der Glaube der Gemeinde und die mündige Welt—Festschrift Oskar Hammelsbeck (Beiträge zur Evangelischen Theologie, vol. 52). Munich, 1969.

Gorer, G. Death, Grief and Mourning in Contemporary Britain. London, 1965.

Green, B. R. and Irish, D. P. Death Education: Preparing for Living. Cambridge, 1971.

Grollmann, E. A., ed. Explaining Death to Children. Boston, 1967.

THE GRIEF PROCESS

Habenstein, R. W. and Lamers, W. M. Funeral Customs the World Over. Milwaukee, Wis., 1961.

Hahn, A. Einstellungen zum Tod und ihre soziale Bedingtheit: Eine soziologische Untersuchung (Soziologische Gegenwartsfragen NF H. 26). Stuttgart, 1968.

Harbsmeier, G. Was wir an den Gräbern sagen, in H. Runte, ed., Glaube und Geschichte (Festschrift Friedrich Gogarten). Giessen, 1948, 83-109.

Hedinger, U. Hoffnung zwischen Kreuz und Reich: Studien und Mediationen über die christliche Hoffnung (Basler Studien zur historischen und systematischen Theologie, vol. 11). Zurich, 1968.

Hertz, R. Contribution à une étude sur la représentation collective de la mort. L'année sociologique 10 (1905/1906), 48-137.

Irion, P. E. The Funeral: Vestige or Value. New York-Nashville, 1966.

Jackson, E. N. The Christian Funeral. New York, 1966.

———. Understanding Grief: Its Roots, Dynamics, and Treatment. New York-Nashville, 1957.

Jacobsen, G. F. et. al. The Scope and Practice of an Early-Access Brief-Treatment Psychiatric Center. American Journal of Psychiatry 121 (1965), 1176-82.

Jahnow, H. Das hebräische Leichenlied im Rahmen der Völkerdichtung (Beiheft zur Zeitschrift für alttestamentliche Wissenschaft, vol. 36). Giessen, 1923.

Janis, I. L. Air War and Emotional Stress. New York, 1951.

———. Problems of Theory in the Analysis of Stress Behavior. Journal of Social Issues 10/3 (1954), 12-25.

———. Psychological Stress. New York, 1958.

Jüngel, E. Tod (Themen der Theologie, vol. 8). Stuttgart-Berlin, 1971.

Klein, M. Zur Psychogenese der manisch-depressiven Zustände (1935), in Das Seelenleben des Kleinkindes und andere Beiträge zur Psychoanalyse (supplement to "Psyche"), 44-71. Stuttgart, 1962.

———. Mourning and Its Relation to Manic-Depressive States. Contributions to Psycho-Analysis. London, 1948.

Kliman, G. Psychological Emergencies of Childhood. New York, 1968.

Kramp, W. Der letzte Feind—Aufzeichnung. Munich, 1969.

ADDITIONAL LITERATURE

Kreck, W. Die Zukunft des Gekommenen: Grundprobleme der Eschatologie. Munich, 1966.

Krupp, G. R. and Kligfield, B. The Bereavement Reaction: A Cross-Cultural Evaluation. Journal of Religion and Health 1 (1961/1962), 222-46.

Krusche, W. Die Beerdigungspredigt in der heutigen volkskirchlichen Situation. Pastoralblätter 105 (1965), 411-26.

————. Unsere Predigt am Grab. Das Grab der Kirche? Pastoralblätter 102 (1962), 617-27; 682-91.

Künneth, W. Theologie der Auferstehung. Munich, 1951. This edition has been newly revised and enlarged by the author.

Kutscher, A. H., ed. Death and Bereavement. Springfield, Ill., 1969.

————., ed. But Not to Lose: A Book of Comfort for Those Bereaved. New York, 1969.

Lazarus, R. S. Patterns of Adjustment and Human Effectiveness. New York, 1968.

————. Psychological Stress and the Coping Process. New York, 1966.

Lewin, B. D. The Psychoanalysis of Elation. London, 1951.

Lifton, R. J. Death in Life: Survivors of Hiroshima. New York, 1968.

Lindemann, E. Die Bedeutung emotionaler Zustände für das Verständnis mancher innerer Krankheiten und ihre Behandlung. Die Medizinische (1953), I. Halbjahr, 515-20; 603-6.

————. Symptomatology and Management of Acute Grief. American Journal of Psychiatry 101 (1944), 141-48; reprinted in R. Fulton, ed., Death and Identity. New York, 1965, 186-201.

Lindemann, F.-W. Vier Trauersituationen: Ein Erfahrungsbericht aus den ersten beiden Amtsjahren. Wissenschaft und Praxis in Kirche und Gesellschaft 61 (1972), 39-48.

Maddison, D. and Viola, A. The Health of Widows in the Year Following Bereavement. Journal of Psychosomatic Research 12 (1968), 297-306.

Marris, P. Widows and Their Families (Report of The Institute of Community Studies, vol. 3). London, 1959.

Marsch, W.-D. Hoffen worauf? Auseinandersetzung mit Ernst Bloch (Stundenbücher vol. 23). Hamburg, 1963.

————. Gegenwart Christi in der Gesellschaft: Eine Studie zu Hegels Dialektik. Munich, 1965.

————. Zukunft (Themen der Theologie, vol. 2). Stuttgart-Berlin, 1969.

Miller, D. R. and Swanson, G. E. Inner Conflict and Defense (1960). New York, 1966.

Mitford, J. The American Way of Death. New York, 1963.

Mitscherlich, A. and Mitscherlich, M. Die Unfähigheit zu trauern: Grundlagen kollektiven Verhaltens. Munich, 1966.

Moltmann, J. Theology of Hope. London, 1967.

Neidhardt, W. Die Rolle des Pfarrers beim Begräbnis, in Wort und Gemeinde (Festschrift für E. Thurneysen). Zurich, 1968, 226-35.

Oates, W. Anxiety in Christian Experience. Philadelphia, 1955.

Parkes, C. M. Bereavement and Mental Illness, Part I: A Clinical Study of the Grief of the Bereaved Psychiatric Patients. British Journal of Medical Psychology 38 (1965), 1-12.

————. Bereavement and Mental Illness, Part II: A Classification of Bereavement Reactions. British Journal of Medical Psychology 38 (1965), 13-26.

————. Bereavement: Studies of Grief in Adult Life. London, 1972.

Pollock, G. H. Mourning and Adaptation. International Journal of Psycho-Analysis 42 (1961), 341-61.

Rahner, K. On the Theology of Death. New York, 1961.

Redlich F. C. and Freedman, D. X. The Theory and Practice of Psychiatry. New York, 1966.

Rochlin, G. Grief and Discontents: The Forces of Change. Boston, 1965.

Sauter, G. Zukunft und Verheissung: Das Problem der Zukunft in der gegenwärtigen theologischen und philosophischen Diskussion. Zürich-Stuttgart, 1965.

Schoenberg, B.; Carr, A. C.; Perretz, D.; Kutscher, A. H. Loss and Grief. Psychological Management in Medical Practice. New York, 1970.

Sölle, D. Christ the Representative. Philadelphia, 1967.

Spiegel, Y. Gesellschaftliche Bedürfnisse und theologische Normen. Versuch einer Theorie der Amtshandlungen. Theologia Practica 6 (1971), 212-31.

ADDITIONAL LITERATURE

——— . Der Pfarrer im Amt: Gemeinde, Kirche, Öffentlichkeit (Pfarrer in der Grosstadt, vol. 2/3). Munich, 1970.

——— . Der Prozeß der Trauer. Wege zum Menschen 24 (1972), 1-14.

——— . Wie menschlich ist das Mittrauern? Wissenschaft und Praxis in Kirche und Gesellschaft 61 (1972), 269-71.

Sudnow, P. Passing On: The Social Organization of Dying. Englewood Cliffs, N.J., 1967.

Switzer, D. K. The Dynamics of Grief. Nashville, 1970.

Stone, H. W. Suicide and Grief. Philadelphia, 1972.

Strauss, A. L. Mirrors and Masks: The Search for Identity. Glencoe, Ill., 1959.

Tillich, P. Systematic Theology, vol. III. Chicago, 1963.

——— . The Courage to Be. New Haven, 1952.

Vernon, G. M. Sociology of Death: An Analysis of Death-Related Behavior. New York, 1970.

Warner, W. L. A Black Civilization: A Social Study of an Australian Tribe (1937). Rev. ed., New York, 1958.

——— . The Living and the Dead: A Study of the Symbolic Life of Americans (The Yankee City Series, vol. 5). New Haven, Conn., 1959.

Winkler, K. Pastoralpsychologische Aspekte der kirchlichen Beerdigung. Wissenschaft und Praxis in Kirche und Gesellschaft 61 (1972), 90-96.

Wolfenstein, M. How is Mourning Possible? Psychoanalytic Study of the Child 21 (1966), 93-123.

——— . Loss, Rage, and Repetition. Psychoanalytic Study of the Child 24 (1969), 432-60.

Wolfenstein, M. and Kliman, G., eds. Children and the Death of a President. Garden City, N.Y., 1966.

Wretmark, G. A Study in Grief Reactions. Acta psychiatrica et neurologica Scandinavia 136 (1959), 292-99.

Notes

1. Introduction

1.1 Objective

1) S. Freud, Mourning and Melancholia, in Sigmund Freud: Collected Papers, 5 vols., vol. 4, trans. under supervision of Joan Riviere, New York 1959, 152-70, 153.

2) W. F. Rogers, Ye Shall be Comforted, Philadelphia 1950; E. N. Jackson, Understanding Grief: Its Roots, Dynamics, and Treatment, New York-Nashville 1957; C. Ch. Bachmann, Ministering to the Grief Sufferer, Englewood Cliffs, N.J. 1964; N. Autton, The Pastoral Care of the Bereaved (The Library of Pastoral Care), London 1967; J. D. Spiro, A Time to Mourn: Judaism and the Psychology of Bereavement, New York 1967; D. K. Switzer, The Dynamics of Grief, Nashville-New York 1970; C. M. Parkes, Bereavement: Studies of Grief in Adult Life, New York-International Universities Press 1974.

PART I: GRIEF—The Individual Aspect

2. Theory and symptomatic of grief

2.1 Sigmund Freud: the murder of the father

1) S. Freud, Trauer und Melancholie (1916) Gesammelte Werke, vol. 10, Frankfurt 1967, 428-46. A first draft was presented in December 1914 before the Psychoanalytical Association of Vienna; the manuscript was completed in May 1915.

2) S. Freud, Totem und Tabu (1912/1913); Zeitgemässes über Krieg und Tod (1915) Gesammelte Werke, vol. 10, 324-55; Vergänglichkeit (1916) Gesammelte Werke, vol. 10, 358-61.

3) S. Freud, Totem and Taboo, in The Basic Writings of Sigmund Freud, trans. and ed. A. A. Brill, New York 1938, 807-930, 819-20.

4) Ibid., 854.

NOTES

5) Freud, Totem und Tabu, 77-79.
6) Ibid., Freud, Totem, 856.
7) Ibid.
8) Ibid. 858.
9) Freud, Totem und Tabu, 91.
10) Ibid., 87.
11) Freud, Totem, 874.
12) J. Breuer and S. Freud, Studien über Hysterie, Leipzig-Vienna 1895. Fall der Anna O., passim.
13) E. Jones, Sigmund Freud, vol. 1, Bern-Stuttgart 1960, 25.
14) S. Freud, Die Traumdeutung (1900) Gesammelte Werke, vols. 2/3, Frankfurt 1968[4], 267; cf. also E. Herzog, Tötungsträume, in A. Sborowitz, ed., Der leidende Mensch: Personale Psychotherapie in anthropologischer Sicht (Wege der Forschung, vol. 10) Darmstadt, 1965, 403-17.
15) Freud, Traumdeutung, 267.
16) S. Freud, Bemerkungen über einen Fall von Zwangsneurose (1909) Gesammelte Werke, vol. 7, Frankfurt 1966[4], 451.
17) S. Freud, Dostojewski und die Vatertötung (1928) Gesammelte Werke, vol. 14, Frankfurt 1968[4], 397-418.
18) Freud, Totem, 884-930.
19) Ibid., 916.
20) Ibid.
21) Ibid., 917.
22) Freud, Totem und Tabu, 176.
23) Ibid., 178.
24) Ibid., 177.
25) Ibid., 161.
26) S. Freud, Thoughts for the Times on War and Death (1915), in Collected Papers, vol. 4, 288-317, 300.
27) Freud, Zeitgemässes, 332.
28) Freud, Thoughts, 310.
29) Ibid., 305.
30) Ibid., 316.
31) Ibid.
32) Freud, Vergänglichkeit, 360.
33) Freud, Trauer, 428.
34) Ibid., 429.
35) Freud, Mourning, 154.
36) Ibid.; see 8.41 below.
37) Compare Ibid., 161: "On the one hand, like mourning, melancholia is the reaction to a real loss of a loved object; but over and above this, it is bound to a condition which is absent in normal grief or which, if it supervenes, transforms the latter into a pathological variety. The loss of a love object constitutes an excellent opportunity for the ambivalence in love relationships to make itself felt and come to the fore."
38) See 2.42 below.
39) See 7.31 below.

2.2 Karl Abraham: incorporation

1) K. Abraham, Ansätze zur psychoanalytischen Erforschung und Behandlung des manisch-depressiven Irreseins und verwandter Zustände

(1912), in Psychoanalytische Studien, vol. 2 (Conditio humana), Frankfurt 1971², 146-62.

2) K. Abraham, Versuch einer Entwicklungsgeschichte der Libido auf Grund der Psychoanalyse seelischer Störungen (1924), in Psychoanalytische Studien, vol. 1 (Conditio humana), Frankfurt 1971², 120.

3) See below 2.42; Abraham, Versuch 120, with reference to Roheim, Nach dem Tode des Urvaters, Imago, 9, 103-4. Abraham, Versuch, 122, refers to the custom of student corporations of sending someone into the "beershitting" and thus isolating him; The phrase "shit on it" is also known as the reaction to a loss.

4) Abraham, Versuch, 128.

5) Ibid., 129.

6) See 3.2 below.

7) Abraham, Versuch, 129-30.

8) Ibid., 131.

9) Freud, Trauer, 442.

10) Abraham, Versuch, 158. B. D. Lewin, The Psychoanalysis of Elation, London 1951, 81, justifiably objected to it by saying: "These are not, I think, as Abraham interpreted them, normal analogues of mania, but the 'good analytic result' of the work of mourning."

11) Ibid., 130, 136, 152, 159.

12) Ibid., 130.

2.3 Melanie Klein: the "depressive position"

1) First used in M. Klein, Psychogenese der manisch-depressiven Zustände (1935) in Das Seelenleben des Kleinkindes und andere Beiträge zur Psychoanalyse (supplement to "Psyche"), Stuttgart 1962, 44-71, 54 and 58; compare also E. R. Zetzel, The Depressive Position, in Ph. Greenacre, ed., Affective Disorder, New York 1953, 84-116. Already Abraham, Versuch, 155, talked about a "basic disorder," which, however, in his opinion grows out of the Oedipus complex.

2) Klein, Psychogenese, 44.

3) Ibid., 47.

4) Ibid., 57.

5) M. Klein, Die Trauer und ihre Beziehung zu manisch-depressiven Zuständen (1940), in Seelenleben, 72-100.

6) Klein, Trauer, 75.

7) Ibid., 82.

8) Ibid., 83.

9) Freud, Trauer, 442; Freud, Massenpsychologie und Ich-Analyse (1921) Gesammelte Werke, vol. 131, Frankfurt 1967⁵, 71-161, 148-49.

10) Klein, Trauer, 83.

11) Ibid., 84.

12) Klein, Psychogenese, 59-60.

13) Klein, Trauer, 82.

14) Klein, Psychogenese, 70; Klein, Trauer, 84.

15) Ibid., 89.

16) Ibid.

17) Ibid., 90.

18) Ibid., 93.

19) A. Freud, Das Ich und die Abwehrmechanismen (1936) Geist und Psyche,

vol. 2001, Munich 1964. Also compare H. Deutsch, Zur Psychologie der manisch-depressiven Zustände, insbesondere der chronischen Hypomanie, Internationale Zeitschrift für Psycho-Analyse, *19*, 1933, 358-71, 366, who at this point has dealt with the significance of denial in mania.

2.4 Grief as disease

2.41 The psychic symtomatology of grief

1) S. Freud, Trauer, 429.
2) E. Lindemann, Die Bedeutung emotionaler Zustände für das Verständnis mancher innerer Krankheiten und ihre Behandlung, Die Medizinische, 1953 (1), 515-20; 603-6, 517. Unfortunately, Lindemann does not give the basis for his sample; it deals in part with patients with physical symptoms, which presumably go back to the experience of a loss. It also refers to "those who seek advice and whom we met by way of referral from welfare agencies or ministers" (Ibid., 517). Nothing is mentioned as to why in such cases the referral to the psychiatrist seemed advisable. Therefore a certain precaution with regard to the percentages is appropriate. Compare also P. Marris, Widows and Their Families (Report of The Institute of Community Studies, vol. 3), London 1959, 22, who ends up with five symptom groups, four of them psychic ones: (1) loss of contact with reality (inability to comprehend the loss, brooding about memories and holding on to pieces of property, feeling that the deceased husband is still present, waiting for him to come home, talking to him as if he were still present) (47 percent of the interviewed); (2) tendency to withdraw (escaping from everything that is a reminder of the loss, withdrawal also from sympathizing friends and relatives, as well as from all interests in life) (54 percent); (3) hostility (against the physician, fate, and against self) (25 percent); (4) difficulty in sleeping (57 percent). Further compare the not very convincing study in: A. H. Kutscher, ed., But Not to Lose· A Book of Comfort for Those Bereaved, New York 1969, 261-64; D. Peretz, Understanding Your Mourning: A Psychiatrist's Viow, in J. L. Liebman, ed., Psychiatry and Religion, Boston 1948, 183-202, particularly 183-86, as well as the following research.
3) E. Lindemann, Symptomatology and Management of Acute Grief, American Journal of Psychiatry, *101*, 1944, reprinted in R. Fulton, ed., Death and Identity, New York 1965, 188-89.
4) C. M. Parkes, Effects of Bereavement on Physical and Mental Health: A Study of the Medical Records of Widows, British Medical Journal, 1964 (2), 274-79. This study, based on a group of 42 widows, aged 38-81, in England, reports only the psychic symptoms anxiety, depression, insomnia, exhaustion, and being run down, and going to a general practitioner for prescriptions of sedatives and tranquilizers. While an average of 42 consultations related to psychic symptoms were counted in the two years prior to a bereavement, the number increased to 87 during eighteen months following a bereavement. An extremely high increase was noted during the first six months, in which almost a third of the widows consulted their general practitioner because of sleep disturbances. The high consultation rate referred mainly to widows under the age of 60, who showed an increase of 240 percent during the six-month period. After that the rate decreases, but remains above the number of consultations prior to a bereavement, even after one and a half years. All data was gathered from medical records of general practitioners in England.

THE GRIEF PROCESS

5) P. Clayton, L. Desmarais, and G. Winokur, A Study of Normal Bereavement, American Journal of Psychiatry, 125, 1968, 168-78; a summary is included in P. J. Clayton, Evidences of Normal Grief, in A. Kutscher, ed., Death and Bereavement, Springfield, Ill, 1969, 168-73.
6) D. Maddison and A. Viola, The Health of Widows in the Year Following Bereavement, Journal of Psychosomatic Research, 12, 1968, 297-306; cf. also D. Maddison and W. L. Walker, Factors Affecting the Outcome of Conjugal Bereavement, British Journal of Psychiatry, 113, 1967, 1057-67; D. Maddison, The Relevance of Conjugal Bereavement for Preventive Psychiatry, British Journal of Medical Psychology, 41, 1968, 223-33.
7) Maddison and Viola, Health, 304.

2.42 The psychosomatic of grief

8) S. Freud, Studie zur Hysterie (excluding J. Breuer's contribution) (1895) Gesammelte Werke, vol. 1, Frankfurt 1964², 75-312, 117.
9) S. Freud, Psychische Behandlung (Seelenbehandlung) (1905) Gesammelte Werke vol. 5, Frankfurt 1968⁴, 287-315, 294.
10) K. Landauer, Äquivalente der Trauer, Internationale Zeitschrift für Psychoanalyse, 11, 1925, 194-205.
11) K. Landauer, Die Heilung eines schweren Falles von Asthma durch Psychoanalyse, Jahrbuch für Psychoanalyse, 5, 1913.
12) Landauer, Äquivalente, 198.
13) Ibid., 199.
14) Ibid., 199-200.
15) Ibid., 200.
16) Ibid., 201.
17) Lindemann, Symptomatology, 188.
18) Marris, Widows, 13; compare also J. Hinton, Dying, Baltimore, Maryland 1968, 172-73; an autobiographical discription of the somatic symptomatology is found by N. N. Clerk, A Grief Observed, London 1961 (Pseudonym for C. St. Lewis), 7-11. In the study, already mentioned, by C. M. Parkes, Health, 275-79, the medical records of widows showed largely the same psychosomatic symptoms; only with regard to rheumatism and other muscular diseases a statistically significant increase appeared. The study by Clayton et al., also mentioned above, investigated only in an unspecified way with regard to psychosomatic symptoms and researched only general somatic symptoms and anorexia and/or weight loss. In the first interview, soon after the bereavement, 50 percent of the interviewed showed weight loss, which had been reduced to half of that at the time of the second interview during the first three months. On the other hand, the psychosomatic illnesses reported by 80 percent at the first interview had slightly increased according to the reports in the second interview.
19) Maddison and Viola, Health.
20) G. L. Engel, Psychological Development in Health and Disease, Philadelphia, 1962, 373.
21) Maddison and Viola, Health, 301.
22) See 7.31 below.
23) Switzer, Dynamics, 113.
24) A. C. Carr and B. Schoenberg, Object-Loss and Somatic Symptom Formation, in B. Schoenberg et al., eds., Loss and Grief, New York 1970, 36-48.
25) See 3.1 and 3.6 below.

26) Cf. A. H. Schmale, Relationship of Separation and Depression to Disease, Psychosomatic Medicine, *20*, 1958, 259-77; J. D. Adamson and A. Schmale, Objektverlust, Resignation und der Ausbruch psychischer Erkrankungen (1965), Psyche, *21*, 1966, 641-69; G. L. Engel and A. H. Schmale, Psychoanalytic Theory of Somatic Disorder: Conversion, Specificity, and the Disease Onset Situation, Journal of the American Psychoanalytic Association, *15*, 1967, 344-65.

27) See 8.11 below.

2.43 Grief as disease entity

28) Lindemann, Bedeutung, 519.

29) The American Psychiatric Association Diagnostic and Statistical Manual for Mental Disorders, Washington, D.C. (American Psychiatric Association) 1952, quoted in F. Redlich and D. Freedman, Theorie und Praxis der Psychiatrie (Literatur der Psychoanalyse), Frankfurt 1970, 393.

30) Redlich und Freedman, Theorie, 772.

31) W. Bräutigam, Reaktionen, Neurosen, Psychopathien—Ein Grundriss der Kleinen Psychiatrie (paperback edition of Deutscher Taschenbuch Verlag Scientific Series vol. 4054), Stuttgart 1969, 2nd revised edition, 24.

32) Ibid., 37-43.

33) G. L. Engel, Is Grief a Disease? Psychosomatic Medicine, *23*, 1961, 18-22, 18; cf. also C. M. Parkes, Grief as an Illness, New Society, *9*, 1964 (April), 11-12, 11.

34) See 3.4 below.

35) M. Klein, Trauer, 83. Klein obviously refers here to S. Freud's remark, Trauer, 153: "It is really only because we know so well how to explain it that this attitude does not seem to us pathological."

36) Engel, Is Grief a Disease, 20-22.

3. The process of bereavement

3.1 The four stages of bereavement

1) A.F.S. Shand, The Foundations of Character, London 1914, quoted in J. Bowlby, Processes of Mourning, International Journal of Psycho-Analysis, *42*, 1961, 323.

2) Bowlby, Processes, 333-38; he prefers the term disorganization to regression since he sees as the major phenomenon the inability to start and maintain organized patterns of behavior; Ibid., Grief and Mourning in Infancy and Early Childhood, Psychoanalytic Study of the Child, *15*, 1960, 20. At the beginning Bowlby distinguished stages closer to Freud, namely protest, despair, and detachment; compare Separation Anxiety, International Journal of Psycho-Analysis, *41*, 1960, 90-91. J.-F. Saucier, Anthropologie et psychodynamique du deuil, Canadian Psychiatric Association Journal, *12*, 1967, 477-96, makes the attempt to compare ethnological material on mourning rituals based on Bowlby's stage descriptions, and thus to point out the universality of this three-step theory of protest, despair, and detachment. In this he hardly succeeds and was repudiated by Bowlby through his correction of the sequence of stages.

3) B. Kreis and A. Pattie, Up from Grief: Patterns of Recovery, New York 1969, 11.

4) Engel, Development, 274-79.

5) G. Pollock, Mourning and Adaptation, International Journal of Psycho-Analysis, 42, 1961, 346-55.
6) W. Oates, Anxiety in Christian Experience, Philadelphia 1955, 48-55.
7) D. Fulcomer, The Adjustive Behavior of Some Recently Bereaved Spouses, PhD diss., Northwestern University, Evanston, Ill. 1942, 73-84.
8) Lindemann, Symptomatology, 192.
9) Clayton et al., Study, 170.
10) Maddison and Viola, Health, 304.
11) Marris, Widows, 22.
12) Parkes, Bereavement, 6. In Bereavement: Studies of Grief in Adult Life, Parkes extends this period and declares that even after thirteen months the grieving cannot be said to be concluded.
13) Hinton, Dying, 171.
14) D. Peretz, Reaction to Loss, in Schoenberg et al., Loss, 25.
15) Cf. W. Warner, A Black Civilization: A Social Study of an Australian Tribe, New York 1958 (reprint), 412-50; J. Goody, Death, Property, and the Ancestors, A Study of the Mortuary Customs of the Lo Dagaa of West Africa, Stanford 1962; E. Volkart and St. T. Michael, Bereavement and Mental Health, in A. Leighton, J. Clausen, and R. Wilson, eds., Explorations in Social Psychiatry, New York 1957, reprinted in R. Fulton, ed., Death and Identity, New York 1965; D. G. Mandelbaum, Social Uses of Funeral Rites, in Fulton, ed., Death, 338-45.
16) G. Revesz, Das Trauerjahr der Witwe, Zeitschrift für vergleichende Rechtswissenschaft, 15, 1902, 361-405.
17) See 3.7 below.
18) See 6, 7, and 8 below.

3.2 The stage of shock

1) M. Lerner, When, Why, and Where People Die, in O. G. Brim et al., eds., The Dying Patient, New York, 1970, 5-29, 23.
2) Cf. the following: P. Sudnow, Passing On, ch. 5: "On Bad News," Englewood Cliffs, N.J. 1967, 117-52; cf. also E. Wallace and B. D. Townes, The Dual Role of Comforter and Bereaved, Mental Hygiene, 53, 1969, 327-32; G. Kliman, Psychological Emergencies of Childhood, New York 1967, 74-76.
3) T. D. Eliot, Bereavement: Inevitable but not Insurmountable, in H. Becker and R. Hill, eds., Family, Marriage, and Parenthood, Boston 1955, 641-68, 645.
4) Fulcomer, Behavior, 92-93 (summary).
5) Fulcomer, Behavior, 85-87 (summary).

3.3 The controlled stage

1) V. E. von Gebsattel, Zur Frage der Depersonalisation: Ein Beitrag zur Theorie der Melancholie, in Prolegomena einer medizinischen Anthropologie, Berlin-Göttingen-Heidelberg 1954, 24-25.
2) Ibid., 31.
3) Bowlby, Processes, 335.
4) v. Gebsattel, Frage, 34.
5) Ibid., 36.
6) Parkes, Bereavement, 7.
7) Lindemann, Symptomatology, 194.
8) L. Siggins, Mourning: A Critical Survey of the Literature, International

NOTES

Journal of Psycho-Analysis, 47, 1966, 20.
9) C. Parkes, The Search of a Lost Object: Evidence from Recent Studies of the Reaction to Bereavement (typescript), 21-22.
10) Switzer, Dynamics, 186.

3.4 The stage of regression

3.41 The concept of regression

1) S. Freud, Vorlesungen zur Einführung in die Psychoanalyse (1916/1917) Gesammelte Werke, vol. 11, Frankfurt 1966⁴, 373.
2) S. Freud, Traumdeutung, 554.
3) Ibid.
4) Ibid.
5) H. Nunberg, Principles of Psychoanalysis: Their Application to the Neuroses, New York 1969, 2nd paperback ed., 70.
6) W. Loch, Regression: Über den Begriff und seine Bedeutung in einer allgemeinen psychoanalytischen Neurosentheorie. Psyche, 17, 1963/1964, 521.
7) O. Fenichel, The Psychoanalytical Theory of Neurosis, New York 1945, 65-66.
8) Loch, Regression, 527; Fenichel, Theory, 160-61.
9) Bowlby, Processes, 324.
10) Maddison and Viola, Health, 300-301.
11) Ibid.
12) Fenichel, Theory, 53; Nunberg, Principles, 147.

3.42 The bereaved in the regressive stage

13) Thilo, Seelsorge, 72.

3.43 The function of regression

14) Redlich und Freedman, Theorie, 205, cf. also Loch, Regression, 543.
15) E. Kris, Ego Development and the Comic, International Journal of Psycho-Analysis, 19, 1939, 77-90.
16) Ibid., 77.
17) G. L. Engel, Anxiety and Depression-Withdrawal: The Primary Affects of Unpleasure, International Journal of Psycho-Analysis, 43, 1962, 95.
18) I. A. Caruso, Die Trennung der Liebenden, Stuttgart-Bern, 1968, 101-2.
19) L. Giudice, Ohne meinen Mann: Aufzeichnungen einer Witwe, Stuttgart 1971, 54-55.

3.5 The stage of adaptation

1) Fulcomer, Behavior, 150-52 (summary).
2) Giudice, Ohne meinen Mann, 89-91.
3) Klein, Trauer, 82.
4) A. Philipe, Nur einen Seufzer lang., Reinbek 1964, 101.
5) Giudice, Ohne meinen Mann, 101.
6) N. N. Clerk (pseudonym for C. St. Lewis), A Grief Observed, London 1961, 41-42.

3.6 Anticipatory grief

1) So H. R. Blank, Mourning, in Kutscher, ed., Death, 204-06, 206.
2) Clayton et al., Study, 172-73.

3) J. A. Knight and F. Herter, Anticipatory Grief, in Kutscher, ed., Death, 196-201, 198-99; cf. also B. M. Bell, Pseudo-Terminal Patients Make Come-Back, Medical World, 1966 (12 August), 108-9.

3.7 Inhibition of grief

1) S. Freud, Hemmung, Symptom und Angst (1926) Gesammelte Werke, vol. 14, Frankfurt 1968[4], 101.

2) H. Deutsch, Absence of Grief, Psychoanalytic Quarterly, 6, 1937, 12-22, 13.

3) D. W. Winnicott, A Child Psychiatry Case Illustrating Delayed Reaction to Loss, in M. Schur, ed., Drives, Affects, Behavior, vol. 2, New York 1965, 212-42.

4) G. Gorer, Death, Grief, and Mourning in Contemporary Britain, London, 1965, 67.

5) Homer, Iliad, XIX.

6) J. Fleming and S. Altschul, Activation of Mourning and Growth by Psycho-Analysis, International Journal of Psycho-Analysis, 44, 1963, 419-431, 420-21 (summary).

7) Deutsch, Absence, 16-17 (summary).

8) M. Wolfenstein, Death of a Parent and Death of a President: Children's Reactions to Two Kinds of Loss, in M. Wolfenstein and G. Kliman, eds., Children and the Death of a President, Garden City, N.Y. 1966, 70-90, 86.

9) S. Freud, Aus der Geschichte einer infantilen Neurose (1918) Gesammelte Werke, vol. 12, Frankfurt 1966[3], 27-157, 46-47.

10) D. Kirschner, Some Reactions of Patients in the Psychotherapy to the Death of the President, Psychoanalytic Review, 51, 1964, 665-69.

11) M. Wolfenstein, How is Mourning Possible? Psychoanalytic Study of the Child, 21, 1966, 93-123, 118.

12) N. N. Root, A Neurosis in Adolescence, Psychoanalytic Study of the Child, 12, 1957, 320-34; cf. also Krupp, Identification, 309f.

13) Deutsch, Absence, 21; cf. also R. Wetmore, The Role of grief in Psychoanalysis, International Journal of Psycho-Analysis, 44, 1963, 97-103, 97.

14) Ibid., 21; cf. also H. F. Searles, Schizophrenia and the Inevitability of Death, Psychiatric Quarterly, 35, 1961, 631-65; St. R. Edelson and P.H. Warren, Catatonic Schizophrenia as a Mourning Process, Diseases of the Nervous System, 24, 1963, 527-34.

15) Quoted in Giudice, Ohne meinen Mann, 83.

3.8 Symptoms of pathological coping with grief

1) Kliman, Emergencies, 93.

2) Kliman; with regard to suicidal thoughts in a normal population of children cf. P. Schilder and D. Wechsler, The Attitudes of Children toward Death, The Pedagogical Seminary and Journal of Genetic Psychology, 45, 1934, 442-43 (L. Bender, Children's Attitudes toward Death, in Aggression, Hostility, and Anxiety in Children, Springfield, Ill. 1953, 52); L. Bender and P. Schilder, Suicidal Preoccupations and Attempts in Children, American Journal of Orthopsychiatry, 7, 1937, 225-34.

3) E. Geisler, Selbstmord und Todessehnsucht im Kindesalter, Psychiatrie, Neurologie und medizinische Psychologie, 5, 1953, 210-16.

4) L. Bender and W. Keeler, Children's Reaction to Death in the Family, in L. Bender, Dynamic Psychopathology of Childhood, Springfield, Ill. 1954, 209.

5) M. D. Schechter, The Recognition and Treatment of Suicide in Children, in

NOTES

E. S. Shneidman and N. L. Norman, eds., Clues to Suicide, New York 1957, 131-42, in particular 132-33. For the connection between loss of parents and suicidal tendencies following later see S. Greer, Parental Loss and Attempted Suicide: A further Report, British Journal of Psychiatry, 112, 1966, 465-70.
6) Cf. P. W. Pretzel, Understanding and Counseling the Suicidal Person, Nashville 1972, chap. 4: "The Aftermath of Suicide," 136-74; H. W. Stone, Suicide and Grief, Philadelphia 1972.
7) Kliman, Emergencies, 89.
8) Ibid., 89-90.

PART II: GRIEF—The Social Aspect

4. Grief as status transition

4.1 Rites de passage (rites of passage)

1) R. Hertz, Contribution à une étude sur la representation collective de la mort, L'année sociologique, 10, 1905/1906, 48-137.
2) Ibid., 124.
3) Ibid., 126.
4) Ibid., 127-28
5) Ibid., 128-29
6) Ibid., 129.
7) Ibid., 137.
8) A. van Gennep, The Rites of Passage, London 1960, 178.
9) Ibid., 182-83.
10) A. L. Strauss, Spiegel und Masken: Die Suche nach Identität (1959) Theorie, vol. 2, Frankfurt 1969, Chap. 4: "Wandlungen der Identität," 95-142.
11) Ibid., 135.
12) A. Hahn, Einstellungen zum Tod und ihre soziale Bedingtheit: Eine soziologische Untersuchung (Soziologische Gegenwartsfragen NF H. 26), Stuttgart 1968, 130.
13) W. L. Warner, The Living and the Dead: A Study of the Symbolic Life of Americans (Yankee City Series, vol. 5), New Haven, Conn. 1959, 248-320.
14) Ibid., 304.
15) An interesting thought by Warner is the observation that social death occurs only when cemeteries "die," i.e., when no one is any longer there who takes care of the individual family grave or the cemetery as such, because memories and ties to the ones buried there no longer exist. Ibid., 318-20.
16) Ibid., 302.

4.2 New structuring

1) v. Gebsattel, Frage, 30-31.
2) Caruso, Trennung, 43.
3) S. de Beauvoir, La force des choses, Paris 1963, 274.
4) Bowlby, Processes, 335.
5) Switzer, Dynamics, 102-5.

4.3 The significance of the ritual

1) Y. Spiegel, Gesellschaftliche Bedürfnisse und theologische Normen: Versuch einer Theorie der Amtshandlungen, Theologia Practica, 6, 1971, 230.

2) N. Luhmann, Legitimation durch Verfahren, Soziologische Texte, vol. 66, Neuwied-Berlin 1969, 226-27.
3) Ibid., 225.
4) W. Neidhardt, Die Rolle des Pfarrers beim Begräbnis, in Wort und Gemeinde, Festchrift for E. Thurneysen, Zurich 1968, 226-35.
5) For a sociological analysis of the funeral ritual see S. Wolfrem, The Decline of Mourning, Listener, 1966 (May 26), 763-64; P. Irion, The Funeral: Vestige or Value, Nashville 1966; D. G. Mandelbaum, Social Uses of Funeral Rites, in: Fulton, Death, 338-360; J. F. Scott, Brief Comments on Situational and Social Structure: Implications for the Loss of the Loved One, in D. M. Moriarty, ed., The Loss of Loved Ones, Springfield, Ill. 1967, 167-76; Hahn, Einstellungen, 95-136; E. Q. Campbell, Death as a Social Practice, in L. O. Mills, Perspectives on Death, Nashville-New York 1969, 209-30. For nineteenth-century practice see first G. Rowell, Nineteenth-Century Attitudes and Practices, in G. Cope, ed., Dying, Death, and Disposal, London 1970, 49-56.
6) G. Kehrer, Das religiöse Bewusstsein des Industriearbeiters: Eine empirische Studie, Studien zur Sociologie, vol. 6, Munich 1967, 158-59.
7) Ibid., 159.

4.4 The status transition of the deceased

4.41 The goal

1) G. Rietschel and P. Graff, Lehrbuch der Liturgik, Göttingen 1951², 757.
2) Quoted in Rietschel and Graff, Lehrbuch, 765-66.
3) G. Quell, Die Auffassung des Todes in Israel (1925), Darmstadt 1967, 4-14.
4) J. Gaedke, Handbuch des Friedhofs-und Bestattungsrechts, Göttingen 1963², 293.
5) H. Maser, Die Bestattung, Handbücherei für Gemeindearbeit H. 28, Gütersloh 1964, 37.
6) B. Bürki, Im Herrn entschlafen: Eine historisch-pastoral-theologische Studie zur Liturgie des Sterbens und des Begräbnisses, Beiträge zur praktischen Theologie, vol. 6, Heidelberg 1969, 224.
7) M. Widmann, Die Feuerbestattung: Ein Wort der Aufklärung. o. J. 1938, 43.

4.42 The release of the deceased

8) Giudice, Ohne meinen Mann, 91-92.
9) H.-J. Geischer, Tod und Leben: Volksfrömmigkeit im Spiegel von Todesanzeigen, Theologia Practica, 6, 1971, 268.

4.43 Intercessory prayers for the deceased

10) Cf. Rissi, Die Taufe für die Toten, Zurich 1962.
11) Rietschel and Graff, Handbuch, 760-64.
12) Luther's Works, American Edition: Liturgy and Hymns, ed. Helmut T. Lehmann, vol. 53, Philadelphia 1965, 326.
13) F. Schulz, Die evangelischen Begräbnisgebete des 16. und 17. Jahrhunderts, Jahrbuch für Liturgik und Hymnologie, 11, 1966, 1-44.
14) Bürki, Herrn, 195.
15) Giudice, Ohne meinen Mann, 24, 25, 31.
16) Neidhardt, Rolle, 229.

4.44 The new status

17) Irion, Funeral, 106: "The very occurrence of the funeral signifies that

death has taken place, life as we know it has drawn to a close. This is an irreversible and irrevocable event. It is a part of man's human condition, for although he can delay death he cannot avoid it ultimately. Man can be truly man only as he faces up to these facts and confronts the reality of death. One of the functions of the funeral is to help him do just this"; see below 6.33.
18) Cf. E. A. Grollman, ed., Explaining Death to Children, Boston 1967.

4.45 Public recognition

19) Spiegel, Bedürfnisse, 220.
20) Chr. v. Ferber, Der Tod: Ein unbewältigtes Problem fur Mediziner und Soziologen, Kölner Zeitschrift für Soziologie und Sozialpsychologie, 22, 1970, 237-50, 239-41.
21) Ibid., 239.
22) Ibid., 241.
23) Ibid.

4.46 The community of the dead with the living

24) Warner, Living, 286.
25) J. N. Carlin, Grief Work and Pastoral Care of Baptist Ministers, diss., Southern Baptist Theological Seminary, Louisville, Ky. 1962, 118.

4.5 The status transition of the bereaved

4.52 The controlled mourning

1) M. B. Concepcion, Ritual Mourning: Culturally Specified Crowd Behavior, Anthropological Quarterly, 35, 1962, 1-9, 2.
2) Ibid., 3-4; cf. also, by the same author, Ritual Mourning: A Cross-Cultural Comparison, Philippine Sociological Review, 10, 1962, 182-86.

4.55 The publication of the new status

3) S. Freud, Totem, 68.
4) G. M. Vernon, Sociology of Death: An Analysis of Death-Related Behavior, New York, 1970, 166.
5) Clerk, Grief, 12-13.
6) Giudice, Ohne meinen Mann, 77; cf. also 17-18.
7) Irion, Funeral, 103.

5. Care giving agents

1) G. Caplan, Principles of Preventive Psychiatry, New York 1964, 50.
2) Irion, Funeral, 96, after Warner, Living, 302.

5.1 The physician in the hospital

3) H. Feifel, Death, in Farberow, ed., Taboo Topics, New York 1963, 8-21. Feifel, Is Death's Sting Sharper for the Doctor? Medical World News, 1967 (6 October), 77, Feifel, S. Hanson, R. Jones, and L. Edwards, Physicians Consider Death, Proceedings of the 75th Anniversary of the American Psychological Association, 1967 (2), 201-2.
4) W. M. Easson, Care of the Young Patient Who Is Dying, Journal of the American Medical Association, 205, 1968 (4), 203-7.

5.2 The general practitioner

1) Parkes, Health, 278.
2) Clayton et al., Study, 75.

5.3 The funeral director

1) The professional conflicts between minister and funeral director are analysed by R. L. Fulton, The Clergyman and the Funeral Director: A Study in Role Conflict, Social Forces, 39, 1960/1961, 317-23; R. L. Fulton and G. Geis, Social Change and Social Conflict: The Rabbi and the Funeral Director, Sociological Symposium, 1968 (1), 1-9.
2) Bachmann, Ministering, 116-17.

5.4 The minister

5.41 The social position

1) Margaretta Bowers et al., Counseling the Dying, New York 1964, 65.

5.42 Pastor and funeral

2) Neidhardt, Rolle. It is necessary to emphasize this again and again because of the strong rejection of such a task by the minister. For example, one sentence from a conversation between a minister and a bereaved who asks for a funeral is cited: "You mistake me," said the minister, "for a receiver of orders from your family council. I am a minister, Mr. Perschke, I take my orders from God, and God only"; Butzheinen, Die Beerdigung, Der evangelische Religionslehrer an der Berufsschule, 1956, 155-60, 158.
3) Rietschel und Graff, Lehrbuch, 766.

5.43 The minister's emotional problems in counseling

4) Bowers et al., Counseling, 63.
5) Bachmann, Ministering, 29.
6) C. G. Carlozzi, Death and Contemporary Man: The Crisis of Terminal Illness, Grand Rapids, Michigan 1968, 57.
7) Bowers et al., Counseling, 64.
8) Bachmann, Ministering, 31.
9) Bowers et al., Counseling, 68.
10) Maser, Bestattung, 65.
11) Ibid.
12) Caplan, Principles, 50.

5.5 Counseling

5.53 The visit prior to the funeral (stage of shock)

1) G. F. Jacobson et al., The Scope and Practice of an Early-Access Brief-Treatment Psychiatric Center, American Journal of Psychiatry, 121, 1965, 1176-82; cf. also L. Bellak and L. Small, Emergency Psychotherapy and Brief Psychotherapy, New York 1965, 84-85.

5.54 The group for whom the funeral is intended (controlled stage)

2) Bürki, Herrn, 156.
3) G. Dehn, Die Amstshandlungen der Kirche, Stuttgart 1950, 99; see above 4.45.

NOTES

4) G. Harbsmeier, Was wir an den Gräbern sagen, in H. Runte, ed., Glaube und Geschichte, Festschrift Friedrich Gogarten, Giessen 1948, 98.

5) Ibid., 99.

6) S. de Beauvoir, Ein sanfter Tod, Reinbek 1965, 111.

7) H. Asmussen, Die Seelsorge: Ein praktisches Handbuch über Seelsorge und Seelenführung, Munich 1934, 160.

8) Quoted in R. Bohren, Unsere Kasualpraxis: eine missionarische Gelegenheit? Theologische Existenz heute, NF H. 147 Munich 1968⁴, 12.

9) W. Krusche, Unsere Predigt am Grab: Das Grab der Kirche? Pastoralblätter, 102, 1962, 686.

10) Ibid., 683.

11) Harbsmeier, Gräbern, 103-4.

12) Geischer, Tod, 268-69.

5.55 Postfuneral calls (regressive stage)

13) H. J. Clinebell, Basic Types of Pastoral Counseling, Nashville 1966; D. K. Switzer, The Minister as Crisis Counselor, Nashville 1974.

14) Bachmann, Ministering, 38-39.

15) See 8.21 below.

16) W. B. Oglesby, Referral in Pastoral Counseling, Englewood Cliffs, N.J. 1968.

PART III: The Mechanisms of Coping

6. The narcissistic coping mechanism

6.1 Survey

6.11 The defense mechanisms in grief

1) S. Freud, Analysis terminable and interminable, in Collected Papers, vol. 5, 316-57.

2) R. S. Lazarus, Psychological Stress and The Coping Process, New York 1966, 36.

3) G. K. Krupp, Identification as a Defence against Anxiety in Coping with Loss, International Journal of Psycho-Analysis, 46, 1965, 303-14, 308-9.

4) E. Bibring, Das Problem der Depression, Psyche, 6, 1952, 85.

5) D. R. Miller and G. E. Swanson, Inner Conflict and Defense (1960), New York 1966, 200.

6) Caruso, Trennung, 33.

6.12 Social promotion and inhibition of grief work

7) R. Silverman, Psychological Aspects of Physical Symptoms, New York, 1968.

6.13 The threefold direction of eschatological statements

8) E. Jüngel, Tod, Themen der Theologie, vol. 8, Stuttgart-Berlin 1971, 156-60.

6.2 The mechanism: breakdown of reality testing

6.21 Psychological aspects

1) Peretz, Reaction, 22.

2) v. Gebsattel, Frage, 25.

THE GRIEF PROCESS

3) Marris, Widows, 15.
4) Kreis and Pattie, Up from Grief, 15.
5) Parkes, Search, 7-8; cf. Philipe, Seufzer, 41-42.
6) M. Curtiss, The Midst of Life, Atlantic Monthly, 151, 114-23; 240-50; 372-80; 476-87, 114-15.
7) Ibid., 115.
8) G. Wretmark, Study in Grief Reactions, Acta psychiatrica et neurologica Scandinavia, 136, 1959, 292-299, 295.
9) Kliman, Emergencies, 87.
10) Parkes, Bereavement, 10.
11) Parkes, Search, 8.
12) J. Agee, A Death in The Family, New York 1967, 176-77; 181-82.
13) Gorer, Grief, 54-55.
14) Freud, Vorlesungen, 12. Vorlesung: "Analysen von Traumbeispielen," 187-202.
15) Ch. Anderson, Aspects of Pathological Grief and Mourning, International Journal of Psycho-Analysis, 30, 1949, 48-55, 53.
16) Ibid., 52.
17) Gorer, Grief, 57.
18) Ibid., 58.
19) Pollock, Mourning, 352.
20) G. R. Krupp, The Bereavement Reaction: A Special Case of Separation Anxiety, Sociocultural Considerations, in W. Muensterberger and S. Axelrod, eds., The Psychoanalytic Study of Society, New York, 2, 1962, 53.
21) Freud, Vorlesungen, 223.
22) Krupp, Bereavement, 53.
23) W. Waller, Family: A Dynamic Interpretation, New York 1938, 496.
24) Gorer, Grief, 55.
25) E. A. Poe, Works, vol. 5, London 1895, 22.
26) Caruso, Trennung, 113.
27) Clerk, Grief, 16.
28) Pollock, Mourning, 352.

6.22 Sociological implications

29) W. D. Rees, Bereavement, in A. H. Kutscher, ed., Death, 207-9, 208.
30) Warner, Civilization, 443-44.

6.23 Image or "night of the loss of images"

31) E. Hirsch, Das Wesen des reformatorischen Christentums, Berlin 1963, 174.
32) G. Bornkamm, R. Bultmann, and F. K. Schumann, Die christliche Hoffnung und das Problem der Entmythologisierung, Stuttgart 1954, 58.
33) R. Bultmann, Kritische Stellungnahme zu Th. Lorenzmeier, Das Weiterwirken der Liebe: Zwei Predigten über Auferstehung, Wissenschaft und Praxis in Kirche und Gesellschaft, 60, 1971, 432-33.
34) Karl Barth, Church Dogmatics, 4 vols., trans. Harold Knight, G. W. Bromiley, J. K. S. Reid, R. H. Fuller, Edinburgh 1956-60, III/2, 632-33.
35) Hirsch, Wesen, 183.
36) H. Cox, The Secular City, New York 1965, especially chaps. 5 and 7.
37) H. Gollwitzer, Krummes Holz—aufrechter Gang—Zur Frage nach dem Sinn des Lebens, Munich 1970, 251.

NOTES

6.3 The mechanism: denial/repression

6.31 Psychological aspects

1) Krupp, Bereavement, 48.
2) Redlich und Freedman, Theorie, 202.
3) Wretmark, Grief, 296.
4) Pollock, Mourning, 350.
5) Gorer, Grief, 79.
6) Ibid.
7) Jackson, Understanding, 81; further examples in Gorer, Grief, 80-81; cf. also J. Bowlby, Pathological Mourning and Childhood Mourning, Journal of the American Psychoanalytic Association, 11, 1963, 517-18.
8) C. K. Aldrich and E. Mendkoff, Relocation of the Aged and Disabled: A Mortality Study, Journal of the American Geriatric Society, 11, 1963, 185-94; A. C. Knight, Personality Factors and Mortality in the Relocation of the Aged, Gerontologist, 4, 1964, 92-93.
9) E. Jacobson, Denial and Repression, Journal of the American Psychoanalytic Association, 5, 1957, 62.
10) H. Deutsch, Absence of Grief, Psychoanalytic Quarterly, 6, 1937, 19-20.
11) Redlich and Freedman, Theorie, 201.
12) W. Schulte, Nichttraurigseinkönnen im Kern melancholischen Erlebens, Der Nervenarzt, 32, 1961, 314-20, 316.
13) Ibid.
14) Anderson, Aspects, 51-52.
15) K. Stern, G. M. Williams, and M. Prados, Grief Reactions in Later Life (1951), in Fulton, Death, 240-49, 247.
16) Ibid.
17) Parkos, Bereavement, 17.
18) Fenichel, Theory, 145.
19) S. Freud, Formulations Regarding the Two Principles in Mental Functioning (1911), in Collected Papers, vol. 4, 13-21.
20) S. Freud, Die Ichspaltung im Abwehrvorgang (1938) Gesammelte Werke, vol. 17, Frankfurt 1967⁵, 57-62; S. Freud, Abriss der Psychoanalyse (1938), vol. 17, 63-138.
21) Freud, Ichspaltung, 59-60; cf. also Freud, Abriss, 132-35.
22) S. Freud, Fetishism (1927), in Collected Papers, vol. 5, 198-204, 203.
23) See 6.4 below.

6.32 Sociological implications

24) H. Brewster, Grief: A Disrupted Human Relationship, Human Organization, 9, 1950, 19-22.
25) Deutsch, Absence, 19.

6.33 The reality of death

26) Bachmann, Ministering, 66-70.
27) Gorer, Grief, 65.
28) Switzer, Dynamics, 165-66. Switzer, a representative of pastoral counseling, bases his study about grief essentially on this point of view.
29) J. Berger, Die christliche Botschaft von Tod und Auferstehung und ihre Verkündigung am Grabe: Dogmatische Untersuchung einer homiletischen Problematik, Habilitation Humboldt-Universität, Berlin 1963, 328, 330, 333.

30) Ibid., 336.
31) M. Mezger, Bestattung, in G. Otto, ed., Praktisch-Theologisches Handbuch, Hamburg 1970, 81-92, 86.
32) Ibid., 86.
33) Ibid., 88.
34) Berger, Botschaft, 342.
35) Mezger, Bestattung, 88.
36) Irion, Funeral, 101.
37) Ibid.
38) E. N. Jackson, The Christian Funeral, New York 1966, 34.
39) Ibid.
40) Cf. M. Lamm and N. Eskreis, Viewing the Remains: A New American Custom, Journal of Religion and Health, 5, 1966, 137-143.
41) P. Tillich, The Courage to Be, New Haven 1952, 43.
42) Caruso, Trennung, 117.

6.4 The mechanism: searching

6.41 Psychological aspects

1) Bowlby, Processes, 334.
2) Lindemann, Symptomatology, 189.
3) St. Cobb and E. Lindemann, Neuropsychiatric Observations, Annals of Surgery, 117, 1943, 814-824, 822.
4) See 3.4 above.
5) Parkes, Search, 5.
6) Ibid., 253.
7) F. Beck, The Diary of a Widow, Boston 1965, quoted in Parkes, Search, 523.
8) E. Stengel, Studies on the Psychopathology of Compulsive Wandering, British Journal of Medical Psychology, 18, 1939, 250-54.
9) Ibid., 250. Compare the circular behavior of depression and mania in a case study by Parkes, Search, 15, in the form of searching and finding: "Thus a widow may be preoccupied with a clear visual memory of her husband. At one moment she is anxiously pining for him, and a moment later she experiences a comforting sense of his presence near her. As time passes and the intensity of the affects diminish pain and pleasure are experienced as the 'bittersweet' mixture of emotions which characterize nostalgia."
10) Ibid., 251.
11) Ibid., 253; cf. Stengel, On the Aetiology of the Fugue States, Journal of Mental Science, 87, 1941, 572-99, 594.
12) Ibid., 593.
13) E. Jacobson, The Return of the Lost Parent, in M. Schur, ed., Drives, Affects, Behavior, vol. 2, New York 1965, 200-203.
14) Ibid., 193.
15) M. Wolfenstein, How Is Mourning Possible? 114-15.

6.42 The "new society" as home

16) E. Bloch, Das Prinzip Hoffnung, vol. 2, Berlin 1955, 321-71: "Grundrisse einer besseren Welt: Eldorado und Eden, die geographischen Utopien," 335.
17) Ibid.
18) Ibid., 371. In comparison see U. Hedinger, Hoffnung zwischen Kreuz und Reich, Zurich 1968, 79, who speaks in critique of eschatology of "viatorial" hope and in connection with Barth arrives at a "viatorial synergism" (Ibid., 166-67).

NOTES

19) J. Moltmann, Theology of Hope, trans. James W. Leitch, New York 1967, 329.
20) Ibid., 337.

6.5 The mechanism: mania

6.51 Psychological aspects

1) M. Klein, Psychogenese, 55-61.
2) Lewin, Psychoanalysis, 54.
3) Against Parkes, Bereavement, 22-23; we distinguish the defense mechanism of mania from that of "seeing."
4) Freud, Totem, 914-15.
5) Freud, Totem, 918.
6) Freud, Mourning, 165.
7) Ibid., 165-66.
8) Ibid.
9) Freud, Trauer, 442-43.
10) Klein, Trauer, 83.
11) See 6.41 above.
12) Fulcomer, Behavior, 125-27 (summary).
13) Freud, Massenpsychologie, 147.
14) Ibid.
15) S. Radó, The Problem of Melancholia, International Journal of Psycho-Analysis, 9, 1939, 420-38.
16) Lewin, Psychoanalysis, 103.
17) See 8.31 below.
18) Freud, Massenpsychologie, 146.
19) Lewin, Psychoanalysis, 83-84.
20) Ibid., 91-92.
21) Ibid., 151.
22) Bibring, Problem, 93.
23) Wolfenstein, How Is Mourning Possible? 98-99.
24) K. Friedlander, On the "Longing to Die," International Journal of Psycho-Analysis, 21, 1940, 416-26.
25) L. M. Moss and D. M. Hamilton, The Psychotherapy of the Suicidal Patient, American Journal of Psychiatry, 112, 1956, 814-20.
26) Abraham, Versuch, 158.

6.52 Sociological implications

27) Maddison and Viola, Health; see above 2.41.
28) Jackson, Understanding, 85-86.
29) M. Wolfenstein, Children's Humor, Glencoe 1954; cf. also S. Freud, Der Witz und seine Beziehung zum Unbewussten (1905) Gesammelte Werke, vol. 6, Frankfurt 1969[4].
30) W. Fuchs, Todesbilder in der modernen Gesellschaft, Frankfurt 1969, 142.

6.53 Joy

31) See 3.7 above.
32) A. C. Rush, Death and Burial in Christian Antiquity (The Catholic University of America Studies in Christian Antiquity, vol. 1), Washington 1941, 72-87.
33) Ibid., 228-35.
34) S. Freud, Das Unbehagen in der Kultur (1930) Gesammelte Werke, vol. 14, Frankfurt 1968[4], 419-506, 422-31.

35) Freud, Massenpsychologie, 150-51.
36) E. Brunner, Die Mystik und das Wort, Tübingen 1924.
37) E. Brunner, Das Ewige als Zukunft und Gegenwart, Siebenstern Taschenbuch, vol. 2, Munich-Hamburg 1965, 224-25.
38) Ibid., 225.
39) Ibid., 226.
40) H. Cox, The Feast of Fools, Cambridge, Mass. 1969.
41) Tillich, Systematic Theology, vol. 3, 405.
42) M. Luther, Mit Fried und Freud ich fahr dahin, EKL 310, 1.
43) P. Althaus, Die letzen Dinge—Lehrbuch der Eschatologie (1922), Gütersloh, 1961, 148-53.

7. The aggressive coping mechanisms

1) See 2.1 above.
2) E. Jacobson, Normal and Pathological Moods: Their Nature and Functions, Psychoanalytic Study of the Child, 12, 1957, 73-117, 87.
3) Marris, Widows, 22.
4) Clayton et al., Study, 171.
5) A. H. Kutscher, Practical Aspects of Bereavement, in Schoenberg, ed., Loss, 280-97, 293-94.
6) C. M. Parkes, Bereavement and Mental Illness, British Journal of Medical Psychology, 38, 1965, 5.
7) Lindemann, Bedeutung, 517, 519.
8) Bowlby, Processes, 321.
9) Caruso, Trennung, 28.
10) J. Bowlby, Childhood Mourning and Its Implications for Psychiatry (The Adolf Meyer Lecture), American Journal of Psychiatry, 118, 1961, 481-98, 485.

7.1 The mechanism: protest and lamentation

7.11 Psychological aspects

11) Bowlby, Processes, 485.
12) Ibid., 334.
13) Wolfenstein, How Is Mourning Possible? 104-5.
14) Fulcomer, Behavior, 107-10 (summary).
15) Peretz, Reaction, 22.
16) G. Mosley, Guilt, in Kutscher, ed., Death, 210-11, 210.
17) Parkes, Bereavement.
18) Philipe, Seufzer, 41.
19) Caruso, Trennung, 24.

7.12 Sociological implications

20) Goody, Death, 51.
21) H. Jahnow, Das hebräische Leichenlied im Rahmen der Völkerdichtung (Beiheft zur Zeitschrift für alttestamentliche Wissenschaft, vol. 36), Giessen 1923, 78.
22) A. F. Key, The Concept of Death in Early Israelite Religion, Journal of Bible and Religion, 32, 1964, 239-247.
23) Bowlby, Processes, 333-34; M. Wolfenstein, Loss, Rage, and Repetition, Psychoanalytic Study of the Child, 24, 1969, 432-60, 446-52.

NOTES

24) J. P. Spiegel, Variations in Attitudes toward Death and Disease, in Grosser, Wechsler, and Greenblatt, eds., The Threat of Impending Disaster, Cambridge, Mass. 1964, 283-99, 298.

25) W. Caudill, Effects of Social and Cultural Systems in Reactions to Stress (Pamphlet No. 14), New York 1958.

7.13 The question of natural death

26) Barth, Church Dogmatics, III/2, 632.

27) Ibid., 638.

28) Ibid., 638-39.

29) Jüngel, Tod, 166-67.

30) Ibid., 167.

31) Fuchs, Todesbilder, 22, 67.

32) H. Plessner, Über die Beziehung der Zeit zum Tode, Eranos, 20, 1951, 349-86, 368.

33) S. Freud, The 'Uncanny' (1919), in Collected Papers, vol. 4, 368-407, 395.

34) S. Freud, Thoughts for the Times on War and Death, 305.

35) S. Freud, Beyond the Pleasure Principle, in The Standard Edition of the Complete Psychological Works of Sigmund Freud, trans. and ed. James Strachey, London 1955, vol. 18, 7-64, 45.

36) Caruso, Trennung, 132.

37) Gollwitzer, Holz, 111.

38) Ibid.

39) Ibid., 110.

40) Fuchs, Todesbilder, 221.

41) Althaus, Dinge, 249.

42) Ibid.

43) J. Pieper, Tod und Unsterblichkeit, in E. Schlink and H. Volk, eds., Pro veritate: Ein theologischer Dialog. Festgabe für Lorenz Jaeger und Wilhelm Staehlin, Münster-Kassel 1963, 274-93, 275.

44) Hedinger, Hoffnung, chap. 9: "Hoffnung als Rechten mit Gott," 241-88.

45) Ibid., 257.

7.2 The mechanism: the search for the guilty

7.21 Psychological aspects

1) G. Rochlin, Grief and Discontents: The Forces of Change, Boston 1965, 69.

2) Ibid., 70.

3) Ibid., 74.

4) Bowlby, Processes, 334.

5) Sudnow, Passing, 143-46.

6) Eliot, Bereavement, 656.

7) B. Arthur and M. Kemme, Bereavement in Childhood, Journal of Child Psychology and Psychiatry, 5, 1946 (1), 39-40, in reference to J. Piaget, The Child's Conception of Physical Causality, New York 1930.

8) R. Sigel, An Exploration into Some Aspects of Political Socialization: School Children's Reactions to the Death of a President, in Wolfenstein and Kliman, eds., Children, 53.

9) I. L. Janis, Air War and Emotional Stress, New York 1951, 58.

10) N. J. Smelser, Theory of Collective Behavior, London 1962, 232; see also R. Bucher, Blame and Hostility in Disaster, American Journal of Sociology, 67, 1957, 467-75.

THE GRIEF PROCESS

11) R. A. Kalish, A Continuum of Subjectively Perceived Death, Geron-tologist, 6, 1966, 73-76.

12) Marris, Widows, 22.

13) Ibid., 17.

14) Lindemann, Bedeutung, 519.

15) I. L. Janis, Psychological Stress: Psychoanalytic and Behavioral Studies of Surgical Patients, New York 1958, 171.

16) Marris, Widows, 18.

7.22 Sociological implications

17) Goody, Death, 212-13.

18) W. H. Kelly, Cocopa Attitudes and Practices with Respect to Death and Mourning, Southwestern Journal of Anthropology, 5, 1959, 151-64.

19) L. V. Grinsell, The Breaking of Objects as a Funerary Rite, Folklore, 72, 1961, 457-61; N. G. Politis, On the Breaking of Vessels as a Funeral Rite in Modern Greece, Journal of the Royal Anthropological Institute, 23, 1894, 29-41; K. Meuli, Entstehung und Sinn der Trauersitten, Schweizerisches Archiv für Volkskunde, 43, 1946, 91-109, 106-8.

20) E. Durkheim, The Elementary Forms of the Religious Life (1909), London 1956, 393-94.

7.23 Death as penalty

21) St. B. Friedman, P. Chodoff, J. W. Manson, and D. A. Hamburg, Behavioral Observations on Parents Anticipating the Death of a Child, Pediatrics, 32, 1963, 610-25, 614.

22) Jackson, Understanding, 98.

23) Giudice, Ohne meinen Man, 25.

24) Ibid., 30.

25) Brunner, Ewige, 114.

26) Jüngel, Tod, 99.

27) Ibid.

28) Ibid., 113.

29) Althaus, Dinge, 201.

30) Ibid., 203-4.

31) Althaus, Dinge, 204.

32) K. Rahner, Zur Theologie, des Todes: Mit einem Exkurs über das Martyrium (Quaestiones disputatae, Vol. 2), Freiburg 1958², 38.

33) K. Rahner, On the Theology of Death, trans. Charles H. Henkey, New York 1965, 50.

34) Rahner, Zur Theologie, 42-43.

35) See 7.32 below.

7.3 The mechanism: identification with the aggressor

7.31 Psychological aspects

1) A. Freud, Ich, 85.

2) Ibid., 93.

3) S. Freud, The Economic Problem in Masochism (1924), in Collected Papers, vol. 2, 255-68, 265.

4) Ibid., 380.

5) Ibid., 381-82.

6) Ibid., 433.

7) Ibid., 438.

NOTES

8) H. Loewald, Internalization, Separation, Mourning, and the Superego, Psychoanalytic Quarterly, *31*, 1962, 483-504.
9) See 8.3 below.
10) E. Weiss, Principles of Psychodynamics, New York 1950, 73.
11) Switzer, Dynamics, 132.
12) J. H. Friedman and D. Zaris, Paradoxical Response to Death of Spouse: Three Case Reports, Diseases of the Nervous System, *25*, 1964, 480-83.
13) L. Grinberg, Two Kinds of Guilt: Their Relations with Normal and Pathological Aspects of Mourning, International Journal of Psycho-Analysis, *45*, 1964, 366-71.
14) Marris, Widows, 19.
15) Hinton, Dying, 169.
16) Friedman et al., Observations, 614.
17) Wretmark, Grief, 294-95; R. J. Lifton, Death in Life: Survivors of Horoshima, New York 1968, 489; R. Miller and Sh. Wiesenfeld, The Treatment of "Moral" Masochism in Mothers Who Experienced the Loss of a Child, Smith College Studies in Social Work, *36*, 1966, 148-60.
18) Autton, Care of the Bereaved, 46.
19) S. Freud, Dostoevsky . . . , in Collected Papers, vol. 5, ed. James Strachey, 229.
20) Lifton, Death, 490.
21) E. Wiesel, Night, New York 1960, 108, 113, 116.
22) Lifton, Death, 491-92.
23) Ibid., 491.
24) Ibid., 491-92.
25) Ibid., 496.
26) C. W. Wahl, The Differential Diagnosis of Normal and Neurotic Grief Following Bereavement, Psychosomatics, *11*, 1970, 104-106, 105.
27) Krupp, Identification, 311-12.
28) Cobb and Lindemann, Observations, 816.
29) Wretmark, Study, 295.
30) De Beauvoir, Tod, 104.
31) J. Mitford, The American Way of Death, New York 1963; 22; see also Vernon, Sociology, 162-63.
32) Jackson, Understanding, 64-65.
33) Ibid., 65.
34) S. Freud, The Psychopathology of Everyday Life, in Complete Psychological Works, vol. 6, 180-81.
35) Lifton, Death, 494.
36) S. Freud, Dostojewski, 410.
37) E. De Wind, Begegnung mit dem Tod. Mit einem Diskussionsbeitrag von W. G. Niederland, Psyche, *22*, 1968, 423-46.
38) Lindemann, Bedeutung, 197.
39) Lindemann, Bedeutung, 519; C. M. Parkes, Bereavement and Mental Illness, 10: Wretmark, Study, 292-99.
40) Krupp, Identification, 308-9.
41) Parkes, Bereavement, 10-11.
42) M. Jastrow, The Tearing of Garments as a Symbol of Mourning with Especial Reference to the Customs of the Ancient Hebrews, Journal of the American Oriental Society, *21*, 1901 (2), 23-29.
43) Ibid.
44) J. Breuer and S. Freud, Studien.

45) S. Freud, Der Mann Moses und die monotheistische Religion (1937-39), Gesammelte Werke, vol. 16, Frankfurt 1968[3], 101-246, 184-85.
46) Krupp, Identification, 306.
47) Pollock, Mourning, 354.
48) Jackson, Understanding, 61-62.
49) Jackson, Understanding, 66-67.
50) Siggins, Mourning, 18.

7.32 Sociological implications

51) Jackson, Understanding, 85.
52) E. H. Volkart and St. T. Michael, Bereavement and Mental Health, 287; Engel, Development, 275-76.
53) Switzer, Dynamics, 135-36.
54) Friedman et al., Observations, 614.
55) Jackson, Understanding, 98.
56) D. W. Plath, Where the Family of God is the Family: The Role of the Dead in Japanese Households, American Anthropologist, 66, 1964, 300-317.
57) J. Yamamoto, K. Okonogi, T. Iwasaki, and S. Yoshimura, Mourning in Japan, American Journal of Psychiatry, 125, 1969, 1660-65.
58) Fuchs, Todesbilder, 154.
59) A. D. Weisman and Th. P. Hackett, Predilection to Death, in Fulton, ed., Death, 293-329, 312.

7.33 The universal redemption

60) Tillich, Theology, vol. 3, 416.
61) H. Gollwitzer, Versöhnung, Schuld, Krankheit, in H. Horn and H. Kittel, eds., Der Glaube der Gemeinde und die mündige Welt, Festschrift Oskar Hammelsbeck (Beiträge zur Evangelischen Theologie, vol. 52), Munich 1969, 119-26, 121.
62) Brunner, Ewige, 200-201.
63) Ibid., 201-2.
64) W. Künneth, Theologie der Auferstehung, Munich 1951, 253.
65) W. Kreck, Die Zukunft des Gekommenen — Grundprobleme der Eschatologie, Munich 1966, 147.
66) Barth, Dogmatik, II/2, 358.
67) G. Greshake, Auferstehung der Toten: Ein Beitrag zur gegenwärtigen theologischen Diskussion über die Zukunft der Geschichte, Essen 1969, 94.

8. The object-libidinal coping mechanisms

8.1 The mechanism: helplessness

8.11 Psychological aspects

1) Bibring, Problem, 96.
2) Ibid., 94.
3) Ibid., 97.
4) Ibid., 100.
5) Radó, Problem, 51.
6) Fulcomer, Behavior, 133-35 (summary).
7) Nach Lindemann, Bedeutung, 517.
8) J. A. Averill, Grief: Its Nature and Significance, Psychological Bulletin, 70, 1968, 721-48.

NOTES

9) Ibid., 737.

10) P. Ekman and W. V. Friesen, Nonverbial Behavior in Psychotherapy Research, in J. Shlien, ed., Research in Psychotherapy, vol. 3, Washington, D. C. 1968, 73-88.

11) S. Freud, Das Motiv der Kästchenwahl (1913) Gesammelte Werke, vol. 10, Frankfurt 1967[4], 23-37, 28-31.

12) P. Greenacre, On the Development and Function of Tears, Psychoanalytic Study of The Child, 20, 1965, 209-19, 210.

13) Klein, Psychogenese, 88.

14) Jackson, Understanding, 154.

15) Greenacre, Development, 212-13.

16) Schmale, Relationship, 262, 265-66.

17) Engel and Schmale, Theory, 354.

18) Ibid., 355.

19) Ibid., 356.

20) A. H. Schmale, Object Loss, "Giving up," and Disease Onset: An Overview of Research in Progress, in Medical Aspects of Stress in the Military Climate, Washington, D.C. (Walter Reed Army Institute of Research) 1964, 433-43.

21) J. D. Adamson and A. H. Schmale, Objektverlust, Resignation und der Ausbruch psychischer Erkrankungen, Psyche, 21, 1966, 651.

22) Freud, Behandlung, 294-95.

23) Schmale, Relationship, 271; cf. also Peretz, Reaction, 33.

24) A. H. Schmale and H. P. Iker, The Affect of Hopelessness and the Development of Cancer I, Psychosomatic Medicine, 28, 1966, 714-21.

8.12 Sociological Implications

25) H. v. Hug-Hellmuth, Das Kind und seine Vorstellung vom Tode, Imago, 1, 1912, 286-98, 295.

26) K. Meuli, Entstehung und Sinn der Trauersitten, Schweizerisches Archiv für Volkskunde, 43, 1946, 91-109, 94.

27) Durkheim, Forms, 397.

28) Clayton et al., Study, 171.

29) Ibid., 172.

30) Caplan, Principles, 47.

31) Gorer, Grief, 59.

32) Ibid.

33) Ibid.

34) Cf. Autton, Care of the Bereaved, 72: "Indeed it may be true to say that there are more family upsets and quarrels as a result of things said during bereavement than in any other situation. Friends and neighbours are apt to take offence on such occasions—'Fancy her saying that after all I've done for her. I'll never go near the house again!'—rather than understand that such remarks are but the natural outcome of a bewildering situation."

8.13 Hope and courage

35) P. Tillich, Das Recht auf Hoffnung: Eine religiöse Rede, in S. Unseld, ed., Ernst Bloch zu ehren, Frankfurt 1965, 265.

36) Künneth, Theologie, 201, 249.

37) Althaus, Dinge, 364-65.

38) G. Marcel, Presence et immortalite, Paris 1959.

39) H. Kimmerle, Die Zukunftsbedeutung der Hoffnung: Auseinandersetzung mit Ernst Blochs "Prinzip Hoffnung" aus philosophischer und theologischer Sicht (Abhandlungen zur Philosophie, Psychologie und Pädagogik, vol. 34), Bonn 1966, 191-97.
40) G. Sauter, Zukunft und Verheissung: Das Problem der Zunkunft in der gegenwärtigen theologischen un philosophischen Diskussion, Zurich-Stuttgart 1965, 50-55.
41) Ibid., 52.
42) Ibid.
43) Ibid., 53.
44) Ibid., 54.
45) Ibid., 151.
46) Moltmann, Theologie, 92.
47) Sauter, Zukunft, 157.
48) Bloch, Prinzip, Bd. 3, 202.
49) P. Tillich, Courage, 169.
50) Ibid., 176.
51) Ibid., 177.
52) Ibid.

8.2 The mechanism: recollection

8.21 Psychological aspects

1) Lindemann, Bedeutung, 518; Autton, Care of the Bereaved, 65-66.
2) S. Freud, Recollection, Repetition and Working Through (1914), in Collected Papers, vol. 2, 367-76, 369.
3) S. Freud, as is well known, saw the compulsion to repeat attached to the death wish and interpreted it as an attempt to return to inanimate matter. Compare H. Lichtenstein, Zur Phänomenologie des Wiederholungswanges und des Todestriebes (phenomenology of the compulsion to repeat and the death wish) Imago, 21, 1935, 466-80.
4) Caruso, Trennung, 188.
5) Ibid., 188-89.
6) E. Kris, Recovery of Childhood Memories in Psychoanalysis, Psychoanalytic Study of the Child, 11, 1956, 54-88.
7) Weiss, Principles, 84.
8) V. E. v. Gebsattel, Prolegomena einer medizinischen Anthropologie: Ausgewählte Aufsätze, Berlin-Göttingen-Heidelberg 1954, 288-89.
9) Ibid., 290.
10) Ibid., 291.
11) Cf. P. L. Berger, Invitation to Sociology: A Humanistic Perspective, Garden City, N.Y. 1963, 54-65.
12) Freud, Totem, 1973.
13) F. I. Greenstein, Young Men and the Death of a Young President, in Wolfenstein and Kliman, eds., Children, 193-216, 214.
14) T. Bonhoeffer, Das Kerygma in der Abdankung, Theologia Practica, 3, 1968, 187-92, 190.
15) Carlin, Grief, 130-31.
16) Jahnow, Leichenlied, 54; Klein, Trauer, 81.
17) Autton, Care of the Bereaved, 48.
18) Klein, Trauer, 77.
19) Klein, Psychogenese, 69.

20) Caruso, Trennung, 75.
21) Ibid., 55.
22) B. Brecht, On a Drowned Girl, trans. Eric W. White, Knotting, Bedfordshire, England 1973.
23) M. Klein, Trauer, 84.
24) Bonhoeffer, Kerygma, 191.
25) J. Mathers, Ministry to the Bereaved, in Cope, Dying, 40-48, 44, speaks of "making a sort of inventory of memories, good and bad."
26) Lindemann, Bedeutung, 518.

8.22 Sociological implications

27) L. W. Simmons, Attitudes toward Aging and the Aged: Primitive Societies, Journal of Gerontology, 1, 1946, 72-94, 82.
28) A. W. McMahon and P. Rhudick, Reminiscing in the Aged, in S. Levin and R. J. Kahana, eds., Psychodynamic Studies on Aging, New York 1967, 64-78; R. N. Butler, The Life Review: An Interpretation of Reminiscence in the Aged, Psychiatry, 26, 1963, 65-75.

8.23 Commemoration and recollection

29) Quoted in Krusche, Predigt, 620.
30) Geischer, Tod, 269.
31) Bonhoeffer, Kerygma, 190.
32) K. Barth, Church Dogmatics I/2 (1956); II/1 (1957); III/2 (1960).
33) Sauter, Zukunft.
34) J. B. Metz, Kirchliche Autorität im Anspruch der Freiheitsgeschichte, in Metz, J. Moltmann, and W. Oelmüller, Kirche im Prozess der Aufklärung: Aspekte einer neuen politischen Theologie (Gesellschaft und Theologie, Systematische Beiträge, vol. 1), Munich-Mainz 1970, 53-90, 72.
35) Metz, "Politische Theologie" in der Diskussion, in H. Peukert, ed., Diskussion zur "politischen Theologie," Munich-Mainz 1969, 267-301, 286; cf. 284-96: "Zum theologischen Charakter der 'politischen Theologie': die memoria-These."
36) Jüngel, Tod, 153.
37) Tillich, Theology, vol. 3, 399, 400.

8.3 The mechanism: incorporation

8.31 Psychological aspects

1) Philipe, Seufzer, 42.
2) Loewald, Internalization.
3) Ibid., 489.
4) Ibid., 491.
5) Ibid., 493.
6) Ibid., 495.
7) Klein, Trauer, 88.
8) Jahnow, Leichenlied, 30-31. I Sam. 31:13; II Sam. 1:12.
9) Krupp, Bereavement, 50.
10) W. W. Hamburger, Appetite in Man, American Journal of Clinical Nutrition, 5, 1960, 571, 573.
11) Ch. G. Babcock, Food and Its Emotional Significance, Journal of the American Dietetic Association, 24, 1948, 390-93.

THE GRIEF PROCESS

8.32 *Sociological implications*

12) G. Quell, Die Auffassung des Todes in Israel (1925), Darmstadt 1967, 25-26.
13) Jahnow, Leichenlied, 36.
14) Josephus, Jewish Wars, II, 1,1.

8.33 *Corporeality*

15) Bultmann, Theologie, 196.
16) G. Sauter, Die Zeit des Todes: Ein Kapitel Eschatologie und Anthropologie, Evangelische Theologie, *25*, 1965, 642.
17) Moltmann, Theology of Hope, 214.
18) Kreck, Zukunft, 175.

8.4 The mechanism: substitution

8.41 *Psychological aspects*

1) Cf. Jackson, Understanding, 75-87, chap. 5: "Grief and Substitution."
2) A. P. Noyes and L. C. Kolb, Modern Clinical Psychiatry, Philadelphia 1963, 55.
3) S. Freud, The Relation of the Poet to Day-Dreaming (1908), in Collected Papers, vol. 4, 173-83, 175.
4) E. Freud and L. Freud, eds., Sigmund Freud: Briefe 1873-1939, Frankfurt 1960², 403 (letter of 12 April 1929).
5) See 2.1 above.
6) Jackson, Understanding, 83.
7) A. C. and B. S. Cain, On Replacing a Child, Journal of the American Academy of Child Psychiatry, *3*, 1964, 443-56, 445-48; A. C. Cain, I. Fast and M. E. Erickson, Children's Disturbed Reactions to the Death of a Sibling, American Journal of Orthopsychiatry, *34*, 1964, 741-52, 747.
8) See 3.7 above.
9) W. A. Greene, Role of a Vicarious Object in the Adaptation to Object Loss: 1. Use of a Vicarious Object as a Means of Adjustment to Separation from a Significant Person, Psychosomatic Medicine, *20*, 1958, 345.
10) Lindemann, Symptomatology, 193.
11) Greene, Role, 346.
12) Cf. A. G. Knudson and J. M. Natterson, Participation of Parents in the Hospital Care of Fatally Ill Children, Pediatrics, *26*, 1960, 482-90.
13) Mary E. Bozeman, Ch. E. Orbach, and A. M. Sutherland, Psychological Impact of Cancer and its Treatment: III The Adaption of Mothers to the Threatened Loss of Their Children through Leukemia: Part I, Cancer, *8*, 1955, 1-19.
14) Greene, Role, 346-47.
15) Lindemann, Bedeutung, 517, defines the "psychological substitution therapy" as an attempt to "provide a substitute for the loss of the commonly shared experience, . . . in which the psychotherapist had to represent the characteristics and functions which were important in the lost brother, namely active participation in the daily events of life."
16) Sudnow, Passing, 161.
17) I. May Greer, Grief Must Be Faced, Christian Century, *62*, 1945, 269-71, 271.
18) Jacobson, Normal, 103-7 (summary).

NOTES

19) Hamburger, Appetite, 572.
20) Wolfenstein, How is Mourning Possible? 119.
21) Peretz, Loss, 34; Maddison and Viola, Health, 303-4; Clayton *et al.*, Study, 171-72.
22) S. Freud, Recollection, 373.

8.42 Sociological implications

23) Maddison and Walker, Factors, 1063.
24) M. Spiro, Ifaluk: A South Sea Culture (unpublished manuscript), National Research Council, Human Relation Area Files, Yale University, New Haven 1949, quoted in Volkart and Michael, Bereavement, 281-83.
25) Volkart and Michael, Bereavement, 289.
26) Similarly, Hahn presents the societal and familial organizations without attempting to show any connection between the two. A. Hahn, Einstellungen zum Tod und ihre soziale Bedingtheit: Eine soziologische Untersuchung (Soziologische Gegenwartsfragen, NF H. 26), Stuttgart 1968, 95.
27) E. Bott, Urban Families: Conjugal Roles and Social Networks, Human Relations, 8, 1956, 345-84; Family and Social Network, London 1957, 52-61, 92-96.
28) M. B. Sussman and L. Burchinal, Kin Family Network: Unheralded Structure in Current Conceptualizations of Family Functioning, in B. L. Neugarten (ed.), Middle Age and Aging, Chicago 1968, 247-254, 250.
29) Marris, Widows, 60.
30) Ibid., 67.
31) The author of the First Letter of Timothy turns his attention here only to older widows; as is well known, he trusted no widow under sixty and his pronouncements about them are negative. I Tim. 5:11-14: "But refuse to enrol younger widows; for when they grow wanton against Christ they desire to marry, and so they incur condemnation for having violated their first pledge. Besides that, they learn to be idlers, gadding about from house to house, and not only idlers but gossips and busybodies, saying what they should not. So I would have younger widows marry, bear children, rule their households, and give the enemy no occasion to revile us."

8.43 Representation and substitution

32) Hahn, Einstellungen, 96.
33) D. Sölle, Stellvertretung: Ein Kapitel Theologie nach dem "Tode Gottes," Stuttgart-Berlin 1965, 22-23.
34) Ibid., 23.
35) D. Sölle, Christ the Representative: An Essay in Theology After the 'Death of God,' trans. David Lewis, Philadelphia 1967, 21.
36) Ibid.
37) Ibid., 42.
38) Ibid., 46.
39) Ibid., 48.
40) Ibid., 50.
41) Ibid., 68.
42) Ibid.
43) Ibid., 67-71.
44) Ibid., 21.

9. Epilogue: The death of Jesus and the grief of the disciples (John 16)

1) For the connection of the Spirit and Jesus see R. Bultmann, Das Evangelium des Johannes, Göttingen 1956[14], 451.
2) R. Bultmann, The Gospel of John, trans. G. R. Beasley, Philadelphia 1971, 368.
3) Ibid., 558; cf. Hedinger, Hoffnung, 74.
4) Bultmann, Gospel of John, 558.
5) E. Käsemann, Jesu letzter Wille nach Johannes 17, Tübingen 1971, 3; veränderte Auflage, 94-96.
6) Bultmann, Gospel of John, 562.
7) Ibid., 575.
8) Ibid., 576.
9) Käsemann, Jesu, 89f.
10) Bultmann, Gospel of John, 582.
11) Ibid.
12) Ibid., 584.
13) Ibid., 583, n. 1.
14) For the critique of this interpretation and the theological premisses behind it see Käsemann, Jesu, 102-6; Kreck, Zukunft, 50-62; Hedinger, Hoffnung, 73-80.